myth and reality

Myth and reality:
readings in education

GLENN SMITH

CHARLES R. KNIKER

Iowa State University

Boston: Allyn and Bacon, Inc.

Library of Congress Catalog Card Number: 79-184719

Illustrations by Allyn and Bacon photographers

Third printing . . . July, 1973

Contents

Part 3. Patterns schools reinforce 167

Part 4. Directions schools explore 267

Preface

In 1966 Allard Lowenstein, a Democratic candidate for the United States Congress from Long Island, New York, achieved the impossible dream — he won in a bedrock Republican district. Later he succeeded in another seemingly impossible venture: he launched the "dump Johnson" movement. Some observers credit his success to the breezy, innovative, at times irreverent style captured in his campaign slogan, "Sacred Cows Make Great Hamburgers."

It is time for educators to adopt that motto. For too long, books discussing educational foundations have been little more than historical recitations of the triumph of public schools, or cautious explorations of ways to improve what is often billed as the best system of instruction in the world's history. From time to time critical books have appeared, which carp on the failure of the school system to meet stated goals. The flaws common to these books are their deadly seriousness, academic impotence, and consistent promotion of student disinterest.

By examining basic assumptions about the functions of American schooling, by weighing the distance between the rhetoric and reality of the schools, by focusing on what American schooling *is* more than on what it is *supposed to be,* we believe, the study of educational foundations can be provocative, exciting, and yes, entertaining. Further, such an approach does aid a person in deciding whether school is the best place to invest his energies.

Unique features

To place in perspective the myths and realities of school situations, we chose types of readings which do not appear in most other anthologies. Many of the articles describe local school situations, to emphasize what is actually happening at the grass roots and concrete pavement levels of instruction today. This made it imperative to include newspaper reports in addition to the more usual journal essay. While we plead guilty to the sin of omission of some popular and scholarly writers, we hope the use of actual situations provides a freshness unmatched in other sources.

The book is contemporary. Most selections are less than two years old. Historical material has frequently been placed in the introductory essays.

The book is an introduction to rather than a comprehensive treatment of issues. We did not always seek to balance liberal and conservative points of view, nor insist that an Establishment pronouncement be followed by a militant spokesman's words. We chose articles which we believe present the issues clearly. Reader interest was also weighed in the selection of certain articles.

Certain topics usually found in introductory readers have been minimized or eliminated. Information on legal responsibilities of teachers and discussions of teaching methods, we believe, belong elsewhere. The same may be said for psychology of education material.

Organization

The book is organized around five themes or issues in American education today, issues which touch some basic assumptions that Americans have held about their schools for the past century.

"The school is the best panacea for America's social ills."   Lawrence Cremin, an historian of education, has pointed out that in periods of crisis the typical American response is to encase the problem in a school curriculum. In the nineteenth century we asked the schools to Americanize the immigrants. In the twentieth century we answered the Sputnik launching by revising the science curriculum, attacked highway deaths with driver education, and met black unrest with Afro-American studies. Part 1 explores the meaning of schooling and education, with articles that ask whether the goals of both can be compatible.

"The school prepares the student for life in a democratic society."   Part 2, "Values Schools Transmit," enumerates professed and actual values of school life. Articles on such topics as student freedom and conduct codes, discipline techniques, and extracurricular events suggest a reappraisal of the belief that school is a microcosm of or preparation for democratic living.

"The school provides equal educational opportunity for all."   One of the most controversial topics today is the glaring difference between the theory and the fact of equal educational opportunity for all American children. Combined in Part 3 are readings usually listed under social

class and race. A wide range of sources documents the extent of the inequities, while other selections describe remedies which attempt to counter the injustice of the present system.

"American schools have gotten progressively better, and will continue to improve if more money is invested."   Part 4 highlights some current directions schools are exploring. The basic question readers will ask of these purported innovative schools is: How radical a change are you really proposing? Some models remain well within traditional controls and would seem to be a change in the flavor of the frosting on the cake. Other suggestions are radical and would demand a reordering of educational priorities if widely adopted.

"The school is responsive to the needs of society."   The final part serves as an epilogue by focusing on issues developing now. While some articles call for a new type of schooling and suggest vastly different curricula, at least one selection suggests that schooling as we now have it must disappear.

We hope these essays will help students appreciate the problems and promises of American schools. If most inquirers, upon reading this book, have increased their ability to fathom the reality in the rhetoric about the American school, we shall feel we have succeeded. In addition, if these readings help some people realistically decide whether or not they want to pursue a teaching career, we shall be doubly rewarded.

G S
C R K

part 1

"The common school is the greatest discovery of mankind."   —Horace Mann

"The public schools are the kind of institution one cannot really dislike until one gets to know them well."
                                      —Charles Silberman

Functions
schools perform

Teaching, learning, certification, and the institutionalized processes in which they are encased preoccupy Americans today more than at any time in the past. A major feature of this concern is the close, almost exclusive, identification of *education* with *going to school*. During most of our colonial and national experience this was not the case. Until quite recently, an overwhelming majority of people acquired most of their education through a combination of apprenticeship, family, personal interest, church, community, friends, and on-the-job training, with perhaps a short period of school thrown in. In the nineteenth century, even physicians and attorneys usually learned their crafts as apprentices to established professionals rather than by going to medical or law schools.

At the beginning of this century, only 6 percent of American seventeen-year-olds graduated from high school, and less than 5 percent between the ages of 17 and 21 went to college. Today, over 70 percent of the former age group graduate from high school, and about 50 percent of the people of college age attend college. Almost a third of the total population is involved full time in American schools as either student, teacher, or administrator. Americans spend over $60 billion each year on elementary, secondary, and collegiate schooling, and there are insistent pressures for increasing both the number of years and the number of people in school, as well as per capita outlay.

The very fact that schooling has become such an entrenched part of contemporary existence has been taken by most Americans—and certainly by educators—as transparent evidence of progress. Until recently, even most people who criticized schools did so on the grounds that schools were not efficient enough, rather than because they were harmful. School officials worried about the 30 percent who dropped out without high school diplomas and the 80 percent who decided not to enter or failed to graduate from college. Perhaps, many people said, the society was losing badly needed talent. What could educators do for the people dropping out?

But now the real question seems to be what shall schools do for the people who stay? For a growing body of evidence suggests that schools are destructive of the diversity, independence, intelligence, and inventiveness which we have long regarded as characteristic of Americans. Growing amounts of schooling may reflect progress, but progress towards what? The readings in Part 1 suggest we are progressing toward institutionalized conformity.

ALEXANDER CALANDRA

Angels on a Pin

The first two selections suggest that whatever the intent of schools, the results are often an unbearable oppressiveness.

Some time ago, I received a call from a colleague who asked if I would be the referee on the grading of an examination question. He was about to give a student a zero for his answer to a physics question, while the student claimed he should receive a perfect score and would if the system were not set up against the student. The instructor and the student agreed to submit this to an impartial arbiter, and I was selected.

I went to my colleague's office and read the examination question: "Show how it is possible to determine the height of a tall building with the aid of a barometer."

The student had answered: "Take the barometer to the top of the building, attach a long rope to it, lower the barometer to the street, and then bring it up, measuring the length of the rope. The length of the rope is the height of the building."

I pointed out that the student really had a strong case for full credit, since he had answered the question completely and correctly. On the other hand, if full credit were given, it could well contribute to a high grade for the student in his physics course. A high grade is

Alexander Calandra, "Angels on a Pin," *Saturday Review,* December 21, 1968, p. 60. Copyright 1968 Saturday Review, Inc. Reprinted by permission.

supposed to certify competence in physics, but the answer did not confirm this. I suggested that the student have another try at answering the question. I was not surprised that my colleague agreed, but I was surprised that the student did.

I gave the student six minutes to answer the question, with the warning that his answer should show some knowledge of physics. At the end of five minutes, he had not written anything. I asked if he wished to give up, but he said no. He had many answers to this problem; he was just thinking of the best one. I excused myself for interrupting him, and asked him to please go on. In the next minute, he dashed off his answer which read:

"Take the barometer to the top of the building and lean over the edge of the roof. Drop the barometer, timing its fall with a stopwatch. Then, using the formula $S = \frac{1}{2}at^2$, calculate the height of the building."

At this point, I asked my colleague if *he* would give up. He conceded, and I gave the student almost full credit.

In leaving my colleague's office, I recalled that the student had said that he had other answers to the problem, so I asked him what they were. "Oh, yes," said the student. "There are many ways of getting the height of a tall building with the aid of a barometer. For example, you could take the barometer out on a sunny day and measure the height of the barometer, the length of its shadow, and the length of the shadow of the building, and by the use of a simple proportion, determine the height of the building."

"Fine," I said. "And the others?"

"Yes," said the student. "There is a very basic measurement method that you will like. In this method, you take the barometer and begin to walk up the stairs. As you climb the stairs, you mark off the length of the barometer along the wall. You then count the number of marks, and this will give you the height of the building in barometer units. A very direct method."

"Of course, if you want a more sophisticated method, you can tie the barometer to the end of a string, swing it as a pendulum, and determine the value of 'g' at the street level and at the top of the building. From the difference between the two values of 'g,' the height of the building can, in principle, be calculated."

Finally he concluded, there are many other ways of solving the problem. "Probably the best," he said, "is to take the barometer to the basement and knock on the superintendent's door. When the superintendent answers, you speak to him as follows: 'Mr. Superintendent, here I have a fine barometer. If you will tell me the height of this building, I will give you this barometer.' "

At this point, I asked the student if he really did not know the conventional answer to this question. He admitted that he did, but said that he was fed up with high school and college instructors trying to teach him how to think, to use the "scientific method," and to explore the deep inner logic of the subject in a pedantic way, as is often done in the new mathematics, rather than teaching him the structure of the subject. With this in mind, he decided to revive scholasticism as an academic lark to challenge the Sputnik-panicked classrooms of America.

R. MUKERJI

About School

He always wanted to say things. But no one understood.
He always wanted to explain things. But no one cared.
So he drew.

Sometimes he would just draw and it wasn't anything. He wanted to
    carve it in stone or write it in the sky.
He would lie out on the grass and look up in the sky and it would
    be only him and the sky and the things inside that needed saying.
And it was after that, that he drew the picture. It was a beautiful
    picture. He kept it under the pillow and would let no one see it.
And he would look at it every night and think about it. And when it
    was dark, and his eyes were closed, he could still see it.
And it was all of him. And he loved it.
When he started school he brought it with him. Not to show anyone,
    but just to have with him like a friend.
It was funny about school.
He sat in a square, brown desk like all the other square, brown desks
    and he thought it should be red.
And his room was a square, brown room. Like all the other rooms. And
    it was tight and close. And stiff.

R. Mukerji, "About School," *Colloquy,* vol. 3, no. 1 (January 1970), p. 2. Reprinted by permission of United Church Press.

He hated to hold the pencil and the chalk, with his arm stiff and his
feet flat on the floor, stiff, with the teacher watching and
watching.

And then he had to write numbers. And they weren't anything. They
were worse than the letters that could be something if you put
them together.

And the numbers were tight and square and he hated the whole thing.

The teacher came and spoke to him. She told him to wear a tie like
all the other boys. He said he didn't like them and she said it
didn't matter.

After that they drew. And he drew all yellow and it was the way he
felt about morning. And it was beautiful.

The teacher came and smiled at him. "What's this?" she asked. "Why
don't you draw something like Ken's drawing? Isn't that beautiful?"

It was all questions.

After that his mother bought him a tie and he always drew airplanes
and rocket ships like everyone else. And he threw the old picture
away.

And when he lay out alone looking at the sky, it was big and blue and
all of everything, but *he* wasn't anymore.

He was square inside and brown, and his hands were stiff, and he was
like anyone else. And the things inside him that needed saying
didn't need saying anymore.

It had stopped pushing. It was crushed. Stiff.
Like everything else.

JERRY FARBER

The Student and Society

*Are schools, as the first two articles imply, agencies of oppression,
purposely crushing creative students? Readers may write off such a
criticism as the "sour grapes" of a few disgruntled students, or a
half-truth based on isolated incidents involving teachers with per-*

Jerry Farber, "The Student and Society," from *The Student As Nigger*, Contact
Books, copyright 1969, pp. 14–55. Reprinted by permission.

sonality defects. Jerry Farber, however, argues that such oppression is an intentional and pervasive part of schooling. While he points out the depth of choking conformity in which the school specializes, he suggests ways students may revolutionize the system.

School is where you let the dying society put its trip on you. Our schools may seem useful: to make children into doctors, sociologists, engineers—to discover things. But they're poisonous as well. They exploit and enslave students; they petrify society; they make democracy unlikely. And it's not *what* you're taught that does the harm but *how* you're taught. Our schools teach you by pushing you around, by stealing your will and your sense of power, by making timid square apathetic slaves out of you—authority addicts.

Schooling doesn't have to be this destructive. If it weren't compulsory, if schools were autonomous and were run by the people in them, then we could learn without being subdued and stupefied in the process. And, perhaps, we could regain control of our own society.

Students can change things if they want to because they have the power to say "no." When you go to school, you're doing society a favor. And when you say "no," you withhold much more than your attendance. You deny continuity to the dying society; you put the future on strike. Students can have the kind of school they want—or even something else entirely if they want—because there isn't going to be any school at all without them.

NOTES

(1) "School is where you let the dying society put its trip on you."

School is a genetic mechanism for society, a kind of DNA process that continually recreates styles, skills, values, hangups—and so keeps the whole thing going. The dying part of society—the society that has been —molds the emerging part more or less in its own image, and fashions the society that will be.

Schooling also makes change possible—evolution, if you like. But here we run into a problem. Although our schools foster enormous technological change, they help to keep social change within very narrow limits. Thanks to them, the technological capacity of society evolves at an explosive rate. But there is no comparable, adaptive evolution in the overall social framework, nor in the consciousness of the individuals who make up society. It isn't just that schools fail to create the necessary social change. They actually restrain it. They prevent it. (*How* they prevent it is the subject of the Notes that follow.)

When I say that schools serve the society-that-has-been, the dying society, I mean just that. It isn't "society" itself that runs our schools. Children and adolescents are a huge segment of society but they don't run schools. Even young adults don't run them. Nor as a general rule do workers. Nor do black people (although a few Negroes do). Nor do the poor in general. By and large our schools are in the hands of the most entrenched and rigidly conservative elements in society. In the secondary and elementary schools, students, of course, have no power and teachers have little power. Administrators possess somewhat more, but the real control comes from those solid Chamber-of-Commerce types— those priests of the American Way—on the school board. They uphold the sovereignty of the past; they are the very avatars of institutional inertia. As for the colleges and universities, California, where I teach, is typical. Higher education is controlled primarily by the business elite, aided by a sprinkling of aging politicos, venerable clergymen and society matrons.* And in the rare cases when these trustees and governing boards relax their tight control, they are backstopped by our elected officials, whose noses are always aquiver for subversion and scandal and who are epitomized in that querulous Mrs. Grundy, our current governor.

While schools stifle social change, technological change is, to repeat, another matter. The society-that-has-been, in its slavering pursuit of higher profits and better weapons, demands technological progress at a fantastic, accelerating rate. Universities have consequently become a giant industry in their own right. A few tatters of commencement-day rhetoric still cling to them but it becomes more obvious every day that the modern university is not much more than a Research, Development and Training center set up to service government and industry. And so we have a technological explosion within the rigid confines of our unchanging social institutions and values. Schools today give us fantastic power at the same time as they sap our ability to handle it. Good luck, everybody.

---

* Read James Ridgeway's "The Closed Corporation: American Universities in Crisis" (New York, 1968). Ridgeway provides extensive information on the interlocking managements of universities and major corporations, as well as an analysis of the "big-business" aspect of the universities themselves.

(2) "It's not *what* you're taught that does the harm
but *how* you're taught."

In fact, for most of your school life, it doesn't make that much difference what subject you're taught. The real lesson is the method. The
medium in school truly is the message. And the medium is, above all,
coercive. You're forced to attend. The subjects are required. You *have*
to do homework. You *must* observe school rules. And throughout, you're
bullied into docility and submissiveness. Even modern liberal refinements don't really help. So you're called an underachiever instead of a
dummy. So they send you to a counselor instead of beating you. It's
still not your choice to be there. They may pad the handcuffs—but the
handcuffs stay on.

Which particular subject they happen to teach is far less important than the fact that it is required. We don't learn that much
subject matter in school anyway in proportion to the huge part of our
lives that we spend there. But what we do learn very well, thanks to
the method, is to accept choices that have been made for us. Which rule
they make you follow is less important than the fact that there are rules.
I hear about English teachers who won't allow their students to begin
a sentence with "and." Or about high schools where the male students
are not permitted to wear a T-shirt unless it has a pocket. I no longer
dismiss such rules as merely pointless. The very point to such rules is
their pointlessness.

The true and enduring content of education is its method. The
method that currently prevails in schools is standardized, impersonal
and coercive. What it teaches best is—itself. If, on the other hand, the
method were individual, human and free, it would teach that. It would
not, however, mesh smoothly into the machine we seem to have chosen
as a model for our society.

It's how you're taught that does the harm. You may only study
geometry for a semester—or French for two years. But *doing what you're
told,* whether or not it makes sense, is a lesson you get every blessed
school day for twelve years or more. You know how malleable we
humans are. And you know what good learners we are—how little time
it takes us to learn to drive a car or a plane or to play passable guitar. So
imagine what the effect must be upon our apt and impressionable minds
of a twelve-year-course in servility. Think about it. Twelve years of tardy
bells and hall passes; of graded homework, graded tests, graded conduct;
of report cards, GPA's, honors lists, citizenship ratings; of dress codes,

straight lines and silence. *What is it that they're teaching you?* Twelve years pitted against your classmates in a daily Roman circus. The game is Doing What You're Told. The winners get gold stars, affection, envy; they get A's and E's, honors, awards and college scholarships. The losers get humiliation and degradation. The fear of losing the game is a great fear: it's the fear of swats, of the principal's office, and above all the fear of failing. What if you fail and have to watch your friends move past you to glory? And, of course, the worst that could happen: you could be expelled. Not that very many kids get swats or fail or are expelled. But it doesn't take many for the message to get across. These few heavy losers are like severed heads displayed at the city gates to keep the populace in line.

And, to make it worse, all of this pressure is augmented by those countless parents who are ego freaks and competition heads and who forcibly pass their addiction on to their kids. The pressure at school isn't enough; they *pay* the kids for A's and punish them for D's and F's.

But can you feel any of this? Can you understand what has been done to your mind? We get so used to the pressure that we scarcely are conscious of it without making some effort.

Why does the medium of education affect us so deeply while its purported content—the subject matter—so often slips our minds? This is partly because the content varies from year to year while the form remains more or less the same; but also because the form—a structure of rules, punishments, rewards—affects us directly in a real way, while the subject matter may have no such immediate grasp on our lives. After all, don't we tend to learn best what matters most? Under a coercive system it isn't really the subject that matters; what matters is pleasing the authorities. These two are far from the same thing.

Remember French class in high school (or college, for that matter)? The teacher calls on you, one at a time, to see if you've prepared the questions at the end of Leçon 19. "Marshall," she asks, *"qu'est-ce que Robert allait faire le mardi?"* Marshall doesn't get to respond that he doesn't give a shit—not even in French. Fat chance. While he's in school, he's got to be servile to stay out of trouble. And the law requires him to be in school. He's got to do the questions in Leçon 19 because the teacher said to. He's got to do what the teacher said in order to pass the course. He's got to pass the course to get to college. He's got to get to college because it's been explained to him that he'll be a clod all his life if he doesn't; at assembly they've put up charts showing how many hundreds of thousands of dollars more he'll make in his lifetime if he goes to college. And, of course, there's an immediate reason as well for Marshall to have done his homework. If he hasn't, he'll be embarrassed in front of the class.

The educational medium has a very real hold on his life. Unfortunately, the subject probably does not. So we can't console him for all this dull toil by pointing out that he is at least learning French. Because, of course, he isn't. He'll take two years of French in high school. And when he gets to college, it will be like they never happened. Right? In fact, some acquaintances from Montreal recently told me that English-speaking students there are required to take French every year from the second grade on. And yet, I was told, after ten years of the language, they still haven't learned it.

Or what about Freshman English? What actually gets taught? The purported subject matter is usually writing. But consider, up front, who teaches the course. It's usually some well-meaning instructor or TA whose own writing achievements have reached their zenith in a series of idle and heroically dull papers, written in pretentious faggot-academic for his graduate classes. And how does he teach? What's his method? Well, that depends—because things are changing. Somewhere in some college there is undoubtedly a heavyweight, on the verge of being fired, who is teaching silence to freshmen so that they can hear themselves. Maybe somewhere else a teacher has renounced grading and is letting the students write what they want. Most Freshman English teachers, however, are doing the standard thing. They're demanding and then grading "themes" on capital punishment and on lowering the voting age. They're compelling students to drudge through topic-sentence exercises, outline exercises, library exercises, inference-judgment-report exercises, and a flood of other dreary busy work. They think they know the difference between a B minus essay and a C plus essay, and they teach their students to believe in such foolishness. They "correct" their students' work with *ex cathedra* judgments, none of which a student is at liberty to ignore.

In Freshman English, the method teaches you—in case you haven't already gotten the message—that writing is a drag. It's a job you do to please someone else (God knows that writing a theme on The Vanishing Individualist is hardly your own idea of how to spend Sunday night). Writing is school work and "English" is learning how to please your English teacher. What interest there is in the course is provided not so much by your writing experience as by the method. That is to say, you may write something tonight but the payoff, the real excitement, won't come until next week when the papers are handed back and you can find out "what you got." That's what makes it all worthwhile; that's what school writing is all about: pleasing the teacher.

The very essence of Freshman English is that term paper they force out of you. In perfect order, impeccably footnoted, unreal and totally useless—that term paper, that empty form, is pretty much the content of the course: submission—alienation—learning to live a pretend intellectual life, pretend-caring about pretend things.

Sometimes you even get a pretend choice; you're allowed to pick your own topic. But you don't get to make the one choice that would give the whole business some meaning: the choice to write no paper at all. Oh, you *can* make that choice. But then you don't get through Freshman English, which means you don't get through college and, therefore, don't get your hands in the gigantic goodie-box which is programmed to open only upon insertion of a college diploma. Or maybe you even get drafted right away. Yeah, you've got a hell of a choice. And college teachers like to style themselves "seekers after truth." Sure. "Know the truth and the truth shall get you a B." The truth in a freshman term paper is about the same truth a banker can expect from his shoeshine boy.

I'm sorry to sound so snotty about composition teachers. God knows, I've been there too. In my first year I even assigned research papers in Freshman English. I didn't really want to but I did it anyway "to prepare students for their other courses." I prepared them all right. My method was the term paper. What I taught was alienation and servility. Now I try to *un*prepare students for their other courses. I only wish I were better at it.

The medium of schooling, by the way, covers much more than assignments, grading, rules and so on. If *how* you're taught exerts a profound effect, what about the physical environment? What does a classroom teach?

Consider how most classrooms are set up. Everyone is turned toward the teacher and away from his classmates. You can't see the faces of those in front of you; you have to twist your neck to see the persons behind you. Frequently, seats are bolted to the floor or fastened together in rigid rows. This classroom, like the grading system, isolates students from each other and makes them passive receptacles. All the action, it implies, is at the front of the room.

What would be better? A circle? For a while I used to ask classes to sit in a circle (in rooms where we weren't bolted down). It was much better. But after a time I become depressed about it. It was still awk-wardly geometrical; it was still my trip, and they were still dutifully following orders. I felt that if I told them to sit on each other's heads, they'd do it. So next semester I simply took a position in the second seat of the fourth row or thereabouts. I still do this most of the time. Some classes begin to move their chairs around, often within a matter of days, into a sort of loose, pleasant jumble, although they usually maintain a certain pious distance from me, leaving me at the center of a small but unmistakable magic circle. Occasionally, a class is unbelievably faithful to the traditional seating plan. They sit mournfully facing an empty altar and they sprain their necks trying to see me and the other students. I curse and mutter but they hold firm. It's almost as though they're saying, "Screw you, you bastard, you're going to have to *tell* us to move." And I swear to myself I won't. But I usually give in about half way through the semester.

But why those chairs at all? Why forty identical desk-chairs in a bleak, ugly room? Why should school have to remind us of jail or the army? (A rhetorical question, I'm afraid.) For that matter, why are there classrooms? Suppose we started over from scratch. What would be a good place to learn stress analysis? What would be a good place to study Zen? To learn about child development? To learn Spanish? To read poetry? You know, wherever I've seen classrooms, from UCLA to elementary schools in Texas, it's always the same stark chamber. The classrooms we have are a nationwide chain of mortuaries. What on earth are we trying to teach?

The scariest thing about a classroom is that it acts as a sort of psychological switch. You walk into a classroom; some things switch on in you and others switch off. All sorts of weird unreal things start to happen. Any teacher who has tried simply to be real in a classroom knows what I'm talking about. This is so hard to express . . . you walk in and everyone's face is a mask.

Last semester I had the best room yet. Because of overcrowding, one class was in an apartment living room on the edge of campus. The school did its well-meaning best to kill the room, boarding up the door to the kitchen and the can and literally filling the small room with long formica-topped grammar-school tables (the formica itself is a message: furniture has won; you ain't carving no initials in these desks, baby). For a while we floundered miserably but then things got better. Some-times we sat in a big square. Sometimes we sat on top of the tables;

once we crawled under them where it was dark and restful. Sometimes we'd pile up the tables and sit in a bunch on the carpet. Sometimes we'd sit on the grass outside. It was only a very small gain though. Given our conditioning and the overall college context, I could have held that class at the beach, at home, in the Avalon Ballroom. *I* would still be *holding* it; they would still want to rest limply in my hands—good natured, obedient students. Neither they nor I can get out from under our schooling so quickly as we might like.

I think that what we need is not to touch up or modernize classrooms but rather to eliminate them.

(Question from the audience: "Where would we learn?" Answer: "We'd manage.")

(3) "They exploit and enslave students; they petrify society . . ."

Let me not be accused of ignoring "what's right with" our schools—to use the patriotic jargon. Schools are where you learn to read, write sort of, and do long division. Everyone knows about that. In college you learn about Pavlov, mitosis, Java Man and why we fought the Civil War. You may forget about Java Man but you get to keep your degree just the same, and it gets you a job. College is also where they discover new medicines, new kinds of plastic and new herbicides to use in Asia. But everybody knows all that. I want to return to the exploit-enslave-and-petrify part.

It's ironic. Radicals dream midnight police raids, or sit around over coffee and talk with glittering eyes about Repression—about those internment camps that are waiting empty. And all the time Miss Jones does her quiet thing with the kids in third grade.

People like to chat about the fascist threat or the communist threat. But their visions of repression are for the most part romantic and self indulgent: massacres, machine guns drowning out La Marseillaise. And in the meantime someone stops another tenth grader for a hall-pass check and notices that his T-shirt doesn't have a pocket on it. In the meantime the Bank of America hands out another round of high-school achievement awards. In the meantime I grade another set of quizzes.

God knows the real massacres continue. But the machine gun isn't really what is to be feared most in our civilized Western world. It just isn't needed all that much. The kids leave Miss Jones' class. And they go on to junior high and high school and college. And most of them will never need to be put in an internment camp. Because they're already there. Do you think I'm overstating it? That's what's so frightening: we have the illusion that we're free.

In school we learn to be good little Americans—or Frenchmen—or Russians. We learn how to take the crap that's going to be shoveled on us all our lives. In school the state wraps up people's minds so tight that it can afford to leave their bodies alone.

Repression? You want to see victims of repression? Come look at most of the students at San Diego State College, where I work. They *want* to be told what to do. They don't know how to be free. They've given their will to this institution just as they'll continue to give their will to the institutions that engulf them in the future.

Schools exploit you because they tap your power and use it to perpetuate society's trip, while they teach you not to respect your own. They turn you away from yourself and toward the institutions around you. Schools petrify society because their method, characterized by coercion from the top down, works against any substantial social change. Students are coerced by teachers, who take orders from administrators, who do the bidding of those stalwarts of the status quo on the board of education or the board of trustees. Schools petrify society because students, through them, learn how to adjust unquestioningly to institutions and how to exercise their critical thought only within narrow limits prescribed by the authorities. In fact, as long as a heavy preponderance of a nation's citizens are "good students" and are in some way rewarded for their performance, then dissenters and radical thinkers are no threat and can be permitted to express their opinions relatively unmolested. In the United States, free expression, to the extent that we have it, is a luxury commodity made available by the high standard of living and by the efficient functioning of such disguised forms of repression as schooling.

Schools preserve the status quo in two complementary ways: by molding the young and by screening them. Today almost all of the positions of relative power in the United States are reserved for those who have completed the full sixteen-year treatment, and perhaps a little more. Persons who are unwilling to have their minds and bodies pushed around incessantly are less likely to get through and therefore tend to be screened out of the power centers; the persons who do get through are more likely to accept things as they are and to make their own contributions in "safe" areas. Thus corporations and government agencies insist that executive trainees have a bachelor's degree, often without specifying any particular major. The degree, therefore, doesn't represent any particular body of knowledge. What *does* it represent? A certain mentality.

It is true, though, that an increasing number of rebels and freaks are getting through (as well as a much larger number of essentially adjusted students who try to have the best of two worlds by pretending that they are rebels and freaks). The small but noisy student rebellion of recent years has had the effect of bringing to campus a number of drop-ins—dissidents who would not otherwise be there. One friend of mine is an excellent example. He belonged to a Trotskyist youth group as a teenager but threw that over in 1963 because the civil rights movement seemed to be accomplishing more than his youth group was. He had made a few futile attempts at college but realized that he had absolutely no interest in it and furthermore had no time for it. After a couple of years in Los Angeles, he disappeared into the Southern movement: Alabama, Mississippi, Georgia. For a while I lost track of him. Then, last year, I heard from him again; he had just enrolled in San Francisco State College—where the action is. He is typical of a growing minority of students; he may do more or less what's needed to stay in school but he is more than willing to risk being expelled or failed out (two years ago he was risking his life). It is unlikely that college will disarm him.

As the tensions in our society work their way up to the surface, some overt rebellion appears in many settings; certainly it appears in schools, which offer at least a meeting place and staging ground for young middle-class rebels. May it grow in good health. But, as our college presidents are fond of pointing out, the great majority—the great silent majority—are there "not to make trouble but to get an education" (for "education," read "degree").

What about this majority? What is the mentality which employers depend upon our school system to deliver? What is most likely to emerge from the sixteen-year molding and screening process?

Well, a "good citizen" of sorts—isn't that the way they put it on report cards? Thoroughly schooled and ready for GE or IBM or the State Department, the graduate is a skilled, neat, disciplined worker with just enough initiative to carry out fairly complicated assignments but not so much initiative that he will seriously question the assignment itself. He is affably but fiercely competitive with his peers and he is submissive to his superiors. In fact, as long as he has some respect from his peers and subordinates, he is willing to be almost naked of dignity in the eyes of his superiors; there is very little shit he will not eat if there is something to be gained by it. In asserting himself he is moderate, even timid—except when he exercises the power of a great institution, when he himself is the superior, when he puts on some kind of real or figurative uniform. At that point he is likely to assume the sacerdotal mask that his teachers wore. At that point—when he becomes official— his jaw hardens.

This college graduate is positively addicted to rules of all sorts at every level. In fact, should he help to form some club or group, it will probably have by-laws and officers and will follow parliamentary procedure. Even in games—cards, Monopoly, whatever—he is likely to have a passionate respect for the rules and to get bent out of shape if their sanctity is violated.

Ever since his gold-and-silver-star days he has been hooked on status and achievement symbol systems. He has a hunter's eye for the nuances of such systems in his work, in his leisure life and in the society at large. He carries a series of grade-point averages in his head and they rise or fall with an invitation to lunch, the purchase of a Triumph TR-2, a friendly punch on the arm from his ski instructor or the disrespectful attitude of a bank teller.

Since grade school, also, he has known how to become mildly enthusiastic about narrow choices without ever being tempted to venture rebelliously out of the field of choice assigned to him. His political world, for example, is peopled with Nixons and Humphreys; its frontiers are guarded by McCarthys and Reagans. He himself has had a taste of politics: he was elected sophomore class president in college on a platform that advocated extending snack-bar hours in the evening. Like Auden's "Unknown Citizen": when there is peace, he is for peace; when there is war, he goes. He doesn't expect a wide range to choose from in politics. His chief arena of choice is the marketplace, where he can choose enthusiastically among forty or fifty varieties of cigarette, without, incidentally, ever being tempted to choose the one variety that will turn him on. His drugs are still likely to be the orthodox ones, the consciousness-contractors: liquor, tranquilizers, a little TV.

He yearns for more free time but finds himself uncomfortable with very much of it. His vacations tend to be well structured. From time to time he feels oppressed and would like to "break out" but he isn't sure what that means. Leaving his family? Starting his own business? Buying a boat? He's not sure.

Let me stop at this point. There is, thank God, a limit to the meaningfulness of such a stereotyped characterization. It hits home in those areas where the college graduate has literally been stereotyped by his upbringing and by the rigid matrix of his schools. But it leaves out what makes him one individual, what makes him real. Doesn't he have a self beyond the stereotype? Isn't he unique—splendid—a center of existence? Isn't he, to use Timothy Leary's phrase, a two-billion-year-old carrier of the Light? Of course. But who sees it? His self has been scared into hiding. The stereotype that has been made of him hides his uniqueness, his inner life, his majesty from our eyes and, to a great extent from his own as well. He's got a sure A in Citizenship but he's failing in self-realization (a subject not too likely to appear in the curriculum).

Let's understand, when we consider this college graduate, that harm has been done not only to him but to society as well. There may, after all, be some of us who assume that dehumanization and standardization are no more than the price that an individual pays in return for a smoothly functioning society. But is that true? Is this man really what's good for society?

Social change is not just the radical's hang-up. It's a means of adaptation, of self-preservation. Now, as our technology and our environment change with increasing rapidity, as we acquire ever more awesome resources and more bewildering problems, we need the capacity to recreate our society continually rather than be victimized by it. This, of course, is the sort of thing that gets said a great deal nowadays but what doesn't get said is that we will not meet this need for rebirth without giving up what we now call schooling. A crisis in civilization—and we are in the midst of several—*demands* the radical thought, the radical will and the profound self-confidence which have been schooled out of our college-educated institutional man. His narrow vision and his submissive conformity aren't good for society; they paralyze it. They are a curse on it.

(4) "They make democracy unlikely."

Our schools make democracy unlikely because they rob the people, who are supposed to be sovereign, of their sense of power and of their ability to will meaningful institutional changes.

The democratic ideal—to which even the most conservative college trustees usually give lip service—means government of, by and for the people. It means power in the hands of the people. Our schools, however, remain less suited to this ideal than to an authoritarian society; they are more effective in teaching obedience than in fostering freedom.

Our textbooks may teach one kind of political system but the method by which our schools operate teaches another. And the method wins out over the textbooks overwhelmingly. A more substantial degree of democracy will become likely only when we understand that political freedom is not merely a constitutional matter; it's also a state of mind, which can be either nurtured or blighted in school.

I don't mean to ignore the reasons that already abound to explain that immense gap between our ideals of democracy and the system we see operating. Some people, for example, argue that democracy only works well in small political units and that centralized democratic government of 200 million persons is just not possible. Others insist that the people are and will always remain too stupid and ill-informed to make political decisions. Then there's the very persuasive socialist argument: democracy is just not compatible with capitalism. Even if you grant the socialist proposition, though, the question remains: is democracy compatible with socialism? I think it could be, more or less—but there are problems involved that are not normally recognized in this kind of analysis.

A socialist country where schooling is standardized and coercive might well, in time, develop an electorate as dismal as ours *even though* its constitution provided the most extensive political freedom for the individual and even though it had eliminated class exploitation in the traditional sense. In fact, the resources adhering to a powerful socialist government create a very special danger in this area. That's why the growing student power movement has the greatest importance politically. The more that political radicalism comes to include educational radicalism, the more nearly attainable democratic government will be.

Capitalist or socialist, a democracy cannot possibly function if its citizens are educated to be clever robots. The way to educate children for democracy is to let them do it—that doesn't mean allowing them to practice empty forms, to make pretend decisions or to vote on trivia; it means that they participate in the real decisions that affect them. You learn democracy in school not by defining it or by stimulating it but by doing it.

If students and teachers ran their own schools, it would do more for democracy than all the government classes ever taught. But it would have to be just that: true participation in running the schools. Not those little make-believe student governments which govern in about the same way that baby's toy steering wheel drives daddy's car. Not even anything like those "faculty senates," which retain the right to create college policy as long as they don't abuse that right by exercising it.

Also, in considering the effect of schooling on democracy, it's wise to think not only about the overall academic decision-making process but also about day-to-day classroom experience as well. That's at the very heart of the problem. It's in the classroom where you learn that happiness is submission and where you grow used to authoritarianism and coercion. It's in the classroom where you learn how to follow orders mindlessly and how to surrender your sovereignty to an institution.

Incidentally, in discussing this question, I've often heard the objection that teachers legitimately possess authority by virtue of their knowledge and that, therefore, democracy is out of place in the classroom. This argument is a favorite with teachers, so it deserves some attention.

It's true that many teachers possess authority in one particular sense of the word but that does not entitle them to authority in every sense of the word. A teacher's authority rests in his special knowledge or ability, not in his power over students. I may be, say, an authority in ancient history but what has that to do with authority in the sense of a right to enforce obedience, to reward and punish? And the fact that I work for the state of California doesn't amplify my academic authority. If I'm sound in my analysis of Athenian society, the state of California adds nothing. If I'm all wrong the state of California doesn't make me less wrong.

Democracy in school doesn't mean that a class votes on whether two and two make four, even though that seems to be the fear of some teachers. Suppose, for example, my entire history class insists that Rome fell because of its sexual laxity. Suppose we argue. I give my reasons and they give theirs. Then, in desperation, I try to impress them by detailing my academic background but they still insist that they're right. In this (unlikely) situation what relevance would grading have? What would it add to my true authority if I were able to pass, fail, expel, what have you? My value to a class is that I can be of some kind of assistance to them. What they make of it is up to them. I'm a teacher not a cop.*

* One counter-argument might be that the authority to pass and fail is necessary, not to coerce knowledge, but to determine a student's fitness to enter a given field or profession. For a discussion of this question and of grading in general, "A Young Person's Guide to the Grading System." [In Jerry Farber, *The Student as Nigger*, pp. 67–73—Editors.]

Democracy in school doesn't mean that we vote on what's true; it means that education isn't anything which is *done* to somebody.

(5) "Authority addicts"

It's time to say a few kind words about our coercive schools. They do —more or less—solve an existential problem. They shape time for us and thus give some meaning, if not to our life, then at least to some segments of it. Do you know what I mean? You study off and on for a final exam, slowly building tension as the date approaches. The night before, you get no sleep; you're in a strange world of glaring lights, notes, coffee cups, piled up books. Whatever other worries you might have are suspended. This task takes precedence; it's something to hold on to. When you approach the classroom, your exhaustion disappears in a fresh wave of tension and nervous energy. This all has to be important, has to be meaningful; anything you stay up all night for and get this worked up about has to mean something. And when you finish the bluebooks, they rest substantial on your desk. It wasn't all a dream; you've got the bluebooks and, eventually, the grade to prove it.

Courses may be pointless and uninteresting. The data may go through you like mineral oil. But at least it is some kind of challenge. And while you're involved in all this, time is off *your* hands and rests in *theirs*—the authorities'. Should you not be attending school, you may feel that you're pissing away time—days and weeks; you may begin to feel very uncomfortable. On your own, you have to face the responsibility for how you spend time. But in school you don't. What they make you do may obviously be a waste but at least the responsibility isn't charged to your account. School in this respect is, once again, like the army or jail. Once you're in, you may have all kinds of problems but freedom isn't one of them.

After you leave school and get a job, you'll find you *need* the job just as you learned to need school. You'll remain an existential minor who needs trustees to spend his time for him.

The schools we have are a cop-out. Why not face the responsibility for what we do with our time? And if we need structures to inform our time, why not find more congenial, more human ones. Why not surround ourselves with tailor-made educational structures rather than torture ourselves to fit the Procrustean set-up we have now.

Besides, things are changing. The leisure-time explosion is removing even the solace of constant work. Leisure calls on the ability to accept autonomy, to be content with internal justification for what you do. The more leisure we have, the more we need to be able to perceive our own needs and then to follow them for no other reason than that we want to.

So where are we headed? Are we going to face the existential problem or run from it? Will we let time fall on our very own hands without trying to kill it. Or will we continue to look for authorities to take the burden of our freedom from us. As we free ourselves from work in the traditional sense, we have the opportunity to lift our heads up and to look around; we become more free to create our lives rather than undergo them.

Drugs, by the way, have some relationship both to school and to the increase in leisure time. A growing number of people have found that smoking a little weed helps them to appreciate the possibilities of unstructured, uninstitutionalized time. Acid and the other psychedelic drugs typically open up possibilities beyond school and beyond the job (dropping out is always dropping *in* to something else). The educational reform movement probably owes a good deal to students and teachers whose drug experiences have made them impatient with the miserable use that schools make of their time.

(6) "If it weren't compulsory . . ."

If we want our children locked up all day until they're sixteen, let's at least be honest about it and stop trying to pass imprisonment off as education.

Say, for example, that a mother and father would like their eight-year-old boy out of the house all day and also off the streets. Then I guess they will want there to be some place for him to go. Call it a youth center, a postgraduate nursery or a daytime internment camp. But why does it have to be a school? It should have plenty of room and lots of variety: places to be alone if you want, places to play games if you want, places to build things, and places to learn how to read and do sums—*if you want*.

Learning isn't a duty that we must be flogged into performing; it's our birthright, our very human specialty and joy. Places to learn are everywhere. So are reasons to learn. All we need, occasionally, is a little help from our friends.

We don't need compulsory schooling to force us to read. There are good reasons to read and things all around us that want to be read.

And if someone should choose to pass his life illiterate, there are other communications media accessible to him. He'll probably make out fine. He may even be able to teach the rest of us some things that print hides.

It would be well if we stopped lying to ourselves about what compulsory schooling does for our children. It temporarily imprisons them; it standardizes them; it intimidates them. If that's what we want, we should admit it.

There's not much point in going on about this. If you've somehow missed reading A. S. Neill's *Summerhill,* you ought to go out and get it.

Incidentally, with compulsory schooling eliminated, there is no reason to assume that most parents will send their children to public internment centers during the day, or that learning itself will be as dependent upon public institutions as it now is. With compulsory education and all the related red tape out of the way, small groups of parents should be able to make their own arrangements to care for their children and even to satisfy the children's desire to learn. Some areas of learning—nuclear physics, for example—require heavy financial support. But many other areas do not; they provide opportunities for those who want to learn or teach to bypass official institutions. Furthermore, advances in computers, in information retrieval and in communication should soon make it much easier and cheaper than it is now to learn outside of public schools. Technological developments should, before long, give a home resources that are presently available only to a large and well-funded school. Sooner or later, if a child (or adult) wants to learn more about, say, snakes or jet engines, he should be able to tune in, at home, to books, films, learning computers and so on, which he can use as much or as little as he wants. Naturally, if the child chooses not to use the computers and books, that should be his unrestricted right. What I'm getting at is that parents should, before long, be able to develop a formidable alternative to our system of compulsory public elementary schools. As for older children—adolescents—the whole matter is less a parental responsibility and more their own.

(7) "If schools were autonomous and were run by the
    people in them . . ."

Learning is not something that is done to you.

Suppose we agree that there must be something better than our schools, something better suited to our human potential, our political ideals and our accelerating technology. What then? It is exactly at this point that there is a temptation to make what I believe is the basic educational blunder: Having tried and convicted the present educational system, one then works out in detail his own educational utopia— setting up a blueprint that covers matters such as curriculum, textbooks, administration policy, student-teacher ratio, classroom construction and so on.

From my point of view, however, a good school can't be described very clearly in advance because one essential characteristic of a good school is *the freedom to establish its own direction*. In fact, there may not even *be* such a thing as a good school within our present conception of what "school" means.

To say that learning is not something that is done to you has meaning on more than one level. With respect to the school as a whole, it means autonomy. There should be no dictatorial governing board or other body above the school making its decisions for it. If we are going to continue our policy of public education, this means that the people and their elected representatives will have to accept a new and radical policy: that they must pay for schools without controlling them. What happens, therefore, on a state university campus or on a junior high school campus would be decided neither by the legislature nor by the governor nor by any board of regents or board of education nor by any chancellor or superintendent of schools but only by the persons participating in the school itself. It is true that there would be a kind of power implicit in the fact that the state or community could refuse to pay for the school or could reduce its funds. But that would be the limit. To the extent that a state or city wanted to have a school, it would have to pay for it and leave it alone. Hopefully, the idea of an externally controlled school will in time become a contradiction in terms.

Autonomy in schools would almost certainly create much greater diversity—something that should be very good for us as individuals and as a society. As it is, almost all of our schools, at any given level, are amazingly alike. Given the way they are governed, this is not surprising. But what if schools were autonomous? Naturally there would be standardizing forces. The overall needs of society—the proliferating communications networks—a considerable degree of cultural cohesion—these would tend to restrain diversity in schools. But still, if schools were autonomous, they would show much more variety than they do now. Schooling arrangements in a given neighborhood would more closely reflect the character of the neighborhood. The country's colleges would offer a much wider and more interesting choice. There would be more experimentation and consequently a greater opportunity for one school to learn from the varied experiences of others. Schools might, in fact, begin to look more like a free enterprise system—but an educational rather than an economic one (free enterprise has always made much more sense to me in connection with the production of ideas than with the production of automobiles).

Also, if schools were autonomous, I would expect our rigid system of educational levels to weaken. There might well be large centers where persons of all ages would learn from each other and where the structural divisions would be based on areas of learning rather than on age. School might emerge less as a molding and screening process that usurps the first third of a person's life than as a continuing opportunity for certain kinds of learning and group activity.

Ideas about curriculum would also become much less rigid, since curriculum would be determined not by centralized authority but by the learners' and teachers' own awareness of what is relevant and necessary to them and their society. On one campus you might find a curriculum in light; on another a school of ecstatic pharmacology. Radical movements would develop through schools, not against them. The departmental concept would probably fade. The concept of "curriculum" itself would perhaps become dated.

It's not my intention to predict everything that would result from autonomy in schools. My basic point is simply that autonomy is necessary if we want schools to become places where you can learn without being deadened and intimidated in the process and where adaptive social change is fostered rather than prevented.

To say that learning is not something that is done to you implies the need for more than just autonomy. *Within* the school it means that everyone must have a voice in the decisions that affect him. This kind of arrangement—democracy—doesn't eliminate discord but it does put the responsibility for a school on all of the people in it.

I can't see any reason why either students or teachers should be shut out of the decision-making process. In fact, the supposed conflict between students and teachers doesn't itself seem to be a basic one; it arises rather out of the coercive and judgmental powers that have been held by teachers and out of the slave role that has been forced on students. In an autonomous and noncoercive school, I would expect most disagreements to cut across this tenuous boundary in other directions.

I hesitate to go on about students and teachers. The very categories need to be questioned. The most meaningful distinction may be no more than an economic one: who gets paid for what he does? And when we all get paid for what we do, that distinction will disappear. Suppose that today I teach gymnastics, tomorrow I study Arabic and the next day I participate in an encounter group. In which category do I belong?

Administrator is still another term. Right now it's in bad repute with many of us because administrators are there to do the bidding of some external authority. In an autonomous and democratic school, *administration* would just be people running their own school. A high school administrator for example, could be either a student or a teacher; he would be more or less a blackboard monitor on a somewhat larger scale. But this category also would be blurred at the very least.

To prevent education from being victimization, it will not be enough to have autonomy and democracy for the school as a whole. One would also want individual groups within a school to be free to develop their own learning structures without being pushed around and standardized by some central administration. However, I want to avoid falling into the trap I described earlier; I want to avoid trying to blueprint an educational utopia in advance. Self-government in practice cannot help but fall short of an ideal and therefore admits of endless approaches. If schools can serve as workshops in self-government, it will be both likely and valuable that they be diverse in this respect.

If schools are free, some of them may choose to renounce a part of their freedom. There may be students who prefer to be dictated to. For all I know there may always be students who want to be graded daily and threatened with probation, dismissal and so on, just as there may always be persons who want to be flogged and will no doubt always find other persons willing to do it. It is certainly not my wish to prevent them.

The freedom I talk about, incidentally, is not merely a matter of "academic" freedom. Schools are not just learning places but communities as well. Many schools are communities in the full sense of the word: people don't just go to them; they live in them. And, in the future, the distinction between "school" and "community" is likely to be much vaguer than it is now. Rochdale, for example, in Toronto, may be a sign of what is to come.

Rochdale is a number of things. To begin with, it's a new 18-story building. The people who live and pay rent in it own it and run it. For some of them it's a very loosely structured place to learn—a sort of experimental college. For others it's just a place to live. There are, furthermore, people who participate in educational activities of Rochdale but who don't live there. Rochdale is also a continuing problem—a place where there is no one to blame things on, where people have to improvise their own structures and to decide what to do with their freedom. Here is a paragraph, titled "The Secret," from one of their pamphlets:

> The secret of dealing with the confusion and uncertainty of Rochdale is to use "we" in place of "they" when referring to the operations of the College. For example, say "what we are going to do with the 17th floor terrace" rather than "what are they going to do, etc." This simple trick clarifies many otherwise ambiguous problems and helps eliminate flatulence.

I hope Rochdale thrives. And even more I hope the idea spreads.*

(8) "The power to say 'no' "

The people who control colleges are fond of pointing out to students that higher education is a privilege. The implication is that if they don't behave, the privilege will be withdrawn. Similarly, in high school the ultimate threat is expulsion. School is supposed to be some kind of favor that society grants you. The condition for continuing to receive this favor is that you accept it on society's terms.

Sweat shop owners used to tell their workers more or less the same thing. It's astonishing that workers swallowed that line for so long. And it's equally astonishing that most students continue to see schooling as a privilege rather than as a transaction in which they happen to be getting a rotten deal.

When you go to school, you do society an enormous favor; you give it the opportunity to mold you in its image, stunting and deadening you in the process. What you get in return is access to a certain income bracket and the material comforts that go with it. But think what you've given up. Other animals have much of their nature born in them. But you were born with the freedom to learn, to change, to transcend yourself, to create your life—that's your human birthright. In school you sell it very cheap.

I have already tried (in Notes 3 and 4) to show that this rotten bargain isn't even good for society, that it forestalls necessary social change. Unfortunately, the dying part of society, which controls schooling, is

---

* If you're interested in free schools, you ought to read a beautiful essay by Dennis Lee, "Getting To Rochdale," in "The University Game" (Toronto, 1968). The essay originally appeared in "This Magazine is about Schools" (Winter, 1968).

also the part least likely to understand the need for profound change. It is the students—the not entirely socialized—who most feel the need for change and who, in trying to transform the society in which they live, become the victims of its self-protective rage.

The power that students have is simply the power not to be students, to refuse a bad bargain, as workers have frequently done—to say "no." If students have power, it is because they have something society needs very badly. Student power is made possible by the dying society's need to remain alive—to preserve itself through its children. Think how our institutions feed on the unformed future. Think even how individuals—those aging businessmen on a college board of trustees —clutch at immortality by putting their trip on the young. Society *needs* students to retain its identity; they are the only future it has. For this reason, students can demand freedom from exploitation and can get that freedom. They can insist that the continuity they provide society be one that is achieved through rebirth rather than through petrification.

There are a multitude of approaches that students can take toward changing schools. But the one that offers the most hope is the strike or boycott. It is more than a gesture, more than a pressure tactic. It cuts right to the heart of the problem. It refuses a bad bargain; it puts the future on strike. Requests can be denied or put off. Demonstrations can be broken up and the protesters put in jail. But a strike is not really vulnerable to force. When Governor Reagan of California recently promised to keep San Francisco State College open at the point of a bayonet if need be, he failed to understand both the limitations of the bayonet and the power of the student revolution.

High school students are in a more difficult position but this has not stopped them from beginning to use boycotts as well as other forms of noncooperation in order to change their schools. A few high school troublemakers can be expelled or disciplined in other ways. But what does it mean to expel most of the students in a school—especially when you've already compelled them to be there? Also, because these students are so regimented and because they are actually compelled to attend, a high school strike, though very difficult to bring about, is an even more dramatic and powerful action than is a college strike.

I have not yet said anything about the possibility of faculty-student cooperation in changing the nature of school. Such cooperation is difficult; most faculty members are still very much caught up in their roles and, even though they have their own reasons to want to change things, are reluctant to make common cause with students. Faculty, further-

more, are very hesitant to engage in the kind of forceful actions that
might endanger their jobs or even their chances for promotion, tenure
and so on. Still, there are enough instances of student-faculty cooperation to keep this an important possibility even at present. In order,
though, for such cooperation to advance rather than impede student
progress, it is essential that students don't wait around for faculty support and that they don't allow professorial timidity to rub off on them.

The American Federation of Teachers represents a relatively militant segment of faculty; they have shown themselves, at San Francisco
State in particular, to be a possible ally for the student movement. But
it must be remembered that the AFT chose to join the students in striking at S.F. State in great part because it was an excellent opportunity to
push their own drive for collective bargaining. AFT militancy—to the
extent that they possess it—is directed toward rather limited goals. It
would be a mistake to assume that the majority of AFT members, in
high school or college, are stalwart supporters of the student liberation
movement or even that they understand it.

In the long run, if students and teachers can outgrow their feudal
relationship, they do indeed have a common cause: the freeing of schools
from domination by outside forces. Perhaps the best thing students can
do with respect to faculty is, first of all, to emphasize that common
cause and to fully support faculty moves for greater self determination
and, second, to work ceaselessly to educate teachers, to show them what's
lacking in school as it is and to show them what education could be.

MERRILL HARMIN & SIDNEY B. SIMON

The Year the Schools Began
Teaching the Telephone Directory

*If Farber's contention is right that the method of school, rather
than the content, is the message, the curriculum could be anything
and school would still do its job. So long as everyone involved*

Merrill Harmin and Sidney Simon, "The Year the Schools Began Teaching the
Telephone Directory," *Harvard Educational Review* 35 (Summer 1965), 125–
130. Copyright © 1965 by President and Fellows of Harvard College. Reprinted
by permission.

takes his task seriously, the schools might just as well teach Silas
Marner, *the* Montgomery Ward Catalog, *or, as the authors of the
next article suggest, the telephone directory.*

No one quite knew what had been the motivating factor. It seemed
unlikely that the Council for Basic Education was behind it. Sputnik
itself seemed a long way off. Some harsh critics, seeking a scape-
goat, suspected the Telephone Company, but upon closer examination
it was clear that they might have had as much to lose as they would
to gain.

No, it was the superintendent's decision, and no apparent pressure
group seemed to have motivated it. The memorandum went out on
March 18th. It was simple and to the point.

> Beginning with the Fall term, all 7th grade classes will be held
> responsible for learning the contents of our local telephone directory.
> Each teacher, working in cooperation with his or her immediate super-
> visor, will evolve the methods and procedures necessary to effect an
> efficient and appropriate achievement of the above-stated goal.

You can imagine the buzzing which went on in the men's faculty
room. Some said that the memo was a first step towards a merit pay
plan. Others were convinced that it had something to do with Admiral
Rickover. An intellectual blamed it on that "Bruner guy." In the women
teachers' room there was a more sedate but none the less bitter inquiry.
"Just what is the old boy up to now?" "Do you think there will be a
system-wide test?" "I wonder if any company has brought out review
books yet?"

Labor Day with its sad, fond farewell to the summer came and
went. School was off and roaring. Most of the teachers weren't settled
enough to give the students the telephone directories until the second
day of class, but out they came and then it began, usually with some
motivation such as this:

"Boys and girls. We are going to have an exciting new unit this
term. As a way of studying our city, we're going through this amazing
collection of information which tells us about the melting pot our city
has been."

One teacher said, "There will be an examination on this material
in February, so you'd better learn it."

Another approached it with, "You wouldn't want to hurt my feelings by not memorizing these few names and numbers, would you,
children?"

Students dutifully received their directories, wrote their names on the labels, and tactfully checked off the condition, "new." Feeling deeply his professional responsibilities, almost every teacher reminded his class that the books would be rechecked in February to see that no pages had been written upon or in any other way disfigured.

Miss Clark, a not atypical telephone directory teacher, was heard to say: "Now boys and girls, let us look over our new textbooks. You will notice that it has a logical organization. It is arranged by the alphabet, as it were, and that's why they don't have a table of contents or an index. Although there are no illustrations in the part of the book we will be concerned with, you can always turn to the yellow pages for a picture or two. I've always enjoyed the listings for exterminators and moving vans. How about you?"

The students were quickly caught up in the enthusiasm the teachers projected and they pounced fiercely upon the new textbooks. Many looked at their teachers with new respect and admiration, for indeed the textbooks *were* arranged by the alphabet. Ah, to have education and wisdom. It was then that Miss Clark wrote on the board, in clear, Palmer-method letters: "Tonight's assignment. Read and memorize the A's."

Most of the students dragged home the telephone directories and after a short scrap with mothers about the t.v.-watching policy of the new term, they sat down to the evening's work. Read and memorize the A's. It was hard going, but this is not an easy world. Teachers, parents and students agreed that school needed to be more rigorous. Nothing comes easily, the students had been told, year after year. So they read and they memorized.

Morning came and the 7th graders filed into their respective classes. "Good morning, boys and girls," greeted our typical telephone directory teacher. "Did you do your homework last night?" (Not wishing to dampen the ardor of learning, she decided against a surprise quiz on this, the first morning of the unit. After all, an understanding of early adolescent behavior had been part of her background.)

"All right, students, let's begin. What is Gregory Arnold's phone number?"

A hush fell over the room, but almost instantly, three hands shot up.

"Eloise," the teacher said.

Eloise answered, her voice more questioning than answering, "Tr 8-9754."

"Very good, Eloise," the teacher said, "but, please, class, let's use the full name of the exchange. Digital dialing is not completely with us yet. Let's say, *Triumph* 8-9754. Next, class, tell us who lives at 174 N. Maple Street?"

Almost all of the hands went up. The teacher smiled benevolently. She had asked them an easy one, thrown out to give everyone a little feeling of success. It was the address of Mr. Appleby, the principal, and almost everyone knew about the old mansion he lived in. The teacher, always striving to provide for individual differences, called on the slowest learner in the class and he gave the right answer. Everyone felt warm and good.

"Now boys and girls, we'll take up a little more difficult topic. Whose number is Wentworth 4-7312?" Panic spread through the class. No one seemed to know. Could she have slipped in a number from the B's? Finally, after the silence seemed unbearable, one hand, timidly, climbed towards the ceiling.

"Yes, Henry?" the teacher asked.

"I'm not sure, Miss Clark, but is it Frank Abelard?"

"Now, Henry, *I'm* asking the questions. Do you know or don't you? Do you wish us to count 'Frank Abelard' as your answer?"

Was she supporting now, giving a hint that Frank Abelard was, indeed, the correct answer? Henry wasn't sure. It was difficult to figure Miss Clark sometimes.

"Well," he said, "I guess I'm not sure."

"But, Henry," she said, "You were right! It was Frank Abelard. You must have more confidence in yourself. Confidence is the substance of maturity. Right? Now, the next question. What is the name of the home appliance repair company on Front Street?" One hand went up instantly and the teacher was taken a bit aback. "Yes, Gloria, do you know the answer?"

"I certainly do. That's my father, Miss Clark."

"That's all very nice, Gloria, but we're here to find out if you did the assignment or not, so I think I had better give you another question. What is the phone number of the American Bar Association?"

A wave of laughter quickly spread through the group. Most of them knew, but Miss Clark didn't, that very often Gloria's father was not available to fix a reluctant washing machine because he just happened to be in a bar, albeit usually not the American one. Gloria didn't answer, she just blushed, and Miss Clark, said, "Now, Gloria, you'll just have to do your work more conscientiously. This is a difficult unit and

I want our class to do well on the finals. You're just going to have to work harder, Gloria, and that goes for the rest of you as well."

The hand of a boy named Edward went up from the back row. "Miss Clark can I ask you a question?"

"Now, now, Edward," Miss Clark said, "Time is running out and we have all of those A's to cover this period. Please save your question. Later, perhaps, in February, we can take it up. Back to our work, class. Which big industrial company in our town has two phone numbers?"

And so it went. Through the B's and through the C's. The students (many of them) studied and the teachers (all of them) cross-examined. After the D's there was increasing anxiety in the air as teachers began to have quizzes. But everyone seemed to know that it was the big marking-period test which was to count the most. That was the time for nerves! Miss Clark was one teacher who did place equal emphasis upon quizzes and tests, and so, of course, anxiety in her room was at a more constant level.

Many questions were raised in the school and in the community about this new seventh-grade curriculum. It wasn't long, however, before a united front of teachers, principals and the superintendent, worked out, in more or less trial-and-error fashion, a set of answers that became quite standard. Soon no one bothered to ask the questions any longer, for the answers had become predictable. For the historically-minded, here is a sample of the more pesky questions.

Q. Why learn the telephone book?
A. It develops good study habits which will be necessary in college and it trains the student to concentrate and apply himself, qualities which are useful in adult life. Among other things, disciplined adults are what we want.
Q. Won't they just forget the information after the tests?
A. The less bright student will most likely forget a lot. However, we intend to have regular reviews in later grades and consequently the retention curve will hold fairly satisfactorily.
Q. Why work so hard learning the telephone book when the directories are so handy when you actually need one?
A. After all, this could be said about any subject we teach. If we want our people to look up information when they need it, why teach anything? Furthermore, life *is* hard and the sooner our students learn this the better off they will be.

There were, of course, some students who did not concentrate enough to learn the phone book. It is not easy to run a school. There are slow learners in every community. These students were identified and plans were made to place them in special remedial classes the following term, classes which would work mainly on the yellow pages. The color, illustrations, greater interest value, and reduced amount of material were expected to result in success for all but the fundamentally bad or lazy. Some children, it was readily acknowledged, just wouldn't learn no matter what a school did.

Back in the classrooms it was letter after letter until the word was out that there would be a system-wide mid-term examination on A through M. Oh, the cram sessions which were organized by eager mothers, the withheld allowances which were used as bludgeons, the diligent studying which went on! Never before did so many telephone numbers, addresses and names get committed to so many memories.

Some boy students in the group spent their hours making small strips of answers which they taped to their shins and which were read later by slowly lifting their trouser legs. Some girls wrote their answers upon flat throat lozenges. A few did nothing; they were non-motivated and didn't seem to care to become other than non-motivated. The only numbers they could get even a little excited about were the ones they phoned regularly themselves.

On the day of the test there were the usual amount of absences due to nervous stomachs. The teachers grudgingly set aside time for make-up exams, vowing to make them harder than the regular exams, "otherwise, everyone will want to wait for the make-up test." So the test was given, the papers marked, the grades carefully recorded in the appropriate grade books, and the teaching routine resumed.

But Miss Clark became increasingly uneasy. She was getting weary of asking, "Who lives at so-and-so? Whose number is such-and-such?" Dull days. Slowly, the rich memories of her undergraduate days in education courses came back. She sifted through the jargon and searched for ideas . . .

The next Monday it was a new Miss Clark. The change rippled through the rows with electrifying results. Miss Clark had gone "progressive." For one thing, she organized a field trip. She and her class went off on a long walk to look upon some of the houses in the "N's." It was difficult to plan, but Miss Clark felt that at least she was doing something worthwhile. Then she came up with the idea of inviting a guest speaker to come to class to talk about the P's. She obtained a film strip on the R's, but it turned out to be about the "Three R's" and she couldn't use it. She attempted to organize committee work on the T's but the committee could find nothing to do, so she had to scrap that idea. Miss Clark programmed the U's and this helped some. They had a bulletin board display on the V's—"Victory Lunch" and "Veteran's Taxi Cab Service." She did role playing on the W's, had a discussion-debate on the X's, and then, with that handsome Mr. Brown in room 107, she did team teaching on the Y's.

By the time the Z's were reached, she was worrying about transfer of training. Would they really know how to use their knowledge? And, then, she had had no "correlated motor behavior training," as they sometimes called it in college. So Miss Clark's class spent two whole days, courtesy of the public relations department of the phone company, practicing dialing the numbers that they had learned (on eighteen telephones of various colors and shapes). It was noisy, and difficult to supervise, even though the students were carefully grouped, sociometrically, but Miss Clark was willing to risk a little to be a good teacher.

Finally, this too had to end. The final exam was a mere six weeks away. So, in Miss Clark's class, as well as in all the others, thirty days were spent in review for the "Big Test."

Review was no fun for anyone. The first week of June came with the sweetness of summer air. The girls in their barearmed summer dresses flitted in and out of the classrooms while the boys seemed slower than ever. Finally, the test was taken, the papers marked and the term was over. A sense of heavy relief settled upon Miss Clark and all the others. The teachers gathered in the telephone directories, properly disciplined those who had written in their books, and stacked the directories in piles of eager readiness. September was not far away.

Miss Clark felt strangely tired. It wasn't that she had really worked harder this term. The feeling of being drained came from something else. Exactly what she wasn't sure and as she walked to her mailbox she was pondering this problem. There was a blue slip of paper in her mailbox among the more routine notices. It was a memo from the superintendent.

> The success of the telephone directory project initiated by this office has earned the well-deserved respect and admiration of the entire community. The rigorous efforts you and your students have made have not gone unnoticed. Certain thoughtful groups of con-

cerned citizens within our district have urged this office to give this project the nation-wide publicity it deserves and also to move the content down further into the elementary school. We agree with those critics who say that we are long over-due in our efforts to reform the softness of the elementary curriculum.

Consequently, we are assigning to the 5th grade the community's telephone directory. Out of appreciation to those faculty members among our 7th grades who gave so much to our pioneer effort in this content area, we are assigning 7th grade teachers the exciting task of teaching the telephone directory of our State Capitol. The 6th grades, to make the study complete, will combine their study of French with at least one unit on various sections of the Paris, France, telephone directory. This is dependent upon whether or not we can obtain government or foundation assistance to purchase the suitable directories, however.

You will hear more in September. Have a most pleasant summer.

The blue sheet slipped from Miss Clark's hand and floated to the floor, but she seemed not to notice.

PATRICIA MICHAELS

Teaching and Rebellion at Union Springs

Are schools as repressive as the preceding articles indicate? Can they be changed? Can teachers who do not want to be repressive survive in ordinary American public schools? These are some of the questions to which the following essay is addressed.

In 1967 I got a job teaching high school in a small industrial community in upstate New York. I didn't think the job would have political significance for me. I had been involved in civil rights demonstrations and anti-Vietnam marches and in general I identified with the movement. I had also taught in an urban ghetto school. No liberal or left activity

Patricia Michaels, "Teaching and Rebellion at Union Springs," *No More Teachers' Dirty Looks,* vol. 52, no. 5 (January 1971), pp. 262–266. Reprinted by permission.

existed in Union Springs, so I saw my job there as a retreat from politics and as an opportunity to teach without the pressures of the ghetto. But, in fact, teaching in Union Springs turned out to be a profoundly political experience. I learned there that decent human relations and meaningful work and education are impossible in this country even in those little red schoolhouses that seemed impervious to the crisis affecting the rest of society.

One of my first discoveries was that most of my students, who looked like Wonder Bread children, were non-college bound and hostile to school. I asked them why they hadn't quit when they were 16. Most replied, like a chorus, "Because to get a good job you have to go to school." They understood that the boredom and discipline were preparation for the future. One boy parroted an administrator on the subject of keeping his shirttails in: "When you work in a factory you're going to have to follow rules you don't like, so you'd better get used to them now."

After a few weeks of teaching, I began to discover that the school was designed to teach the majority of students to adjust to the lives already laid out for them after high school. It reinforced what they had learned at home and in grade school: to blunt feelings, distrust feelings you do have, accept boredom and meaningless discipline as the very nature of things. The faculty and the administration saw themselves as socializers in this process. This point was brought home to me at one faculty meeting following an assembly. In an effort to bring culture to Union Springs, the school sponsored a cello concert, one of several longhair events. The students, tired of having their "horizons broadened," hooted and howled throughout the concert. The cellist was almost as indignant as the teachers and administration. The teachers expressed the sentiment that somehow they had failed to do their job; to train kids to accept things they did not like. Teacher after teacher admitted that while the assembly may have been boring, so were many things in life. *They* had made it; so could the kids. "Culture isn't supposed to be fun," said the principal, "but if you get something out of it, that's all that counts. For most of our kids this is the only time they'll ever get to hear a cellist and their lives will be richer for it."

The school was also designed to promote a definition of work that excluded emotional satisfaction. To the degree that the kids accepted this definition, they distrusted the very classes they enjoyed. Students would often tell me, "This isn't English, it's too much fun," or "School is where you learn—not have a good time." Enjoyment was drinking, speeding cars, minor lawbreaking activities that involved little creativity or effort. Having defined school (i.e., work) as joyless, joy, they thought, must be effortless.

They didn't connect their feelings of depression and anger with the socialization they were undergoing. While putting themselves down as failures, they would tell me everything that was wrong with the school. The petty vandalism, the screaming in the halls, the "cutting up" in class were their means of psychological survival. They didn't see this behavior as an attack on the school system. They were certain, too, that if they didn't shape up, they would pay a terrible price.

Their response to the first novel we read in class, Warren Miller's *The Cool World*, reflected their sense of futility. They admired Duke, the gang-leader hero, and thought he was "cool" because he said what he felt and did what he wanted. At the same time, he was "stupid" because his actions could only lead to poverty, violence, and death. They were infuriated at the ending of the novel when Duke "gets rehabilitated." In the endings that they wrote as an exercise, they had Duke killed or imprisoned. As one boy wrote, "This was the only honest ending because the price you pay for doing what you want is defeat in one form or another."

Resigned to the "realities" of life, they had difficulty accepting praise. They had been taught that they were unworthy and to distrust anyone who thought they were not. Praise challenged their self-image. John B., for example, was a senior who planned to pump gas after he got out of the army. He also wrote poetry. He alternated between being proud of his work and telling me that it was "bull-shit." He was threatened by his creativity. The school had "tracked" him into a "low achiever" class since grade one, and after 18 years he wasn't about to challenge that authoritative definition. The only other job he considered was as a state policeman. "At least you'd have some power," he told me.

The student body was split between the working-class "greasers" and the middle-class "scholars" or honors students. The students from working-class homes saw the honors kids as sellouts, phonies, and undeservedly privileged. The honors kids, for example, had a lounge. The rest of the student body congregated in the bathrooms.

The honors students were more ambivalent in their attitudes toward the greasers. Their own school experience was a grind, and they both resented and envied the relative casualness of the other students.

A few college-bound kids protested against my lenience in grades and the lack of discipline in my classes. They demanded that I lower the grades of the "less gifted" and enforce school rules. Some honors students admitted that behind their demands was a conception of learning as drudgery. Success, in turn, meant the failure of others. But this, they added, was the way things are. Society, they were convinced, owed them nothing. Reality was the status quo, and people should be judged by how well they coped with that reality.

The "scholars'" game in school consisted of conning the teachers. Establish your reputation and slide through. At times, they acknowledged the hypocrisy of the game, but rarely acted on it. While the "scholars" had nothing but contempt for the administration and most of the faculty, they couldn't get close to the other kids because of their unwillingness to give up the privileges that came with being honors students.

The student body was also divided along sexual lines. Men at Union Springs were more individually rebellious; they expressed their hatred of the school in ways that were considered "manly": haphazard disobedience, drinking before coming to school, vandalism. The women, however, were passive about school on a daily basis, since their major concern was the prestige that came from having a boyfriend and their status among the men.

One day I assigned my senior class an article about a girl who had been thrown out of college for living with her boyfriend. The boys in the class acknowledged that while they wouldn't marry a girl who did "that," they didn't think it was the school's right to punish her. The girls said nothing. In their compositions they expressed anger at the injustice of punishing the girl and not the boy. One girl wrote: "It's always the girl who suffers in this situation; nothing ever happens to the boy."

The following day I spoke with the girls (the boys were out of the room) and asked why they hadn't said in class what they had written on their papers. They said that they were afraid. One girl told me that the only time she would talk freely in a class was if no boys whom she liked romantically were present.

On another occasion a boy criticized my assigning a novel that contained obscene language, because, he said, it embarrassed him to read those words in front of girls. At the end of the class, a few girls told me that while people should be free to read and write what they wanted, they were glad at least one boy respected them enough to watch his language.

In spite of these divisions among the students, the oppressiveness of the school sometimes brought them together in action. Smoking in the bathrooms was the most controversial issue in the school. Breaking the smoking rules enraged the teachers. Several of them spent their free time catching the smokers, bringing them into the office, and getting them suspended for three days. The administration, in an act of desperation (20 cigarette butts had been found on the floor in one day), removed the entrance doors to the bathrooms. After unsuccessfully petitioning the principal, 25 students lined up in front of the men's room and refused to proceed to their first-period class. The principal threatened to call the police if they wouldn't obey his order to move.

Inside the faculty room, some teachers said they wanted to bust heads and hoped that the administration would allow it. Others joked about how our students were trying to imitate the college kids.

In an assembly later that afternoon, the principal announced that he was replacing the bathroom doors, but only because of the responsible behavior of the majority of students. "All over the country," he said, "bearded rebels are tearing up the schools and causing trouble, and now we have their younger versions at Union Springs. We know," he added, "that while the troublemakers demonstrate, the cream of the crop is dying in Vietnam. These are the true heroes. The boys who stood in front of the men's room this morning are the riffraff."

The students had not thought of the demonstrators as riffraff. They were among the most popular kids in school. But neither had they seen them as part of a national movement. By making that association, the principal had helped to break down some of the students' antagonisms toward the left. Later, when SDS people tried to link up with students at Union Springs, some of the groundwork had already been laid by the principal.

By my second year at Union Springs, I was intensely sensitive to the repressiveness of the school system and my own role in it. My way of dealing with that was to make my classes more relevant to students' lives. I told them to write about about what they felt in the language with which they were most comfortable. The first papers I received were filled with obscenity, and I criticized them on stylistic rather than moral grounds. In the second papers, the students' efforts to shock me changed into honest attempts at good writing. I told one class of seniors who were working on short stories that I would mimeograph and distribute some of their work. The most popular story was a satire concerning soldiers in Vietnam; it was sprinkled with obscenity. I said that I would reprint the story as promised, but I wanted the class to be aware of the risk. They all agreed that the author had written what he felt and that there was nothing objectionable about the piece.

A few weeks later the principal told me that I would have to "cease and desist" from accepting students' work that made use of "poor" language. The principal also criticized me for playing rock music in my classes. "You're allowing too much freedom in your classes." He told me that while these methods were all right for "Negro kids," since "that's the kind of life they're used to," or for very responsible college-bound students, they were not all right for youngsters whose future success in the army or on their jobs depended on their following rules.

As a result of my classes, he said, students were becoming defiant and teachers and parents were complaining. He said that I was doing a disservice to students in allowing them a freedom that they were not going to have later on.

Up to that point I had not thought of my work as political. In fact, I had berated myself because I hadn't spent more time talking about the war, blacks, tracking, and so on. Movement friends I had spoken with warned me that far from "radicalizing" my students, I was providing them with a "groovy classroom," making school more palatable and adjustment to a corrupt system easier for them. After speaking with the principal, however, I concluded that my classroom methods were political. In order for the students to fit into the society, they had to believe certain things about themselves, about their teachers, and about their work. By permitting my students to use their own language in the classroom and to wander the halls without passes, by helping them to discover that schoolwork could be creative, I was challenging the values of the school and, therefore, those of society. That was the beginning for the students of understanding the relation between their lives and the movement.

I told the principal that I could not comply with his order but would discuss the issue with my class. He warned me that I was close to losing my job and that he couldn't figure out why I wanted to be a martyr for the students.

The next day I told my class what had happened. They agreed that we should continue to do what we were doing, although a few students argued that I was teaching revolution and disrespect for authority. One boy told me that his father said that if I were teaching in Russia I would have been jailed long ago. Other students defended our classroom activities, saying that this was the first time they'd been able to express themselves in school. "Everybody in town is calling Mrs. Michaels a Communist," one girl said. "Everything they don't like around here they call Communist. We've done nothing wrong and neither has she. Those who don't like it here should transfer to another class, and not ruin it for the rest of us."

Although the students expressed concern about my losing my job, they knew that the issue was them, as well as myself. It wasn't *my* class that was on the line, but *our* class. Crucial to their understanding of the issue as it deepened was my continuing to inform them of developments. By breaking down the traditional teacher-student relationship, I could speak with them not only about their own oppression but mine as well. In that process, the students had begun to listen to me when I raised questions about the war, the draft, and the tracking system, although they weren't ready yet to ask those questions for themselves.

In January of my second year, a local SDS chapter sponsored a festival and several workshops for high school students. I announced the events to my students and urged them to go. In spite of warnings from administrators, teachers, and parents, a number of students attended. Several teachers showed up to "learn about SDS," but the students knew that they were spies.

The SDS organizer asked the students if they wanted the teachers to stay. "They are part of the reason we're here," one boy said. "We can never talk honestly in their presence and we can't now. They have to leave." When the teachers refused to go, the students walked out of the room and set up another workshop—a liberating experience, defiance without punishment, a taste of collective power.

The festival changed the students' attitude toward the left. Their disdain for the "peace freaks" was based on a stereotype of the cowardly college student. Their brothers were fighting in Vietnam and if the leftists took their beliefs seriously, they "would be fighting too." One boy told me that the only time he took college demonstrators seriously was when he saw them on TV at the Chicago convention. The students at Union Springs disliked the college protestors because they saw them as a privileged group and they couldn't figure out why they were rebelling.

Students at Union Springs felt ambivalent about leftist culture. Although they talked about "filthy hippies," they listened to the Doors and the Rolling Stones. Rock music was vital to their lives. To hate hippies was difficult for them because Mick Jagger was one, too. The longhaired radicals who spoke to them at the SDS festival acted tough, brave, and "tuned" into the kids' experiences. That the principal and teachers defined these people as outlaws only made them more attractive.

The festival and the presence of high school students at an SDS function frightened the community. The newspapers were filled with letters for the next few weeks condemning the SDS and the students who attended. Kids brought the newspapers to school and we discussed reasons for the community's and administration's terror at SDS presence. Gradually the kids began to connect the local issue with the anti-Communist, pro-war rhetoric they had heard all their lives. They had begun to identify their own rebellion with the rebellion of the people they had earlier called "rioters," "peace creeps," and "commies."

Earlier that year I had talked with some students about Cuba. They had insisted that Castro was a dictator who filled the prisons with anyone who disagreed with him, and that the United States ought to invade the island. When I questioned the reliability of media reporting, they didn't respond. Only after they read the distortions about themselves in the local newspaper stories did my argument have some meaning for them. When they were not involved in their own struggle, they accepted what the TV and the newspapers told them. They had even resented my raising questions about Cuba, Vietnam, or blacks. As one student told me after I talked with him about the war, "Our government couldn't be doing all of those terrible things." What made those "terrible things" believable to him was his new-found consciousness of what the school had been doing to him every day and how the principal and teachers responded when he began to act.

In the months that followed the SDS conference, I talked with students in class, during free periods, and in my home, where many of them became frequent visitors, about everything from Vietnam to dating problems. In April of that year, some of them joined an SDS demonstration against Westmoreland.

As the opportunity to rebel began to develop at Union Springs High, many of the women held back. They didn't see the relevance of the rebellion to their own lives, and some even discouraged the boys from participating since it disrupted the normal social life of the school. The girls who did participate, however, were the most militant and committed of the rebels. Some were girls whose dating unpopularity had made high school hell for them and who identified with me because in my classroom they could assert themselves in ways that won them respect. Others were girls who were more assured of their popularity and, because they were not hung up in the individualism of the boys, could act together more easily.

The male students, on the other hand, were beginning to challenge the traditional values of individualism and competitiveness that had made it difficult for them to rebel together. Previously much of their prestige had depended upon *individual* defiance. As one boy told me earlier that year: "I talk back to teachers, but when everybody starts doing it, it doesn't mean anything anymore."

About two weeks after the Westmoreland demonstration, seven students decided that they were going to boycott an honors assembly and asked if they could use my room. The assembly was an annual ritual to humiliate the majority of students and to honor the handful who had "achieved." The students felt that their refusal to participate was justified, but were uncomfortable about the action. One boy said, "Listen, I don't like this: 'Cutting up' in class is fun, but this is different. It's too serious. I'm not scared or anything, but everybody's acting like it's such a big deal." The boy may have expected punishment for his action, but he felt threatened because he had involved himself with six others in a collective decision to defy the school system. If they escaped without punishment, he would be only one among seven heroes. If they got into trouble, his act couldn't be dismissed as a prank. Another boy replied, "This is different from setting a cherry bomb off in the halls and running away. We're identifying ourselves and we're trying to figure out why we're doing it. If you don't see that, you'd better leave."

In early May, I was fired. Many students prepared to sit in. They made signs, held meetings, and argued with their parents, who urged them not to get involved. The administration responded with threats of police, suspensions, and warnings to seniors who "might not graduate" if they participated. Administrators phoned the parents of the student leaders and urged them to keep their kids at home. Police watched the entrance of my house. On the morning of the sit-in, teachers in the halls urged the students to hurry to class. Many students did stay home. Others were confused and stood around the halls. About 50 sat in. Six students were suspended for five days, and one boy was beaten by the vice-principal when he refused to move on to class.

The next morning the principal met with the students and tried to calm them. There wasn't anything they or he could do to get me back in school, he said. But he would listen to their grievances about the school. After a few days of restlessness and more meetings with students, Union Springs High had ostensibly returned to normal.

But many students had changed during my two years there. When I first met them, they had been resigned to the limited world that the school had defined for them. They didn't believe that they were capable of creating anything larger. Experiences in my classes and their struggle opened the possibility of new definitions of work, of teachers, and of themselves. When they had to defend those discoveries to parents, contemporaries, and school personnel, the students learned how to work together.

I did not come to Union Springs to be a political organizer. I came to teach. But I refused to be the teacher that both the administration and the students expected me to be. I had rejected the role of cop and socializer not out of any revolutionary commitment, but out of my need to relate to my students. This same need made me reject the labels "lower track," "non-college bound," and "slow learner" that were placed on my students. My refusal to play the traditional teacher role was linked to my refusal to accept them as inferior because they had been treated as such. By breaking down their stereotypes of themselves and of me, I also helped them break down their self-confining images of the world around them.

One letter I received from a female student indicated the achievement as well as the limitations of my work at Union Springs: "Up until you came to us, I'm sure no student knew where he or she stood in the school. They didn't know the powers they had. Now we know them and are trying to use them as best we can. It's going to take time to get organized, but the way things are going now, I'm sure the time will come. I remember the time I was accused of smoking. The principal told me that I had no alternative but to admit I was smoking. I told him that I wasn't and that he could get the Supreme Court on it if he wanted to, but he couldn't prove it. That was the first time I really used the power I had and I won. It didn't seem like much power when it was all over, but I can still remember looking at his face and noticing that his smirk was gone and that he really looked afraid of me. I don't know if you realize it or not, but that small power has affected almost every kid in school and I think that's why you were fired."

Energy had been released at Union Springs, but where will students go with this energy, what will they do with it in that same school this year, in the army, in the factories, and in their marriages? The students were ready to join a movement. Right now there is no movement for them to join. Those who are still in school write me that Union Springs is quiet again. Those who are out say pretty much the same thing. The movement that speaks to the needs they experienced and acted on at Union Springs is yet to be created.

part 2

"The basic moral and spiritual value in American life is the supreme importance of the individual personality. . . . In educational terms, this value requires a school system which, by making freely available the common heritage of human association and human culture, opens to every child the opportunity to grow to his full physical, intellectual, moral, and spiritual stature. . . . By exploring and acknowledging the capacities of each child, education seeks to develop all his creative powers, to encourage him to feel that he can do things of value, that he belongs, and that he is wanted. It discourages every tendency toward despotism. It assigns no superior moral status, but rather a more definite moral responsibility, to the strong and the able. It endeavors to arouse in each individual a profound sense of self-respect and personal integrity."

—Educational Policies Commission,
National Education Association

"Today it embarrasses many teachers to be reminded that all sorts of values are transmitted to students, if not by their textbooks then by the informal curriculum—seating arrangements, the school bell, age, segregation, social class distinctions, the authority of the teacher, the very fact that students are in a school instead of the community itself. . . . Yet the formal curriculum continues to be presented as though it were value-free. . . ."

—Alvin Toffler, *Future Shock*

Values
schools transmit

Sociologist Patricia Sexton has observed that "all societies use the schools for ideological instruction, to transmit core values to the young and teach order and loyalty to the society."[1] Her analysis in 1967 concluded that United States schools were *relatively* open to various ideologies. The readings in Part 1 and Part 2 generally concur with her first statement, but disagree with her conclusion. Critics of schools today argue that despite such academic excursions as the "discovery" method, flexible scheduling, programmed reading books, and individually prescribed instruction (IPI), the American school expects, demands, and rewards students who are obedient rather than questioning.

When asked what values should be transmitted in the schools, Americans of many generations have responded, "Those which prepare students for life." Another commonly cited value has been that school is the place where future citizens learn to participate in and contribute to the democratic way. More specifically, what goals does the school seek to pass from one generation to another?

Interestingly, the most widely known statements which call for transmission of specific values in schools have come within a decade or two after the close of large military confrontations. Apparently, the major wars have caused Americans to reexamine and reshape the country's purposes and priorities. For example, encouraged by a large financial prize offered by the American Philosophical Society in 1796, major thinkers spoke passionately for a national system of education. Patriotism became more important than moral instruction. A post-revolutionary best-seller such as Noah Webster's "blue-backed" speller was more concerned about speech than grammar because he hoped to build a national language and to eliminate sectional dialects.

In 1918 the National Education Association's Commission on the Reorganization of Secondary Education issued its recommendations, *Cardinal Principles of Secondary Education.* Citing international rela-

[1] P. Sexton, *The American School: A Sociological Analysis* (Englewood Cliffs: Prentice-Hall, 1967), p. 6.

tions, increasingly complex economic order, the "immigrant" problem and more leisure, the commission urged health courses and promotion of "worthy home-membership, worthy use of leisure, and ethical character."

Six years after World War II ended, another NEA body asked schools to promote "moral and spiritual values" in the public schools. This list of values began with "the supreme importance of the individual personality," and included moral responsibility, brotherhood, the pursuit of happiness, and the belief that institutions are the servants of mankind. The commission believed courses that taught *about* religious groups and their contributions to civilization would be helpful.

It seems clear that the American school has transmitted values the country perceived of highest national importance. Patriotism has been highest on the list. Certainly, order and obedience have ranked consistently high in the school's value system. Students are also taught that good is rewarded and wrong punished.

Most obvious, however, is that the rhetoric about the functions of schooling and values in the classroom should always be weighed carefully, for rhetoric is frequently misleading. If one takes the description that the school "prepares one for life" to mean that it prepares the individual to be a quiet, pliant member of society, then it can be accepted as true. On the other hand, the school as a model of democratic procedures is far from ideal.

Consider the faded dreams of American statesmen and educators of the past: the national system of education envisioned by Revolutionary War leaders is yet to be fulfilled; the 1918 hope for comprehensive physical fitness programs is challenged by the data that in 1970 less than five percent of America's elementary schools had gymnasiums; the Korean era call for moral and spiritual values was drowned in the roar of the Sputnik rocket and the scientific curriculum aftermath.

The central question raised in Part 2 is: Can the schools be as democratic as they claim to be, when society expects the schools to inculcate specific values? Stated differently: Can the student be socialized without being indoctrinated?

Hopefully, the articles that follow will encourage more specificity. Professors and students often conclude that middle-class values permeate the classroom. But that begs the question of which middle-class values. Are they the only values conveyed by the curriculum?

As the historical notes suggest, it is easy to have commissions detail broad values society would like conveyed to students. It is easy to be critical, to point to bland instruction, and to ask the school to become more controversial. Prospective teachers especially should ask themselves: Will I be able to stand the heat and pressure if I use an unpopular book, or challenge a predominant community more?

A final realm of issues relates to the school curriculum *per se:* Schools tend to add courses to please pressure groups. Science, driver education, black studies, and sex education are recent additions. Now religion, drug education, and ecology are being considered. What criteria should be used in adding and dropping courses? What groups should determine curriculum—school board, parents, faculty, students, pressure groups? Finally, does the addition or deletion of courses affect the transmission of values, or do values come from how we act rather than from what we espouse?

WILLIAM BOYER

War Education

William Boyer suggests that our values and life styles frequently are built upon "conventional wisdom." Through an extended discussion of the military mystique, he asks the reader to determine whether the schools reenforce this wisdom, or whether they can challenge it.

Conventional wisdom tells us that things are the way they appear to be. Institutions are merely the means to the goals they claim to serve. The military establishment is merely a means to national defense. A nation needs to defend itself, so in a militarized world we must have armed forces, and they must be the best the nation can afford.

We have built national policy on conventional wisdom. We first created a capacity to defend ourselves against attack. When ICBM's with nuclear warheads made defense impossible, we changed to a strategy of offense, and counted on a balance of terror for our defense. We worked to achieve a "balance" in our favor, and so effected a persistent escalation of terror. Finally the burgeoning armament on both sides produced the capacity for mutual annihilation. Yet the arms race continued and resulted in the era of overkill. We then gained national security through a policy based on the escalation of overkill.

A shift in political language has corresponded with the military

William Boyer, "War Education," *Phi Delta Kappan*, vol. 48 (May 1967), pp. 418–421. Reprinted by permission.

transformation. National security has been based on containment, deterrence, and nuclear brinkmanship. Justification has been grounded in the need to defend the "free world." Such policy, based on an assumed absolute goodness of our goals, has needed no reconsideration. The effort has gone instead to research and development of an ever more advanced and powerful military technology. Conventional wisdom has assured us that reliance on technical superiority is the only sane road to national security. Unconventional wisdom would assert that it is a likely road to international annihilation.

No nation easily admits that the traditional beliefs are no longer valid. Most Americans are especially unlikely to accept basic criticism of national political-military policy, for the conventional way produced military victory for all those Americans who have survived two world wars. The dead were not victorious, but most Americans survived. So the escalation of nuclear terror has seemed wise to most surviving Americans, more wise than it may seem, for example, to Japanese survivors of the bombing of Hiroshima.

Those who do not accept conventional wisdom question whether things are the way we assume they are. Institutions may not be doing what they claim to be doing. Means may not be merely instrumental to ends, they may *determine* ends. Preparation for war may not serve merely the goals of national defense, but, as has often occurred in the past, may produce attitudes and beliefs which cause war. Reliance on the threat of annihilation may create conditions which make annihilation necessary. Unconventional wisdom looks beyond the formal structure to examine the informal structure, for it believes, among other things in the existence of self-fulfilling prophecies.

The way in which one frames a problem limits the possibilities of its solution. Saul Friedman in his study of RAND, a civilian research arm of the Air Force, found that the organization "has done little positive research toward ending nuclear confrontation because of the belief of RAND's leading thinkers that the theory of 'mutual vulnerability' is a positive way to peace." This is a conventional perception of the world, yet the danger of such narrow framing of problems is that research limited to this narrow perspective may influence political policy. The danger in this case was well founded, for in 1957 RAND predicted a Russian crash program in ICBM development, consistent with the military metaphysic of their client. The prediction was incorrect, but it encouraged the United States to embark on a crash program. By 1961, when it became evident to the Russians that the United States had an overwhelming superiority, the Russians did increase their production of ICBM's. Friedman says: "The RAND prediction, as it turned out, precipitated another round of the arms race."[1]

The RAND incident is neither unique nor isolated. The particular incident is not of central importance. What is most important is its illustration of the process of the self-fulfilling prophecy. This process is not taken into account in the bulk of decision making, even though it will largely determine the kind of world we will have—or will not have —tomorrow.

The self-fulfilling prophecy can be further illustrated. Young men are drafted into military service because of the "requirements" of national *defense*. When they get into the armed forces they are taught *war*, with its various arts, sciences, beliefs, and attitudes. It is thought that learning to wage war is an unfortunate necessity in keeping the peace. This way of framing the problem does not admit that military forces can be used for aggression or to pressure other nations into economic and political subservience. Even the label "Department of Defense" is a euphemism in support of the official function. (It was more accurately labeled the War Department a couple of decades ago.) So when our Marines land, as they did recently in the Dominican Republic, and as they have in many periods of American history, tortured rationalization is applied to call the act national defense.

Cloaking the armed forces in the role of national defense obscures much of what is taught by the military establishment. Ordinarily we think of "education" as formal schooling. Yet evidence strongly suggests that the pervasive qualities of an environment are more potent determiners of attitudes, values, beliefs, and behavior than formal classes labeled "education." When our government officials decide to draft young men into the armed forces they seldom treat it as compulsory education. National defense and manpower requirements are cited as the central issues. But the hard fact is that young men are sent into two or more years of compulsory war indoctrination.

Armed forces education seeks to build fighting morale by teaching a special military ideology which filters ideas and information.[2] Information is selected to fit the morale objectives. Descriptions of "enemy" powers are constructed to promote a fanatic fighting psychology. The metaphysical certainty of the military ideology provides a basis for unequivocal pronouncements, even in official materials, about the true meaning of human nature, freedom, the American way of life, and good and bad economic systems. The training goes well beyond teaching men how to fight. It tells them what to believe and why they should fight. The message is even reinforced by the Chaplain's Corps, which rationalizes the need to kill and provides divine sanction for each military adventure.

Such education assumes first that the indoctrination of beliefs and attitudes is necessary for national survival. But thought control is necessary only when the general reasons for fighting will not meet the test of open inquiry. Second, this education implies that the end justifies the means. This is true only within a system that has abandoned the democratic belief in the worth of the individual. When military training is seen as an educational system the anomaly becomes clear, for the American armed forces provide an education suitable more for a totalitarian society than for a democratic society.

Morris Janowitz points out that "military mission is the key to military organization. . . . The unique character of the military establishment derives from the requirement that its members are specialists in making use of violence and mass destruction."[3] The organization and management of violence excludes training in nonviolent conflict resolution and in determining the conditions under which violence might be defensible. Education in the military is education in learning to want to kill and how to kill. An education which emphasizes preparation for war as the only plausible alternative is likely to create its own world. Though the atomic age requires peace education, the lion's share of national wealth goes into a system which claims that thinking war is the only way to peace, and the message is even transmitted through a burgeoning international network of military radio stations.

CIVILIAN WAR EDUCATION

War education, however, is not monopolized by the military. American television glorifies war for the young and the old, and American industry has shown the know-how to capitalize on the mass production of war toys and war games for American children. Divisive ethnocentrism and moralistic self-righteousness permeate television war stories and war games. It becomes normal and exciting to see the dehumanized enemy killed. Even now in the Vietnam war the real thing has become the game, and the mass media parade statistics (often of dubious accuracy) on the daily kill. A high score of kills of the enemy produces delight; high scores against our side are lamented.

As American culture becomes more war-oriented, the value system of the armed forces often becomes a model for the American way of life. President Truman after World War II wanted universal military training "to develop citizenship responsibilities and to foster the moral and spiritual welfare of our young people."⁴ And in 1964 Congress expanded the high school ROTC programs by nearly 500 percent, even though the Department of Defense said it was actually a hindrance to national defense. It was defended for its "educational" values, and there was scarcely any opposition, even from professional educators. Some educators even actively supported the program.

Our concern for appropriate educational experience has lagged far behind our national concern for military technology because the implications of the new technology are not adequately understood. The atom and hydrogen bombs and their new delivery systems made most of the old weapons and old strategies obsolete. Everyone grants this, but what is typically not understood is that the old military *structures* are obsolete. Not only do they gobble up national resources and hinder economic improvement and social reform, but nation-states with massive atomic power have neither the capacity to produce successful aggression nor defense.

Smaller wars, such as those in Vietnam, no longer are worth the risk of escalation into thermonuclear disaster. A strong international police force under the United Nations is necessary to resolve violent conflicts, but national armed forces are obsolete. We now are developing a world comparable to a United States where the president has a small conventional military force and the governors of each state have nuclear power. To be sure, other nations would need to cooperate in disarming, but the failure to change cannot be blamed solely on other nations, for we do not lead disarmament policy.

The political implications of modern military technology are rarely comprehended by the professional militarists, so education within our national military establishment perpetuates the pre-atomic structure. It is an anachronistic education, therefore part of the problem rather than part of the solution. Those caught up in the burgeoning military establishment of World War II and the subsequent hot and cold war have become the least likely to create a world without atomic holocaust. Yet those locked in the military value system constitute the core of the American establishment, whether they are normally civilian or military. Life within a military establishment may be more charged with military values, but the expanding military-industrial-cultural complex has made the militaristic outlook a pervasive feature even of civilian culture. Nationalistic militarism, like all systems of belief, cannot be contained merely because a civilian president is commander-in-chief of the armed forces. Nations take on the characteristics of the enterprise they become involved in. We become what we do.

It is doubtful that the expanding militarization of American society can long continue without catastrophe, for a garrison state can hardly be expected to concentrate on the urgent goals of peace. C. Wright Mills has pointed out that the main cause of World War III will be preparation for war. We cannot blissfully continue to ignore the consequences of the attitudes and beliefs that war education produces.

PUBLIC SCHOOL PEACE EDUCATION

Public schools are among the institutions which usually reinforce conventional, pre-atomic "wisdom." To help prepare students for the atomic age, however, they could point out that the established outlook and the mass media which usually support such an outlook are representative of a traditional point of view. The school could help students examine unconventional alternatives and compare them with established orthodoxy. History could be studied culturally and the strains of violence and the war culture could be identified in the same way that a culture of poverty is now being identified. Education could focus on cross-cultural education and cross-cultural experience, especially with nations as important to the future as Russia and China. Issues of war and peace could take a more central role, while war indoctrination programs such as Junior ROTC would need to be discontinued. If military recruiters are permitted in the schools, the need for the students to know non-military information should also be respected. Those who can explain the laws and procedures for conscientious objectors should be made equally available.

Pre-atomic thinking still permeates not only our schools and the armed forces but virtually all American institutions, yet our age urgently requires more planning based on reflective thought about where we have been, where we are going, and where we want to go. A few people are beginning to question whether our deterrence strategy really deters and whether our national defense defends. The unconventional wisdom emerging from such inquiry may offer solutions difficult to accept for those who are dependent on the beliefs of a pre-atomic world. Yet the option is not whether to reassess but when to reassess, and the kind of education Americans receive or fail to receive will affect their capacities to choose. Basic reassessment will come, but it would be more useful prior to World War III than afterwards.

NOTES

1. Saul Friedman, "The RAND Corporation and Our Policy Makers," *The Atlantic,* September, 1963, p. 68.
2. See William Boyer, "The Armed Forces as Educator," *Proceedings of the Philosophy of Education Society,* 1963, pp. 85–92.
3. Morris Janowitz, *Sociology and the Military Establishment.* New York: Russell Sage Foundation (for the American Sociology Society), 1959, p. 106.
4. Harry S Truman, *Memoirs.* New York: Doubleday, 1955, Vol. 1, p. 511.

JUDITH MARTIN

The Untainted World
of Our Miss Americas

If Boyer is correct that we become what we do—that societies take on the characteristics of the enterprises they become involved in—then the indirect commentary provided by the annual Miss America Pageant and the hundreds of similar "beauty" and "queen" contests raises some serious questions about who we really are.

Atlantic City, N. J.—"Anybody here over 35?" shouted Bert Parks as he gave an extra wiggle to his hips.

"Yaaay" came back the answer from the crowd gathered in Convention hall last week to watch the Miss America pageant.

They had come to cheer *their idea of what youth should be like* and 50 girls tried all week to personify that idea.

Miss America girls do not smoke, drink, date, discuss controversial topics or go around unchaperoned during the pageant—the winner agrees to behave that way for a year—and they are very polite to their elders.

They support their government, condemn dissent, and set their goals on spending a year or two in traditional female occupations—modeling or elementary school teaching—until the right man comes along.

Miss America of 1970, Pamela Anne Eldred of Detroit, Mich., gave a press conference Sunday in which she said she was a spokesman for her generation and she made a statement about the establishment: "I feel that the people who were voted into office must have the intelligence to know what to do and that everybody should have faith in them."

As a spokesman, she said she does not object when the pageant officials refuse to let her speak on certain subjects. "I feel that they are older and wiser than I am and I can always learn something especially from someone who is older. If I am told I can't do something, I am told for a reason and I don't challenge it."

"God love you," said a state pageant official from Michigan.

Other pageant officials, the audience and the judges all talked about how comforting it was to see this girl and the others like her. They called them "true representatives of American youth."

For a few magic days the drug scene, the sexual revolution, and the civil rights, anti-war, female liberation and student protest movements seemed to them to have been just bad dreams or as they kept saying "a tiny minority of kooks."

Miss America told her admirers that the war was right because otherwise the government never would have gotten into it.

Miss Minnesota, Judith Claire Mendenhall, a runner-up to the title, told them that women shouldn't try to run things "because they are more emotional and men can overcome their emotions with logic."

Miss Virginia, Sydney Lee Lewis, won a talent award for a speech in which she condemned student reform movements but lauded her generation for things like "conceiving the rally for decency."

The theme of this year's pageant was "The Sound of Young." There was much talk in it about the new sound and then one talent winner sang "Get Happy" and another played "Bumble Boogie" on the piano.

"Each generation has its own translation of young, and this generation's is a search for the golden rainbow of peace and understanding," said Parks to introduce Miss America 1969, Judi Ford, who wore a Ginger Rogers white pleated chiffon dress and danced the kind of number which used to be the finale of motion picture musical comedies of the 40's. The pastel chiffon dresses with sequined tops, which girls wore with 18-button length white cotton gloves in the evening dress competition, had to be specially made. So did the one-piece, solid color, no-cut-outs bathing suits, which are no longer stocked commercially. Spiked heeled, pointed-toed shoes dyed to match were worn with the bathing suits.

Evening culottes were permitted during the talent competition but most of the girls favored sequined drum majorette type of costumes. Several chose mid-knee cocktail dresses just a shade longer than the new habits of a group of nuns, who attended the preliminary competition one night.

Make-up was used in the shows to create the kewpie doll look of decades ago—bright red lipstick, blue eye shadow and hair teased into bee-hives with wiglets of curls added.

Offstage, however, the girls were more contemporary with shoulder length hairstyles and little wool dresses which gave them the look of 50 Tricia Nixons.

The judges said they were gratified at what they saw and had a hard time picking a winner. "It renews my faith in youth," said Hollywood make-up man Bud Westmore, a judge, whose wife was Miss California of 1952.

"We have a complete misconception of what is going on when we see the New York hippies who don't wash," said Leon Leonidoff, another judge, who has been staging Radio City Music Hall spectaculars since 1932. "This country is wholesome and healthy." His wife is a former Miss New Jersey and he has been going around all week offering contracts to his favorite contestants.

"We really haven't got a thing to worry about," said Judge Jane Pickens Langley, who describes herself as "singer, artist and philanthropist."

"These aren't the girls you hear about because there is never any scandal attached to them," said Judge Zelma George, executive director of the Cleveland Job Corps Center for Women. "Someone should do a master's thesis on them."

"You don't hear about them later because basically they are not ambitious," said writer Joan Crosby, a judge. "They want to be good wives and mothers."

No one seemed to know, however, why most of the past Miss Americas have been divorced at least once.

The pageant officials expressed their delight with the way Miss America 1970 handled reporters' questions Sunday.

Topics on which she smiled and said, "I really couldn't voice an opinion—I don't know enough about that," included drugs, nudity in the theater, unisex fashions, student unrest, what the priorities of America should be, and whether or not 18-year-olds should have the vote. She also stated that she was happy about the moon shot "which proves that the United States is a great country" and that her goal in life is "to be a nice person."

Her mother, Mrs. William B. Eldred, who broke in once just after the crowning to tell Miss America "you are no expert" said that she and her daughter feel alike on all topics. "There is no generation gap," said Mrs. Eldred.

Miss America's one moment of confusion was when she was asked where her father works. He is an employee of Chrysler, and loyalty to the pageant's sponsors, one of which is Oldsmobile, is an important quality of Miss America.

Miss America 1969 said that during her year, love of Toni hair products, Pepsi Cola and Oldsmobile became a spontaneous part of her.

The past and present Miss Americas looked very much alike— both with blonde bouffant hairdos, green eyes, pale skin and wide smiles. They are both, said Bert Parks, "composites of positive wonders."

"All Miss Americas are," he said.

HOLLIS LIMPRECHT

Devaney: A Unifying Force

If the vestal virginity of Miss America is the epitome of values for women, where do we put men? Apparently on the gridiron. The Omaha World-Herald *staff apparently had an easy task selecting University of Nebraska "Big Red" Coach Bob Devaney as the best example of manhood in the American heartland. If Devaney*

Hollis Limprecht, "Devaney: A Unifying Force," *Magazine of the Midlands,* the Sunday magazine of the *Omaha World-Herald,* December 27, 1970, pp. 2–5. Reprinted by permission.

and his admirers plus the thousands of local Devaneys and Vince Lombardis across the country are any evidence, schools should prepare pupils for the gigantic football game of life—the boys competing directly and the girls cheering them on. This is a piece of "conventional wisdom" most schools accept. The reader may well ask if the author of the following article should not take his own observation more seriously, to wit: "Perhaps in a year of turmoil it is pure escapism to drape the Man of the Year mantle on one whose contribution to society is teaching big boys how to play a small boys' game."

In some respects, 1970 was not a very good year. The war cranked on; slowly, to be sure, but nonetheless it cranked on. The economy creaked, prices rose and so did unemployment; taxes climbed and as they climbed the voters of Nebraska turned their governor out of office.

It was called the most divisive non-presidential election campaign in more than a generation; students rioted, women went on a liberation kick and, in Omaha, a policeman was murdered by terrorists.

It was a year when people needed something honest and solid to rely on, and in the midlands, at least, they had that something in their beloved, their revered, their own Big Red.

The University of Nebraska football team created unity while disunity was trying to take root; clean across the state the cry was as unanimous as anything can reasonably be these days: "Go Big Red!"

And the man responsible for this red-hued mania, the man who had brought "next year" to the football fans of Nebraska, the man who, in the words of Sports Illustrated magazine, "harnessed the region's old-fashioned Americanism, dressed it up in red and put it in the stadium to cheer his team," is also the 1970 Midlands Man of the Year: Robert S. (Bob) Devaney.

He is, on the basis of games won and lost during his 14 years as a head coach at Wyoming and Nebraska, the finest college football coach in America. His career record is 113 victories, 28 losses and six ties. In nine seasons at Nebraska his teams have won 78, lost 18 and tied one. Compare that with the 33-56-2 record of Coaches Bill Glassford, Pete Elliott and Bill Jennings in the nine years before Devaney came to Lincoln.

His most recent successes are vivid in the minds of all Cornhusker fans: 10 wins, no losses and one tie; another (the sixth) Big Eight championship and another (the seventh) bowl invitation—back to the Orange Bowl for the third time.

So much for the vital statistics. They are only the bare bones of the Devaney posture at Nebraska. It is more than statistics that make Bob Devaney Midlands Man of the Year.

Cornhusker football has always been a unifying force in Nebraska, and Devaney has been the most successful practitioner of the 25 head coaches who have been involved with this force. He gives 1,400,000 Nebraskans a sense of excellence; he does so well that Chancellor Durward Varner, newly arrived on the scene, strives to make the university as good in education as it is in football.

To paraphrase Ted Sorensen: "Nebraska is a good place to be from, or to die, or to be a football fan." Across the nation, wherever football fans congregate, they know of the Cornhuskers' prowess even if they still think we have to chase the buffalo off the field in order to clear a place to play.

Perhaps in a year of turmoil it is pure escapism to drape the Man of the Year mantle on one whose contribution to society is teaching big boys how to play a small boys' game.

But consider the Greeks; their civilization was the first for the Western world, and the Greeks were playing at Olympic games some 300 years before Socrates appeared on the scene to admonish his fellow Athenians to "know thyself." It isn't too far-fetched to say that "know thyself" is part of the lesson to be learned from football. A young man who has to mesh his personal desires into the machinery of an entire football squad learns, sooner or later, to know himself.

In Devaney, the 60 or 70 young men who make up the Big Red squad have, if not a Socrates as their leader at least a 20th Century philosopher. Those closest to him say he has an almost uncanny faculty for saying the right thing at the right time.

He teaches boys how to live as well as how to hit. An example: After this year's Kansas game, in which the Huskers fell behind, 20-10, but won, 41-20, Coach Devaney told them in the dressing room, after the customary silent prayer: "You learned something today. You learned you can come back. Remember that. That's the lesson of life."

Or his words after last year's 17-7 loss to Missouri, which gave the Huskers a drab 2-2 record and opened the conference season with a defeat. The woebegone players expected a tongue-lashing; instead, Devaney said: "Everybody predicts that the Big Eight champion will lose one game this year. We've just lost ours." He was right. Nebraska won six conference games in a row to tie Missouri for the title and went to the Sun Bowl.

Consider his psychology at that game. He spoke quietly to the boys before the game (it was the first bowl appearance in three years), then he opened the dressing room door to lead them onto the field. Suddenly he stopped, turned back and said: "Boys, half the state of Nebraska is out there cheering you on. And the other half is back home praying for you. Let's go get 'em." The score was 45-6 over Georgia.

He has the knack of creating in the players a desire for team success above individual stardom. Either of the two I-backs, Joe Orduna or Jeff Kinney, is good enough to be Big Man on Campus at most schools. At Nebraska, Devaney has them both willing to share playing time and win.

When he isn't a philosopher or a psychologist, he is raconteur. He is, without a doubt, one of the funniest men in football. His weekly Monday luncheon engagement at the Lincoln Hotel is a stand-up comedian's dream. The quips come freely and easily as he narrates the previous Saturday's film.

On a touchdown by Dan Schneiss: "Dan's a pretty good football player. I think I'll tell him so personally after the season is over."

On a lateral by Jerry Murtaugh that went wild and was recovered by Colorado: "Jerry wanted us to put that one into our permanent play book but we talked him out of it."

On a play in which Jerry Tagge went one way and his blockers went the other and he was caught behind the line: "Jerry left his friends. We always tell him to stay with the people who love him the most."

Possibly his all-time favorite story, told when he's trying to be modest after an especially enthusiastic standing ovation, goes like this: "There are 800 million Chinamen who don't give a damn what happens to the Nebraska football team on Saturday afternoon."

Well, just a darned minute on that one, coach. Maybe Chairman Mao's Chinamen don't care, but don't include Thick Chu Huey, proprietor of a Chinese restaurant in Omaha, in that group. Chu cares. He is a fan, he subscribes to a weekly college football rating system, and he loves the Huskers. "I listen on the radio and I watch the films on TV," he said. "But I don't go to the games. I can't get a ticket."

Can't get a ticket. If there is a flaw in the Husker operation, there it is. Four lucky men who, for the past nine seasons have perched in the front row of the western balcony down by the south goal line, like so many redbirds on a barbed wire fence, are among the lucky thousands who do have season tickets.

The four are farmers—brothers Alan and Brooke Beregren, Neal

McBeth and David Jacobson of near Stromsburg. Doesn't a farmer have something better to do during the autumnal bringing-in-the-sheaves time than go to a football game?

Says Alan Beregren: "During the football season, we work five days a week. Just like the bankers." Bankers. Taxi drivers. Salesmen. Teachers. Loafers. Bartenders. Laborers. Everybody tries to get a seat.

Jim Pittenger, assistant athletic director and ticket manager, says the Huskers could have sold 100,000 tickets to both the Missouri and Kansas State games this year. Since the stadium's record crowd is 68,128 for the 1968 Kansas game, that means thousands of frustrated fans and several hundred thousands of lost dollars.

Every home game for the '70 season was sold out by January 1. The story is the same for the 1971 season despite the fact the Huskers will play an unprecedented seven home games.

And still they keep trying to get tickets. Persons try to will their season tickets to an heir; season tickets become the subject of property distribution in divorces. Tough luck; the option to renew tickets is not transferable. Some 200 tickets are given up each year, usually singles behind a post, said Pittenger. Or by death.

"I've had people drop in en route to or on the way home from the funeral of a deceased friend to inquire about his tickets," said Pittenger.

The athletic department (Devaney has doubled as athletic director since 1967) is toying with the possibility of adding a balcony to the south end zone stands—something that would put capacity slightly in excess of 70,000.

It isn't a matter of money; despite four stadium expansions since Devaney has been at Nebraska, despite a grandiose new press box and despite new AstroTurf, the department will be debt free by the end of the fiscal year next June 30.

Is the athletic program really that successful? The answer is yes, and it is done despite the fact the department receives no tax funds. The double-barreled reason is enthusiasm and financial support.

"Probably no state in the union supports its football program like Nebraska," say Devaney in an interview shortly after the end of the regular season. "They support us with enthusiasm and finances. This makes it much easier for us."

Devaney has no illusions about fielding a loser. "Our fans are understanding in defeat," he said, "but I hope I don't have to put them to a serious test. I'm not naive enough to believe it's not necessary to win in Nebraska any more than in Kansas or Colorado. This is not a criticism of Nebraska fans; any coach must understand this. The big thing is that Nebraska support makes it easier to assemble a winning team."

Nebraska fans do more than pack Memorial Stadium. They shell out money in a variety of ways—the Extra Point Club ($1 to $25 donations), the Touchdown Club (the $100 givers), the Husker Beef Club (whose members contribute some 200 head of cattle a year to feed the hungry mouths), and the big spenders of the Cornhusker Educational and Athletic Award program ($1,000 each). There are 88 of the latter. Total contributions come to some $150,000 a year, which sum just about pays for the athletic scholarships of the players.

Speaking of scholarships, it is in recruiting that football success begins these days. Nebraska had two "poor" seasons in a row—six wins and four losses in 1967 and '68. Devaney shoulders the blame: "We might have had a couple of years of loafing a little at recruiting. We had the conference championships wrapped up in '63 and '64 before the last game of the season and we got a little complacent; no, that isn't the word, but we didn't realize we had let up a little on recruiting. The results were that maybe we didn't have enough to win in '67 and '68. Since then we've worked like hell."

The work this year began in earnest the Monday after the Oklahoma game for Devaney and his staff of nine assistants. A bowl game hurts and it helps. Practice for the bowl game interferes with recruiting trips, but a successful game on nationwide TV will attract prospects.

Like all coaches, Devaney prefers big football players, but he has no stereotypes about size. And he admits to recruiting mistakes. "We don't overlook the guy who can get the job done," he said. He recruited Guy Ingles, the 5-foot 9-inch, 158-pound split end, but he wanted no part of little (for a middle guard) Ed Periard, 5-9, 201 pounds. "We tried to discourage Eddie," said Devaney. But Eddie came out on his own from Birch Run, Mich., without a scholarship, to enroll as a freshman. He did get the scholarship, of course, after his freshman season.

Bowl game business will keep Devaney away from serious recruiting chores until late January, and if there is anything that would cause his enthusiasm for his job to wane, it is this phase of the program.

"It's getting harder for me to travel on those long recruiting trips," he said. But the assistants take up the slack. And Devaney has a superb staff in Jim Ross, who has been with him for 21 years, including high school coaching days in Alpena, Mich.; Carl Selmer, Mike Corgan and John Melton, who also came to Nebraska with Devaney from Wyoming; Cletus Fischer, inherited from the Bill Jennings staff, Warren Powers,

Monte Kiffin, and Bill (Thunder) Thornton, all ex-Huskers with pro experience, and Tom Osborne, ex-Hastings College, ex-pro and holder of a doctor of philosophy degree.

"You've got to have a group of guys around you who are willing to work hard, who won't count the hours on those two and three-week recruiting trips; guys who enjoy talking to high school coaches and to players' mothers, who are loyal to the head coach and to each other, who are willing to prod a kid into getting his degree once he enrolls at Nebraska."

Devaney's staff is a mix of experienced coaches, most with some time as high school coaches where a man has to teach football as well as coach it, and younger staffers with a keen knowledge of the game learned on pro fields.

The head coach relies heavily on them. At a pre-game practice, Devaney seems to be the least busy man on the field. Wearing baggy tan trousers, a Husker "N" jacket and red bill cap with white "N," equipped with whistle and clipboard, he watches from the sidelines as the various units are run through their drills by the assistants.

This is the age of specialization, and N.U. assistants specialize. Coaches Melton, Kiffin and Powers work at the north end of the stadium with the Blackshirt defensive unit, studying formations of the next opponent as displayed by a group of subs. Incidentally, there are only 11 black pullovers for the practice sessions; defensive subs wear other colors.

At the south end, specialization becomes even more acute. The first team offense is tutored by assistants Corgan and Selmer for plays run from the I-formation, by assistants Osborne and Fischer for spread formation plays, and by Fischer for punting drills.

No army keeps a tighter schedule. Devaney is adamant about that. During the regular season, the Monday practice lasts an hour and 10 minutes. Tuesday's practice lasts an hour and 49 minutes. Wednesday's an hour and 20 minutes. Thursday and Friday sessions are shorter.

"A big thing in coaching is not to leave your game on the practice field," he explained. "If a kid knows exactly how long he'll be on the practice field, he will give out 100 percent every minute. It's when he has to hang around after dark to correct some mistakes that he gets bored."

If something isn't going well in an N.U. practice, it is scheduled into tomorrow's session and today's practice ends on time.

And speaking of ending, what about Coach Devaney's career?

When will he give up coaching for the cushy job of full-time athletic director?

"Quitting? I think about quitting every Saturday morning," he answers. "I think that there must be a better way to make a living. I won't coach forever, but I will as long as I feel good. Sure this is a pressure job, but lots of men have pressure jobs."

His biggest problem, he said, is finding time for himself and his wife Phyllis. One evening in late November—not typical because the Huskers had just accepted the Orange Bowl bid—he left his office for home with his clipboard to catch up on next Saturday's game plan and with eight or nine phone calls unanswered. "I just ran out of time," he said apologetically. His telephone number is in the book, and he expected that some of the callers would catch him at home. Would he resent the interruptions?

"No, not really. I like to talk football."

So do the people of the Midlands.

PHILIP MEYER

If Hitler Asked You To Electrocute a Stranger, Would You?

One of the persistent verbal commitments in American experience has been to a style of personal independence. But the three preceding articles, as well as those in Part 1, raise serious doubts about our real, as opposed to spoken, values. Sports, the military, and the Miss America contest emphasize subordination of individual judgment to the authority of others. Stanley Milgram suggests that our professed belief in the primacy of individual conscience be treated as another myth. To bring this question into contemporary focus, ask whether the following article sheds any light on the incidents at My Lai in South Vietnam. If an American officer asked you to "waste a gook," would you?

Philip Meyer, "If Hitler Asked You To Electrocute a Stranger, Would You?" *Esquire*, February 1970, pp. 72–73+. Reprinted by permission of Esquire Magazine © 1970 by Esquire, Inc.

In the beginning, Stanley Milgram was worried about the Nazi problem. He doesn't worry much about the Nazis anymore. He worries about you and me, and, perhaps, himself a little bit too.

Stanley Milgram is a social psychologist, and when he began his career at Yale University in 1960 he had a plan to prove, scientifically, that Germans are different. The Germans-are-different hypothesis has been used by historians, such as William L. Shirer, to explain the systematic destruction of the Jews by the Third Reich. One madman could decide to destroy the Jews and even create a master plan for getting it done. But to implement it on the scale that Hitler did meant that thousands of other people had to go along with the scheme and help to do the work. The Shirer thesis, which Milgram set out to test, is that Germans have a basic character flaw which explains the whole thing, and this flaw is a readiness to obey authority without question, no matter what outrageous acts the authority commands.

The appealing thing about this theory is that it makes those of us who are not Germans feel better about the whole business. Obviously, you and I are not Hitler, and it seems equally obvious that we would never do Hitler's dirty work for him. But now, because of Stanley Milgram, we are compelled to wonder. Milgram developed a laboratory experiment which provided a systematic way to measure obedience. His plan was to try it out in New Haven on Americans and then go to Germany and try it out on Germans. He was strongly motivated by scientific curiosity, but there was also some moral content in his decision to pursue this line of research, which was, in turn, colored by his own Jewish background. If he could show that Germans are more obedient than Americans, he could then vary the conditions of the experiment and try to find out just what it is that makes some people more obedient than others. With this understanding, the world might, conceivably, be just a little bit better.

But he never took his experiment to Germany. He never took it any farther than Bridgeport. The first finding, also the most unexpected and disturbing finding, was that we Americans are an obedient people: not blindly obedient, and not blissfully obedient, just obedient. "I found so much obedience," says Milgram softly, a little sadly, "I hardly saw the need for taking the experiment to Germany."

There is something of the theater director in Milgram, and his technique, which he learned from one of the old masters in experimental psychology, Solomon Asch, is to stage a play with every line rehearsed, every prop carefully selected, and everybody an actor except one person.

That one person is the subject of the experiment. The subject, of course, does not know he is in a play. He thinks he is in real life. The value of this technique is that the experimenter, as though he were God, can change a prop here, vary a line there, and see how the subject responds. Milgram eventually had to change a lot of the script just to get people to stop obeying. They were obeying so much, the experiment wasn't working—it was like trying to measure oven temperature with a freezer thermometer.

The experiment worked like this: If you were an innocent subject in Milgram's melodrama, you read an ad in the newspaper or received one in the mail asking for volunteers for an educational experiment. The job would take about an hour and pay $4.50. So you make an appointment and go to an old Romanesque stone structure on High Street with the imposing name of The Yale Interaction Laboratory. It looks something like a broadcasting studio. Inside, you meet a young, crew-cut man in a laboratory coat who says he is Jack Williams, the experimenter. There is another citizen, fiftyish, Irish face, an accountant, a little overweight, and very mild and harmless-looking. This other citizen seems nervous and plays with his hat while the two of you sit in chairs side by side and are told that the $4.50 checks are yours no matter what happens. Then you listen to Jack Williams explain the experiment.

It is about learning, says Jack Williams in a quiet, knowledgeable way. Science does not know much about the conditions under which people learn and this experiment is to find out about negative reinforcement. Negative reinforcement is getting punished when you do something wrong, as opposed to positive reinforcement which is getting rewarded when you do something right. The negative reinforcement in this case is electric shock. You notice a book on the table, titled, *The Teaching-Learning Process,* and you assume that this has something to do with the experiment.

Then Jack Williams takes two pieces of paper, puts them in a hat, and shakes them up. One piece of paper is supposed to say, "Teacher" and the other, "Learner." Draw one and you will see which you will be. The mild-looking accountant draws one, holds it close to his vest like a poker player, looks at it, and says, "Learner." You look at yours. It says, "Teacher." You do not know that the drawing is rigged, and both slips say "Teacher." The experimenter beckons to the mild-mannered "learner."

"Want to step right in here and have a seat, please?" he says. "You can leave your coat on the back of that chair . . . roll up your right sleeve, please. Now what I want to do is strap down your arms to avoid excessive movement on your part during the experiment. This electrode is connected to the shock generator in the next room.

"And this electrode paste," he says, squeezing some stuff out of a plastic bottle and putting it on the man's arm, "is to provide a good contact and to avoid a blister or burn. Are there any questions now before we go into the next room?"

You don't have any, but the strapped-in "learner" does.

"I do think I should say this," says the learner. "About two years ago I was at the veterans' hospital . . . they detected a heart condition. Nothing serious, but as long as I'm having these shocks, how strong are they—how dangerous are they?"

Williams, the experimenter, shakes his head casually. "Oh, no," he says. "Although they may be painful, they're not dangerous. Anything else?"

Nothing else. And so you play the game. The game is for you to read a series of word pairs: for example, blue–girl, nice–day, fat–neck. When you finish the list, you read just the first word in each pair and then a multiple-choice list of four other words, including the second word of the pair. The learner, from his remote, strapped-in position, pushes one of four switches to indicate which of the four answers he thinks is the right one. If he gets it right nothing happens and you go on to the next one. If he gets it wrong, you push a switch that buzzes and gives him an electric shock. And then you go to the next word. You start with 15 volts and increase the number of volts by 15 for each wrong answer. The control board goes from 15 volts on one end to 450 volts on the other. So that you know what you are doing, you get a test shock yourself, at 45 volts. It hurts. To further keep you aware of what you are doing to that man in there, the board has verbal descriptions of the shock levels, ranging from "Slight Shock" at the left-hand side, through "Intense Shock" in the middle, to "Danger: Severe Shock" toward the far right. Finally, at the very end, under 435- and 450-volt switches, there are three ambiguous X's. If, at any point, you hesitate, Mr. Williams calmly tells you to go on. If you still hesitate, he tells you again.

Except for some terrifying details, which will be explained in a moment, this is the experiment. The object is to find the shock level at which you disobey the experimenter and refuse to pull the switch.

When Stanley Milgram first wrote this script, he took it to fourteen Yale psychology majors and asked them what they thought would happen. He put it this way: Out of one hundred persons in the teacher's predicament, how would their break-off points be distributed along the 15-to-450-volt scale? They thought a few would break off very early, most would quit someplace in the middle and a few would go all the way to the end. The highest estimate of the number out of one hundred who would go all the way to the end was three. Milgram then informally polled some of his fellow scholars in the psychology department. They agreed that very few would go to the end. Milgram thought so too.

"I'll tell you quite frankly," he says, "before I began this experiment, before any shock generator was built, I thought most people would break off at 'Strong Shock' or 'Very Strong Shock.' You would get only a very, very small proportion of people going out to the end of the shock generator, and they would constitute a pathological fringe."

In his pilot experiments, Milgram used Yale students as subjects. Each of them pushed the shock switches, one by one, all the way to the end of the board.

So he rewrote the script to include some protests from the learner. At first, they were mild, gentlemanly, Yalie protests, but, "it didn't seem to have as much effect as I thought it would or should," Milgram recalls. "So we had more violent protestation on the part of the person getting the shock. All of the time, of course, what we were trying to do was not to create a macabre situation, but simply to generate disobedience. And that was one of the first findings. This was not only a technical deficiency of the experiment, that we didn't get disobedience. It really was the first finding: that obedience would be much greater than we had assumed it would be and disobedience would be much more difficult than we had assumed.

As it turned out, the situation did become rather macabre. The only meaningful way to generate disobedience was to have the victim protest with great anguish, noise, and vehemence. The protests were tape-recorded so that all the teachers ordinarily would hear the same sounds and nuances, and they started with a grunt at 75 volts, proceeded through a "Hey, that really hurts," at 125 volts, got desperate with, "I can't stand the pain, don't do that," at 180 volts, reached complaints of heart trouble at 195, an agonized scream at 285, a refusal to answer at 315, and only heart-rending, ominous silence after that.

Still, sixty-five percent of the subjects, twenty- to fifty-year-old American males, everyday, ordinary people, like you and me, obediently kept pushing those levers in the belief that they were shocking the mild-mannered learner, whose name was Mr. Wallace, and who was chosen for the role because of his innocent appearance, all the way up to 450 volts.

Milgram was now getting enough disobedience so that he had something he could measure. The next step was to vary the circumstances to see what would encourage or discourage obedience. There seemed very little left in the way of discouragement. The victim was already screaming at the top of his lungs and feigning a heart attack. So whatever new impediment to obedience reached the brain of the subject had to travel by some route other than the ear. Milgram thought of one.

He put the learner in the same room with the teacher. He stopped strapping the learner's hand down. He rewrote the script so that at 150 volts the learner took his hand off the shock plate and declared that he wanted out of the experiment. He rewrote the script some more so that the experimenter then told the teacher to grasp the learner's hand and physically force it down on the plate to give Mr. Wallace his unwanted electric shock.

"I had the feeling that very few people would go on at that point, if any," Milgram says. "I thought that would be the limit of obedience that you would find in the laboratory."

It wasn't.

Although seven years have now gone by, Milgram still remembers the first person to walk into the laboratory in the newly rewritten script. He was a construction worker, a very short man. "He was so small," says Milgram, "that when he sat on the chair in front of the shock generator, his feet didn't reach the floor. When the experimenter told him to push the victim's hand down and give the shock, he turned to the experimenter, and he turned to the victim, his elbow went up, he fell down on the hand of the victim, his feet kind of tugged to one side, and he said, 'Like this, boss?' Zzumph!"

The experiment was played out to its bitter end. Milgram tried it with forty different subjects. And thirty percent of them obeyed the experimenter and kept on obeying.

"The protests of the victim were strong and vehement, he was screaming his guts out, he refused to participate, and you had to physically struggle with him in order to get his hand down on the shock generator," Milgram remembers. But twelve out of forty did it.

Milgram took his experiment out of New Haven. Not to Germany, just twenty miles down the road to Bridgeport. Maybe, he reasoned, the people obeyed because of the prestigious setting of Yale University. If they couldn't trust a center of learning that had been there for two centuries, whom could they trust? So he moved the experiment to an untrustworthy setting.

The new setting was a suite of three rooms in a run-down office building in Bridgeport. The only identification was a sign with a fictitious name: "Research Associates of Bridgeport." Questions about professional connections got only vague answers about "research for industry."

Obedience was less in Bridgeport. Forty-eight percent of the subjects stayed for the maximum shock, compared to sixty-five percent at Yale. But this was enough to prove that far more than Yale's prestige was behind the obedient behavior.

For more than seven years now, Stanley Milgram has been trying to figure out what makes ordinary American citizens so obedient. The most obvious answer—that people are mean, nasty, brutish and sadistic—won't do. The subjects who gave the shocks to Mr. Wallace to the end of the board did not enjoy it. They groaned, protested, fidgeted, argued, and in some cases, were seized by fits of nervous, agitated giggling.

"They even try to get out of it," says Milgram, "but they are somehow engaged in something from which they cannot liberate themselves. They are locked into a structure, and they do not have the skills or inner resources to disengage themselves."

Milgram, because he mistakenly had assumed that he would have trouble getting people to obey the orders to shock Mr. Wallace, went to a lot of trouble to create a realistic situation.

There was crew-cut Jack Williams and his grey laboratory coat. Not white, which might denote a medical technician, but ambiguously authoritative grey. Then there was the book on the table, and the other appurtenances of the laboratory which emitted the silent message that things were being performed here in the name of science, and were therefore great and good.

But the nicest touch of all was the shock generator. When Milgram started out, he had only a $300 grant from the Higgins Fund of Yale University. Later he got more ample support from the National Science Foundation, but in the beginning he had to create this authentic-looking machine with very scarce resources except for his own imagination. So he went to New York and roamed around the electronic shops until he found some little black switches at Lafayette Radio for a dollar apiece. He bought thirty of them. The generator was a metal box, about the size of a small footlocker, and he drilled the thirty holes for the thirty switches himself in a Yale machine shop. But the fine detail was left to professional industrial engravers. So he ended up with a splendid-looking control panel dominated by the row of switches, each labeled with its voltage, and each having its own red light that flashed on when the switch was pulled. Other things happened when a switch was pushed. Besides the ZZUMPHing noise, a blue light labeled "voltage energizer" went on, and a needle on a dial labeled "voltage" flicked from left to right. Relays inside the box clicked. Finally, in the upper left-hand corner of the control panel was this inscription, engraved in precise block letters:

SHOCK GENERATOR TYPE ZLB
DYSON INSTRUMENT COMPANY
WALTHAM, MASS.
OUTPUT: 15 VOLTS—450 VOLTS

One day a man from the Lehigh Valley Electronics Company of Pennsylvania was passing through the laboratory, and he stopped to admire the shock generator.

"This is a very fine shock generator," he said. "But who is this Dyson Instrument Company?" Milgram felt proud at that, since Dyson Instrument Company existed only in the recesses of his imagination.

When you consider the seeming authenticity of the situation, you can appreciate the agony some of the subjects went through. It was pure conflict. As Milgram explains to his students, "When a parent says, 'Don't strike old ladies,' you are learning two things: the content, and, also, to obey authority. This experiment creates conflicts between the two elements."

Here is a partial transcription from one of the experiments. The naïve "teacher" is a heavyset, worried-looking man with prematurely grey hair. He is wearing a polo shirt. He is very polite. He has just pushed the 180-volt lever. A hidden camera is recording the performance.

Learner (*who, from the teacher's point of view is heard but not seen, an offstage voice*): Ow, I can't stand the pain. Don't do that . . . .

Teacher (*pivoting around in his chair and shaking his head*): I can't stand it. I'm not going to kill that man in there. You hear him hollering?

Experimenter: As I told you before, the shocks may be painful, but—

Teacher: But he's hollering. He can't stand it. What's going to happen to him?

Experimenter (*his voice is patient, matter-of-fact*): The experiment requires that you continue, Teacher.

Teacher: Aaah, but, unh, I'm not going to get that man sick in there . . . know what I mean?

Experimenter: Whether the learner likes it or not, we must go on, through all the word pairs.

Teacher: I refuse to take the responsibility. He's in there hollering!

Experimenter: It's absolutely essential that you continue, Teacher.

Teacher (*indicating the unused questions*): There's too many left here, I mean, Geez, if he gets them wrong, there's too many of them left. I mean who's going to take the responsibility if anything happens to that gentleman?

Experimenter: I'm responsible for anything that happens to him. Continue please.

Teacher: All right. (*Consults list of words.*) The next one's "Slow—walk, truck, dance, music." Answer, please. (*A buzzing sound indicates the learner has signaled his answer.*) Wrong. A hundred and ninety-five volts. "Dance." (*Zzumph!*)

Learner: Let me out of here. My heart's bothering me! (*Teacher looks at experimenter.*)

Experimenter: Continue, please.

Learner (*screaming*): Let me out of here, you have no right to keep me here. Let me out of here, let me out, my heart's bothering me, let me out! (*Teacher shakes head, pats the table nervously.*)

Teacher: You see, he's hollering. Hear that? Gee, I don't know.

Experimenter: The experiment requires. . . .

Teacher (*interrupting*): I know it does, sir, but I mean—hunh! He don't know what he's getting in for. He's up to 195 volts! (*Experiment continues, through 210 volts, 225 volts, 240 volts, 255 volts, 270 volts, delivered to the man in the electric chair, at which point the teacher, with evident relief, runs out of word-pair questions.*)

Experimenter: You'll have to go back to the beginning of that page and go through them again until he's learned them all correctly.

Teacher: Aw, no. I'm not going to kill that man. You mean I've got to keep going up with the scale. No sir. He's hollering in there. I'm not going to give him 450 volts.

Experimenter: The experiment requires that you go on.

Teacher: I know it does, but that man is hollering in there, sir.

Experimenter (*same matter-of-fact tone*): As I said before, although the shocks may be painful. . . .

Teacher (*interrupting*): Awwww. He—he—he's yelling in there.

Experimenter: Start with "Blue," please, at the top of the page. Continue, please, Teacher. Just go ahead.

Teacher (*concentrating intently on list of words in front of him, as if to shut everything else out*): "Blue—boy, girl, grass, hat." (*Buzz indicates answer.*) Correct. "Night—day, sky, job, chair. (*Buzz*) Wrong. The answer is "day." Two hundred and eighty-five volts. (*Zzumph!*)

Learner: Ohhhuhhoohhh!

Experimenter: Continue, please.

Teacher: "Fat—man, lady, tub, neck." Answer, please. (*Buzz*) Wrong. The answer is "neck." Three hundred volts. (*Zzumph!*)

Learner: Ohhh. I absolutely refuse to answer any more. (*Shouting urgently, now*) Let me out of here. You can't hold me here. Get me out. Get—me—out—of—here.

Experimenter: Continue. The next word is "Green," please.

Teacher: "Green—grass, hat, ink, apple." (*Nothing happens. No answering buzz. Just gloomy silence.*)

Teacher: I don't think he is going to answer.

Experimenter: If the learner doesn't answer in a reasonable time, about four or five seconds, consider the answer wrong. And follow the same procedures you have been doing for wrong answers. Say "Wrong," tell him the number of volts, give him the punishment, read him the correct answer. Continue, please.

Teacher: "Green—grass, hat, ink, apple." Answer, please. (*More silence. Teacher just sits there.*)

Experimenter: Go on with the procedure, please, Teacher.

Teacher: Three hundred and fifteen volts. The answer is "ink." (*Zzumph!*)

Learner: Ohh. Ooohh.

Teacher (*relieved to hear response*): Next one. . . .

Learner: I absolutely refuse to answer.

Teacher: You got to. You get a shock if you don't answer. (*Experiment continues with learner refusing to answer, and, finally, failing even to grunt or groan. At 375 volts, the teacher stands up. Has he had enough? Will he break off the experiment? Will he disobey?*)

Teacher: I think something's happened to that fellow in there. I don't get no answer. He was hollering at less voltage. Can't you check in and see if he's all right, please?

Experimenter (*same detached calm*): Not once we've started. Please continue, Teacher.

Teacher (*sits down, sighs deeply*): "Cool—day, shade, water, paint." Answer, please. Are you all right in there? Are you all right?

Experimenter: Please continue, Teacher. Continue, please. (*Teacher pushes level. Zzumph!*)

Teacher (*swiveling around in his chair*): Something's happened to that man in there. (*Swiveling back*) Next one. "Low—dollar, necklace, moon, paint." (*Turning around again*) Something's happened to that man in there. You better check in on him, sir. He won't answer or nothing.

Experimenter: Continue. Go on, please.

Teacher: You accept all responsibility.

Experimenter: The responsibility is mine. Correct. Please go on. (*Teacher returns to his list, starts running through words as rapidly as he can read them, works through to 450 volts.*)

Teacher: That's that.

Experimenter: Continue using the last switch on the board, please. The four-fifty switch for each wrong answer. Continue, please.

Teacher: But I don't get no anything!

Experimenter: Please continue. The next word is "White."

Teacher: Don't you think you should look in on him, please.

Experimenter: Not once we've started the experiment.

Teacher: But what if something has happened to the man?

Experimenter: The experiment requires that you continue. Go on, please.

Teacher: Don't the man's health mean anything?

Experimenter: Whether the learner likes it or not. . . .

Teacher: What if he's dead in there? (*Gestures toward the room with the electric chair.*) I mean, he told me he can't stand the shock, sir. I don't mean to be rude, but I think you should look in on him. All you have to do is look in the door. I don't get no answer, no noise. Something might have happened to the gentleman in there, sir.

Experimenter: We must continue. Go on, please.

Teacher: You mean keep giving him what? Four hundred fifty volts, what he's got now?

Experimenter: That's correct. Continue. The next word is "White."

Teacher (*now at a furious pace*): "White—cloud, horse, rock, house." Answer, please. The answer is "horse." Four hundred and fifty volts. (*Zzumph!*) Next word, "Bag—paint, music, clown, girl." The answer is "paint." Four hundred and fifty volts. (*Zzumph!*) Next word is "Short—sentence, movie. . . ."

Experimenter: Excuse me, Teacher. We'll have to discontinue the experiment. (*Enter Milgram from camera's left. He has been watching from behind one-way glass.*)

Milgram: I'd like to ask you a few questions. (*Slowly, patiently, he dehoaxes the teacher, telling him that the shocks and screams were not real.*)

Teacher: You mean he wasn't getting nothing? Well, I'm glad to hear that. I was getting upset there. I was getting ready to walk out.

(*Finally, to make sure there are no hard feelings, friendly, harmless Mr. Wallace comes out in coat and tie. Gives jovial greeting. Friendly reconciliation takes place. Experiment ends.*)
© *Stanley Milgram 1965.*

Subjects in the experiment were not asked to give the 450-volt shock more than three times. By that time, it seemed evident that they would go on indefinitely. "No one," says Milgram, "who got within five shocks of the end ever broke off. By that point, he had resolved the conflict."

. . .

[F]or most subjects in Milgram's laboratory experiments, the act of giving Mr. Wallace his painful shock was necessary, even though unpleasant, and besides they were doing it on behalf of somebody else and it was for science. There was still strain and conflict, of course. Most people resolved it by grimly sticking to their task and obeying. But some broke out. Milgram tried varying the conditions of the experiment to see what would help break people out of their state of agency.

"The results, as seen and felt in the laboratory," he has written, "are disturbing. They raise the possibility that human nature, or more specifically the kind of character produced in American democratic society, cannot be counted on to insulate its citizens from brutality and inhumane treatment at the direction of malevolent authority. A substantial proportion of people do what they are told to do, irrespective of the content of the act and without limitations of conscience, so long as they perceive that the command comes from a legitimate authority. If, in this study, an anonymous experimenter can successfully command adults to subdue a fifty-year-old man and force on him painful electric shocks against his protest, one can only wonder what government, with its vastly greater authority and prestige, can command of its subjects. . . ."

JOEL T. SANTORO

Control and Discipline
in School Cafeterias

Milgram's conclusion that a substantial number of people do what they are told as long as it comes from a "legitimate" authority is certainly encouraged by the military, on the playing fields, and on the Miss America stage. But what about schools? They are supposed to teach people how to think for themselves. Do people leave school as autonomous individuals to be corrupted by other agencies? The following suggestions, seriously proposed by a New York teacher and approvingly published by a respected national educational journal, raise doubts. How many schools follow this spirit of control, if not the specific suggestions, advocated by Joel Santoro?

Organization, control and discipline in school cafeterias is a job that can be handled most effectively by teachers. It is also a task that is viewed as distasteful, since at many times it becomes more exhausting than teaching itself. This assignment will never be easy, but with the proper techniques, the situation can be improved.

Certain physical aids are extremely necessary. A clear sounding portable microphone is a "must" for effective control of any large group. The teacher can move among the students, instantly adjust the volume, take the instrument out of doors, and easily have it repaired.

Another aid is the division of the cafeteria into approximately four sections. This can be accomplished by numbering the tables or taping large numbers opposite designated sections. By dividing the area in this way, dismissal at the close of the period is facilitated, since one section at a time can be released and the area checked for cleanliness and order.

Next, a clear, short definition of cafeteria rules can be posted in several visible places. Having something tangible to point to seems to help. When a rule is violated, have the student read it back so there

Joel T. Santoro, "Control and Discipline in School Cafeterias," *Clearing House*, vol. 40, no. 3 (November 1965), pp. 152–154. Reprinted by permission.

is no ground for complaint when appropriate measures are taken if the problem reoccurs. Here are a few examples that may be of help:

1. Do not run in aisles.
2. Obtain passes before leaving cafeteria.
3. Take a seat when the whistle is blown.
4. Eat ice cream in the cafeteria only.
5. Empty garbage into receptacles.

The signs can be made in the art department or by gluing one and one-half inch plastic letters to a heavy piece of poster paper.

A whistle, used in conjunction with the microphone, may be used to signal students to their seats before daily announcements. If blown more than several times during the period the whistle will become ineffective. Overuse, a common mistake, becomes annoying, and soon no one listens.

Last of all, be sure that the cafeteria clock is synchronized with the school master clock. It is wise to dismiss students by sections at the close of the period—generally a few minutes early, to avoid a clash with the next lunch period.

Controls for the cafeteria have to be established with the administration. One administrator, assigned to handle chronic problem cases, should pass through the cafeteria daily, to help set a proper tone. Through early planning and scheduling, an effective method of immediately curbing uncooperative students is to request a lunch detention room. Obtaining volunteers to supervise this room will be difficult, but on a rotation basis the assignment is tolerable and the cafeteria situation always improves.

Administrators must place in charge one teacher with authority commensurate to the large responsibility at hand. They must also avoid placing in supervisory positions custodians, aides, parents, or other well-meaning individuals who do not have the proper training and authority. Such people have been tried in many metropolitan schools and have not proven effective. Teachers know the students, understand the supervisory problem, and are more apt to possess the skills to deal with and prevent discipline problems.

Assuming most of the preceding suggestions are in effect, let's look at a typical daily procedure from entrance to exit and consider some techniques of control and discipline.

Every day must have a similar pattern from start to finish, consistent with a prearranged organizational plan. Entering the cafeteria is the first phase of the pattern. Students should form an orderly line and wait to pick up their food. Immediately have those who attempt to sneak ahead, push, or create a disturbance go to the end of the line. Do not hesitate! Act at once and the days to come will be automatically easier, once students recognize that poor conduct will be dealt with firmly. Keeping those lines moving and in order prevents confusion from the start. Maintaining another line with trays for those who bring a lunch from home speeds the serving a great deal.

When the students are in the cafeteria and eating, very little "horse-play" or unnecessary traffic occurs. As the actual eating of lunch is completed, the "fooling" and jostling about begin. There are specific techniques that, if utilized by the professional staff, can be effective in curbing these difficulties.

The raising of the voice is the most effective tool the teacher has. Use a strong voice whether a student is next to you or ten tables away. Remember, this is not a classroom of 25 students but a cafeteria of possibly 500 talking boys and girls. Use a powerful voice and be heard!

Another useful thing is a whistle, used only by the teacher in charge to seat students once a period for announcements, and once for dismissal. On a whistle signal, students should be seated. Make this clear from the first day or when the time comes for an emergency announcement, fire drill instructions, or some important message, order will be difficult to obtain.

A method of enforcing cafeteria regulations is to assign one or more teachers to a section of the cafeteria for which they are responsible. Teachers must not all stand together, but should constantly move around their section, talking to students and keeping order. Teachers should make a conscious effort to learn the names of students. It is much easier to correct students and prevent problems when youngsters are known on a first name basis.

Students will test the rules; so enforce the determined regulations. Immediate discipline might range from having a student pick up several pieces of paper to lunch detention. If possible, avoid letting the detention room become a crutch for problems. Get used to handling them yourself, since most schools cannot spare the staff to organize a lunch detention room anyway. Setting up what is called a "manners table" within the cafeteria can substitute for a detention room. By placing a sign saying "Manners Table" over several tables set aside in one corner of the cafeteria, a convenient area for disruptive students can be established. Discipline cases can eat there or remain seated for the entire lunch period. Be careful not to overload these tables or the method will not succeed, because it will become impossible to contain all the problem students in one small section.

On occasion a silent lunch can be given to quiet things down, but this becomes more of a strain on the teachers and its results are negligible. An uncooperative group can be improved by first having them report to the auditorium for 15 minutes and then dismissing them for lunch. The shorter lunch period automatically reduces the time available for horseplay.

At the end of the period, dismissal can be a hectic time, and a definite system goes a long way to alleviate confusion and congestion at exits. Start by blowing the whistle approximately five minutes before the bell and seat all students. When this is accomplished, teachers can check their sections and the cafeteria can be looked over for cleanliness and order. The section which is in order first can be dismissed, then one section at a time. Good timing will have the cafeteria cleared just as the next lunch class begins to enter, and the regulation of sections for dismissal will reduce the accident potential on crowded stairways.

Whatever the methods used in the cafeteria for its many phases, always be consistent and follow a well organized routine. The assignment will always be difficult, but it certainly can be handled effectively with a good staff and careful organization.

ANTHONY TOVATT

This World of English

Although authors of some of the preceding readings believe that how the schools operate is more important than what they purport to teach, a society which places a strong emphasis on control is not likely to leave content to whim. The next two selections speak about pressures for a "safe" curriculum. Both overt censorship and more subtle, willing self-censorship are involved.

Anthony Tovatt, "This World of English," *English Journal*, September 1966, pp. 795–796. Copyright © 1966 by the National Council of Teachers of English. Reprinted by permission of the publisher and Anthony Tovatt.

In a recent survey of censorship in 87 Arizona high schools, 36 schools reported incidents involving at least one book. In 21 of these, books were ultimately removed from libraries, classroom shelves, or reading lists.

Size of the school seemed to make no difference in institutions where books had been removed—"some were small, isolated schools, others were part of a large, metropolitan system." In all 21 schools, "right wing pressure groups were frequently cited as the cause of complaints. None of the schools had an established procedure for handling complaints prior to a book's removal." Many of the schools which yielded or lost when a book used in their high school was challenged were already extremely conservative because of a fear of censorship. In fact, one school reported, "We have had no trouble since 1961 but have purchased no books that anyone could object to, thus limiting our college-bound senior students and in reality handicapping them in future study of modern literature and authors, such as Salinger, Steinbeck, Hemingway, Dreiser, Dos Passos, Orwell, Warren, etc."

Many of the books challenged and withdrawn were books of proven literary merit—*Black Like Me* (Griffin, criticized because of its language and situations; *Brave New World* (Huxley), sordidness and sex; *Catcher in the Rye* (Salinger), vulgarity, sacreligious and unsuitable; *The Diary of Anne Frank*, sex; *A Farewell to Arms* (Hemingway), glorifies unmarried sex; *Good Morning, Miss Dove* (Patton), Communist propaganda because it contains numerous woodcut illustrations of doves on chapter heading pages; *The Grapes of Wrath* (Steinbeck), vulgarity; *Lord of the Flies* (Golding), violence and a distorted view of youth; *Moby Dick* (Melville), homosexuality; *The Ox-Bow Incident* (Clark), language; *The Scarlet Letter* (Hawthorne), adultery; *To Kill a Mockingbird* (Lee), racial situation and reference to rape.

Interestingly enough, some of the objectors to many of the above books were school people themselves, i.e., superintendents, teachers, and school board members.

To strengthen English departments and schools of the state, the Arizona English Teachers Association has approved the following recommendations:[1] (1) That all English departments make a determined effort to have their schools adopt an established policy for handling complaints. (2) That English teachers participate fully as individuals and as departments in making selections for classrooms and libraries. (3) That teachers remain constantly aware of literature both old and new that is appropriate for high school use and that in developing their programs they exercise professional judgment regarding the books needed by the students they teach. (4) That English teachers encourage, in so far as possible, the free circulation of school library books. (5) That English teachers both enlist and offer support of other departments in their schools, realizing that freedom to read is sometimes at stake in science, history, home economics, and other departments, as well as in their own. (6) That English teachers enlist the support of responsible persons in the community before trouble starts. (7) That English teachers make it plain that censorship pressures on schools will not be accepted quietly but will result in local and statewide publicity. (8) That English departments build a file of resource materials to aid in combating pressures. These materials should be available to all teachers and administrators of the school to provide a rationale and build a climate of opinion that will ultimately lead to freedom of inquiry and expression.

NOTE

1. Retha Foster, *Arizona English Bulletin,* May 1966.

HILLEL BLACK

What Our Children Read

Miss Mabel O'Donnell, one of the most highly paid authors in America, begins her working day in a cramped study in her six-room, ranch-style home in Aurora, Ill. There, promptly at nine in the morning, this shy, matronly woman enters a never-never world filled with talking owls, chattering squirrels and the antics of a red-haired girl named Janet and her blond, brown-eyed brother, Mark. On this day Miss O'Donnell, sitting at a mahogany desk at the keyboard of a standard-size typewriter, began composing a reading exercise titled *A Bad Morning.*

Mark was as cross as a bear.
When a boy is that cross,
he is just as cross
as a boy can get.
If you are wise,
you will look out
for someone like that.

As the story tumbled onto the 5½-by-8-inch sheet of paper, Miss O'Donnell solved a number of technical writing problems that few other authors ever face. In this tale, which will be used in schools to teach six-year-olds to read, she employed words of no more than two syllables and introduced no more than one new word to a page. Despite the limited vocabulary, every sentence and paragraph had to flow smoothly, and her plot had to be sufficiently imaginative and universal in theme for a child in the suburbs, a youngster in the slums, and a farmer's son to want to read more.

Miss O'Donnell, a former grade-school teacher, was once told by a creative-writing instructor at the University of Chicago that she would never make any money as an author. But as the creator of the Janet and Mark books—and before that Alice and Jerry, a first-through-sixth-grade reading series—she has earned over $2,700,000 in royalties, according to Harper & Row, her publisher. Since 1936, when Alice and Jerry first appeared, over 67 million copies of her books have been sold in hard cover, more than the total United States sales of all the books written by Ian Fleming. Over the past three decades more than 300 million children have read Miss O'Donnell's books. Not only do her books continue to teach millions of children to read but they also teach such virtues as honesty, perseverance and self-denial.

"Oh, Father," says Jerry in the reader for first-graders, "I want the ball. I want the boat. I want the train."

Father firmly replies, "You may have just one toy, Jerry. Just one toy."

"One toy! One toy!" says Jerry.

Few people are aware of the important role some 265 million textbooks play in the education of the nation's 50 million elementary and high school students. During your child's school career he will attempt to absorb at least 32,000 textbook pages. In the first grade he will complete at least four textbooks, and by the time he finishes his last year in high school, he will intensely study another 60. These books impart most of the skills and knowledge he will learn in school, covering every subject from beginning reading and arithmetic to high school biology, economics, French and literature. Seventy-five percent of your child's classroom time—and 90 percent of his homework time—will be spent on textbooks.

"Textbooks," declared *School Management*, a magazine published for school administrators and school-board members, "are still the single most important teaching tool. Put all your new teaching tools together—the projectors, the films, the teaching machines—and they're just a drop in the bucket compared to that old standby, the textbook. Invariably, the textbook is the basis of every curriculum. To an overwhelming extent, it determines what will be taught and when."

The textbook and its even heftier manual also will determine *how* almost any given subject will be taught. The manual organizes the course for the teacher, describes most of the teaching techniques she will use, and provides hundreds of student homework assignments, discussion and test questions, as well as the answers. The teachers' manuals supplied by Mabel O'Donnell illustrate the extent to which the textbook and its guide can dominate classroom teaching in America. For instance, the four pre-primers in the Alice and Jerry series contain a total of 236 pages, but the teacher's guide contains 528, and it offers instructions on how to teach not only each page but each word in the pre-primers.

Despite the fact that publishers usually list outside readings and encourage teachers to use them, most teachers rarely wander far from the guides or texts. Dr. Ruth G. Strickland, professor of education at Indiana University, estimates that about half the nation's primary teachers stick closely to the guides. According to Dr. Bruce Joyce, the former head of elementary teacher education at the University of Chicago, about 80 percent of the nation's elementary teachers use textbooks as their main teaching tool and source of knowledge.

Dr. Joyce, now associate professor of education at Teachers College, Columbia, adds that reliance on textbooks is probably even greater in high school: "Because the high-school teacher works with as many as 150 youngsters a day, it is impossible for him to prepare tailor-made materials for each child or even each class. He has to come up with the prepared package, the textbook."

In appearance, at least, the American textbook has few peers. Profusely illustrated, laid out in the same fashion as the mass magazines, most school books are far more inviting than the textbooks used 30 years ago. By contrast there has been little change in the actual content of most history books, readers, grammars and civics books. Devoid of controversy, stylistically dull, they remain vacuous and boring. The wonder indeed is not that Johnny can read but that Johnny, after a 12-year diet of schoolbooks, wants to read at all.

At the same time, one must temper such harsh comments with the hopeful observation that the textbook industry—and as a result American education—is emerging like the Devonian lungfish from a dark and murky sea. For at long last one finds a number of revolutions taking place in the American schoolroom. New textbooks and learning tools have already affected the sciences—physics, biology, chemistry, mathematics—and foreign languages. And now that federal aid is available, even the social scientists and teachers of literature are displaying the kind of courage and individuality of thought that could cause an extraordinary improvement in education.

For the textbook publishers themselves, this has become an era of transition and turmoil. Until recently the antediluvians of education, they have had the modern age thrust upon them. As the creators or producers of the nation's teaching tools, they must deal with the awesome increase in knowledge brought about by the splitting of the atom, the space age, the computer. The nation's giant electronics firms have joined the effort. As John I. Goodlad, professor of education at the University of California at Los Angeles, summed it up. "Beginning with the birth of Christ, it is estimated that the first doubling of knowledge occurred in 1750, the second in 1900, the third in 1950 and the fourth in 1960." The process continues.

Textbook publishers also face the difficult task of creating books that prepare both privileged and underprivileged children for economic survival. They must answer the demands of the civil-rights groups that call for integrated textbooks as well as integrated schools, and they must do business with those southern states that will buy only all-white editions. "On the one hand," declared Craig T. Senft, former president of Silver Burdett, a major schoolbook publisher, and now vice president of General Learning Corp., "come the scholars and intellectuals, who complain that textbooks are badly written, so bland as to be inconclusive, so pedantically conceived that they insult the capabilities of children. On the other hand come the minority groups—everyone from the D.A.R. to the Texans for America—with their own set of complaints. It's subversive to mention the United Nations, or to include Carl Sandburg in an English anthology. Or B'nai B'rith complains if a phrase appears stating, 'And then Christ was turned over to the Jewish mob.' Other groups object just as strenuously if you take it out."

Faced with so many complex problems, some old, but most of them new, the American textbook industry finds itself in greater ferment than it has ever been during its 200-year history.

Bob Hay once was a newspaperman, and before that he was science editor for an encyclopedia. He has never taken a course in education and has never taught a class of students. His annual salary is around $12,000.

Yet it was Bob Hay who guided the textbook division of Harper & Row in a gamble of more than half a million dollars. The gamble produced a tremendously successful series of science textbooks that has flourished in an already crowded field; it greatly enriched two authors and contributed heavily to the firm's prosperity.

Hay's name does not appear anywhere in the seven texts and seven teachers' guides of the Harper & Row series, *Today's Basic Science*, but he probably had as much to do with the books' success as the two authors did—they are John Gabriel Navarra, chairman of the science department at Jersey City State College, and Joseph Zafforoni, who was an associate professor of education at the University of Nebraska when the project started. Navarra and Zafforoni already have split $100,000 in royalties, and will probably share an additional million by 1977. For Hay, who is editor in charge of the series, and science director of the textbook division at Evanston, Ill., the reward is the praise of his colleagues and his employer.

The plan to bring forth a new textbook series did not originate with Hay but with Gordon Jones, then president, and Walter Brackman, at the time editor-in-chief of Row, Peterson, a midwestern textbook publisher. In 1956, a year before Sputnik and seven years before the first books in the series were published, Jones and Brackman concluded that Row's 80-odd science pamphlets would never capture a large enough chunk of the market. "We sold millions of these pamphlets," Jones said. "But they were always used as supplements to the basic science courses. We realized that the teachers wanted hardbound textbooks which organized the courses for them."

To find out whether the schools would buy a new hardbound elementary science series (there were already a dozen on the market), the publisher mailed questionnaires to 2,000 elementary-school teachers and assigned 80 salesmen to interview dozens more. The firm sought to learn what the teachers wanted in a basic textbook and what they liked and disliked in the series put out by Row's competitors.

The teachers' sharpest criticism was that many of the current text-books were little more than Dick-and-Jane readers with a smattering of science. And the science that appeared in even the better books turned out to be repetitive. For example, in the first grade all a child learned about electricity and magnetism was that a magnet picked up some objects but not others. In the second grade he identified the objects the magnet attracted as made of metal. What the teachers wanted was a textbook series that taught electricity, meteorology, astronomy and atomic energy in depth to children at earlier ages. They also wanted more experiments youngsters could do in the classroom and some accounts of how scientists thought and worked. "There was," said Jones, "a real opening in the market."

The next step was to find a science editor capable of overseeing the series. Brackman first offered the job to Zafforoni. Though Zafforoni declined, he agreed to collaborate with John Navarra in writing a book for teachers on how science should be taught in the elementary schools.

In the meantime, Hay had been hired as an editor, and his first task was the Navarra-Zafforoni book for science teachers. Late one after-noon in the spring of 1959, Bob Hay and Gordon Jones, in a seemingly casual discussion, decided to publish a standard hardbound elementary science series, to be written by Zafforoni and Navarra. (Row, Peterson merged with Harper & Brothers in 1962, becoming Harper & Row.)

Actually, Jones's decision was not quite that casual. Nor did Navarra and Zafforoni take their assignment lightly. By 1959 the au-thors were working 80 hours a week, and they began submitting the manuscripts for the first four grades in 1960. And in the fall of 1961, Hay started working 10 hours a day, six to seven days a week, a pace that would continue without letup for two years. First he analyzed the authors' first drafts, then he rewrote their revised versions. In this, Hay encountered a major problem: He had to fit the authors' ideas into the limited vocabularies demanded by the elementary-school teachers, who insist that the average grade-school child can cope with only the simplest words. Using standard graded readability formulas, Hay compromised, rewrote and juggled. For example, he changed the phrase "bubbles, bubbles everywhere" to "bubbles, bubbles all around," because "everywhere" was not on the vocabulary list. Nor, for that matter, was the word "bubbles." However, "bubbles" continued to float through the text.

While his superiors permitted Hay to crack the taboo against words like "bubbles," he was simply forbidden to mention Darwin's theory of evolution. "Because of the opposition of Protestant fundamentalists, our series does not mention it," he said. "In fact, no reference is made to evolution in any elementary-school science series."

While the series managed to ignore Darwin and his theory, it could not deny the existence of an even more fundamental subject, sex. "By the time youngsters get into the sixth grade," Hay said, "their hormones begin stirring around a little. They become aware of their own sexual interest. To a younger child in the fifth grade, you can teach human reproduction in a detached way. The older youngsters who are aware of sex and who know more are inclined to snicker in the classroom."

While Hay felt some schools might object to an explanation of *human* reproduction, he and the authors hoped that a description of *animal* reproduction would prove acceptable to the teachers who select books and the communities that would pay for them.

Hay defended the plan in a memo to his superiors, then showed the passage describing animal reproduction to an elementary-school principal in Evanston, a science teacher in Wilmette, Ill., the firm's seven regional managers and the Florida salesman who would be responsible for obtaining the first major state adoption of the series.

"While the principal and the teacher okayed inclusion of the sperm and egg cells," Hay recalled, "the salesman said we had gone a little too far to be safe. I got a little nervous and queasy. Suppose people in Florida look on the subject gingerly and for this reason alone your books are eliminated. Then you have made a mistake. The conclusion was to soft-pedal all the details of animal reproduction."

Hay then boiled down the passage to this single paragraph:

> Almost all mammals bring forth living young. The offspring develops inside the female's body. The growing organism receives food and oxygen from the mother. A system of blood vessels carries this nourishment to the embryo.

In effect, what he had done was dilute the description of animal reproduction by removing any mention of such terms and concepts as the egg cell and fertilization. As Hay himself put it, "We now teach reproduction without ever introducing the sperm cell."

In his office at Jersey City State College, John Navarra, the senior author, described the omission as an act of "educational statesmanship." "The final decision of what goes into the schools rests with the lay boards of education," he said. "The schools do belong to the people and the schools are an extension of the home and community. It is not our job to introduce something that subverts the community.

"It would have been distinctive to have included reproduction, but the important thing is to move the educational program forward and not start brush fires. As strongly as I feel about teaching the concepts of reproduction, you can be ahead of your time."

Toward the end of 1962 and the beginning of 1963, *Today's Basic Science* began rolling off the presses, and with the appearance of the freshly printed copies loomed the most nervewracking question of all: Would the series sell? Navarra and Zafforoni had already spent years developing, testing and writing the texts. More than a million words had passed through Bob Hay's hands. The production department had spent $100,000 on four-color illustrations. Advertising was preparing to spend $92,000 in educational journals and brochures, and sales was in the process of giving away 100,000 copies to teachers who indicated that they might be interested in using the books. In brief, the textbook publisher had already spent $525,000 and had yet to sell a single book.

The first major sales test came in February, 1963, in Florida. Seven years had passed since that state had adopted a new elementary science series, and competition promised to be stiff, for Harper & Row had not been alone in its planning. Eight publishers had submitted as many different series for consideration by a statewide textbook selection committee consisting mostly of classroom teachers. However, under the law, the committee could recommend only three different series, which the Florida State Board of Education would then approve. The decisions would prove crucial since local schools could use only those textbooks which the two groups sanctioned. In sum, if Florida selected the Harper & Row series, it would not only mean a probable sale of 200,000 books but would also indicate that the publisher had guessed right, that other schools in other states would want to adopt a series that attempted a more difficult approach to science.

The fate of *Today's Basic Science* rested with Tom Shannon, the firm's Florida salesman. Ten months before the Board of Education met to decide which books the state would adopt, Shannon and another salesman began a thousand-mile journey that took them from Pensacola to Key West. Along the way they visited 6,000 teachers, supervisors and principals and interviewed the 12 members of the all-powerful state selection committee.

Finally, at 2 p.m. on February 26, 1963, the Florida salesmen, the firm's general sales manager, Harvey Hanlon, and several dozen other bookmen filed into the ornate State Senate Chamber in Tallahassee. They were handed a booklet listing all the choices of the committee, which had met in secret during the previous week. At the top of the list were the Harper & Row books.

It was now up to Harvey Hanlon to leap the last hurdle. Under the Florida system, each publisher whose book has been recommended by a state selection committee must submit a sealed bid guaranteeing the prices he will charge for five years. Hanlon knew that if he offered to charge 10 percent more than the sum asked by his competitors, the Florida State Board of Education might reject the series even though the committee had recommended it. And rejection, Hanlon realized, could easily mean an enormous loss in sales.

Hanlon, his palms slightly moist, wrote out the Harper & Row prices, placed them in a sealed envelope and then joined the other bookmen outside the Senate Chamber. For the next hour the salesmen anxiously paced up and down the hallway while the board and the elementary-textbook selection committee met in executive session. At last the large oaken doors swung open, and the bookmen once again took their seats. A hush settled over the huge room. Thomas Bailey, state superintendent of schools, arose to announce the textbooks Florida would adopt for the next five years. Again Harper & Row had won. "I can only tell you I was relieved that it was over," said Tom Shannon. "The risks and gamble are tremendous. You spend all that time and it could all come to nothing."

As the year proceeded it seemed that *Today's Basic Science* could not be stopped. More than a half-dozen states, mostly in the South, had sought new science textbooks, and the schoolbooks they selected invariably included those published by Harper & Row. In addition, cities like New York, Philadelphia, Boston, Cincinnati and Omaha adopted or approved the new series.

"All this adds up to a remarkable achievement in sales—a successful selling job," Hay said in a private memorandum that he sent to the sales force. As is the typical practice of the industry, Hay also ripped into the competing texts, giving the Harper & Row salesmen a varied assortment of verbal buckshot with which they could blast the series issued by the other publishers. His strongest comments were reserved for the D. C. Heath science series, the most successful of all the elementary science texts on the market. Heath understandably had the most to lose in a sales battle with an upstart challenger, and according to the Harper & Row salesmen, the Heath bookmen were doing their best to criticize the Navarra and Zafforoni texts.

In a separate memorandum devoted just to an attack on the Heath series, Hay told his own bookmen the Heath editors had supplied the Heath salesmen with a "hair-splitting critique" of *Today's Basic Science*. He wrote: "Obviously the Heath people are employing these tactics because they find it difficult to deal with our basic program. They are desperate, frustrated and frightened. . . . If necessary, we can respond in kind to Heath's attacks."

Then in December, 1963, a bombshell exploded in Harper & Row's offices. The Newark Textbook Council, which selects books for New Jersey's largest public-school system, rejected the series even though it thought the books were the best grade-school science texts on the market. In a brief letter, the council accused the publisher of using "stereotyped middle-class" illustrations and charged that Harper & Row had failed to include any pictures or text "relating to minority groups." What the council really meant was that not one illustration in the entire series showed a Negro, child or adult.

The company decided to publish an "Intercultural Edition." The text would be exactly the same as the all-white edition, but about one third of the illustrations would portray Negroes, with a sprinkling of Orientals and Mexicans. All would be shown in poses identical to those held by the whites.

The new edition appeared within the year and Newark was delighted with it. But in Peoria, Ill., integrationists complained that no Negro appeared in an illustration of a symphony orchestra. The Peoria critics also found fault with a picture of a Negro father and his little girl standing on a wooden porch and gazing up at the moon and stars. The critics felt that the wooden porch reflected a lower-class background and thus was biased. Peoria ended by adopting the non-integrated edition, which showed a white father and his little girl perched on the identical wooden porch. At the same time, several school districts in Georgia turned down the "Intercultural Edition" because of an illustration showing a white and Negro boy sitting together on a large chair, and another showing Negro and white children swimming in the same pool. "Try as we will," said Bob Hay, "we will be criticized."

As a product carefully concocted for the national market, the textbook must reflect the broadest cultural and social level of the American schoolchild. This means that the textbook publisher will omit material or works that might possibly stir up regional or community prejudices or offend a particular group's point of view. Thus no hardbound literary anthology used in high school contains Shakespeare's *Othello*, because publishers are convinced that part of the southern market would reject a schoolbook that had a play about "miscegenation." Similarly, no hardbound literary anthology contains *The Merchant of Venice*, because it might offend communities that have large Jewish populations. In addition to omitting literary works that may cause trouble, publishers leave out information or change passages and illustrations that may be considered controversial.

Because mass sales are the goal, textbooks tend to sink to a level of intellectual blandness. A description of the final product appears in *High School English Textbooks*, an exhaustive survey of schoolbooks used in teaching secondary-school English. The authors, Professors James J. Lynch and Bertrand Evans, note that only a little more than half the dramas represented in the anthologies can be classified as stage plays. Most of the others are either radio or TV plays, with an occasional sprinkling of musical comedies. "Many choices," the authors comment, "seem to have been determined by quite irrelevant criteria: introduction to television and radio, teen-age mores, the celebration of holidays, and —most frequently—'entertainment,' rather than literary quality and permanence. Shakespeare is given the greatest amount of space—27 appearances of five plays, including excerpts, abridgements and adaptations—but in all the anthologies examined, this greatest of all writers in the English language . . . is given only 4.1 percent of their total space—only one sixth the attention given to miscellaneous and largely nonliterary prose. In 45 volumes (62.5 percent of the total) Shakespeare's plays are not represented at all."

Since the teachers believe that the communities that support them disapprove of controversy, it is not surprising that the schoolbooks teachers approve and select avoid topics or issues that might provoke thought among their students. And textbook publishers prefer to invest in those books that promise the widest approval and sales and hence the biggest profits. Not surprisingly, the schoolbooks that still offer the most outmoded view of man and his world are the social-studies texts, American and world history books and civics and problems-in-democracy texts.

In 1966 the Lincoln Filene Center for Citizenship and Public Affairs at Tufts University published a preliminary report on 24 elementary social-studies texts. Miss Astrid C. Anderson, the research assistant who wrote the report, notes that most grade-school social-studies texts "dwell on the theme that America got to be the way it is today because of the ax, hoe, gun and plow, aided by thrift, endurance and bravery in the face of overwhelming physical odds." Those who brought this about invariably were the English, Spanish, French and Dutch. Little or no mention is made of the crucial period of American history, the era of the greatest migration which led to the development of the cities. To view America this way, Miss Anderson writes, "is to exclude the Jew, the Greek, the Negro, the factory sweatshop worker, the Cuban, the Irish, the Italian . . ."

In "Racism in Geography," a paper prepared for the department of geography at Wayne State University, William Bunge summed up the simplistic, narrow view of today's schoolbooks. Children, he wrote, cannot help but "gain this strange historic-geographic dream that 'our' people were in Western Europe starting with the Renaissance. Before that 'our people' were in Greece, not as the dominant group of slaves, of course, but sitting around the temples calculating the shape and size of the earth. The Torch of Civilization just followed us about the map."

By the time he has reached the fifth grade, the student gets the first of many year-long introductions to American history. Here ethnocentricity becomes the official point of view. A typical illustration of this view can be found in Harper & Row's *The Story of Our Country*. In the chapter titled "The United States Fought a Second World War," the authors manage to attribute almost the entire Allied victory to America, with occasional assistance from England:

> Winning the Second World War required the best efforts of all Americans. More than twelve million men and women became members of the army, navy, marine corps, and coast guard. One army unit, which fought in Italy, was made up entirely of Japanese-Americans.
>
> Citizens at home worked in factories that made war equipment for the nation. They gave up food so that there would be enough to feed the soldiers. Citizens at home were permitted to use only limited amounts of gasoline so that there would be fuel for tanks and airplanes. Americans everywhere made great sacrifices to achieve victory.

In this section on how the war was fought and won, there is no mention of Stalingrad, European and Asian undergrounds, the troops of India, Australia, New Zealand, the Free French. It's as if Uncle Sam had done it all.

Many current social-studies and history books are also invested

with an exaggerated sense of American perfection. Patriotic indoctrination begins with the Founding Fathers. In "History in High-School
Textbooks," an illuminating essay published in *School Review,* three
historians, H. J. Noah, C. E. Prince and C. R. Riggs wrote: "Despite
many studies of individual Fathers which cast doubt on the images of at
least some of them as unselfish patriots, their unitary and common
stereotypes have remained with remarkable persistence in the high-school
textbooks. The Founding Fathers remain uniformly and without exception good and great men, disinterested promoters of the public welfare,
sternly doing their duty to God and country."

More dangerous are the schoolbook accounts of the Cold War.
Here the world is divided between good guys (the West) and bad guys
(Communist countries). Since McKinley, America has never committed
any act which may be questioned on moral grounds. Russia, on the
other hand, personifies evil. The authors of "History in High-School
Textbooks" report that in only one of the 12 schoolbooks they examined
were they able to find an account that recognizes that "the Soviet Union
is guided by historic Russian ambitions as well as by Marxist dogma.
Other weaknesses follow from the original distortions," they add. "Although the mistakes, stupidities and power plays of the East are fully
exposed, the mistakes, stupidities and power plays of the West tend to
be omitted or played down."

To illustrate their point, they cite the accounts of Fidel Castro's
rule in Cuba. In *Our Country's History,* by David Muzzey, published
by Ginn, students are told: "The red hand of Communism was likewise
seen at work in Cuba where dictator Castro broke with the Catholic
Church, confiscated all American-owned properties, and openly boasted
of military aid from Russia and China."

What, ask the three historians, is one to make of the implication
that breaking "with the Catholic Church" and confiscation "of all Amer-
ican-owned properties" are clear evidence of Communist inspiration?
Could it not be also said that these acts reflect nationalistic aspirations?
And if this is one's interpretation, how does the historian—and student—
view Martin Luther, Henry VIII and George Washington? According to
Muzzey's interpretation, they would have to be counted among the first
Communists.

"The textbooks examined," the three historians declare, "leave the
impression that Russian actions are sly, evilly motivated and subversive,
while Western moves represent honest, disinterested and generous statesmanship. Nowhere is it even hinted at that responsible thinkers about

the Cold War might hold the kind of view expressed by George F. Kennan in *Russia, the Atom and the West:* 'The Russians are not always wrong, any more than we are always right. Our task, in any case, is to make up our minds independently.'

"Because we in the West prize highly independent, critical thought in the attainment of truth," conclude Noah, Prince and Riggs, "it is especially incumbent on us to make sure that our textbooks reflect this free tradition and do not distort history or invent historical 'facts.' It is a grave charge to make, but the conclusion is inescapable: under this treatment our students' minds tend to be closed, not widened. Students whose history reading is largely confined to the textbook (and there are many such) are subjected to a brainwashing as complete as it is dangerous."

Among the perversions committed in the name of education, few equal the American schoolbook's treatment of the Negro and his history. For more than 150 years he was presented to millions of children, both black and white, as a subhuman, incapable of achieving culture, happy in servitude, a passive outsider in the development and struggles of the American people. Until the 1960's, the American youngster saw an almost completely white world in his textbooks. No Negro child ever romped with Spot, no Negro child ever performed a scientific experiment, no Negro child was ever portrayed as reading a book, hitting a baseball, playing a musical instrument.

As the student continued his education, he would rarely find a schoolbook that mentioned the 5,000 Negro troops who fought in the American Revolution, the 168,000 Negro soldiers who joined the Union Army and who took part in 450 battles, the 30,000 Negroes who joined the Union Navy, the 14 Negro Congressional Medal of Honor winners in the Civil War. Nor would he learn about the suffering of the slaves as they were transported to American shores or the slave rebellions. The student would encounter brief mention of Crispus Attucks, Booker T. Washington, George Washington Carver and, if the publisher was possessed of sufficient courage, Ralph Bunche. In this way the schools and the textbooks not only deprived the Negro child of a sense of his own worth and dignity but robbed the white child of any understanding of the Negro's history.

Then in the 1960's, nearly a hundred years after the Emancipation, textbook publishers began putting the Negro into the schoolbooks. Not only did black children romp with Dick and Jane but they and their parents joined their white counterparts in many of the normal activities that Americans, including Negroes, have been participating in for generations. Even more significant, the Negro's contribution to American history was being recognized, so that he no longer appeared as the happy, dancing slave who had had emancipation thrust upon him. The driving force behind this change was the Negro Revolution, which opened the schoolbook market by forcing the big-city boards of education and school systems to demand integrated textbooks. In part because of organized Negro protests and the subsequent pressures brought to bear on publishers by Detroit, New York City, Pittsburgh, Los Angeles, there have been impressive improvements in the treatment of the Negro in junior- and senior-high-school history texts.

While taking an important step forward in integrating grade-school books, a number of publishers have simultaneously perpetuated segregated education by continuing to sell all-white, or what one editor called "mint julep," editions of the same books. For example, Scott, Foresman, the nation's largest elementary-school publisher, is still selling integrated and all-white editions of its grade-school social-studies, health and reading series. In the integrated readers apple-cheeked, blond Jane and Sally and their brother Dick play with three Negro children, Penny, Pam and Mike. In the segregated edition all the children are white.

These are not the only differences. Chicago's fourth-graders, who use the integrated Scott, Foresman reader, learn about Benjamin Banneker, the Negro astronomer, while youngsters in the same grade in some southern—and some northern—communities read instead about Paul Revere. In the integrated sixth-grade reader, children learn about the African slave trade and how a Negro boy saves a white playmate from drowning. In the "mint julep" edition both stories are omitted.

At least three large publishers, Holt, Rinehart & Winston, Harcourt, Brace & World, and Silver Burdett, have agreed to give up the lucrative southern market if textbook selection committees insist on all-white texts of new series in subject areas they have not previously covered. Publishers with big investments in existing "mint julep" editions generally continue to sell them.

So far three southern states, Virginia, Mississippi and Louisiana, have adopted integrated texts. Craig Senft, of General Learning Corp., spoke of his experience as president of Silver Burdett: "The first question the chairman of the Louisiana textbook selection committee used to ask was: 'You got any niggers in your book?' The publisher's representative would say, 'No, sir.' Two years ago we decided we would not produce one series for Detroit and New York and another for the South. Some of our friends said, 'You are absolutely crazy. You'll ruin the company.' Our really difficult decision was whether we should submit integrated texts in states like Louisiana. We did, and in December, 1965, Louisiana adopted both our integrated music and science series."

Although textbook publishers may be considered creators of a mass-market product—over 151 million grade- and high-school textbooks were purchased in 1966—the industry itself remains only a multi-million-dollar midget among the multibillion-dollar giants like steel and cars. In fact, despite the important role textbooks play in education, schools spend one and one half to two percent of their total budget on books. This can be explained by the fact that textbooks are relatively inexpensive. In 1966 the average cost of a hardbound book for a grade-school child came to $2.26; for a high-school student, $3.42.

Yet, as small as it is in comparison to other mass producers, the textbook industry is in the process of becoming a very big business indeed. Schoolbook publishers in 1966 sold $440 million worth of elementary- and high-school textbooks. This is an increase of more than 750 percent over 1945 sales and reflects the postwar baby boom.

As so often happens when an industry becomes highly successful, individual companies begin to lose their corporate identity. In fact, during the past decade, few industries in America have been so consumed by the twin fevers of merger and acquisition as textbook publishing. In 1958 there were more than 62 elementary- and high-school houses. Today there are 56. At one time many of these firms specialized in grade or secondary texts and thus went after only one part of the school market. But as the market expanded, they sought an inexpensive device for their own quick growth so that they could meet the soaring demand for schoolbooks. The solution was merger, and the results were publishing giants like Harcourt, Brace & World and Holt, Rinehart & Winston, that now embrace the entire school market from kindergarten through college.

But this was only the beginning. What may turn out to be the wave of the future was the entry of the huge electronic firms into educational publishing. In 1963, I.B.M. made its first acquisition in 30 years when it purchased Science Research Associates, a Chicago-based educational publisher, for $62 million worth of I.B.M. stock. Others that followed in quick succession were Xerox, which bought American Education Publications, a publisher of weekly newspapers and math and science journals for 16.5 million schoolchildren, and General Electric, which joined forces with Time, Inc., to form General Learning Corp., a $37.5 million publisher of educational materials. Added to that marriage were Silver Burdett, the textbook subsidiary of Time, Inc., and the brains of a thousand General Electric Ph.D.'s. All these mergers and acquisitions were followed in 1966 by Raytheon's purchase of D. C. Heath and R.C.A.'s ingestion of Random House. In 1967, CBS and Holt, Rinehart & Winston announced their merger.

A dozen or so major firms account for over 60 percent of the schoolbooks sold. There are now four giants in the field: Scott, Foresman in suburban Chicago and Ginn in Boston, the two biggest elementary publishers, and in New York, Harcourt, Brace & World, and Holt, Rinehart & Winston, the two largest secondary-school publishers. These firms are followed in New York and New Jersey by McGraw-Hill, Prentice-Hall, Crowell-Collier & Macmillan, Silver Burdett, and American Book Company. In Chicago there is Follett and in nearby Evanston, Ill., the textbook division of Harper & Row. And finally, there are the Boston firms of D. C. Heath, Allyn & Bacon, Houghton Mifflin, and Addison-Wesley, the outrider and fastest-growing company in the industry.

Almost all of these firms are 50 to a hundred years old. In contrast, Addison-Wesley, a small printing company and college publisher during World War II, did not enter schoolbook publishing until 1958. Four years later, Addison-Wesley brought forth its first-grade school series, a collection of math books that use color and graphic designs to show how math works. This visual approach proved so popular that Addison-Wesley's sales rocketed from $8.3 million in 1964 to near $16 million in 1965, and the firm is now preparing to take on the entire school market, something which no company has done from a dead start for over a quarter of a century. As a way of urging its employees to reach even greater heights, the company recently posted a brief note on the cafeteria bulletin board. The notice said that if anyone had bothered to buy a single share of Addison-Wesley stock for $200 in 1947, it would be worth $80,000.

The whole industry is engaged, along with the schools, in a tremendous revolution. The forces that started the American educational revolution were nurtured by the scientific and technological shock brought about by World War II. They gained great strength in the competition of the Cold War and through the intense concern of a few brilliant educators like Dr. Jerome Bruner, the director of Harvard's

Center for Cognitive Studies, and Dr. Jerrold R. Zacharias, the M.I.T. physicist. It had finally become apparent that the schools of the 1950's were failing to prepare the nation's children for the complexities of the new age. (There was an early response to this at Scott, Foresman, which was spending $10 million to develop the New Math that was to revolutionize the teaching of this subject.) The knowledge explosion could overwhelm the world's most advanced technological society if future generations were incapable of developing the new skills demanded of them.

In November, 1956, a solution was suggested when the Federal Government made its first grant for textbook development. Since then the Government has given over $56 million to scholars and teachers who have created new teaching techniques and textbooks and teachers' guides in high-school physics, biology, chemistry, foreign languages, and elementary- and high-school mathematics. Most of this money was funneled through the National Science Foundation, an independent agency of the Federal Government. Once the books with their new approaches to learning were written and tested in the schools, they were then turned over to commercial textbook publishers who sold the books and paid royalties to the Government. At the same time, additional millions in government funds were poured into teacher-retraining programs.

An instructive illustration of the educational revolution can be seen in the achievements of, and the difficulties that beset, the Biological Sciences Curriculum Study (B.S.C.S.), a nonprofit, independent group of scientists and teachers who have dramatically changed the teaching of high-school biology. Established by the American Institute of Biological Sciences in January, 1959, the B.S.C.S. spent four years and nearly eight million dollars in federal funds developing, writing and testing three new biology textbooks, laboratory guides and teachers' manuals.

Before the publication of the B.S.C.S. biology books in 1963, the typical high-school student spent endless hours memorizing the names of animals and plants and analyzing the tissue and cell structure of hearts, brains, stomachs and livers. Little attention was given to laboratory experiments or to how scientists think. Under the B.S.C.S. program, today's 10th-grade students spend twice as much time in the laboratory, where they are taught to cross fruit flies to learn about sex-linked inheritance, and where they inject testosterone into male chickens to discover the effects of reproductive hormones. And in the texts themselves the youngsters study human reproduction, birth control, race and intelligence, and evolution, topics that until 1963 were considered too controversial by most publishers and many teachers.

Even though the B.S.C.S. calls for more sophisticated teaching, the textbooks have proved a success in the schools. Three out of four schools that have adopted new biology texts since 1963 have chosen B.S.C.S. materials. This means that by 1965 some 700,000 out of two million 10th-graders were learning biology the new way, and by the end of this year that figure could grow to 1.6 million.

While the B.S.C.S. represents a great forward leap in textbook publishing, the new biology program also reflects some of the hurdles even the most eminent educators must leap before they can get their books accepted by the schools. The trouble began with the way the B.S.C.S. dealt with sex; it culminated in an extraordinary "Monkey War" fought on the battlefields of Texas.

The B.S.C.S. group realized from the start that their most difficult fight would be winning acceptance of material that had been considered controversial in the past. One of the B.S.C.S.'s first battles raged around an illustrated account of human reproduction, a startling advance over the conventional high-school texts which, until 1963, rarely went beyond the sex life of sunflowers and earthworms.

As part of its nationwide testing program in 1961, B.S.C.S. sent 2,300 orange-covered copies of what was to become one of their three books, *Molecules to Man,* to 10 schools in Dade County, Florida. Shortly before Christmas, county school officials became alarmed when they discovered that the experimental textbooks contained diagrams of the human male and female reproductive systems.

They asked the B.S.C.S. to remove the offending illustrations. When this request was denied, they threatened to cut out the pages. But the B.S.C.S. explained that the books were the property of the study group, and the pages could not be deleted. Undaunted, school officials gave the 2,300 copies to a group of teachers who spent the Christmas vacation blacking out the illustrations with crayons.

"You can imagine the chagrin among the officials," said Arnold B. Grobman, former B.S.C.S. director, "when the students quickly discovered that they could view the pictures very easily by holding the books up to the light. Finally some sanity prevailed, and the books are now widely used in Miami with the 'offensive' illustrations found on pages 279 and 280 of the commercial edition."

The Dade County attack proved to be only a preliminary skirmish. The major battles came after the books were published; they centered on the text's defense and full-length treatment of Charles Darwin's theory of evolution.

The fight over whether evolution should be taught in American schools first made national headlines in 1925, when Tennessee charged John Thomas Scopes with breaking a new state law that forbade any teacher in a publicly supported school to teach "any theory that denies the story of the Divine creation of man as taught in the Bible and to teach instead that man has descended from a lower order of animals."

The great "Monkey Trial" in Dayton, Tenn., was a national sensation. Scopes was found guilty and the judge fined him $100. A year later the Tennessee Supreme Court reversed Scopes's conviction on a legal technicality but left the state's anti-evolution law untested. In May, 1967, the Tennessee Legislature finally repealed the law. However, similar statutes are still in force in Arkansas and Mississippi. The B.S.C.S. texts encountered some anti-evolution tremors in Alabama, New Mexico, Kentucky, California and Arizona, with mixed results, but it was in Texas that the "Down with Darwin" earthquake struck in full force in the summer of 1964—some 105 years after Darwin announced his theories.

Before describing these events and their outcome, let us pause briefly to consider how textbook selection works in Texas.

In all the eastern states and throughout most of the Midwest and Far West, textbook publishers sell their wares in what is known as open territory. This means that each school or district selects the books its children will use. In contrast, all the southern and most of the southwestern states appoint state screening committees that must first select or approve the textbooks before the individual schools can buy them. Under a state adoption system, a small group of officials or a state textbook selection committee can wield a considerable amount of economic power over the publishers.

Texas—which annually buys some $16 million worth of schoolbooks—each year sets up a screening committee of 15 educators who select textbooks. The Texas committee can recommend up to five schoolbooks in each subject, and this list then goes to the State Board of Education for final approval. Since all the textbooks the board approves are paid for with state funds, the local schools invariably choose books that the committee and Board of Education have sanctioned. Thus the only way a publisher can hope to sell to the largest state-controlled market in the country is to win the approval of the state's officials.

In due course, the three B.S.C.S. books came up for possible selection in Texas, and the Texas "Monkey Trial" was set off by a mild-mannered, gray-haired, 53-year-old preacher named Reuel Lemmons. Lemmons, who lives in Austin, edits *Firm Foundation,* a weekly newspaper that is mailed to 30,000 members of the Church of Christ, a fundamentalist sect with over 600,000 adherents in Texas alone.

In the spring of 1964, Lemmons had learned that Texas was considering adopting the B.S.C.S. books. Girding for battle, he wrote a scathing editorial which *Firm Foundation* published on June 30. Titled "An Extremely Dangerous Biology Textbook Coming," the editorial described the B.S.C.S. texts as "Godless" and "atheistic." Lemmon's greatest ire was reserved for Houghton Mifflin's *Molecules to Man,* one of the three B.S.C.S. texts.

"It is pure evolution from cover to cover, completely materialistic and completely atheistic," he thundered. "Unless something is done quickly, these are the texts your children will be studying in biology next fall." He asked his readers to petition, phone and write their congressmen, the Texas Education Agency, newspapers, the P.T.A., and local school officials.

The response was extraordinary even for Texas, whose citizens are encouraged by state authorities to protest against the adoption of any textbook they do not like. During his campaign which lasted through the summer and fall, the fundamentalists made speeches on the radio, collected hundreds of petitions, and bombarded state and local officials with thousands of letters.

Their attack reached fever pitch on October 14, when the state selection committee held its annual public textbook hearing in a Texas Education Agency conference room crammed with folding chairs and TV cameras. By 9 a.m. more than 200 people had gathered.

The hearing began with a prayer asking guidance in the committee's deliberations. One of the first witnesses was Reuel Lemmons. A tall, spare man, he stepped before the committee and declared, "If the First Amendment forbids the teaching of the Bible's account of creation, then that same amendment should forbid the teaching of an anti-creation theory." Reaching his peroration, the preacher warned, "This theory (of evolution) which these texts would teach our children for many years to come will undermine faith in God and in the spiritual, and to that extent undermine America, whose motto is—'In God We Trust.' " Lemmons was followed by a farmer, a housewife, a dentist and two college professors, eventually over a dozen witnesses who sought to have the textbooks banned or changed.

As the publishers' salesmen and editors rose to the defense of the textbooks, they tried to mollify the critics by reaffirming that no atheist had a hand in writing, producing or selling the B.S.C.S. material. "The authors," declared Gordon Hjalmarson, the B.S.C.S. editor at Houghton Mifflin, "are for most cases native-born American Christians. . . . as Mr. [Fay] Brown [the firm's top Texas salesman] has indicated, he teaches Sunday school in Dallas. The supervisor of the Blue Version writing team representing the Biological Sciences Curriculum Study, Dr. [Claude] Welch, has been an elder in the United Church of Christ. I am at the present time and have been for the last two years a deacon in the Congregational Church in my home town."

The next day the selection committee met in secret and, the following day, announced that it had recommended not one but all three of the new biology books.

The battle, however, was not over. Dr. J. W. Edgar, the state commissioner of education, could remove three of the five biology books the committee had recommended. Again the fundamentalists protested, but the commissioner upheld the committee's selections. The final decision now rested with the 21 elected members of the State Board of Education. Another campaign, another hearing, and finally in November, 1964, the *Sweetwater Texas Reporter* emblazoned its edition with the headline: Darwin Declared Winner in Texas 'Monkey War.'

The victory had a price. Along with the tremendous power it wields in textbook selection, the state of Texas also has an impressive power of censorship—they go hand in hand. Under Texas law, every publisher who submits a textbook for adoption must sign a contract in which he agrees "to make revisions in content as the State Board of Education may direct, authorize and demand."

And Texas authorities do insist upon changes, and publishers do make them. And because publishers find it less costly to issue a single, nationwide edition, they will frequently incorporate these changes in future editions sold throughout the country. In short, it is possible for one state to determine the content of textbooks used from Maine to Oregon. And on occasion the state of Texas does just that.

Thus while the Texas fundamentalists were fulminating, and before the first public hearing was held, a quiet censorship battle was being waged behind the scenes. Members of the textbook committee told Houghton Mifflin's salesmen that several changes would have to be made in *Molecules to Man,* chief target of the fundamentalists, before there could be any sales in Texas.

But no changes could be made without the approval of the Biological Sciences Curriculum Study. The only recourse was to send the Texas comments to Michigan State University's Claude Welch, the B.S.C.S. writing supervisor of *Molecules to Man*.

On October 2, some 12 days before the selection committee held its public hearing, Fay Brown, the manager of Houghton Mifflin's Dallas office, wrote the state commissioner of education that the changes would be made. In his letter Brown declared: "Even though *Molecules to Man* represents the most thoroughly tested project in history, the authors and publishers welcome any constructive suggestions which will enhance the scientific-inquiry approach to biology for all students." The changes Fay Brown listed as enhancing scientific-inquiry include the following:

In the original version the authors had written: "Evolution is not a faith, but a scientific theory. The theory has been developed to account for a body of facts."

This was changed to read: "Evolution is not a *belief*, nor an *observational fact*—it is a scientific theory."

In another change the publisher and Dr. Welch had substituted the word "modified" for "strengthened" in the sentence, "Like all scientific theory, the theory of evolution has been both strengthened [now read 'modified'] and revised as research disclosed more and more facts."

In still other changes, the B.S.C.S. replaced, "Biologists are *convinced* that the human species evolved from nonhuman forms," with: "Many biologists *assume* that the human species evolved from nonhuman forms." They also deleted the sentence, "To biologists there is no longer any reasonable doubt that evolution occurs."

Dr. Claude Welch, who authorized the changes, insists they are "minor" and in no way "reduced the logic of our presentation of evolution." Of the pages upon pages of requests for revisions submitted, he declared he "flatly rejected" 99.9 percent of them. "I approved the ones listed in [Fay] Brown's letter," Dr. Welch went on, "simply because the changes seem to make good sense. I certainly don't see what the fuss is about."

In the opinion of Prof. George Gaylord Simpson, Alexander Agassiz professor of vertebrate paleontology at Harvard and one of the nation's top scientists, "the fuss" transcends Darwin's theory. "With only one exception," he said, "the changes follow a tradition of ignorant, red-neck anti-rationalism and anti-evolutionism. They deliberately batten on the vulgar misapprehension that a scientific theory is guesswork, hence as likely to be wrong as right." He added that such a view "is particularly dangerous when it is incorporated in a young person's study of science, which should show him at least the rudiments of rational thinking in the scientific way."

For all that, the texts *do* cover evolution and other previously taboo subjects and Texas *did* adopt them.

Yet with all this one must remember that the dubious changes made as the result of the Texas adoption will be incorporated into future printings that will be sold to schools throughout the United States. As previously noted, this is common practice.

His greeting was warm, almost effusive. He wore a red jacket over a bright red tie rippling down a gray shirt. His silver hair was parted in the middle. All along one wall of his spacious office were group photographs of the nation's most eminent scientists, all friends or acquaintances of the man I had come to see, Dr. Jerrold R. Zacharias, professor of physics at M.I.T.

During most of his academic career, Dr. Zacharias had been absorbed in such esoteric fields of research as the hyperfine structure of atomic hydrogen, deuterium and chlorine, and the nuclear moments of those elements and their isotopes. He was one of the developers of the atomic beam clock, an extraordinarily precise device that loses only one hundredth of a second a year. More recently, however, Dr. Zacharias has been busy in another area—he and his colleagues have wrought an educational revolution.

In our time and in our country, anti-intellectuals found sustenance in the tensions of the Cold War and a leader in the late Senator McCarthy. In such an atmosphere the search for truth was frequently considered an act of subversion, and the intellectual was looked upon as the purveyor of heresy. During this period Dr. Zacharias began serving as a member of the committee of scientists who advised the President. Distressed by the public witch hunts, he also witnessed the privately expressed fears of Russian scientific achievements. Then, in 1956, Professor Zacharias arose to address his colleagues.

"We had been briefed to the point of boredom on how the Russians were getting ahead of us technologically," he recalled. "Finally I spoke up. The problem was not the Russians, but the anti-intellectualism which had pervaded our colleges and schools and which was getting into our children. 'Shouldn't we understand this problem?' I asked."

At first no one responded.

"The only way I know how to do anything," Professor Zacharias said, "is to start with the specific and go to the general." The specific that he knew best was physics. He was concerned, too, with the dull way this discipline was being taught in the schools, and he was deeply concerned with the textbooks then in use; he felt that they grossly misrepresented the subject he loved.

Dr. Zacharias went to the National Science Foundation, and in November, 1956, he received his first grant of $303,000 to do something about improving the teaching of the most difficult of sciences. In the meantime he had received promises of aid from top scientists at Harvard, Cornell, the University of Illinois, M.I.T and the Bell Telephone Laboratories. "None of this was done by institutional relationships," he said. "It was just us boys." The group rapidly expanded and became known as the Physical Science Study Committee—the first of the curriculum reform groups. Four years and over five million dollars later, the first hardbound P.S.S.C. textbook appeared in the schools, along with a series of movies and laboratory guides filled with new experiments. Turned over to D. C. Heath for commercial publication, the P.S.S.C. text is now being used by half the high-school physics students in the United States.

But the new physics program was only the beginning. Since the National Science Foundation made its first grant to the P.S.S.C. in November, 1956, millions in federal funds have been distributed by the N.S.F. to other study groups. Among them: $21 million for math; $10 million for biology; $4 million for chemistry; and more than $13 million for a variety of elementary-science study groups.

Perhaps the most important promise of these new programs is that learning can become a fascinating experience for both teachers and students. An example is the discovery method now used to teach many subjects. Its most dramatic application is in the Cuisenaire Rods, consisting of 72 wooden sticks ranging in length from 1 to 10 centimeters. By playing with the sticks, with the aid of a teacher, children discover all the mathematical operations, including multiplication, factoring and division, fractions and proportions.

Then consider what has happened to the teaching of foreign languages, a subject in the past that was learned by rote and taught by drill.

Until 1961 almost every youngster who studied French, German, Spanish or Russian was given a combination grammar book and reader. "He would spend two years translating sentences like, 'My aunt's purple umbrella is under the bench in the park,'" recalled Mary Thompson with a quiver of horror. Miss Thompson, who directed the federally funded language revolution, added, "The only objectives in teaching foreign languages were reading and translation. It was a deadening process with no relation to the fact that these are living languages. Few children ever learned how to listen and speak."

Today a child in the seventh grade who studies French under the new program learns to speak before he learns to read and write. Within two years a youngster is reading excerpts from modern French novels, poetry and newspapers, and carrying on ordinary conversations in French.

The dramatic changes that are sweeping the teaching of foreign languages, science and math are only beginning to touch the two vital remaining disciplines, humanities and social studies. But here, too, a whole new world of learning is about to burst upon the schools. As in the sciences, millions of dollars in federal, foundation and university grants are being poured into over 140 research and development programs in literature, American history, economics and civics.

At Harvard, Dr. Donald Oliver, a professor of education and a social scientist, is experimenting with a senior-high-school social-studies program that presents the great controversial issues of the past and present. Readings include an excerpt from Kenneth Roberts's novel, *Oliver Wiswell*, describing the persecution of a liberal Tory family by the rebelling Americans, the trial of Galileo, and an account of how a Boston mob killed a United States marshal who was returning a Negro slave to his owner in the South under the Fugitive Slave Law. The youngsters are then bombarded with a series of highly charged questions that involve them in conflicts of conscience and values.

Many scholars complain that the traditional history textbooks attempt to cover too much history and thus do not have the space to present more than a brief summary of events and preordained conclusions. All that youngsters get is "one damned event after another," says Peter Wolffe.

Wolffe until recently had a top editorial role in a social-studies program that is being created by Education Development Center (formerly Educational Services, Inc.), a nonprofit organization of university scholars and schoolteachers. One of E.D.C.'s most interesting projects is a course on colonial history for 12-year-olds that is based almost entirely on original sources and documents. The aim is twofold: to teach eighth-graders American history and at the same time to train them to think like historians.

For example: an experimental section on the Battle of Lexington poses a startingly simple question: "What happened on April 19, 1775, at Lexington, Massachusetts?" The student quickly learns that the answer is not simple. The youngsters are given six written versions of the battle. They include three accounts composed by English soldiers and three by Americans. The eighth-graders are then asked to show where the British and Americans agreed and disagreed, and finally to construct their own version of what happened.

Though much of this new material has been subsidized by the Federal Government and private foundations, the publishing houses are risking their own money for some of the research and in some cases paying all the costs. Indeed, for the first time in the history of textbook publishing almost every major house can boast of at least one innovation in a field that had barely changed for nearly half a century.

Yet all these improvements just begin to touch on the increasingly complex problems that the schools will face in the future. For example, numbers.

"Just to maintain the class ratio of thirty students to one teacher," declared Craig Senft, "half our college graduates will have to go into teaching by 1970. But lacking the human resources, we will have to turn to technology, to introduce totally new concepts of teaching. We may have to build schools completely run by computers. We may have to build learning rooms in every home where a child sits at a console, presses a button and retrieves whatever information he needs. We may turn to educational TV and have a master teacher teach a thousand classrooms at once. All these things are technologically possible now. What we don't know is how to use these tools effectively in the teaching process."

And indeed, here lies the problem: what to put in the machines so that they will become effective teachers? It is for this reason that six of the nation's largest electronics firms—Xerox, General Electric, I.B.M., Raytheon, CBS and R.C.A.—have recently acquired or joined forces with publishers who, it is hoped, will supply or supplement the human brain matter that will turn computers into teachers.

The most advanced electronically run educational system produced to date is the creation of Dr. Patrick C. Suppes, director of Stanford's Institute for Mathematical Studies in the Social Sciences. Dr. Suppes, financed by $2.5 million from the Carnegie Corporation, the National Science Foundation, and the U.S. Office of Education, has programmed an I.B.M. computer that is attempting to teach reading and math to

100 first-graders in East Palo Alto's Brentwood School, where 80 percent of the children are Negro.

For example, in one reading lesson a child is asked to combine the initial sounds *r, p* and *b* with the endings *an, at* and *ag,* and to make *ban, pan, ran, bat, pat, rat, bag* and *rag.* As each word is flashed on the screen the youngster, who is also wearing earphones, hears a woman's taped voice pronounce it. Then the voice, always pleasant, always patient, asks the child to touch or write the word *ran* on a cathode-ray tube using an electronic light pen. (He can also respond by typing his answer or by pushing one of several multiple-choice buttons.) If the youngster picks the correct answer, the voice tells him so. If he touches *ban,* then he gets a remedial drill in initial sounds. If he chooses *rag* instead of *ran,* the machine goes over previous lessons because he probably does not understand the lesson being taught.

The Suppes system was first put into use in September, 1966, and it is too early to tell whether it will prove effective. However, if the Suppes programmed computer or others like it should work, it could totally revolutionize education in the elementary and high schools and colleges. For the computer possesses a crucial device that no human being can produce: total and instant recall of all the information that has been fed into it. This means that it eventually may be able to serve as an individual instructor that will take into account the strengths and weaknesses of each child. It would do this by modifying the curriculum fed into it on the basis of each student's responses. More drill in the same lesson for one child. A remedial lesson for another. Quick advancement for a third.

In the new age, not only will humans have to program the computer and therefore do its original thinking, but once it has been programmed, the teacher will have more time to think, to give individual attention to each child and to teach what the computer cannot manage. Moreover, no machine, however clever its masters, can provide the inspiration that comes from a human being who himself is inspired by the subject he loves and the young minds he is trying to awaken. Finally, no computer with its extraordinary recall, no mass TV class, no self-winding film that a five-year-old can operate, will ever replace the reading book, although some of these devices may radically change the textbook as we have studied it.

"There will be hundreds of books, some in paperback, some in hard cover, some stored on the classroom shelves, others in the school computer," says Craig Senft. "Each book will be different and cover a part of each subject in depth. As Dean Francis Chase of the University of Chicago put it, the biggest revolution in education will come from a better use of books."

The promise is great. At last, after two centuries of what must now seem like imperceptible progress, education is being touched by the visionaries. With the questions they ask, with the dreams that possess them, they may yet open a world of wonder to the children they seek to teach.

GORDON GAMMACK

Anatomy of a Town vs. Long Hair

That schools usually represent the interests of conformity, control, and censorship is further illustrated by the personal appearance or "dress" codes that are still a widespread phenomenon. Controversies have been reported in the press all over the country recently. Typical of these is the account of what happened in Maquoketa, Iowa, a midwestern town of 6,000 people.

Maquoketa, Ia.—A mood of smoldering fury has engulfed Maquoketa over resistance to a ban against long hair in the public schools. That's the issue on the surface. But there are those who sense also the wrath of a no-longer-silent majority against rebellious, non-conforming youth and disrespect for authority. In the midst of all this the Iowa Civil Liberties Union, considered subversive by many Maquoketans, has become the whipping boy. The controversy started when William Brooks, principal of Maquoketa Community High School, sent a letter to parents warning that hair covering boys' ears and below the collar line at the neck would not be tolerated.

There was nothing new about this code. What made it especially provocative was that it was issued in the face of a United States District Court ruling written by Iowa Judge William C. Hanson, in the case of Susan Sims vs. the Colfax (Iowa) Community School district that the

Gordon Gammack, "Anatomy of a Town vs. Long Hair" *Des Moines Register*, September 20, 1970, T1+. Copyright 1970. Reprinted by permission.

Constitution guarantees "a student's free choice of his appearance." At the high school's opening assembly, about nine boys showed up with hair violating the code. The number isn't precise because several drop-outs seeking readmission were involved. The facts are that four students with long hair remain out of school and the storm center is 15-year-old Kevin Allen because his mother, Mrs. Kenneth (Darlene) Allen, sought and obtained the intervention of the Iowa Civil Liberties Union. She has become the target of extensive hostility. She says she has received a barrage of ugly phone calls; has been subjected to obscene gestures as she walks along the streets, and has been shunned by clerks when she goes shopping. It is crystal clear that the school authorities have the backing of the overwhelming majority in Maquoketa, at least ten to one, probably. The five-member Board of Education backs Principal Brooks unanimously.

The strongest opposition to Brooks seems to come from within his own faculty, and some of the teachers, claiming that the school officials and public are taking a courts-be-damned attitude, are out-spoken. Says Richard Wolf, history, English and humanities instructor and also Democratic chairman in Jackson County: "This equation they have developed is dangerous—Long hair equals drug addiction equals peaceniks equals Communism."

Wolf says that some of the backers of the hair code have "total contempt for the law of the land. These are the same people who mouth law and order," he continues. "I find law and order coming out of their mouths as valid as love out of the mouth of a street walker."

Like so many storms, this one developed in relative serenity. Early in August, the "dress code" of Principal Brooks was discussed at a meeting of school board members and school administrators. Attitudes were more resilient than they are now. One school board member, Mrs. Ross River, an unbending supporter of the boys' hair code, challenged a Brooks' directive that girls wear stockings. Stockings are both hot and expensive, she said, and Brooks replied that "this is easy to amend."

Superintendent of Schools Melvin Sikkink, who now maintains that Judge Hanson's ruling in "the Colfax case" doesn't apply to the Maquoketa situation, said then that at summer seminars he attended it was brought out that most court cases have held that hair length is none of the school's business. And Gaylord Willman, long-time principal of the junior high schools, said, "Your dress code is illegal. You are going to lose every case that goes to court. You can't force a majority thing on a minority."

The polarization seems to have come with the intervention of the Iowa Civil Liberties Union and Principal Brooks may have provoked some of the hostility a year ago. He had asked Robert Melvold, publisher of the Maquoketa Newspapers, for permission to write a weekly column about school affairs and Melvold agreed. Brooks wrote in a column:

"Just who or what is this Iowa Civil Liberties Union?" he started. "Where does this so-called champion of the people get the right to tell the public schools how to handle students? 'I.C.L.U. WARNS SCHOOLS VS. LONG HAIR RULES!' Big deal! They really sound tough! A teacher or administrator says something to a student and if his student doesn't happen to like it, he yells 'Foul' or 'Iowa Civil Liberties Union' and a couple of two-bit shyster lawyers come crawling in and scream that we are violating this poor child's freedom. What freedom? The schools are trying to educate students. We are attempting to help bring these students up to that certain age when they are supposed to be mature enough to make their own wise decisions. How can we possibly do this when every time we turn around, some nut hollers, 'You can't do that.'"

The attacks on the Civil Liberties Union are viewed with both sadness and amusement by Agnes Evans, high school journalism and English teacher, who will retire in four years. She says that most people in Maquoketa completely misunderstand the Civil Liberties Union and don't realize it has been supported vigorously by such men as Dwight Eisenhower and a host of other conservative leaders. Back in the 1940s she was a zealous I.C.L.U. member and was on a committee that fought against unjust dismissals of teachers. "Teachers were being dismissed without reason, without being warned that they were doing anything displeasing," she recalls. "Much of the controversy sprang from gossip and personal dislikes. Especially in the humanities, teachers make statements that are rather involved and a pupil will pick up a word and when he repeats it at home, a parent misunderstands and a teacher becomes suspect. Until the 1950s teachers had no security in this state."

Mrs. Evans—a Republican and a member of the Daughters of the American Revolution—says of the Maquoketa hair controversy, "People who are well enough educated, good enough citizens and are fair enough, want to support the law. Many don't realize that the courts have spoken."

There was a stormy public hearing, attended by 400, over the hair code. There was a reference to Joseph Johnston, Iowa City attorney representing the Civil Liberties Union, "coming out from under a rock" to attend the meeting and the revelation that he is a member of the Iowa Legislature proved to be something of a shock to townspeople. When Johnston said that the purpose of the Civil Liberties Union is to protect Constitutional rights, a Maquoketa businessman, Ben Hulsen, said the organization "ought to get a better press agent" because "it appears they only defend those in shady operations."

Mrs. Allen says she sought help of the I.C.L.U. because she didn't have the funds to hire a private attorney. Her husband has been a coronary invalid for 12 years. She has three sons at college—two studying to be teachers at the University of Northern Iowa—and she works part time to support the family. "This is the first time I've ever taken a stand on anything," she says. "But I think it is so important. People should be able to question rulings like this without being considered a Communist or a rabble-rouser. I've been called a permissive parent, no discipline whatever, but I've probably broken as many yardsticks over the boys' little fannies as any mother. The love and respect of my son and my husband mean more to me than this whole community. These town people have checked all the church rolls and decided I'm a heathen because I don't belong to a church. Organized religion has become so big, an individual is lost in the shuffle. I have my own personal relationship with God. I am a Christian. I know I am."

Mrs. Allen has been gratified by the support she has received—especially from Sue River, daughter of the school board member and a freshman at Carleton College who spoke out against the hair code at the public hearing and told Mrs. Allen, "I'm with you all the way." And Mrs. Allen received a letter, signed by two teachers, who praised her for standing up against "embittered and frustrated people infected with fear and irrationality . . . Hate may be stronger than love, but love is more enduring."

Some Maquoketa community leaders have found it difficult to take a middle ground and some businessmen even suspected of being critical of school authorities reportedly have suffered business sanctions. Publisher Melvold has opened his pages to every possible expression and editorially urged the long-hairs to conform pending a conclusive ruling. Yet, he is criticized by Principal Brooks for giving the controversy "too much attention."

The clergy has been involved, too. Mrs. Allen is especially distressed over the reference by the Rev. Jerry B. Walcott (Methodist) to "a mangy looking character from nowhere." Her son, she says, bathes and shampoos his hair daily. Said the Rev. Mr. Walcott: "Even though

Mr. Brooks' action to dismiss long hairs until they clean up and come back to the human race is supposedly illegal, I will be most disappointed if the school board does not give him full backing all the way."

Superintendent Sikkink says he is satisfied that Judge Hanson's ruling in the Colfax hair case does not apply because "it applied to one student, a female; we're dealing with boys and that's quite different right there. Just look at the difference between men's and women's hair all over the country."

Said Judge Hanson: "School hair rules are reasonable and thus Constitutional only if the school can objectively show that such a rule does in fact prevent some disruption or interference of the school system." Civil Liberties Union supporters stress that at Maquoketa the boys with long hair were suspended before classes started, thus depriving the schools of claims the long hair was disruptive.

One school board member, William Lamb, was high school principal before Brooks and now is in business. He says: "Whenever you open the door, there's hardly room to find a stopping place. How far do rights extend? Authority is being challenged everywhere these days. The public hasn't caught up with this liberal thinking. Maybe the public doesn't want to catch up."

Says Mrs. River: "I don't prefer to call it a hair issue because it is not really that. It's a matter of do we have rules and regulations or don't we. One judge's ruling doesn't make a law."

One of the most controversial figures in the Maquoketa rhubarb is Gary Holst, who came from the St. Louis area this year to teach shop. At the public hearing some observers thought he favored putting the "ugly heads" of the long haired boys into the machines of his shop but he says, "No, no, no, I don't think I said that. Anyway, what I meant was that with their long hair, their heads might be caught in the machines." Holst thinks the number of boys wanting long hair is inconsequential. "We're talking about two or three out of 500. If you're talking about 30, 40 percent, you've got something different. I can't see bucking the establishment. Outside forces are involved in this. Someone, somewhere is putting a little pressure on someone." Was he referring to something subversive, Communist-inspired? "I've seen things that have been," he replied.

Teacher Wolf says there are undercurrents of violent hatred in Maquoketa and a feeling against college campus militants of "shoot 'em; kill 'em." And he sees much of the bitterness caused by rifts within the family. "In every single case here where we have a really vociferous opponent, it's because of their home situation. These people have been threatened at home. Their children are rejecting them. The children are going through this traumatic declaration of independence and all this bitterness seems to follow right out of it."

Through all of this, little attention has been paid to one section of Judge Hanson's opinion: "There has undoubtedly been too much said if not written concerning long hair or unusual hair styles. Mankind's experience has demonstrated that in this area of fashion, fads constantly come and go as the pendulum unceasingly swings from extreme to extreme. Thus, no doubt, the proper characterization of the current controversy over students' hair is that of the proverbial tempest in a teapot."

MYRON BRENTON

Profile of the Average Teacher

Where do teachers fit into the pattern of things? Are they fundamentally disaffected with a school system based on coercion? Are they chafing to give students more freedom? A few, like Patricia Michaels, whose activities at a Union Springs high school are described in Part 1, apparently are. Their numbers may even be growing, but for every Pat Michaels fired for supporting student freedom, there are many more who believe that things are pretty much the way they should be. Here is a report of recent research about what makes typical teachers typical.

The contemporary American public school teacher is, on the average, about thirty-six years of age. Chances are he's been teaching for about eight years. Odds are seven to three that he went to a publicly supported college or university for his training. He has a bachelor's degree and is taking additional college courses. (Nearly one-fourth of all teachers have a master's degree, most on the secondary level; the number of classroom teachers holding doctorates is negligible.) College courses and other career growth activities cost the average teacher from $100 to $200 a year. He spends some $20 in out-of-pocket expenses for school materials.

Chances are, if the teacher is a man, that he moonlights. (More than half do.) He's in debt. He and his spouse are buying a home. They own at least one car (over one-third of all teachers own two cars or more). First choice: Chevrolet.

The average teacher attends church or synagogue. He votes in both primary and general elections. Politically, he's a conservative; even if he considers himself a liberal, he tends more toward the conservative side of that spectrum. As Harmon Zeigler points out in his political study of teachers, *The Political Life of American Teachers*, teachers are purveyors of middle-class values and therefore defenders of conventionality.

The average schoolteacher reads one or two newspapers a day. About half the teachers read a paper published outside the area in which they live. Almost all teachers read the national and local news stories; a slightly lower percentage (88.2 percent) reads the international news stories. Slightly less than one-fourth of all teachers read the editorials, and 69.2 percent read letters to the editor. The letters, in fact, are preferred to columnists, with just over half the teachers reading them. Book reviews aren't too popular either; more teachers read the comic strips, the society page, and the display ads than they do book reviews. Lovelorn columnist Ann Landers has the edge over Walter Lippmann, who has been the teachers' favorite political columnist. Quite possibly, teachers do not read book reviews because they read few nonprofessional books. One recent survey shows that of the teachers sampled, nearly one-fourth had not read a single nonprofessional book in the preceding three months. On the other hand, an amazing 10.9 percent had read between six and nine such books. Fiction has the edge.

America's favorite magazine, the *Reader's Digest*, is also the teachers' favorite. *Life* runs a close second. It is a relatively rare teacher who reads *The Atlantic, Harper's,* or even the *Saturday Review.* Hardly any teachers go in for heavy-think or current affairs publications like *New Republic, American Scholar,* or *Daedelus.*

Like his counterpart in the larger society, the public school teacher complains of having little time for recreational activities. Eight out of ten teachers say that preparing lessons and grading papers are a major limitation on recreation; nearly seven out of ten also point to family and home responsibilities. The teacher's principal leisure-time activities are, again like his nonteaching counterpart's, apt to be sedentary. Favorite pastimes are watching television, visiting people, reading, writing correspondence, attending religious services, dining out, going to parties, listening to records (semiclassical, musical comedy, and folk), and going to the movies (historical films are best liked, but only about one-fourth of the teachers attend a movie theatre as often as once or twice a month).

Few teachers like to do more active things, like going out for team sports, acting in dramatic groups, playing musical instruments, tinkering with their cars, sketching, or painting. Favorite sports: football, basketball, and baseball, in that order—but only as spectators. Of teachers who like to be physically active, the plurality (about four in ten) prefer walking or hiking. About one-third like to go swimming. Fewer than three out of ten like to bowl, fish, or camp.

Analyzing teachers' playtime habits, Perry London of the University of California and Donald E. Larsen of Yale University make three points with respect to leisure: (1) Teachers choose activities requiring minimal use of physical energy; (2) teachers choose activities that make few mental demands; (3) teachers aim for escape from workaday life, a life so much more demanding and complicated.

"The net result for teachers," say London and Larsen, "is a somewhat listless, colorless and subdued existence."

Said a junior high school English teacher in Raleigh, North Carolina, "We've had some top-notch people coming now. They're well-equipped; they certainly have an enthusiasm and interest in students that you just are delighted to find. I think the quality has improved tremendously over the past four, five years."

Said a professor of education at City University in New York, "Some brilliant kids from Harvard, MIT, and other places are coming into the schools. They're looking at the schools as ways of going into social service and government service. This is new. They're motivated by Kennedy, the Peace Corps, the idea of giving. Will they change things? I don't know. They're loners. They don't join teachers' groups or move up in the bureaucracy itself. They see education as a profession with dignity, but after a couple of years some of them also see that teaching children isn't for them. So they move on. You also find some middle-aged people, very successful career people, motivated by the idea of serving. A successful attorney who gives up his practice and teaches high school. A physics professor who goes back into the public schools to teach. But they're a small minority."

Said a professor of psychology at Brooklyn College, "The education majors aren't very bright, but they're nice, decent, polite kids. I like them very much."

At two-year intervals from 1928 to 1932 two educational researchers conducted an exhaustive study of over 45,000 high school and college students in Pennsylvania. Their findings were startling. They learned that, among college students, education majors ranked at the bottom scholastically in comparison with students in other categories. The median IQ score for 26,000 high school seniors, selected at random, was higher than the median for education students and those ready to receive their degrees at several teachers' colleges. Moreover, in comparing college seniors in education with unselected high school seniors, the two researchers found that many of the high school seniors had actually made better grades in the very subjects the education majors were getting ready to teach.

In the early 1950's, Dael L. Wolfle scrutinized the Army General Classification Scores to determine how intelligence was distributed among professionals and those preparing to enter professional life. College graduates in education scored fourth from the bottom, followed by social science, home economics, and physical education majors. In a subsequent study, researchers determined that Australian teachers' college students with two years' training did as well on the National Teachers Examination as a group of American students trained for four years at twenty-one colleges in the United States. Comparing four-year Australian and four-year American students, they found that the Australians were superior.

In 1965, a USOE study of graduate students' undergraduate achievement showed that only business and commerce majors did worse, that is, got a lower percentage of A's and A–'s, and a higher percentage of C's and C–'s, than education majors. In 1952 education majors ranked lowest of sixteen professional categories on the Graduate Record Examinations. In 1963–64 they ranked lowest again. In 1968 they ranked lowest once more.

Intellectuals will despair; so do some educators, while others place less importance on these findings. Teachers are part of the college-educated group which has an average IQ at least 15 to 20 points higher than the average IQ of the population as a whole. Surprisingly, many research studies fail to show a direct relationship between teacher intelligence and pupil achievement—at least when intelligence is considered as a *single variable* and certain sophisticated math and science courses are excepted. Some educational experts say research instruments aren't sophisticated enough to measure such aspects of teacher effectiveness; others suggest that most teachers are clustered around the 112–115 IQ range, too short a spread from which to draw any conclusions. But the fact that education majors as a group have consistently lower grade-point averages in college may well suggest that their motivation to achieve is relatively low, something that could affect their teaching efforts. And it explains the reputation education has for attracting college students who want an easy path to a degree or a career. "If the most capable people are rejecting classroom teaching as a career, either at the outset or after trying it for a while, American education is crippled," wrote a Newton, Massachusetts, English teacher in the *NEA Journal,* which doesn't have a reputation for talking tough to teachers.

> "*Q: Why did you choose teaching?*
>
> "Mrs. Y: Well, everyone says he likes kids, and I used to. Seriously, though, since I am married, it is a good insurance policy for me, but more than that, I want to help other children to learn.
>
> "Miss X: It's what I've always wanted to do. There have been a few times when I've been frustrated, but I like teaching.
>
> "Mr. W: I went into teaching because in going through high school I had some classes that were so dull and boring that I kept telling myself that it doesn't have to be like this, that I could do better. And I'm trying."
>
> —from "Troubled Young Voices: Interviews with Four Young Teachers," *Ohio Schools* (January, 1966).

Teachers are caught in a trap of sorts. Despite the fact that they're stereotyped unflatteringly in some respects, deep down the public seems to believe they are (or should be) prompted to their calling by two lofty motives—love for children and love of teaching. Regardless of the extent to which it's grounded in reality insofar as real teachers are concerned, the image is really untenable. Whenever teachers behave in ways inconsistent with it—and it's inevitable that at times they do—the public tends to feel let down, betrayed.

Yet teachers themselves strongly adhere to that same image, the most flattering view possible. That is to say, whenever they're asked why they went into teaching, they usually give reasons that have them putting the best, noblest slant on their motives. Prospective teachers, too, give replies to questions about motivation that have a decidedly inspirational cast. Typical is a detailed study that was conducted with elementary and secondary school teachers-to-be at Northern Illinois University. Nearly all of the prospective grade school and well over three-fourths of the prospective high school teachers ranked "desire to work with children and adolescents" as the primary influence on their decision to become teachers.

Other ranking followed in kind. Nearly three-fourths of both elementary and high school teachers-to-be gave "desire to impart knowledge" second place as a significant influence. Seventy-two percent of the prospective elementary school teachers and 61 percent of the prospective high school teachers ranked "opportunity to continue one's own education" third. "Desire to be of service to society" was the fourth-ranking factor for about two-thirds of the elementary and half the secondary people. As for the fifth-ranking factor, "Liking for a particular subject," only 20 percent of the prospective elementary school teachers but 85 percent of those going into secondary education chose it as a significant influence. And, "Experience in working with youngsters" was a significant factor for 73 percent of the prospective elementary and 43 percent of the prospective high school teachers.

There's no reason to doubt that concern for the welfare of children (most often expressed by elementary school teachers) and strong interest in teaching a particular subject (the big factor with high school teachers) genuinely prompt people to go into the teaching profession. (Quite a few teachers mention other factors, too: such as parents or other relatives who are teachers; the impact of memorable teachers; experience gained teaching in the Army, in summer camps, in the Peace Corps, or elsewhere.) Those, however, are the conscious reasons, the ones readily put down on a questionnaire or given in answer to an interviewer's query.

As will be discussed shortly, there are deeper reasons as well. What motivates people to choose one career over another involves complex psychological forces, many completely hidden even from self, and this applies to the most altruistic of occupations as well as to the more materialistic. It is as unreasonable to expect teachers to be moved solely by "pure" motives (wanting to help children, desiring to further society) as it is to expect doctors and lawyers to be what they are solely out of a profound respect for human life or justice. But teachers, being as human as the others, automatically put their best social foot forward. When nearly two hundred female elementary and secondary school teachers employed by the New York City school system were asked to rate the major factors that influenced them to teach, not even the promise of anonymity deterred them from selecting socially acceptable reasons for making their career choices. Being defenders of middle-class morality, they either wouldn't or couldn't admit to motives at variance with that morality. So concluded the researcher who, writing in the *Journal of Experimental Education*, added, "Apparently teachers are either reluctant and/or unable to admit the powerful sway of motives which are socially less desirable. In private communications, teachers will agree that teaching is a convenient job for a woman. Yet only ten percent regarded this reason as most influential in their choice of teaching."

In 1950 Yale University published a doctoral dissertation whose contents, at least in part, will bring joy to few teachers. Ponderously titled "The Behavior System and Occupational Type Associated with Teaching," it attempts in a few of its pages that most hazardous of exercises: generalizing on the personality characteristics of an occupational group, that group of course being teachers. In effect, it's a word portrait of the average American schoolteacher, complete with strengths and weaknesses.

Teachers (the dissertation says) are not strongly motivated to enter the occupation or to advance in it. They are at least vaguely dissatisfied with their work, inclined toward the status quo, disinclined toward change. They tend to be cooperative and helpful, and adept at school work. They are more followers than leaders, more disposed to political conservatism than liberalism, more apt to grow authoritarian with time than vice versa. Teachers think of teachers as being different— which renders them quite vulnerable to stereotyping. They lack aggression but have a strong sense of service. Women teachers are rather optimistic, disposed to make the best of a situation. Male teachers are inclined to pessimism.

To be fair, it may be pointed out that the world of the 1950's and the world of the 1960's are quite different and that the portrait might be quite different if drawn in recent years. Fortunately, for the sake of comparison, in 1964 researcher John Gillis undertook to analyze the personality needs of men and women about to enter teaching. Published in *Educational and Psychological Measurement,* the study doesn't paint too dissimilar a portrait. In comparison with people going into other professions, teachers show more cognitive organization. They tend to depreciate and devalue themselves more. They have more of a need for close, friendly relationships. They show more deference to persons they consider superiors. They're more emotional, more needful of giving and receiving love, protection, assistance. They have more of a concern for detail and neatness. They're more erotic in their interests and expressions. On the other hand, they have less need to analyze and reflect, less interest in solving problems, less willingness to gamble or take risks. They're less objective but also less spontaneous. They exhibit less assertive behavior with others.

When men and women teachers are compared with one another rather than with persons going into other professions, the men teachers show more of a need to achieve. They show more need to overcome humiliation and failure, more need for personal power, more aggression and hostility, and more of an urge to manipulate others. Women teachers are more self-abasing, more willing to be submissive, more narcissistic and erotic. They have more of a need to be friendly, to love and be loved. These comparisons would seem to reflect the differences generally found between men and women in American culture. They also reflect the direction teachers' organizations have been taking since a substantial number of men have entered the teaching field.

It's a mistake, though, to view teachers as a professionally homogeneous group. They are one when it comes to teacher welfare and to improving educational conditions, perhaps, but there are many divergencies: among elementary and secondary school teachers; even among teachers teaching different grade levels within a given school; increasingly among white and black teachers; among young teachers and those who have been in their school systems for decades; among teachers who specialize in different areas. Tests with high school teachers confirm the obvious: Music and art teachers are, as a group, much more inclined to esthetics than any other teachers. Math and science teachers score highest on "external validity" tests. English teachers have little stomach for computational work. Mathematics teachers show a strong preference for scientific subjects. In sum, teachers don't all speak the same language.

Many aspects of teacher personality—most, in fact—are far less evident and far more subtle. Numerous aspects of personality prompting men and women to become teachers find their roots in yearnings and frustrations that go back to childhood experiences, back to all the myriad impacts upon the psyche that shape a human being's inner self. An educator once isolated some twelve possible needs and pressures that motivate teachers. People teach because their own school experiences were exciting and they want to stimulate intellectual inquiry in others. Or because they'd rather repeat childhood successes than function in a wholly adult world that seems too challenging and competitive. Or because they did badly in school and wanted to return to scenes of failure in order to prove themselves. Or because they lacked affection as children and thus have the need to give to, and become the recipients of, many children's love. Or because their need is to get beyond self, to champion a morally worthy enterprise, and school is it. Or because they need to display strength to others who are not as strong.

Of course such a list, highly clinical in its implications, is a bit mechanical. People's motives generally are diffuse, they overlap, they change with the passing of time and the maturing of self. A middle-aged Negro high school teacher in Los Angeles said that when she first got out of college, teaching was the last thing in the world she wanted to do. She went into it, she felt, because "it was the easiest, most expedient way of building a career—especially because of my race." But after her first child was born, she continued, "teaching became something else again. I realized that it's the most important job in the world."

GALLUP POLL

Third Annual Survey of the Public's Attitudes Toward the Public Schools

How does the American public see its schools? The following report of a 1971 poll conducted by George Gallup reveals a number of interesting attitudes. Those interviewed in 1969 and 1970 listed insufficiency of discipline as the most serious problem of schools today. The cost of providing schools and problems associated with integration have displaced discipline as primary concerns in 1971, but there is evidence that discipline has already become more vigorous since 1970. Despite this evidence, 48 percent of the population surveyed in 1971 said schools are too soft.

PURPOSE OF THE STUDY

The survey reported here was sponsored by CFK Ltd. as part of an annual series designed to measure and to record the attitude of American citizens toward their public schools.

George Gallup, "The Third Annual Survey of the Public's Attitudes Toward the Public Schools, 1971," *Phi Delta Kappan*, vol. 53 (September 1971), pp. 33–40. Reprinted by permission.

Each year new areas are covered, as new problems arise. Some questions are repeated from earlier years to measure trends.

The survey this year dealt at length with the problem of school finances, and particularly with possible economies that might be effected. This proved fortuitous since the survey itself brings to light the fact that in the minds of the people finance is the biggest problem facing the public schools of the nation.

Other issues widely debated in educational circles have been dealt with. These include the voucher system, performance contracts, discipline, accountability, and innovations.

It should be emphasized that the findings in this study apply to the nation as a whole, not necessarily to any single community.

Invaluable help in selecting the areas of interest and concern to be covered in the survey came from: B. Frank Brown, division director, Information and Services, Institute for Development of Educational Activities (I/D/E/A), Melbourne, Fla.; Senator Allen Dines, Colorado State Senate, Denver; Stanley Elam, editor, *Phi Delta Kappan,* Bloomington, Ind.; Gordon L. McAndrew, superintendent of schools, School City of Gary, Gary, Ind.; Mrs. Greta D. Murchison, principal, J. Hayden Johnson Junior High School, Washington, D.C., Public Schools; and Thomas A. Shaheen, superintendent of schools, San Francisco Unified School District, San Francisco, Calif.

The study itself represents the joint planning of the staff of CFK Ltd. and the staff of Gallup International.

RESEARCH PROCEDURE

The Sample. The sample embraced a total of 1,562 adults. It is described as a modified probability sample of the nation. Interviewing was conducted in every area of the country and in all types of communities. These communities, taken together, represent a true microcosm of the nation. A full description of the adult sample will be found at the end of this report.

A separate survey was undertaken to learn the views of young men and women. This sample embraced 229 students who are presently enrolled in either the junior or senior class in high school. Demographic information about these students appears in the section entitled "Composition of the Sample."

The Interviewing Form. Questions included in the questionnaire were selected after many pre-tests conducted in the interviewing center maintained by the Gallup organizations in Hopewell, N.J.

Time of Interviewing. The field work for this study was conducted during the period of April 20 through 25, 1971.

MAJOR PROBLEMS CONFRONTING THE PUBLIC SCHOOLS IN 1971

The major problem facing the public schools in 1970 and in 1969, in the opinion of the American people, was discipline. In 1971, finance—how to pay for the schools—is cited most often as the biggest problem with which the local public schools must deal.

During the year, financial problems have grown with the rise in local property taxes in most areas, the increasing costs of education, and a lagging economy that has placed increased burdens on family pocket-books.

Next in importance, in terms of number of mentions, is the problem of integration/segregation. It is in second place, as it was in 1970.

Difficulties arising out of school integration—busing and in-school troubles in getting whites and blacks to work together amicably—have been widespread enough to keep this problem in its number two position.

It is worth noting that high school juniors and seniors, and parents with children in the public schools, cite the problem of integration less often than do adults who have no children in school and who draw most of their conclusions from the press and television. This latter group believes integration to be the top problem.

Discipline has dropped from first place in 1970 and 1969 to third place in 1971 as a major problem. Undoubtedly the change in the attitude of students on college campuses during this year finds its parallel in the local schools. Also, as will be pointed out in the chapter on discipline, there is evidence that discipline has been tightened in the public schools, just as it has been in the colleges and universities.

The lack of school rooms and school facilities is considered to be the fourth major problem.

Drug taking is listed among the top five problems by adults; high school juniors and seniors cite it the most important problem.

The problem of "poor" teachers is cited often enough to place sixth in number of mentions. Lack of interest on the part of parents and pupils, the curriculum, the school administration are all mentioned as problems but not frequently enough to place them among the major concerns.

WHAT'S RIGHT WITH THE PUBLIC SCHOOLS?

When citizens are asked to give their views on the biggest problems facing the public schools, they obviously think of negative factors. To give them a chance to tell what is "right," this question was asked in this year's study: "In your own opinion, in what ways are your local *public* schools particularly good?"

The response most often given to this question is, "The teachers." The very high respect in which teachers are generally held throughout the nation is evidenced in many ways in this study.

The curriculum (courses offered) comes in for the next highest praise, followed by facilities and extracurricular activities.

Such a question provokes generalized comments; however, the answers do indicate a lack of information about the special merits of any school system.

Cutting school costs

In the present state of the economy and the tight squeeze on the public's financial resources, the question of where school costs can be cut takes on added importance.

Because of the current interest in finding economies in school budgets, a major part of this year's study of the public's attitudes toward the public schools was devoted to discovering which proposals for reducing costs would meet with public approval and which would be opposed.

The problem of financing the schools can be approached from many points of view. In this study a total of 16 proposals for cost cutting were presented to those included in the survey. Also, questions were added to find out the public's reactions to performance contracts and to the use of management firms to look into school costs.

The proposals for reducing school costs was introduced with these words by the interviewer: "Suppose your local school board were 'forced' to cut some things from school costs because there is not enough money. I am going to read you a list of many ways that have been suggested for reducing school costs. Will you tell me, in the case of each one, whether your opinion is favorable or unfavorable?"

The 16 proposals have been ranked in descending order on the basis of those which drew the most "unfavorable" responses:

	Unfavorable %	Favorable %	No Opinion %
1. Reduce special services such as speech, reading, and hearing therapy	80	10	10
2. Reduce the number of teachers by increasing class sizes	79	11	10
3. Cut all teachers' salaries by a set percentage	77	12	11
4. Reduce janitorial and maintenance services	72	15	13
5. Cut out kindergarten	69	19	12
6. Cut out after-school activities like bands, clubs, athletics, etc.	68	23	9
7. Keep present textbooks and library books although it may mean using outdated materials	68	20	12
8. Cut out the 12th grade by covering in three years what is now covered in four	58	29	13
9. Reduce the amount of supplies and materials teachers use in classrooms	58	26	16
10. Reduce the number of subjects offered	57	30	13
11. Charge rent for all textbooks instead of providing them free	56	34	10
12. Make parents responsible for getting children to and from school	51	39	10
13. Reduce the number of counselors on the staff	49	32	19
14. Have the school run on a 12-month basis with 3-month vacations for students, one-month for teachers	38	47	15
15. Cancel any subjects that do not have the minimum number of students registered	35	52	13
16. Reduce number of administrative personnel	32	50	18

Readers of this report should be reminded that these suggestions for cost cutting by no means exhaust the list of places where economies could be made. It should be pointed out, also, that the responses do not apply to schools where there is no real need to make economies.

The findings reveal a strong reluctance to take drastic measures, or to alter in an important manner any of the current programs and practices.

As will be pointed out later, this does not mean that the public is unwilling to take a new look at school costs and to examine carefully the relationship between performance and costs.

As will be noted from the preceding table, the suggestion for cost cutting that wins the greatest support is the one that calls for a reduction in the number of administrative personnel. This reaction is undoubtedly a generalized one that springs from the belief that all institutions are subject to Parkinson's Law and acquire unneeded personnel unless halted.

Analysis of the views of the different groups included in the survey shows that persons who have no children in the public schools tend to look more favorably upon many of the suggested economies than do those with children in the schools. For example, those without children in the schools believe that parents should be made responsible for getting their children to and from school. They would also favor reducing the number of counselors on the staff.

This group, likewise, is much more favorable to putting schools on a 12-month basis, with students having 3-month vacations and teachers one month. While the national finding on this suggestion shows more in favor than opposed, parents divide rather evenly: 47% approve, 46% oppose. In the survey conducted in 1970, a somewhat different plan—one that offered the choice of three of four quarters of the year—was voted down by a ratio of 49% to 42%.

It is still to be proved that the 12-month plan represents a real saving. If it does, then pressures will almost certainly mount to utilize school buildings and facilities the year-around.

The major groups included in this study, excepting only the students, favor canceling subjects that do not have the minimum number of students registered.

Performance contracts

The public wants to be sure that it is getting its money's worth, whether it is a matter of buying shoes or paying taxes for the schools.

In many communities the people are perplexed as to why school costs rise so fast. In some cities they cannot understand why their children at the third- or fourth-grade level cannot read.

In the minds of the people, performance contracts apparently satisfy both of these situations. A fixed amount of money is paid, but only if the child meets a given standard.

To see how the public responds to the idea of performance contracts, this question was included on the interviewing form: "In some public schools, educational companies are given contracts to put in new methods to teach the children in elementary schools certain basic skills, such as how to read. These are called 'performance contracts.' If the children don't reach a certain level of achievement, the company doesn't get paid for those children who fail to reach the standard. Would you like to have such contracts made here, in this community, if the overall school costs remain about the same?"

The number who favor the idea of performance contracts outnumbers the percentage opposed by the ratio of 49% to 28%, but a very sizable group, 23%, have yet to make up their minds about such a development.

Thus the burden of proof rests upon educators who oppose this idea. Unless cogent arguments can be advanced, unless experience proves that this is not an effective way of reaching educational goals at present levels, this movement is likely to gain momentum.

Management experts

Further evidence that the public is not averse to having competent outsiders look into school costs is to be found in the results from another question bearing upon this matter. The question: "Would you favor or oppose the idea of having your school board hire management experts to look into the costs of local schools to see if the educational goals could be achieved at less cost?"

Again, the public votes in favor: 54% like this idea, 31% are opposed, and 15% have no opinion.

Strangely enough, parents of school children support this proposal by higher percentages than do those adults who have no children in the schools.

Accountability

Further evidence that the public wants to be sure that it is getting its money's worth for the tax dollars spent on public education and that the standards of the public schools are high comes from a third question.

This one asked about national tests that permit one community's students to be compared with others of a similar kind. The question asked: "Would you like to see the students in the local schools be given national tests so that their educational achievement could be compared with students in other communities?"

The results: 70% favor, 21% oppose, 9% have no opinion. These findings are substantially the same as those found in last year's survey.

Many educators insist that educational achievement is difficult to measure, that communities vary to such an extent that comparisons are meaningless, and that a testing program puts undue pressures on both teachers and students to get high scores. But here again the burden of proof rests with those who oppose. The public wants some proof that their schools are good, that they are getting their money's worth. In the absence of other evidence, they will most certainly accept performance on national tests.

Voting tax increases

School bond issues have fared no better in 1971 than they did in 1970. The public is reluctant to vote for additional funds; in fact, a majority of all school bond issues throughout the nation have lost out at the voting booths. The percentage of issues voted upon favorably has changed little during the year; it is still in the low forties.

To gauge voter sentiment towards voting tax increases for the public schools, this question was framed: "Suppose the local *public* schools said they needed much more money. As you feel at this time, would you vote to raise taxes for this purpose, or would you vote against raising taxes for this purpose?"

When this same question was asked in the survey conducted last year, the results showed: For raising taxes 37%, against raising taxes 56%, no opinion 7%.

When the same question was asked this year throughout the nation, the results were substantially the same: For raising taxes 40%, against raising taxes 52%, no opinion 8%.

The pattern of those who vote favorably on tax increases for the public schools and those who vote against remains constant.

Those who are most inclined to approve tax increases are the better educated, the younger age groups, business and professional people.

The greatest opposition comes from the poorly educated, persons over 50 years of age, low-income groups, and manual laborers.

Another breakdown of the statistical data reveals the attitudes of those with and without children in the schools. In the 1970 survey, these groups voted as follows:

	For Tax Increases %	Against Tax Increases %	No Opinion %
Public school parents	43	53	4
Parochial/private school parents	37	58	5
No children in schools	35	57	8

In 1971 the vote is as follows:

Public school parents	44	49	7
Parochial/private school parents	37	59	4
No children in schools	37	53	10

The pattern again remains constant. Understandably, parents with children in the public schools are more favorably inclined to favor tax increases to support the public schools than those who have no children, or those who have children in parochial or private schools.

The heavy tax burden placed upon local property to support the public schools has brought the demand in many areas that the state government assume a greater share of these costs.

To see whether the public would prefer a shift to higher state taxes in return for lower real estate taxes, this question was asked: "It has been suggested that state taxes be increased for everyone in order to let the state government pay a greater share of school expense and to reduce local property taxes. Would you favor an increase in state taxes so that real estate taxes could be lowered on local property?"

More persons favor than disapprove this shift, but the margin has declined during the last year. In 1970, the ratio of those in favor to those against was 54% to 34%; in 1971 the ratio is 46% to 37%.

The voucher system

Most state governments have had to increase taxes for other purposes. The suggestion that these state taxes be increased still further—even as an offset to real estate taxes—apparently meets with little enthusiasm.

The voucher system for allocating public funds to parochial and private schools has been widely debated during the last year. However, this discussion, as measured by the percentage of persons for and against the voucher system, has not changed attitudes to any great extent. The public was opposed to the voucher plan by a small majority in 1970. The same situation obtains in 1971.

The voucher plan was explained to those interviewed in these words in 1970: "In some nations, the government allots a certain amount of money for each child for his education. The parents can then send the child to any public, parochial, or private school they choose. Would you like to see such an idea adopted in this country?"

In 1971 one sentence was added: *"This is called the voucher system."* This sentence, it was felt, would make it clear to the person being interviewed that we were discussing the voucher system.

The national results show about the same division of opinion:

	Favor %	Oppose %	Don't Know %
1970	43	46	11
1971	38	44	18

It can be seen that the ratio of those opposed to those who favor the voucher system shows little change; the percentage of "undecideds" has gone up markedly.

Moreover, the percentage of parochial and private school parents who favor the plan has also shown a marked increase. The plan is so obviously favorable to this group that its increase in popularity is not unexpected.

Fund raising in the school

In low-income communities the question arises as to whether school children should be asked to bring money to school to pay for a host of things, apart from school lunches. To save embarrassment for the children of the poor, to increase equality of opportunity, and to minimize dropouts, should not the school itself pay these costs, instead of the child?

Most parents, 59% of those with children in the public schools, say their children must bring money from home to pay for supplies and activities and similar items. In the case of high school juniors and seniors, 76% claim they must bring money to pay for such things as books, insurance, field trips, school pictures, class dues, locker fees, school newspapers and yearbooks, athletic equipment, and the like.

When asked whether the pupil or the school should pay for such things, the majority say such fees should continue to be paid for by the student, not the school.

The vote is 4-to-1 in favor of continuing the present practice.

Another aspect of this same problem has to do with fund-raising events held by teachers and students to pay for special projects such as after-school activities, school equipment, and the like. There is little opposition to these fund-raising affairs. In fact, the vote in favor is an overwhelming 84%.

The approval vote for this type of fund-raising is so high that it leads to the suggestion that the schools of the nation not only should permit, but actively encourage, this method of raising money for school activities. Yet professional educators find many drawbacks to certain fund-raising activities of this sort, often with good logic.

Parent accountability

Much discussion in educational circles has centered about teacher and school accountability. In the survey this year, for the first time, the matter of *parent* accountability was explored—with results so significant that a change in focus of the present debate is indicated.

The question that was designed to gather the views of the public on this matter of parent accountability, as opposed to teacher, school, and pupil accountability, was stated as follows: "When some children do poorly in school, some people place the blame on the children, some on the children's home life, some on the school, and some on the teachers. Of course, all of these things share the blame, but where would you place the *chief* blame?"

The answer given by the greatest percentage of those interviewed: the children's home life. In fact, more than half of the adults interviewed (54%) give this answer. Only 14% name children, 8% teachers, and 6% the schools.

It is significant that parents with children now in the public schools name the child's home life as the chief cause of a student's failure in school; they do not, as might be expected, shift the responsibility to the teachers or to the school or to the children.

It is equally interesting that high school juniors and seniors do not absolve themselves for doing poorly. When the same question was put to them, they said the student, himself, is to blame. Approximately one-half (51%) blame the children, 25% say "home life," only 11% blame the teachers, and only 5% the school.

To explore further the matter of parental accountability, the following question was included: "A suggestion has been made that parents of school children attend one evening class a month to find out what they can do at home to improve their children's behavior and increase their interest in school work. Is it a good idea or a poor idea?"

Eight in ten (81%) of all adults questioned thought this was a good idea. Most important, virtually this same ratio (80%) of the parents of school children said it was a good idea.

This very impressive percentage reveals a growing recognition of the role of parents in the educational process, and of the need for a new kind of partnership between teachers and parents.

Since an important part of the whole educational process must necessarily be carried on in the home, it is obvious that parents must be better trained to carry out their responsibilities.

Until this point in history, the schools have had to shoulder the burden—teaching discipline and how to get along with others, developing proper work habits, providing motivation, and doing a dozen other things—all in addition to teaching the basic school subjects and skills.

Other surveys have shown how important home training and motivation are in determining a child's success in school—in fact, in determining how far he is likely to go in his education.

Preparing parents to carry out their educational responsibilities is just as important as training teachers for their work. How best to do this must await the results of experiments planned in this new field of educational training.

What is of utmost importance is that parents themselves see the need for this kind of training. They are willing to devote time to learn how to do a better job of motivating their children, improving their behavior, and covering those areas of education not included in the school curriculum.

Discipline

Because of the great concern on the part of the public about discipline in the public schools, an effort was made in the 1971 survey to probe more deeply into this problem with the hope of shedding more light on the views of parents and other groups.

This year, as last, those interviewed express their belief that discipline is "not strict enough." There has been a slight decrease in the number who hold this opinion during the last year, and, as pointed out earlier, the problem of discipline has been superseded by finance as the number one worry about the public schools; yet there has been only a slight change in views recorded.

Here is a comparison of the findings for the two years—1970 and 1971.

	1970 %	1971 %
Discipline is too strict	2	3
Discipline is not strict enough	53	48
Discipline is about right	31	33
Don't know/no opinion	14	16

The matter of discipline has not commanded the front-page space it did a year ago, nor as much television or radio time. Some evidence that the schools may be imposing stricter discipline comes from the interviews with high school juniors and seniors—who would be immediately concerned.

When they were asked a year ago whether they thought discipline was "too strict" or "not strict enough," 15% said it was "too strict," 23% said it was "not strict enough," and the remainder said it was "about right." This year almost exactly the same number say discipline is "too strict" as say it is "not strict enough"—22% to 23%.

Since discipline means different things to different people, a question was asked this year of those who replied that discipline is "not strict enough." If they gave this response, they were then asked: "Can you tell me what you mean? In what way is discipline not strict enough?"

Those who said that discipline was not strict enough gave answers that have been categorized as follows: Teachers lack authority to keep order 11%; students have too much freedom, they can get away with anything 11%; students have no respect for their teachers, pay no attention to them 6%; rules are not enforced 3%; vandalism 2%; other responses and no opinion 11%.

The problem of discipline has two sides. One concerns the enforcement of rules; the other, avoiding the need to enforce rules.

The public, judging from their responses, is strongly of the opinion that "if the schools and the teachers interest the children in learning, most disciplinary problems disappear."

Every group interviewed, and by substantial majorities, agrees that the need for discipline tends to disappear when students become genuinely interested in learning.

Further evidence on this point comes from the findings on another question included in the survey. This one dealt with problem children and what should be done about them. The question was worded in this fashion: "Some students are not interested in school. Often they keep other students from working in school. What should be done in these cases?"

Answers fall into two broad categories: "use punitive measures" (expel them, use harsher discipline, put them into a school for problem students) and "try remedial measures" (special classes, a more interesting curriculum, vocational training, etc.).

Those who fall into this latter category outnumber those who believe in punitive measures by a 2-to-1 ratio.

Racial integration in the schools

The 1954 Supreme Court decision dealing with racial integration in the schools was based largely upon the assumption that black students, segregated in their own schools, were being deprived of the higher quality of education offered whites. Some 17 years have passed since that time and integration* is far from complete.

In fact, problems arising out of school integration are cited, in this survey, as the nation's greatest public school problem, next to finance.

Some individuals doubt that integrated education is actually improving the quality of education received by the blacks, or whether it is improving the quality of education received by the whites; and whether integration actually is improving relations between the races.

To see how the public would respond to questions dealing with these aspects of school integration, the following questions were included in the present survey:

1. Do you feel it (school integration) has improved the quality of education received by black students?
2. Do you feel it (school integration) has improved the quality of education received by white students?
3. Do you feel it (school integration) has improved relations between blacks and whites or has it worked against better relations?

*Not distinguished in this report from desegregation.

The national consensus, judged by survey results, is that integration has improved the quality of education received by the blacks, that is has not improved the quality of education received by white students, but that, on the whole, it has improved relations between blacks and whites.

Parents of children now enrolled in the public schools say, by a ratio of 44% to 35%, that relations have been improved; parents of children in parochial and private schools, by a ratio of 49% to 39%, believe that relations have improved. And perhaps of greatest significance, high school juniors and seniors are even more of the opinion that integration has improved relations. They hold 59% to 28% that relations have improved.

Educational innovation

The American people are almost evenly divided on the question of whether too many or not enough educational changes are being tried in the public schools.

The question asked in the survey taps generalized attitudes and, as will be pointed out later, does not apply to specific innovations contemplated. These must be considered on their own merits.

What the question does probe is the overall feeling of the public about the extent to which the schools are keeping up with the times.

In the survey of last year, this question was asked: "Do you feel that the local public schools are not interested enough in trying new ways and methods, or are they too ready to try new ideas?"

The same attitude was probed this year from a slightly different direction, one dealing more with behavior. The question this year reads: "In the schools in your community, do you think too many educational changes are being tried, or not enough?"

No matter which way attitudes are measured, the answers come back almost exactly the same, as the following findings reveal.

1970—*Do you feel that the local public schools are not interested enough in trying new ways and methods or are they too ready to try new ideas?*		1971—*In the schools in your community, do you think too many educational changes are being tried, or not enough?*	
Not interested enough	20%	Too many being tried	22%
Too ready to try new ideas	21%	Not enough	24%
Just about right	32%	Just about right	32%
Don't know	27%	Don't know	22%

Students do not agree with their elders on this matter. In both surveys, they vote heavily on the side that not enough innovations are being tried, that not enough interest is being displayed in trying new methods. In fact, they hold this belief by a ratio of 3-to-1.

As noted earlier, the reaction of those interviewed was to the generalized issue of change, not to specific innovations proposed.

For example:

By a very large majority all the major groups surveyed hold the opinion that not enough attention is being given to students who do not plan to go on to college.

Nationally, the findings show that 68% agree with those who believe "that too much emphasis is placed in the high schools on preparing students for college and not enough emphasis on preparing students for occupations that do not require a college degree." In contrast to the 68% who hold this view, only 23% hold the opposite view.

Another case in point concerns the amount of time spent in classrooms as opposed to the time spent in independent study. A plurality of the adults included in the survey believe the local schools should give more time for independent study, the ratio being 31% in favor to 22% opposed.

The junior and senior high school students questioned are strongly of the opinion that more time should be spent in independent study, relatively less in the classroom. Their vote is 56% in favor to 18% opposed.

THE MAJOR PROBLEMS

What do you think are the biggest problems with which the *public* schools in this community must deal?

	National Totals %	No Children In Schools %	Public School Parents %	Parochial School Parents %	High School Juniors & Seniors %
Finances	23	22	24	21	9
Integration/segregation	21	26	16	14	17
Discipline	14	13	14	23	14
Facilities	13	10	17	20	18
Dope/drugs	12	11	13	9	19
Teachers' lack of interest/ability	5	4	5	12	7
Teachers (general)	6	4	8	5	5
Parents' lack of interest	4	3	5	5	*

	National Totals %	No Children In Schools %	Public School Parents %	Parochial School Parents %	High School Juniors & Seniors %
School administration	3	3	3	7	3
Curriculum	3	3	2	5	5
Pupils' lack of interest	2	2	2	—	3
Vandalism	2	2	2	*	6
Disrespect for teachers	2	2	1	*	1
School board policies	1	*	2	*	1
Using new/up-to-date methods	1	*	2	*	*
We have no problems	4	3	6	*	3
Miscellaneous	6	6	5	9	14
Don't know/no answer	12	16	8	10	2

*Less than 1%

In your own opinion, in what ways are your local *public* schools particularly good?

	National Totals %	No Children In Schools %	Public School Parents %	Parochial School Parents %	High School Juniors & Seniors %
Teachers	21	17	27	22	27
Curriculum	15	10	22	18	28
Facilities	9	6	13	13	10
Up-to-date teaching methods	5	4	7	3	1
Extracurricular activities	3	2	5	5	14
No racial conflicts	3	3	4	3	3
Small school/classes	2	2	3	2	3
Good administration	2	2	3	3	*
Good student/teacher relationships	2	1	3	*	4
Parents are interested/ participate	2	*	3	4	—
Discipline	1	1	1	*	2
Transportation system	1	*	2	—	*
Equal opportunity for all	1	1	1	4	*
Nothing good	7	7	7	13	8
Miscellaneous	4	4	8	2	10
Don't know/no answer	27	38	12	23	10

* Less than 1%

Cutting school costs

Suppose your local school board were "forced" to cut some things from school costs because there is not enough money. I am going to read you a list of many ways that have been suggested for reducing school costs. Will you tell me, in the case of each one, whether your opinion is favorable or unfavorable.

	National Totals %	No Children In Schools %	Public School Parents %	Parochial School Parents %	High School Juniors & Seniors %
Reduce the number of teachers by increasing class sizes.					
Favorable	11	12	9	14	8
Unfavorable	79	72	88	86	91
No opinion	10	16	3	—	1
	100	100	100	100	100
Cut all teachers' salaries by a set percentage.					
Favorable	12	13	11	14	15
Unfavorable	77	70	85	84	80
No opinion	11	17	4	2	5
	100	100	100	100	100
Cut out after-school activities like bands, clubs, athletics, etc.					
Favorable	23	22	23	31	8
Unfavorable	68	64	74	68	89
No opinion	9	14	3	1	3
	100	100	100	100	100
Have the schools run on a 12 month basis with three month vacations for students, one month for teachers.					
Favorable	47	45	47	57	37
Unfavorable	38	33	46	34	58
No opinion	15	22	7	9	5
	100	100	100	100	100
Make parents responsible for getting children to and from school.					
Favorable	39	41	36	48	27
Unfavorable	51	43	62	51	68
No opinion	10	16	2	1	5
	100	100	100	100	100
Cut out kindergarten.					
Favorable	19	18	21	23	24
Unfavorable	69	64	75	72	71
No opinion	12	18	4	5	5
	100	100	100	100	100

	National Totals %	No Children In Schools %	Public School Parents %	Parochial School Parents %	High School Juniors & Seniors %

Charge rent for all textbooks instead of providing them free.

Favorable	34	33	33	47	33
Unfavorable	56	52	63	51	65
No opinion	10	15	4	2	2
	100	100	100	100	100

Cut out the twelfth grade by covering in three years what is now covered in four.

Favorable	29	31	26	28	45
Unfavorable	58	51	69	65	53
No opinion	13	18	5	7	2
	100	100	100	100	100

Cancel any subjects that do not have the minimum number of students registered.

Favorable	52	51	52	60	53
Unfavorable	35	31	42	35	45
No opinion	13	18	6	5	2
	100	100	100	100	100

Reduce the number of subjects offered.

Favorable	30	30	29	32	17
Unfavorable	57	50	68	65	82
No opinion	13	20	3	3	1
	100	100	100	100	100

Reduce janitorial and maintenance services.

Favorable	15	15	14	16	19
Unfavorable	72	67	80	78	77
No opinion	13	18	6	6	4
	100	100	100	100	100

Keep present textbooks and library books although it may mean using outdated materials.

Favorable	20	20	20	14	16
Unfavorable	68	63	76	82	81
No opinion	12	17	4	4	3
	100	100	100	100	100

Reduce the amount of supplies and materials teachers use in classrooms.

Favorable	26	27	22	31	26
Unfavorable	58	51	70	60	73
No opinion	16	22	8	9	1
	100	100	100	100	100

	National Totals %	No Children In Schools %	Public School Parents %	Parochial School Parents %	High School Juniors & Seniors %

Reduce the number of counselors on the staff.

	National Totals %	No Children In Schools %	Public School Parents %	Parochial School Parents %	High School Juniors & Seniors %
Favorable	32	31	33	40	28
Unfavorable	49	42	58	49	70
No opinion	19	27	9	11	2
	100	100	100	100	100

Reduce special services, such as speech, reading, and hearing therapy.

Favorable	10	10	9	9	13
Unfavorable	80	74	89	89	84
No opinion	10	16	2	2	3
	100	100	100	100	100

Reduce the number of administrative personnel.

Favorable	50	48	50	55	43
Unfavorable	32	27	41	32	52
No opinion	18	25	9	13	5
	100	100	100	100	100

In some public schools, educational companies are given contracts to put in new methods to teach the children in elementary schools certain basic skills, such as how to read. These are called "performance contracts." If the children don't reach a certain level of achievement, the company doesn't get paid for those children who fail to reach the standard. Would you like to have such contracts made here, in this community, if the overall school costs remain about the same?

	National Totals %	No Children In Schools %	Public School Parents %	Parochial School Parents %	High School Juniors & Seniors %
Yes	49	44	55	58	57
No	28	25	33	24	33
No opinion	23	31	12	18	10
	100	100	100	100	100

Would you favor or oppose the idea of having your school board hire management experts to look into the costs of local schools to see if the educational goals could be achieved at less cost?

	National Totals %	No Children In Schools %	Public School Parents %	Parochial School Parents %	High School Juniors & Seniors %
Favor	54	49	61	67	69
Oppose	31	30	33	24	23
Don't know	15	21	6	9	8
	100	100	100	100	100

Would you like to see the students in the local schools be given national tests so that their educational achievement could be compared with students in other communities?

	National Totals %	No Children In Schools %	Public School Parents %	Parochial School Parents %	High School Juniors & Seniors %
Yes	70	69	72	70	66
No	21	20	22	24	31
No opinion	9	11	6	6	3
	100	100	100	100	100

The voucher system

In some nations, the government allots a certain amount of money for each child for his education. The parents can then send the child to any public, parochial, or private school they choose. This is called the voucher system." Would you like to see such an idea adopted in this country?

	National Totals %	No Children In Schools %	Public School Parents %	Parochial School Parents %	High School Juniors & Seniors %
Favor	38	34	39	66	58
Oppose	44	40	51	31	35
No opinion	18	26	10	3	7
	100	100	100	100	100

Voting tax increases

Suppose the local *public* schools said they needed much more money. As you feel at this time, would you vote to raise taxes for this purpose, or would you vote against raising taxes for this purpose?

	National Totals %	No Children In Schools %	Public School Parents %	Parochial School Parents %	High School Juniors & Seniors %
For	40	37	44	37	45
Against	52	53	49	59	49
No opinion	8	10	7	4	6
	100	100	100	100	100

Suppose the local *public* schools said they needed much more money. As you feel at this time, would you vote to raise taxes for this purpose, or would you vote against raising taxes for this purpose?

	For %	Against %	Don't Know/ No Answer %
Sex			
Men	40	53	7
Women	39	52	9
Race			
White	40	53	7
Nonwhite	38	49	13
Education			
Elementary grades	27	62	11
High school incomplete	32	60	8
High school complete	37	55	8
Technical, trade, or business school	42	49	9
College incomplete	48	46	6
College graduate	58	35	7
Occupation			
Business & professional	52	41	7
Clerical & sales	48	48	4
Farm	34	56	10
Skilled labor	38	54	8
Unskilled labor	35	59	6
Nonlabor force	27	60	13
Age			
21 to 29 years	53	40	7
30 to 49 years	43	52	5
50 years and over	31	58	11
Religion			
Protestant	41	51	8
Roman Catholic	34	57	9
Jewish	50	39	11
All others	42	47	11
Region			
East	34	58	8
Midwest	40	52	8
South	41	50	9
West	46	46	8
Community Size			
500,000 and over	39	51	10
50,000 to 499,999	38	52	10
25,000 to 49,999	57	36	7
Under 25,000	40	55	5
Income			
$15,000 and over	51	42	7
$10,000 to $14,999	41	51	8
$ 7,000 to $ 9,999	42	55	3
$ 5,000 to $ 6,999	38	52	10
$ 3,000 to $ 4,999	36	55	9
Under $3,000	24	60	16

It has been suggested that state taxes be increased for everyone in order to let the state government pay a greater share of school expense and to reduce local property taxes. Would you favor an increase in state taxes so that real estate taxes could be lowered on local property?

	National Totals %	No Children In Schools %	Public School Parents %	Parochial School Parents %	High School Juniors & Seniors %
For	46	43	50	46	50
Against	37	36	38	46	31
No opinion	17	21	12	8	19
	100	100	100	100	100

Fund raising in the public schools

Does your child bring money from home to pay for anything, except lunch, in school? (Asked only of parents of school children)

	National Totals %	Public School Parents %	Parochial School Parents %	High School Juniors & Seniors %
Yes	59	60	56	76
No	39	38	37	24
Don't know	2	2	7	—
	100	100	100	100

If "YES," for what?

Books	9	19	27	30
Supplies for classes (general)	7	17	17	24
Travel expenses for field trips	5	11	11	7
Athletic fees/equipment	3	6	6	11
School newspaper/school related newspaper	3	7	2	7
Fees for special programs	3	8	5	4
Club dues/class dues	2	5	3	16
Parties/dances	2	4	3	2
Charitable contributions/events	2	3	6	3
General school activities	1	3	4	5
Miscellaneous	9	20	12	26

Do you think such fees should be charged?

Yes	47	47	46	56
No	10	11	10	17
No opinion	2	2	—	3
	59	60	56	76

In some schools, teachers and students have fund-raising events to finance special projects for school equipment, after-school activities, and the like. Do you think it is a good idea or a poor idea for the schools to permit these events?

	National Totals %	No Children In Schools %	Public School Parents %	Parochial School Parents %	High School Juniors & Seniors %
Good idea	84	81	88	90	97
Poor idea	11	12	10	8	3
No opinion	5	7	2	2	—
	100	100	100	100	100

Parent accountability

When some children do poorly in school, some people place the blame on the children, some on the children's home life, some on the school, and some on the teachers. Of course, all of these things share the blame, but where would you place the *chief* blame?

	National Totals %	No Children In Schools %	Public School Parents %	Parochial School Parents %	High School Juniors & Seniors %
Children	14	11	17	14	51
Home life	54	58	49	44	25
School	6	6	6	14	5
Teachers	8	7	10	8	11
No opinion	18	18	18	20	8
	100	100	100	100	100

A suggestion has been made that parents of school children attend one evening class a month to find out what they can do at home to improve their children's behavior and increase their interest in school work. Is it a good idea or a poor idea?

	National Totals %	No Children In Schools %	Public School Parents %	Parochial School Parents %	High School Juniors & Seniors %
Good idea	81	82	80	81	75
Poor idea	13	11	16	15	21
No opinion	6	7	4	4	4
	100	100	100	100	100

Discipline

How do you feel about the discipline in the local public schools—is it too strict, not strict enough, or just about right?

	National Totals %	No Children In Schools %	Public School Parents %	Parochial School Parents %	High School Juniors & Seniors %
Too strict	3	3	3	—	22
Not strict enough	48	47	47	58	23
Just about right	33	26	46	29	53
Don't know	16	24	4	13	2
	100	100	100	100	100

If "not strict enough": Can you tell me what you mean? In what ways is discipline not strict enough?

	National Totals %	No Children In Schools %	Public School Parents %	Parochial School Parents %	High School Juniors & Seniors %
Teachers lack authority	11	10	12	14	2
Students have too much freedom	11	11	12	15	7
Disrespect for teachers	6	7	4	8	4
Rules are not enforced	3	4	2	3	4
Dress code is too liberal	3	2	3	4	*
Vandalism	2	2	2	5	*
Parents not interested in school affairs	2	1	3	5	*
Miscellaneous	3	3	3	5	*
Don't know/no answer	3	3	4	2	*

* Less than 1%

Some students are not interested in school. Often, they keep other students from working in school. What should be done in these cases?

	National Totals %	No Children In Schools %	Public School Parents %	Parochial School Parents %	High School Juniors & Seniors %
Special classes for all who are not interested	29	26	34	27	27
Expel them	12	12	12	13	22
Offer better/more interesting: curriculum/teaching methods	11	11	10	13	14
Special counseling	9	9	10	11	13
Harsher discipline	9	9	10	7	4
Vocational training	8	8	7	9	8
Make their parents responsible	7	6	7	8	3
Put in school for problem students	6	5	7	13	3
Teachers should take more interest in such students	4	3	5	3	4
Miscellaneous	5	5	5	4	5
Don't know/no answer	18	21	16	14	14

Some people say that if the schools and the teachers interest the children in learning, most disciplinary problems disappear. Do you agree or disagree?

	National Totals %	No Children In Schools %	Public School Parents %	Parochial School Parents %	High School Juniors & Seniors %
Agree	76	75	76	78	81
Disagree	18	17	20	20	18
No opinion	6	8	4	2	1
	100	100	100	100	100

Racial integration in the schools

How do you feel about school integration? Do you feel it has improved the quality of education received by black students?

	National Totals %	No Children In Schools %	Public School Parents %	Parochial School Parents %	High School Juniors & Seniors %
Yes	43	39	48	51	56
No	31	31	31	33	31
Don't know	26	30	21	16	13
	100	100	100	100	100

Do you feel it has improved the quality of education received by white students?

	National Totals %	No Children In Schools %	Public School Parents %	Parochial School Parents %	High School Juniors & Seniors %
Yes	23	21	26	30	35
No	51	48	54	53	47
Don't know	26	31	20	17	18
	100	100	100	100	100

Do you feel it has improved relations between blacks and whites or has it worked against better relations?

	National Totals %	No Children In Schools %	Public School Parents %	Parochial School Parents %	High School Juniors & Seniors %
Improved relations	40	36	44	49	59
Worked against	35	35	35	39	28
No opinion	25	29	21	12	13
	100	100	100	100	100

Do you feel it (school integration) has improved relations between blacks and whites or has it worked against better relations?

	Improved Relations %	Worked Against %	No Opinion %
Sex			
Men	40	37	23
Women	40	33	27
Race			
White	37	37	26
Nonwhite	63	15	22
Education			
Elementary grades	26	43	31
High school incomplete	36	37	27
High school complete	37	38	25
Technical, trade, or business school	41	34	25
College incomplete	49	32	19
College graduate	51	29	20
Occupation			
Business & professional	49	28	23
Clerical & sales	44	31	25
Farm	29	37	34
Skilled labor	40	39	21
Unskilled labor	40	34	26
Nonlabor force	29	40	31
Age			
21 to 29 years	50	31	19
30 to 49 years	42	36	22
50 years and over	33	36	31
Religion			
Protestant	39	37	24
Roman Catholic	39	33	28
Jewish	48	35	17
All others	48	22	30
Region			
East	37	34	29
Midwest	40	36	24
South	41	39	20
West	42	29	29
Income			
$15,000 and over	44	35	21
$10,000 to $14,999	41	35	24
$ 7,000 to $ 9,999	40	37	23
$ 5,000 to $ 6,999	42	33	25
$ 3,000 to $ 4,999	38	37	25
Under $3,000	31	35	34
Community size			
500,000 and over	41	37	22
50,000 to 499,999	43	33	24
25,000 to 49,999	32	61	7
Under 25,000	37	34	29

Educational innovation

In the schools in your community, do you think too many educational changes are being tried, or not enough?

	National Totals %	No Children In Schools %	Public School Parents %	Parochial School Parents %	High School Juniors & Seniors %
Too many	22	21	23	24	14
Not enough	24	23	26	33	53
About right	32	24	44	28	31
Don't know	22	32	7	15	2
	100	100	100	100	100

In some schools, time spent by students in classrooms is being reduced to give more time for independent study, that is, carrying out learning projects on their own. Should the local schools give more time to independent study than they presently do, or should they give less time?

	National Totals %	No Children In Schools %	Public School Parents %	Parochial School Parents %	High School Juniors & Seniors %
More	31	30	31	39	56
Less	22	18	26	28	18
About right now	25	21	32	25	20
No opinion	22	31	11	8	6
	100	100	100	100	100

Some people feel that too much emphasis is placed in the high schools on preparing students for college and not enough emphasis on preparing students for occupations that do not require a college degree. Do you agree or disagree?

	National Totals %	No Children In Schools %	Public School Parents %	Parochial School Parents %	High School Juniors & Seniors %
Agree	68	68	69	67	61
Disagree	23	21	25	27	35
No opinion	9	11	6	6	4
	100	100	100	100	100

COMPOSITION OF THE SAMPLE

Analysis of respondents

Adults
No children in school   56%
Public school parents   39%*
Parochial school parents   8%*

* Totals exceed 44% because some parents have children attending more than one kind of school.

High school juniors and seniors
Public school students	90%
Parochial & private school students	10%

	All Adults %	High School Juniors & Seniors %
Sex		
Men	48	52
Women	52	48
	100	100
Race		
White	91	90
Nonwhite	9	10
	100	100
Religion		
Protestant	64	53
Roman Catholic	26	33
Jewish	3	4
Others	7	10
	100	100
Age		
21 to 29 years	20	
30 to 49 years	38	
50 years and over	42	
	100	
15 years and under		10
16 years		30
17 years		42
18 years and over		18
		100
Region		
East	29	31
Midwest	28	30
South	26	25
West	17	14
	100	100
Community size		
500,000 and over	32	32
50,000 to 499,999	24	23
25,000 to 49,999	3	3
Under 25,000	41	42
	100	100
Education		
Elementary grades	16	
High school incomplete	19	
High school complete	31	
Technical, trade, or business school	7	
College incomplete	13	
College graduate	14	
	100	

	All Adults %	High School Juniors & Seniors %
Occupation (head of household)		
Business & professional	24	29
Clerical & sales	11	13
Farm	5	6
Skilled labor	18	23
Unskilled labor	21	21
Nonlabor force	19	4
Undesignated	2	4
	100	100
Income (total household)		
$15,000 and over	17	18
$10,000 to $14,999	26	32
$ 7,000 to $ 9,999	18	14
$ 5,000 to $ 6,999	15	15
$ 4,000 to $ 4,999	5	4
$ 3,000 to $ 3,999	5	5
Under $2,999	12	4
Undesignated	2	8
	100	100

PAUL GOODMAN

The New Reformation

If large numbers of students—not to speak of teachers, parents, administrators, and school board members—think schools are not too bad as they are (only one-fifth of students polled by Gallup thought schools too strict), where does this leave the minority of protestors? Are they merely spoiled brats? Are they inspired by communists, as some of the Maquoketans think? Paul Goodman, in the last article of Part 2, analyzes the worldwide youth protest movement as a crisis of faith and values in the modern religion of science and progress—a crisis as fundamental as that in Christendom preceding the Reformation. If he is correct, the schools should take note, for they represent the established faith as the Roman Catholic Church did in the time of Luther. "The bloated universi-

Paul Goodman, "The New Reformation," *The New York Times Magazine*, September 14, 1969, pp. 32–34ff. © 1969 by The New York Times Company. Reprinted by permission.

> *ties and the expanded school systems under them,"* Goodman
> contends, *"constitute the biggest collection of monks since the
> time of Henry VIII."*

For a long time modern societies have been operating as if religion were
a minor and moribund part of the scheme of things. But this is unlikely.
Men do not do without a system of "meanings" that everybody believes
and puts his hope in even if, or especially if, he doesn't know anything
about it; what Freud called a "shared psychosis," meaningful because
shared, and with the power that resides in deep fantasy and longing. In
advanced countries, indeed, it is science and technology themselves that
have gradually, and finally triumphantly, become the system of mass
faith, not disputed by various political ideologies and nationalisms that
have also had religious uses.

Now this basic faith is threatened. Dissident young people are
saying that science is antilife, it is a Calvinist obsession, it has been a
weapon of white Europe to subjugate colored races, and scientific technology has manifestly become diabolical. Along with science, the young
discredit the professions in general, and the whole notion of "disciplines"
and academic learning. If these views take hold, it adds up to a crisis of
belief, and the effects are incalculable. Every status and institution
would be affected. Present political troubles could become endless religious wars. Here again, as in politics and morals, the worldwide youth
disturbance may indicate a turning point in history and we must listen
to it carefully.

In 1967 I gave a course on "Professionalism" at the New School
for Social Research in New York, attended by about 25 graduate students from all departments. My bias was the traditional one: professionals are autonomous individuals beholden to the nature of things
and the judgment of their peers, and bound by an explicit or implicit
oath to benefit their clients and the community. To teach this, I invited
seasoned professionals whom I esteemed—a physician, engineer, jour-
nalist, architect, etc. These explained to the students the obstacles that
increasingly stood in the way of honest practice, and their own life experience in circumventing them.

To my surprise, the class unanimously rejected them. Heatedly
and rudely they called my guests liars, finks, mystifiers, or deluded.
They showed that every professional was co-opted and corrupted by
the System, all decisions were made top-down by the power structure
and bureaucracy, professional peer-groups were conspiracies to make

more money. All this was importantly true and had, of course, been said by the visitors. Why had the students not heard? As we explored further, we came to the deeper truth, that they did not believe in the existence of real professions at all; professions were concepts of repressive society and "linear thinking." I asked them to envisage any social order they pleased—Mao's, Castro's, some anarchist utopia—and wouldn't there be engineers who knew about materials and stresses and strains? Wouldn't people get sick, and need to be treated? Wouldn't there be problems of communication? No, they insisted; it was important only to be human, and all else would follow.

Suddenly I realized that they did not really believe that there was a nature of things. Somehow all functions could be reduced to interpersonal relations and power. There was no knowledge, but only the sociology of knowledge. They had so well learned that physical and sociological research is subsidized and conducted for the benefit of the ruling class that they did not believe there was such a thing as simple truth. To be required to learn something was a trap by which the young were put down and co-opted. Then I knew that I could not get through to them. I had imagined that the worldwide student protest had to do with changing political and moral institutions, to which I was sympathetic, but I now saw that we had to do with a religious crisis of the magnitude of the Reformation in the fifteen-hundreds, when not only all institutions but all learning had been corrupted by the Whore of Babylon.

The irony was that I myself had said 10 years ago, in "Growing Up Absurd," that these young were growing up without a world *for* them, and therefore they were "alienated," estranged from nature and other people. But I had then been thinking of juvenile delinquents and a few Beats; and a few years later I had been heartened by the Movement in Mississippi, the Free Speech protest in Berkeley, the Port Huron statement of S.D.S., the resistance to the Vietnam war, all of which made human sense and were not absurd at all. But the alienating circumstances had proved too strong after all; here were absurd graduate students, most of them political "activists."

Alienation is a Lutheran concept: "God has turned His face away, things have no meaning, I am estranged in the world." By the time of Hegel the term was applied to the general condition of rational man, with his "objective" sciences and institutions divorced from his "subjectivity," which was therefore irrational and impulsive. In his revision of Hegel, Marx explained this as the effect of man's losing his essential nature as a cooperative producer, because centuries of exploitation, culminating in capitalism, had fragmented the community and robbed the workman of the means of production. Comte and Durkheim pointed to the weakening of social solidarity and the contradiction between law and morality, so that people lost their bearings—this was anomie, an acute form of alienation that could lead to suicide or aimless riot. By the end of the 19th century, alienation came to be used as the term for insanity, derangement of perceived reality, and psychiatrists were called alienists.

Contemporary conditions of life have certainly deprived people, and especially young people, of a meaningful world in which they can act and find themselves. Many writers and the dissenting students themselves have spelled it out. For instance, in both schools and corporations, people cannot pursue their own interests or exercise initiative. Administrators are hypocrites who sell people out for the smooth operation of the system. The budget for war has grotesquely distorted reasonable social priorities. Worst of all, the authorities who make the decisions are incompetent to cope with modern times: we are in danger of extinction, the biosphere is being destroyed, two-thirds of mankind are starving. Let me here go on to some other factors that demand a religious response.

There is a lapse of faith in science. Science has not produced the general happiness that people expected, and now it has fallen under the sway of greed and power; whatever its beneficent past, people fear that its further progress will do more harm than good. And rationality itself is discredited. Probably it is more significant than we like to think that intelligent young people dabble in astrology, witchcraft, psychedelic dreams, and whatever else is despised by science; in some sense they are not kidding. They need to control their fate, but they hate scientific explanations.

Every one of these young grew up since Hiroshima. They do not talk about atom bombs—not nearly so much as we who campaigned against the shelters and fall-out—but the bombs explode in their dreams, as Otto Butz found in his study of collegians at San Francisco State, and now George Dennison, in "The Lives of Children," shows that it was the same with small slum children whom he taught at the First Street School in New York. Again and again students have told me that they take it for granted they will not survive the next 10 years. This is not an attitude with which to prepare for a career or to bring up a family.

Whether or not the bombs go off, human beings are becoming useless. Old people are shunted out of sight at an increasingly earlier age, young people are kept on ice till an increasingly later age. Small farmers and other technologically unemployed are dispossessed or left to rot. Large numbers are put away as incompetent or deviant. Racial minorities that cannot shape up are treated as a nuisance. Together, these groups are a large majority of the population. Since labor will not be needed much longer, there is vague talk of a future society of "leisure," but there is no thought of a kind of community in which all human beings would be necessary and valued.

The institutions, technology and communications have infected even the "biological core," so that people's sexual desires are no longer genuine. This was powerfully argued by Wilhelm Reich a generation ago and it is now repeated by Herbert Marcuse. When I spoke for it in the nineteen-forties, I was condemned by the radicals, for example, C. Wright Mills, as a "bedroom revisionist."

A special aspect of biological corruption is the spreading ugliness, filth, and tension of the environment in which the young grow up. If Wordsworth was right—I think he was—that children must grow up in an environment of beauty and simple affections in order to become trusting, open, and magnanimous citizens, then the offspring of our ghettos, suburbs, and complicated homes have been disadvantaged, no matter how much money there is. This lack cannot be remedied by art in the curriculum, nor by vest-pocket playgrounds, nor by banning billboards from bigger highways. Cleaning the river might help, but that will be the day.

If we start from the premise that the young are in a religious crisis, that they doubt there is really a nature of things, and they are sure there is not a world for themselves, many details of their present behavior become clearer. Alienation is a powerful motivation, of unrest, fantasy and reckless action. It leads, as we shall see, to religious innovation, new sacraments to give life meaning. But it is a poor basis for politics, including revolutionary politics.

It is said that the young dissidents never offer a constructive program. And apart from the special cases of Czechoslovakia and Poland, where they confront an unusually outdated system, this is largely true. In France, China, Germany, Egypt, England, the United States, etc., most of the issues of protest have been immediate gut issues, and the tactics have been mainly disruptive, without coherent proposals for a better society. But this makes for bad politics. Unless one has a program, there is no way to persuade the other citizens, who do not have one's gut complaints, to come along. Instead one confronts them hostilely and they are turned off, even when they might be sympathetic. But the confrontation is inept too, for the alienated young cannot take other people seriously as having needs of their own; a spectacular instance was the inability of the French youth to communicate with the French working class, in May 1968. In Gandhian theory, the confronter aims at future community with the confronted; he will not let him continue a course that is bad for *him,* and so he appeals to his deeper reason. But instead of this *Satyagraha,* soul force, we have seen plenty of hate. The confronted are *not* taken as human beings, but as pigs, etc. But how can the young people think of a future community when they themselves have no present world, no profession or other job in it, and no trust in other human beings? Instead, some young radicals seem to entertain the disastrous illusion that other people can be compelled by fear. This can lead only to crushing reaction.

All the "political" activity makes sense, however, if it is understood that it is not aimed at social reconstruction at all, but is a way of desperately affirming that they are alive and want a place in the sun. "I am a revolutionary," said Cohn-Bendit, leader of the French students in 1968, "because it is the best way of living." And young Americans pathetically and truly say that there is no other way to be taken seriously. Then it is not necessary to have a program; the right method is to act, against any vulnerable point and wherever one can rally support. The purpose is not politics but to have a movement and form a community. This is exactly what Saul Alinsky prescribed to rally outcast blacks.

And such conflictful action has indeed caused social changes. In France it was conceded by the Gaullists that "nothing would ever be the same." In the United States, the changes in social attitude during the last 10 years are unthinkable without the youth action, with regard to war, the military-industrial, corporate organization and administration, the police, the blacks. When the actors have been in touch with the underlying causes of things, issues have deepened and the Movement has grown. But for the alienated, again, action easily slips into activism, and conflict is often spite and stubbornness. There is excitement and notoriety, much human suffering, and the world no better off. (New Left Notes runs a column wryly called, "We Made the News Today, O Boy!") Instead of deepening awareness and a sharpening political conflict, there occurs the polarization of mere exasperation. It often seems that the aim is just to have a shambles. Impatiently the ante of tactics is raised beyond what the "issue" warrants, and support melts away. Out on a limb, the leaders become desperate and fanatical, intolerant of criticism, dictatorial. The Movement falls to pieces.

Yet it is noteworthy that when older people like myself are critical of the wrongheaded activism, we nevertheless almost invariably concede that the young are *morally* justified. For what is the use of patience and reason when meantime millions are being killed and starved, and when bombs and nerve gas are being stockpiled? Against the entrenched power responsible for these things, it might be better to do something idiotic now than something perhaps more practical in the long run. I don't know which is less demoralizing.

Maybe the truth is revealed in the following conversation I had with a young hippie at a college in Massachusetts. He was dressed like an (American) Indian—buckskin fringes and a headband, red paint on his face. All his life, he said, he had tried to escape the encompassing evil of our society that was trying to destroy his soul. "But if you're always escaping," I said, "and never attentively study it, how can you make a wise judgment about society or act effectively to change it?" "You see, you don't dig!" he cried. "It's just ideas like 'wise' and 'acting effectively' that we can't stand." He was right. He was in the religious dilemma of Faith vs. Works. Where I sat, Works had some reality; but in the reign of the Devil, as he felt it, all Works are corrupted, they are part of the System; only Faith can avail. But he didn't have Faith either.

Inevitably, the alienated seem to be inconsistent in how they take the present world. Hippies attack technology and are scornful of rationality, but they buy up electronic equipment and motorcycles, and with them the whole infrastructure. Activists say that civil liberties are bourgeois and they shout down their opponents; but they clamor in court for their civil liberties. Those who say that the university is an agent of the powers that be, do not mean thereby to reassert the ideal role of the university, but to use the university for their own propaganda. Yet if I point out these apparent inconsistencies, it does not arouse shame or guilt. How is this? It is simply that they do not really understand that technology, civil law, and the university are *human* institutions, for which they too are responsible; they take them as brute given, just what's there, to be manipulated as convenient. But convenient for whom? The trouble with this attitude is that these institutions, works of spirit in history, are how Man has made himself and is. If they treat them as mere things, rather than being vigilant for them, they themselves become nothing. And nothing comes from nothing.

In general, their lack of a sense of history is bewildering. It is impossible to convey to them that the deeds were done by human beings, that John Hampden confronted the King and wouldn't pay the war tax just like us, or that Beethoven too, just like a rock 'n' roll band, made up his music as he went along, from odds and ends, with energy, spontaneity, and passion—how else do they think he made music? And they no longer remember their own history. A few years ago there was a commonly accepted story of mankind, beginning with the Beats, going on to the Chessman case, the HUAC bust, the Freedom Rides, and climaxing in the Berkeley Victory—"The first human event in 40,000 years," Mike Rossman, one of the innumerable spokesmen, told me. But this year I find that nothing antedates Chicago '68. Elder statesmen, like Sidney Lens and especially Staughton Lynd, have been trying with heroic effort to recall the American antecedents of present radical and libertarian slogans and tactics, but it doesn't rub off. I am often hectored to my face with formulations that I myself put in their mouths, that have become part of the oral tradition two years old, author prehistoric. Most significant of all, it has been whispered to me—but I can't check up, because I don't speak the language—that among the junior high school students, aged 12 and 13, that's really where it's at! Quite different from what goes on in the colleges that I visit.

What I do notice, however, is that dozens of Underground newspapers have a noisy style. Though each one is doing his thing, there is not much idiosyncrasy in the spontaneous variety. The political radicals are, as if mesmerized, repeating the power plays, factionalism, random abuse, and tactical lies that aborted the movement in the thirties. And I have learned, to my disgust, that a major reason why the young don't trust people over 30 is that they don't understand them and are too conceited to try. Having grown up in a world too meaningless to learn anything, they know very little and are quick to resent it.

This is an unpleasant picture. Even so, the alienated young have no vital alternative except to confront the Evil, and to try to make a new way of life out of their own innards and suffering. As they are doing. It is irrelevant to point out that the System is not the monolith that they think and that the majority of people are not corrupt, just browbeaten and confused. What is relevant is that they cannot see this, because they do not have an operable world for themselves. In such a case, the only advice I would dare to give them is that which Krishna gave Arjuna: to confront with nonattachment, to be brave and firm without hatred. (I don't here want to discuss the question of "violence," the hatred and disdain are far more important.) Also, when they are seeking a new way of life, for example when they are making a "journey inward," as Ronald Laing calls it, I find that I urge them occasionally to write a letter home.

As a citizen and father I have a right to try to prevent a shambles and to diminish the number of wrecked lives. But it is improper for us elders to keep saying, as we do, that their activity is "counterproductive." It's our business to do something more productive.

Religiously, the young have been inventive, much more than the God-is-dead theologians. They have hit on new sacraments, physical actions to get them out of their estrangement and (momentarily) break through into meaning. The terribly loud music is used sacramentally. The claim for the hallucinogenic drugs is almost never the paradisal pleasure of opium culture nor the escape from distress of heroin, but tuning in to the cosmos and communing with one another. They seem to have had flashes of success in bringing ritual participation back into theater, which for a hundred years playwrights and directors have tried to do in vain. And whatever the political purposes and results of activism, there is no doubt that shared danger for the sake of righteousness is used sacramentally as baptism of fire. Fearful moments of provocation and the poignant release of the bust bring unconscious contents to the surface, create a bond of solidarity, are "commitment."

But the most powerful magic, working in all these sacraments, is the close presence of other human beings, without competition or one-upping. The original sin is to be on an ego trip that isolates; and angry political factionalism has now also become a bad thing. What a drastic comment on the dehumanization and fragmentation of modern times that salvation can be attained simply by the "warmth of assembled animal bodies," as Kafka called it, describing his mice. At the 1967 Easter Be-In in New York's Central Park, when about 10,000 were crowded on the Sheep Meadow, a young man with a quite radiant face said to me, "Gee, human beings are legal!"—it was sufficient, to be saved, to be exempted from continual harassment by officious rules and Law and Order.

The extraordinary rock festivals at Bethel and on the Isle of Wight are evidently pilgrimages. Joan Baez, one of the hierophants, ecstatically described Bethel to me, and the gist of it was that people were nice to one another. A small group passing a joint of marijuana often behaves like a Quaker meeting waiting for the spirit, and the cigarette may be a placebo. Group therapy and sensitivity training, with Mecca at Esalen, have the same purpose. And I think this is the sense of the sexuality, which is certainly not hedonistic, nor mystical in the genre of D. H. Lawrence; nor does it have much to do with personal love, that is too threatening for these anxious youths. But it is human touch, without conquest or domination, and it obviates self-consciousness and embarrassed speech.

Around the rather pure faith there has inevitably collected a mess of eclectic liturgy and paraphernalia. Mandalas, beggars in saffron, (American) Indian beads, lectures in Zen. Obviously the exotic is desirable because it is not what they have grown up with. And it is true that fundamental facts of life are more acceptable if they come in fancy dress, e.g. it is good to breathe from the diaphragm and one can learn this by humming "OM," as Allen Ginsberg did for seven hours at Grant Park in Chicago. But college chaplains are also pretty busy, and they are now more likely to see the adventurous and off-beat than, as used to be the case, the staid and square. Flowers and strobe lights are indigenous talismans.

It is hard to describe this (or any) religiosity without lapsing into condescending humor. Yet it is genuine and it will, I am convinced, survive and develop—I don't know into what. In the end it is religion that constitutes the strength of this generation, and not, as I used to think, their morality, political will, and common sense. Except for a few, like the young people of the Resistance, I am not impressed by their moral courage or even honesty. For all their eccentricity they are singularly lacking in personality. They do not have enough world to have much character. And they are not especially attractive as animals. But they keep pouring out a kind of metaphysical vitality.

Let me try to account for it. On the one hand, these young have an unusual amount of available psychic energy. They were brought up on antibiotics that minimized depressing chronic childhood diseases, and with post-Freudian freedom to act out early drives. Up to age 6 or 7, television nourished them with masses of strange images and sometimes true information—McLuhan makes a lot of sense for the kindergarten years. Long schooling would tend to make them stupid, but it has been compensated by providing the vast isolated cities of youth that the high schools and colleges essentially are, where they can incubate their own thoughts. They are sexually precocious and not inhibited by taboos. They are superficially knowledgeable. On the other hand, all this psychic energy has had little practical use. The social environment is dehumanized. It discourages romantic love and lasting friendship. They are desperately bored because the world does not promise any fulfillment. Their knowledge gives no intellectual or poetic satisfaction. In this impasse, we can expect a ferment of new religion. As in Greek plays, impasse produces gods from the machine. For a long time we did not hear of the symptoms of adolescent religious conversion, once as common in the United States as in all other places and ages. Now it seems to be recurring as a mass phenomenon.

Without doubt the religious young are in touch with something historical, but I don't think they understand what it is. Let me quote from an editorial in New Seminary News, the newsletter of dissident seminarians of the Pacific School of Religion in Berkeley: "What we confront (willingly or not we are thrust into it) is a time of disintegration of a dying civilization and the emergence of a new one." This seems to envisage something like the instant decline of the Roman Empire and they, presumably, are like the Christians about to build, rapidly, another era. But there are no signs that this is the actual situation. It would mean, for instance, that our scientific technology, civil law, professions, universities, etc., are about to vanish from the earth and be replaced by something entirely different. This is a fantasy of alienated minds. Nobody behaves as if civilization would vanish, and nobody acts as if there were a new dispensation. Nobody is waiting patiently in the catacombs and the faithful have not withdrawn into the desert. Neither the Yippies nor the New Seminarians nor any other exalted group have produced anything that is the least bit miraculous. Our civilization may well destroy itself with its atom bombs or something else, but then we do not care what will emerge, if anything.

But the actual situation *is* very like 1510, when Luther went to Rome, the eve of the Reformation. There is everywhere protest, revaluation, attack on the Establishment. The protest is international. There is a generation gap. (Luther himself was all of 34 when he posted his 95 theses in 1517, but Melanchthon was 20, Bucer 26, Münzer 28, Jonas 24; the Movement consisted of undergraduates and junior faculty.) And the thrust of protest is not to give up science, technology, and civil institutions, but to purge them, humanize them, decentralize them, change the priorities, and stop the drain of wealth.

These were, of course, exactly the demands of the March 4 nation-

wide teach-in on science, initiated by the dissenting professors of the
Massachusetts Institute of Technology. This and the waves of other
teach-ins, ads and demonstrations have been the voices not of the alienated, of people who have no world, but of protestants, people deep in
the world who will soon refuse to continue under the present auspices
because they are not viable. It is populism permeated by moral and
professional unease. What the young have done is to make it finally
religious, to force the grown-ups to recognize that they too are threatened
with meaninglessness.

The analogy to the Reformation is even closer if we notice that
the bloated universities, and the expanded school systems under them,
constitute the biggest collection of monks since the time of Henry VIII.
And most of this mandarism is hocus pocus, a mass superstition. In my
opinion, much of the student dissent in the colleges and especially the
high schools has little to do with the excellent political and social demands that are made, but is boredom and resentment because of the
phoniness of the whole academic enterprise.

Viewed as incidents of a Reformation, as attempts to purge themselves and recover a lost integrity, the various movements of the alienated
young are easily recognizable as characteristic protestant sects, intensely
self-conscious. The dissenting seminarians of the Pacific School of Religion do not intend to go off to primitive love feasts in a new heaven
and new earth, but to form their own Free University; that is, they
are Congregationalists. The shaggy hippies are not nature children as
they claim, but self-conscious Adamites trying to naturalize Sausalito
and the East Village. Heads are Pentecostals or Children of Light.
Those who spindle IBM cards and throw the dean down the stairs are
Iconoclasts. Those who want Student Power, a say in the rules and
curriculum, mean to deny infant baptism; they want to make up their
own minds, like Henry Dunster, the first president of Harvard. Radicals
who live among the poor and try to organize them are certainly intent
on social change, but they are also trying to find themselves again. The
support of the black revolt by white middle-class students is desperately
like Anabaptism, but God grant that we can do better than the Peasants'
War. These analogies are not fanciful; when authority is discredited,
there is a pattern in the return of the repressed. A better scholar could
make a longer list; but the reason I here spell it out is that, perhaps,
some young person will suddenly remember that history was about
something.

Naturally, traditional churches are themselves in tradition. On college campuses and in bohemian neighborhoods, existentialist Protestants and Jews and updating Catholics have gone along with the political and social activism and, what is probably more important, they have changed their own moral, esthetic and personal tone. On many campuses, the chaplains provide the only official forum for discussions of sex, drugs and burning draft cards. Yet it seems to me that, in their zeal for relevance, they are badly failing in their chief duty to the religious young: to be professors of theology. They cannot really perform pastoral services, like giving consolation or advice, since the young believe they have the sacraments to do this for themselves. Chaplains say that the young are uninterested in dogma and untractable on this level, but I think this is simply a projection of their own distaste for the conventional theology that has gone dead for them. The young are hotly metaphysical—but alas, boringly so, because they don't know much, have no language to express their intuitions, and repeat every old fallacy. If the chaplains would stop looking in the conventional places where God is dead, and would explore the actualities where perhaps He is alive, they might learn something and have something to teach.

part 3

"Schools free children to rise to the level of their natural abilities."   —Committee for the White House
Conference on Education, 1960

"In its desegregation decision of 1954, the Supreme
Court held that separate schools for Negro and white
children are inherently unequal. This survey finds that,
when measured by that yardstick, American public education remains largely inequal in most regions of the
country, including all those where Negroes form any
significant proportion of the population."
—Coleman Report

Patterns
schools reinforce

One of the most deeply entrenched myths in America is that all people begin life with an equal chance to enjoy whatever pursuits strike their fancies. We have taken comfort in the belief that America, unlike Europe, is a classless society. The public school, we have told ourselves, is the keystone in this arch of equality.

The myth of classlessness is becoming more and more obviously untenable. Beneath our egalitarian protestation abides a stratified class structure—the richest 5 percent of the population has 20 percent of the wealth, leaving the poorest fifth of the population only 5 percent. The result is a boiling caldron of social unrest. Minority groups of blacks, Chicanos, Indians, and Puerto Ricans have repeatedly protested unfair treatment. Commissions have investigated, courts have rendered libertarian decisions, and Congress has passed civil rights legislation. Head Start, Follow Through, Upward Bound, outreach, compensatory education, desegregation, and a host of other Great Society terminology has come into common parlance. But glaring inequities remain.

Since schooling is so often portrayed as the primary route for individual social advancement, where does the school system fit in an unequal society? Are schools the royal avenue to success for everyone or, to borrow from George Orwell's *Animal Farm*, are some children more equal than others? If schools do not treat everyone the same, what mechanisms are used to ensure unequal results? Finally, if one assumes that schools should provide equal opportunity, how should they be changed?

These questions apply, of course, not only to classroom facilities or teacher certification. The basic matter of financing public schools is being scrutinized. In 1971 the California Supreme Court raised what may be the most critical issue for school districts since the 1954 *Brown* decision. It declared that the local property tax form in California, the basis on which the majority of public money for schools is raised, discriminates against the poor. Justice Raymond L. Sullivan, in the majority opinion, declared that education in the modern industrial state is a fundamental right, which like justice in the court, must be protected for all. To build an educational system on a financial strategy which favors rich districts over poor is to violate the constitutional guarantee of equal protection under the law.

Part 3 explores in some depth the extent and denial of equal educational opportunities, blatant and subtle. The first five articles discuss the majority attitudes that form the foundation for continuing racial, ethnic, and social stratification. The other selections treat the place of schools in the structure of race–social class and some proposed solutions to this American dilemma.

HARRY EDWARDS

The Revolt of the Black Athlete

In 1968 the Columbia Broadcasting System commissioned a nationwide poll to ascertain racial attitudes. The pollsters concluded that 34 percent—or about 70 million—of the whites in America could be accurately described as racists. Presumably, the remaining 65 percent, a clear majority, were willing to admit to at least some need for change in order that American society come closer to its egalitarian ideals. Why, then, is change so slow in coming? The following essay by black ex-athlete Harry Edwards gives some clues. In the area of collegiate and professional athletics, many people have concluded the color barrier has disappeared. Athletics is the way up the social ladder for minority youth, especially blacks —or so runs the popular belief. But is it? Edwards' observations are particularly interesting when read in conjunction with the article in Part 2 by Hollis Limprecht, who praises athletics.

I am a college sociology teacher, age 25. Before I gave up games and went academic, I set a national junior college discus throw record of nearly 180 feet and track coaches fell all over me, as a likely internationalist. One Western coach called me (I'm 6-feet-8, 250 pounds), "a terrific animal"—without a moment's concern that I overheard his description.

But discus-tossing in no way dimmed my memory of the south side of East St. Louis, Illinois, where I grew up. Like everyone else, the Edwards family lived on beans and paste and watched neighbor kids freeze to death. We used an outhouse which finally collapsed in the hold and drank boiled drainage-ditch water.

Young mothers just *flew out* of the place. My own mother abandoned us when I was eight years old, later showing up with 86 stitches in her body after a street brawl. Cops jailed me for juvenile offenses. They jailed me when I was innocent. A brother of mine, today, serves 25-years-to-life in the Iowa State Penitentiary. Intelligent hearthside conversation didn't exist—intergroup allegiance and family discipline died under the weight of poverty.

I was the first boy from my area to graduate from high school. Until I was 17 I had never held a meaningful conversation with a white adult and until shortly before that I was unaware that one could vote in an election without first receiving pay—the $5 handed to a "block nigger" for his preempted ballot being a postulate of staying alive in East St. Louis.

One in tens of thousands of teen-agers has the muscle, speed, and coordination to "escape" such scenes—that is, physically leave the ghetto by signing with one of the universities which hotly recruit, buy, and ballyhoo the Negro high school sport whizzes. And, once out of it and in a high-education environment, he's considered lucky. I was one of these.

Yet no medals I've won nor the B.A. and M.A. degrees which follow my name [and the Ph.D. that is coming] can balance the East St. Louis I saw upon returning there last year. Jobs in trade unions, in public utilities, behind downtown store counters, remained blocked to 35,000 of the city's 105,000 population. Rags plugged paneless windows of tin shacks, children had been incinerated in fire-traps, riot had come and gone. A dungheap comatoseness still ruled six square miles.

"Are you still selling your vote for five bucks?" I asked the shot-to-hell young adults I grew up with.

"What else is it good for?" they replied.

If the weapons at their command aren't used in behalf of those left behind—it begins to occur to many athletes—how do they go on living with themselves? We have an avenue of power open to us: the most interracially significant gathering of peoples short of the U.N. If the most mobile minority in the public eye—Afro-American dashmen, leapers, musclemen, etc.—can arouse continuing worldwide publicity by not moving at all, at least the ditch-water drinkers will be remembered. Possibly the gain will be larger.

Until now, foreign interest in U.S. bigotry has been scattered and blurred, but when the Olympic Games walk-out first was announced, it rated Page One space in London, Paris, Tokyo, Rome. France's top sports periodical, *L'Equipe,* saw it as "the revolution incredible." The London *Daily Times'* Neil Allen wrote, "As we diagnose it, you are hitting at the middleclass America, the social force most perpetuating racism—telling it that no longer can sport be excluded from goals of assimilation." Japan's Sports Federation chief Tetsuo Ohba expressed surprise "at the depth of your racial problem," pointedly adding, "The Negro super-stars made the Games worth seeing." As the national boycott leader, I have received dozens of *why?*-type inquiries from Europe, Asia, and Africa.

Focus of attention in this direction, abroad, actually began nearly two years ago when Muhammad Ali's world heavyweight title was lifted. U.S. black fight champs have been castrated before—in 1913, for instance, when Jack Johnson was forced into exile by white supremacists. Johnson was the classic, tragic loser. But the modern spotlight has caused the plight of one who believes that war is evil and stuck with his belief to be well-noted.

Ali's treatment stunned black multitudes everywhere. To us, he was—is—a god. Demands that we appear in the Olympics, when placed alongside Ali's case, are revealed for what they are, especially when based on the pitch that our youngsters are missing the chance of a life-time—the glory of being part of a world-championship show. Ali, as Cassius Clay, won an Olympic gold medal in 1960. Swell, baby. "Trust no Future, howe'er pleasant," as Longfellow said.

Another form of distortion of sportsmanship in which we are deeply involved is the class struggle heightened by Olympic medal-fever (outscore the Russians, show our superiority by use of complicated point tabulations). At the 1964 Tokyo-held games the U.S. won 20 gold medals in track-and-field, nine of them contributed by blacks. In Mexico City, without our help, vicarious patriotism no doubt will suffer. But what happens to the national point total concerns us not at all; we say, only, if Olympics zealots think white, then let them go to the starting line white.

If all our past heroes of the Games, their medals jangling, paraded into Washington, Detroit, or Cleveland, and confronted riot squads, all their speed wouldn't enable them to outrun bayonets and bullets. The sole factor separating a Tommie Smith, Ralph Boston, or John Carlos from becoming an ambushed Rev. Reeb or Medgar Evers is that they've been on no firing lines. Beyond the win-or-lose motivatation there exists another intimate—and overlooked—concern of our membership.

Since the time of Jesse Owens it has been presumed that any poor but rugged youngster who was able to jump racial fences into a college haven was happy all day long. He—the All-American, the subsidized, semi-professional racer—was fortunate. Mostly, this is a myth.

In 1960, for example, I was recruited by San Jose State College, a prominent "track school." Fine things were promised. "You'll be accepted here," the head coach and deans assured me. It developed that of 16 campus fraternities (as Greek in name as Plato, who revered the democracy of the Olympic Games) not one would pledge Harry Edwards (or anyone of color). The better restaurants were out of bounds and social activity was nil—I was invited nowhere outside of "blood" circles.

Leaving California, I spent two years acquiring a Master's degree at Cornell University. Returning to San Jose State as a teacher, I knocked on door after door bearing "vacancy" signs, but Mr. Charley was so sorry—the rental room suddenly wasn't available. The end-up: a cold cement-floor garage, costing $75 a month.

Not long later I came to know Tommie Smith, whose 0:19.5 is the world 220-yard record and whom this same state college uses to impress and procure other speedsters and footballers of his race. "I have you beat," he said. "My wife's pregnant. We have no decent house. So far 13 lovely people have turned me down."

Much of the headbusting and police crackdowns at schools originate in Afro-American student frustration over housing, an area where valuable, "taken-care-of athletes" are thought to be uninvolved. Athletic Department p.r. men skillfully make this seem so. However, the great majority of black varsity men live, like Smith, in backstreet bed-in-the-wall pads located far from their classes, and overpriced. Existing as celebrity-pariahs, they go along with it because (1) they're dependent upon Charley's scholarship funding; (2) they're shy and tractable, taught early to "respect everyone, whether they respect you or not," or— "remember, as part of the Big Team you're safe from those Spookhunters outside"; (3) if they openly rebelled, back to pushing a poolhall broom they'd go.

The answer was expressed some weeks ago by Lee Evans, a collegian who ranks as the world's second-best quarter-miler of all time.

"That bag," he says, "is rapidly changing. We're all through having our insides churned just when we think we're emancipated."

The examples are many and they vary little: in 1967, Southern California U's great footballer-trackman, O. J. Simpson, was worth at least $500,000 to USC at the box office. Many awards followed. Simpson, should he desire, could not become a member of more than 90 percent of the groups which honored him with banquets and trophies. (Typical are the many restricted athletic clubs and country clubs throughout the nation.) Such organizations, however, feel quite justified in using Simpson's name to enhance their own identification with athletics.

At Southern Methodist University last year, "one-man-team" halfback Jerry Levias drew so many death threats and so much abuse by mail and phone that he was given a bodyguard and begged by his family to quit sports. Varsity Negroes at the University of Washington, excluded from organized dances, golf, and ski-trips, boycotted the school's sports program. At UCLA a public-relations gag was put on 7-ft.-1 Lew Alcindor; he shook it off to reveal that he's been nigger-blasted by fans, cold-shouldered by students, and told to get lost.

In Kansas City, former Heisman Trophy-winner-turned-pro Mike Garrett found a bachelor apartment unobtainable and exploded in print. "Troublemaker" the local community said of him.

In sections of the Bible Belt and in Southern states where many Olympic point-winners are developed, trackmen routinely break records, but their friends must sit far from the finish line in segregated seats.

At a recent Los Angeles Boycott Olympics Project conference, word arrived that Dickie Howard had been found dead, not far away, of an overdose of drugs. Howard was a fairly good student and he won an Olympic 400-meter bronze medal at Rome in 1960. Finding too many doors shut, he disintegrated and at 29 took his own life.

Post-Olympic careers for black grads in coaching, teaching, advertising, and business are so few (a Bob Hayes in pro football, a Rafer Johnson in radio, a Hayes Jones in recreation direction, are but tokens in the overall picture) that the following happened: a college alumnus famous for his accomplishments as an Olympic athlete approached a TV agency. As he well knew, the endorsement, testimonial, and product-pushing industry generally employs as many of his kind as you'll find swimming in pools in Southampton. However, he had a winning smile. To his suggestion that he could sell breakfast food or toothpaste, network executives said, "Use you on commercials? Not hardly. We'd lose 60 percent of our audience. But we do have a job open." He promptly was handed a card to be held up before studio audiences, reading—"Laugh."

Not laughing himself, he held it up. No other work was open to him.

As much as Olympic officials denounce the profit motive and try to legislate it away, most athletes waste no time in cashing in on their reputations. The Games and commercialism are so closely tied that no longer is it arguable that they are not. One big goal is a job with a school. What major universities employ a black athletic director, head coach, assistant coach, or even a head scout? Answer: almost none. Equipment-man and bus-driving positions are open, always, in number.

Once upon a time, children, we inform men who are undecided about joining the boycott and come to us torn between their personal need and a larger need, there was Binga Dismond. He's forgotten now. Binga was the original Negro track sensation in America—a meteor who flared in Chicago in 1916–17, long before the Eddie Tolans, Ralph Metcalfes, and De-Hart Hubbards. "Binga," wrote Charley Paddock, the Caucasian sprint champion of that time, "could beat any man alive at 440 yards. But he was required to run on the outside of the pack, all the way around, so as to avoid physical contact with any white. Eventually, discouraged, he disappeared."

From "Long Way" Dismond we move to the subject of Jesse Owens: "immortal" Jesse, whose four gold medals won at the 1936 Olympics in Berlin left Hitler much discomfited. For 30 years Olympic Committee and Amateur Athletic Union officials have used Owens as the prime illustration of how pride and hope of a minority can be uplifted through the feats of a blood brother. The recorded facts—not mentioned—are:

The "Buckeye Bullet" finished his amazing Reich Sportsfield appearances on a Sunday. Within 12 hours he was put aboard a train to Cologne and sent on a grueling European trip by his promoters, the AAU. In the next 10 days, Owens raced eight times and lost 14 pounds. Exhausted, he was ordered to Sweden for still more exhibitions. All gate receipts would accrue to the Swedes and the AAU. Owens refused to go. Within weeks, he was suspended by the AAU and thrown out of amateur sports, for life.

When Owens next raced it was for money against horses and motorcycles in sleazy hippodromes in Mexico and Reno. Over ensuing years a modicum of advantages have come Jesse Owens' way; but to friends he says, "I've never been in the mainstream. They won't put me on any key Olympic committees, the policy groups. I've been used."

None of the organizers of Boycott Olympics was surprised when Owens, last November, expressed sympathy with our motives, but found boycott over-severe—a "wrong approach" to the problem. For he belongs to a controlled generation, the inheritors of Binga Dismond running on the outside.

Does it occur to Jesse Owens that blacks are ineligible by color-line and by endless economic obstacles to compete in some 80 percent of scheduled Olympic events? Rowing, skating, swimming, shooting, horse-backing, yachting, skiing, fencing, gymnastics, modern pentathlon, water polo, among others, are activities outside our cultural reach, although wasn't it Baron Pierre de Coubertin, the French scholar and humanist, who inspired the revival of the Olympics in 1896, who wrote, "The important thing in the Games is not winning, but taking part"? And who inscribed, "The foundation of human morality lies in mutual respect—and to respect one another, it is necessary to know one another."

"Know" requires association, yes? Nineteen Olympiads later, no black ever has been a member of the American Olympic Committee's governing board, nor held a responsible post on any of the multiple individual sport federations. When we demand a place, back comes the disguised echo—of Maddox, Barnett, Wallace, Bull Connor.

Concededly, poor whites aren't yachtsmen, equestrians or badge-wearers, either. But as United States District Court Judge Wade H. McCree of Detroit remarked, "No one in this country is poor or outside because he's white." I'm sure Jesse Owens grasps the whole Olympic picture, agrees deep-down with us and would move to our support but for the bonds forged long ago.

Humble is out now. Action that is non-action is in. Quadrennially, the newspapers exclaim over feats of the Ralph Bostons, Bob Hayses, and Henry Carrs—record-breakers. Olympic symbols.

Symbolically, they can only serve a wrong purpose. Overseas audiences hear little of bloodshed in the human-rights struggle. But when the Asian, Nordic, or Slav sees a white Richmond Flowers of Tennessee passing a relay baton to a Charles Greene or an O. J. Simpson they deduce, "Those boys, indeed, are equal." Greene or Simpson, of course, couldn't race on many southern U.S. tracks or join a fraternity or a downtown A.C. in the North, any more than Thurgood Marshall, of our highest courts, could be named a county attorney in Alabama.

On the Olympic Committee for Human Rights, we think simply.

We believe that the answer to why Afro-Americans are relegated to a subhuman sphere is one of two—either they want to be classed that way or society feels that they should be there. The first reason is obviously ludicrous. Application of the second of the two answers has led the Union to the edge of ultimate revolution.

If the fastest among us can show that our sense of personal worth and obligation outweighs any rewards offered us and that we represent the many, something may be accomplished. The aim of Pierre de Coubertin may be recognized more than 70 years later.

DICK GREGORY

The Shortest Month

Another indication of racial prejudice is shown in our selective treatment of history, particularly in the national holidays we observe—or in the days we do not observe. The addition of courses in black history in some schools has partially filled the gap indicated in the following article, but even that small step has not been taken in many schools.

February is American history month, it seems, for white America. Banks, schools, public buildings and many offices close twice during February to commemorate the birth of two of traditional American History's most legendary heroes—George Washington and Abraham Lincoln. The Father of our country and the supposed Healer of its wounds are given their revered and honored place in America's official memory.

February is also a month rich in the history of the black experience in America, although there is no official recognition at the national level. Perhaps that fact partially explains why the nation's wounds are still bleeding profusely.

Frederick Douglass, runaway slave, author, probably the leading voice of the 19th century abolitionist movement, editor of the famed abolitionist newspaper *The North Star*, was born and also died in the

Dick Gregory, "The Shortest Month," *Renewal*, vol. 9, no. 2 (February 1969), pp. 4, 5. Reprinted by permission.

month of February. This month saw the birth of Dr. W. E. B. DuBois, prolific writer, noted historian, founder of the NAACP, certainly the father of the current mood among black youth of black identity, black culture and black studies, and Langston Hughes, one of the most renowned black men of letters in this century.

February is both the month of black recognition and black assassination. Hiram Rhoades Revels of Mississippi, the first black United States Senator, took the oath of office in 1870 during the month of February. The wise and courageous spokesman of racial truth in America, Brother Malcolm X, was murdered on February 21, 1965.

An increasing national phenomenon is the demand of black youth that black history be taught in colleges, high schools and grade schools throughout the land. It is primarily a northern phenomenon, since the segregated school system of the South has long provided black youth with black principals, black teachers and a black curriculum. Graduates of all-black southern schools are familiar with the names and accomplishments of black men in America—a history conspicuously eliminated from the supposedly liberal northern educational system.

So there is obviously more to the concept of integration than physical proximity. School buses can "bring students together" to borrow a Nixon phrase, but they are irrelevant to establishing cultural identity and racial pride. The popular phrase "quality education through integration" means more than establishing a physical racial balance in the public schools. It means establishing an educational system which encourages the full integration of the individual human being.

If a black student is fully exposed to his own unique history, not the degrading history of slavery but the noble accomplishments of his ancestors, that student will no longer harbor those feelings of inferiority which the American system has imposed upon him. If the white student is fully exposed to that same black history, he will no longer be able to accept his parents' version of black worth. Such exposure may show the white student who the real "nigger" is.

White folks must study black history to set the record straight. Traditional American history is a slanted version of the story of America. For the black student, black history is only a prelude to a more thorough orientation in black studies. Black studies must relate the entire educational process to the black experience. The only way for the black student to break out of the system in America, which has made him a "nigger" for so long, is to find out who he is and where he came from, so that he himself can determine where he is going. A man without identity is like a tree without roots.

The list of black accomplishments is long indeed. Look at the list of black inventors alone. White America tends only to think of George Washington Carver and peanut butter. But there was also Benjamin Banneker, who made the first clock in America, a wooden "striking" clock, and who laid out the blueprint for the nation's capitol. Henry Blair was the first black man to be issued a patent—first for a corn planting machine and later for a cotton planter.

Dr. Daniel Hale Williams performed the first open heart surgery. Dr. Charles Drew developed the techniques for separating and preserving blood—though he died of injuries received in an automobile accident because a southern hospital would not give blood transfusions to blacks. Jan Matzeliger revolutionized the shoe industry with his machine to mass produce shoes. Granville T. Woods revolutionized the railroad industry with his Synchronous Multiplex Railway Telegraph. Norbert Rillieux revolutionized the sugar-refining industry in the United States, by inventing a vacuum evaporating pan which reduced the industry's dependence upon gang labor and produced a superior product.

Elijah McCoy revolutionized machines, period, by developing a process for automatic lubrication. Garrett Morgan invented both the gas mask and the traffic light. Andrew Beard invented a coupling device for railroad cars which prevented the maiming or death of countless railroad workers.

The list of black inventions is endless and includes such common household items as the dust pan, the pencil sharpener, the fountain pen and the paper bag. Just one more reminder that black is not only beautiful, but also creative and inventive and necessary for America's survival.

PHI DELTA KAPPAN

Discrimination Against Mexican-Americans

*Social, political, economic, and educational inequality is not con-
fined to black Americans. In southwestern United States are many
citizens of Mexican descent who experience subtle or overt discrimination. The following report of recent research documents
this problem and describes how "Anglos" retain control in communities even if they are outnumbered.*

A vivid and sometimes poignant picture of discrimination against Mexican-Americans in a California community and its school system was
disclosed in a recent Stanford doctoral dissertation by Theodore W.
Parsons, now assistant professor of education and cultural anthropology
at Florida State University.

For three years Parsons studied an agricultural town in central
California, called "Guadalupe" in his report, spending 40 days in personal observation of the elementary school where more than half (57
percent) of the nearly 600 pupils are Mexican-Americans.

Some examples of how those of Mexican origin are kept firmly
subordinated to the "Anglos" (white Americans of Anglo and other
national origins) in both school and community:

1. A teacher, asked why she had called on "Johnny" to lead five
Mexicans in orderly file out of a schoolroom, explained: "His father
owns one of the big farms in the area and . . . one day he will have to
know how to handle the Mexicans."

2. Another teacher, following the general practice of calling on
the Anglos to help Mexican pupils recite in class, said in praise of the
system: "It draws them [the Americans] out and gives them a feeling of
importance."

3. The president of the Chamber of Commerce declared in praise
of the school principal: "He runs a good school. We never have any

trouble in our school. Every kid knows his place. . . . We believe that every kid has to learn to respect authority and his betters."

4. The school principal expounded the "grouping" and departmentalized reading programs instituted under his administration: "We thought that the white children would get more out of school if they could work faster and not be slowed down by the Mexicans. We thought the Mexican kids would do better work if they were in classes geared more to their level. We thought that maybe we could give them some special attention. . . .

"Everybody is happy about the grouping programs. . . . The Mexican parents have never said anything, but the kids in school are doing better. . . . I guess the Mexicans are more comfortable in their own group."

5. By admitted subterfuge, the Chamber of Commerce committee sees to it that the artichoke festival "queen" is always an Anglo, with the Mexican candidate in second place as her attendant. An influential citizen told Parsons: "We could never have a Mexican queen represent us at the county fair."

6. Two of the three churches do not accept Mexicans. At the Catholic church, when both groups are assembled for special occasions, the Mexicans sit in the back or stand if seating is inadequate.

Mexicans buy tickets to church affairs but seldom attend because the people "aren't friendly." The one Mexican family who showed up at a barbecue sat alone throughout the afternoon.

7. At school graduation, the Mexicans march in last and sit at the back of the platform. A male teacher explained that this is traditional and "makes for a better-looking stage." Also, the Americans, who have all the parts in the program, can get more easily to the front. He added:

"Once we did let a Mexican girl give a little talk of some kind and all she did was to mumble around. She had quite an accent, too. Afterwards we had several complaints from other parents, so we haven't done anything like that since. . . . That was about 12 years ago."

8. The Mexican cub scout pack was in high excitement at the close of one annual town cleanup drive, when their pile was the highest at the 10 A.M. deadline. At 10:40 the garbage collector's large truck arrived and deposited a big load of trash on the Anglo cub pack's pile. The Anglo pack then was awarded the $50 prize.

9. A light-skinned Mexican high school graduate promptly lost the job as bank teller she had just been engaged to fill when the manager heard her speak to an acquaintance in Spanish. He said he had

not realized she was Mexican—it was not bank policy to employ Mexicans.

The school teachers, all Anglo and for the most part indigenous to the area, appeared unanimous in sharing the stereotype of Mexican-Americans—inferior in capacity as well as performance—Parsons reported. So firmly is the pattern in mind that a teacher, in full view of a group of well-dressed, quietly behaved Mexican children, could describe Mexican children as noisy and dirty.

Sociometric tests conducted by Parsons disclosed that even the Mexican children come to share the view constantly held up to them that the Anglos are "smarter" and their good opinion of special value.

"In general, Anglo informants characterized the Mexicans as immoral, violent, and given to fighting, dirty, unintelligent, improvident, irresponsible, and lazy," wrote Parsons.

"Mexican informants often described Anglos as being unsympathetic, aggressive, interested only in themselves, cold, and demanding. . . . Not one of the several hundred people contacted during the field investigation had ever visited a home outside of his own ethnic group."

U.S. SENATE

Indian Education: A National Tragedy— A National Challenge

American Indians, too, have long suffered discrimination and dishonesty. These excerpts from Senate hearings give graphic examples of another area where our official rhetoric has covered an unpalatable reality. One of the predominant themes that characterize minority groups' efforts to change the schooling patterns

From *Indian Education: A National Tragedy—A National Challenge,* 1969 Report of the Committee on Labor and Public Welfare, United States Senate, special subcommittee on Indian education. 91st Congress, 1st Session. Senate Report No. 91-501 (Washington: U. S. Government Printing Office, 1969).

offered their children is reflected in the slogan "community con-
trol." These brief, edited selections—from the historical descrip-
tions to listings of current statistics—should be a blow to anyone
who believes in what Jonathan Kozol labels "the myth of progress."

A CASE STUDY: CHEROKEE EDUCATION—PAST AND PRESENT

One of the most remarkable examples of adaptation and accomplishment
by any Indian tribe in the United States is that of the Cherokee. Their
record provides evidence of the kind of results which ensue when
Indians truly have the power of self-determination:

a constitution which provided for courts, representation, jury trials and
the right to vote for all those over 18 years;

a system of taxation which supported such services as education and
road construction;

an educational system which produced a Cherokee population 90 percent literate in its native language and used bilingual materials to
such an extent that Oklahoma Cherokees had a higher English
literacy level than the white populations of either Texas or Arkan-
sas;

a system of higher education which, together with the Choctaw Nation,
had more than 200 schools and academies, and sent numerous
graduates to eastern colleges;

publication of a widely read bilingual newspaper.

But that was in the 1800s, before the federal government took
control of Cherokee affairs. The record of the Cherokee today is proof
of the tragic results of 60 years of white control over their affairs:

90 percent of the Cherokee families living in Adair County, Oklahoma,
are on welfare;

99 percent of the Choctaw Indian population in McCurtain County,
Oklahoma, live below the poverty line;

The median number of school years completed by the adult Cherokee
population is only 5.5;

40 percent of adult Cherokees are functionally illiterate; Cherokee drop-
The level of Cherokee education is well below the average for the State
out rates in public schools is as high as 75 percent.

of Oklahoma, and below the average for rural and non-whites in the state.

The disparity between these two sets of facts provides dramatic testimony to what might have been accomplished if the policy of the federal government had been one of Indian self-determination. It also points up the disastrous affects of imposed white control.

Cherokee education was truly a development of the tribes itself. In 1821 Sequoyah, a member of the tribe, presented tribal officials with his invention—a Cherokee alphabet. Within six years of that date Cherokees were publishing their own bilingual newspaper, and the Cherokee Nation was on its way toward the end of illiteracy and the beginning of a model of self-government and self-education.

The Cherokee Indians established a government of laws in 1820 and, in 1927, a constitution patterned after that of the United States. Their nation was divided into districts, and each district sent representatives to the nation's capital, which had a two-house legislative structure. The system compared favorably with that of the federal government and any state government then in existence.

The Cherokee education system itself was just as exemplary as its governmental system. Using funds primarily received from the federal government as the result of ceding large tracts of land, a school system described by one authority as "the finest school system west of the Mississippi River" soon developed. Treaty money was used by Sequoyah to develop the Cherokee alphabet, as well as to purchase a printing press. In a period of several years the Cherokee had established remarkable achievement and literary levels, as indicated by statistics cited above. But in 1903 the federal government appointed a superintendent to take control of Cherokee education, and when Oklahoma became a state in 1906 and the whole system was abolished, Cherokee educational performance was to begin its decline.

Authorities who have analyzed the decline concur on one point: the Cherokees are alienated from the white man's school. Anthropologist Willard Walker simply stated that "the Cherokees have viewed the school as a white man's institution over which parents have no control." Dr. Jack Forbes of the Far West Regional Laboratory for Research and Development said that the federal and state schools operated for the Cherokee have had negative impact because of little, if any, parent-community involvement. Several researchers have also commented upon the lack of bilingual materials in the schools, and the ensuing feeling by Cherokees that reading English is associated with coercive instruction.

Alfred L. Wahrhaftig makes the point that the Indian child communicates in Cherokee and considers it his "socializing" language. English is simply an "instrumental" language one learns in school, a place which the Cherokee student sees no value in attending anyway.

In the 1890s Cherokees knew there was a forum for their opinions on how their children should be educated, and they used that forum. Wahrhaftig's study showed Cherokee parents haven't lost interest in their children's education, just faith in a white-controlled system's ability to listen to them and respond. "Cherokees finally have become totally alienated from the school system," he reported. "The tribe has surrendered to the school bureaucracy, but tribal opinion is unchanged."

THE FAILURE OF A NATIONAL POLICY

A careful review of the historical literature reveals that the dominant policy of the federal government toward the American Indian has been one of forced assimilation which has vacillated between the two extremes of coercion and persuasion. At the root of the assimilation policy has been a desire to divest the Indian of his land and resources.

The Allotment Act of 1887 stands as a symbol of the worst aspects of the Indian policy. During the 46-year period it was in effect it succeeded in reducing the Indian landbase from 140 million acres to approximately 50 million acres of the least desirable land. Greed for Indian land and intolerance of Indian cultures combined in one act to drive the American Indian into the depths of poverty from which he has never recovered.

From the first contact with the Indian, the school and the classroom have been a primary tool of assimilation. Education was the means whereby we emancipated the Indian child from his home, his parents, his extended family, and his cultural heritage. It was in effect an attempt to wash the "savage habits" and "tribal ethic" out of a child's mind and substitute a white middle-class value system in its place. A Ponca Indian testifying before the subcommittee defined this policy from the standpoint of the Indian student: "School is the enemy!"

It is clear in retrospect that the "assimilation by education" policy was primarily a function of the "Indian land" policy. The implicit hope was that a "civilized Indian" would settle down on his 160 acres and become a gentleman farmer, thus freeing large amounts of additional land for the white man. But in addition, there has been a strong strain of "converting the heathen" and "civilizing the savage," which has subtly, but persistently, continued up to the present. Two stereotypes still prevail—"the dirty, lazy, drunken" Indian, and, to assuage our conscience, the myths of the "noble savage."

Regretfully, one must conclude that this nation has not faced up to an "American dilemma" more fundamental than the one defined so persuasively for us by Gunnar Myrdal in 1944. The "Indian problem" raises serious questions about this nation's most basic concepts of political democracy. It challenges the most precious assumptions about what this country stands for—cultural pluralism, equity and justice, and integrity of the individual, freedom of conscience and action, and the pursuit of happiness. Relations with the American Indian constitute a "morality play" of profound importance in our nation's history.

The Indian in American Life Today

This nation's 600,000 American Indians are a diverse ethnic group. They live in all fifty states and speak some 300 separate languages. Four hundred thousand Indians live on reservations, and 200,000 live off reservations. The tribes have different customs and mores, and different wants and needs. The urban Indian has a world different from that of the rural Indian.

Fifty thousand Indian families live in unsanitary, dilapidated dwellings, many in huts, shanties, even abandoned automobiles; the average Indian income is $1,500, 75 percent below the national average; the unemployment rate among Indians is nearly 40 percent—more than ten times the national average; the average age of death of the American Indian is 44 years, for all other Americans 65; the infant mortality rate is twice the national average; and thousands of Indians have migrated into cities only to find themselves untrained for jobs and unprepared for urban life. Many of them return to the reservation more disillusioned and defeated than when they left.

Indian Schooling Today

Indian children attend federal, public, private, and mission schools. In the early days of this republic, what little formal education there was available to Indians was under the control of the church. Gradually, however, as the nation expanded westward and Indian nations were conquered, the treaties between the conquering United States and the defeated Indian nation provided for the establishment of schools for Indian children. In 1842, for example, there were 37 Indian schools run by the U. S. government. This number had increased to 106 in 1881, and to 226 in 1968.

This pattern of federal responsibility for Indian education has been slowly changing. In 1968, for example, the education of Indian children in California, Idaho, Michigan, Minnesota, Nebraska, Oregon, Texas, Washington, and Wisconsin was the total responsibility of the state and not the federal government.

In 1968, there were 152,088 Indian children between the ages of 6 and 18. 142,630 attended one type of school or another. Most of these—61.3 percent—attended public, non-federal schools, and 6.0 percent attended mission and other schools. Some 6,616 school-age Indian children were not in school at all. The Bureau of Indian Affairs in the Department of the Interior, the federal agency charged with managing Indian affairs for the United States, was unable to determine the educational status of some 2,842 Indian children.

The Bureau of Indian Affairs operates 77 boarding schools and 147 day schools. There are 35,309 school-age children in these boarding schools, and 16,139 in the day schools. Nearly 9,000 of the boarding-school children are under 9 years old.

Has the federal government lived up to its responsibility? The extensive records of this subcommittee, seven volumes of hearings, five committee prints, and this report, constitute a major indictment of our failure.

Drop-out rates are twice the national average in both public and federal schools. Some school districts have drop-out rates approaching 100 percent. Achievement levels of Indian children are two to three years below those of white students; and the Indian child falls progressively further behind the longer he stays in school; only 1 percent of Indian children in elementary school have Indian teachers or principals; one-fourth of elementary and secondary school teachers—by their own admission—would prefer *not* to teach Indian children; and Indian children, more than any other minority group, believe themselves to be "below average" in intelligence.

VERA JOHN, VIVIAN HORNER & JUDY SOCOLOR

American Voices:
Politics, Protest, and Pedagogy

The belief that America is a pluralistic society has been a pervasive one. But pluralism presupposes genuine respect for many divergent social and cultural traditions. One good indication of the extent to which a country really does welcome different cultural approaches is its policy towards languages. The following excerpts from a book on American language policy gives some clues about our commitment to pluralism.

The widespread belief in the United States in the "melting pot" has obscured the complex history of minorities here, and still clouds understanding of their present status. While English is the national language, it is neither native nor indigenous, but was one of the group of languages brought here by the colonial powers. Before World War I there was little organized pressure in the United States to impose English as the sole language in the communities settled by the non-English-speaking colonial powers and by the recent immigrants from Europe. Thus, during the 19th century, bilingual schools existed in several states; and, in the state of New Mexico, for example, the Spanish language had equal constitutional status with English as the official state language.

The notable exceptions to this lenient pre-World War I attitude concerned the black slaves from Africa and many of the Indian tribes. (Neither the slaves nor Indians were Christians. Thus denying them their language gave no offense to Christian ethics.) The African languages spoken by the slaves were so totally and brutally suppressed that none survived. And with the Indian tribes the federal government, as Joshua Fishman notes in *Language Loyalty in the United States*, so "vacillated between policies oriented toward forced detribalization and tribal autonomy," that it "greatly weakened the ability and interest of Indian tribes to retain their languages."

Vera John, Vivian Horner, Judy Socolor, "American Voices: Politics, Protest, and Pedagogy," *Center Forum*, a publication of the Center for Urban Education, vol. 4, no. 1 (September 1969), pp. 1–3. Reprinted by permission.

Before they were conquered and "detribalized," as an example, the Cherokees, a highly literate Indian nation, had developed a written form of their language, printed a weekly newspaper and other publications in Cherokee and organized academies where subjects were taught in Cherokee. But with the treaties signed between the United States Army and the Indian nations, which stipulated that every child of the tribe be formally educated in the English language, the use of the Cherokee language fell in abeyance, printing presses were dismantled and sent off to the Smithsonian Institute, and the academies abandoned.

With the heightened nationalism in the United States kindled by World War I, the existence of different cultures and languages here came to be viewed as a serious threat. Various measures, including restrictive legislation, were imposed to enforce a policy of "English-only" in the schools and other institutions.

Among the immigrant groups, some did fight to maintain their mother tongue, a struggle that has been well documented by scholars. But, as Fishman points out, in spite of commitment by some to their native language, many immigrants learned to feel that conforming to the political, educational, and language policies of their adopted country was part of the price of citizenship and a downpayment toward the American dream.

On the other hand, the fight against this English-only policy waged by non-immigrant, indigenous American groups—the Indians and the Mexican-Americans—has been poorly documented. This struggle and the realization that Indians and Mexican-Americans (who are part Indian themselves) are people whose language, culture and knowledge of the land pre-dates the formation of the American states are hardly noted. Indeed, the study of language loyalty among Indians, Mexican-Americans and the more newly arrived Puerto Ricans, remains extremely fragmentary and without the recognition that these are conquered peoples whose attachment to their language is a bond to their past independence of greater self-determination.

Until very recently the literature on minorities in the United States, a literature mainly the work of scholars of Anglo-Saxon or immigrant backgrounds, stressed acculturation and assimilation. With the decreased immigration since World War II and the increased political activity among nonwhite and non-English-speaking minority groups, new social concepts are being developed and advocated. The notion of a pluralistic society is becoming more and more popular among these groups; their spokesmen advance the model of a pluralistic, egalitarian society in which ethnic minorities maintain and develop their own cultural heritage. In addition, the migration of non-English-speaking groups from rural areas to urban centers, a move forced by the mechanization of America's farms, has increased the concern of some of these groups with their cultural and linguistic survival. Their young spokesmen repeatedly express their fear of being members of an uprooted, alienated and underemployed mass in the urban slums.

The returning Mexican-American veterans of World War II and the subsequent wars have formed political organizations in the barrios of Denver, Los Angeles, Albuquerque, San Antonio and other cities. Through their activities they have developed a new pride in the Spanish language; political meetings are conducted in Spanish; bilingual newspapers, in increasing numbers, appear in both Spanish and English.

Similarly, Indian war veterans, many of whom attended college after demobilization, are projecting a new interest in their Indian heritage and tribal languages. They have joined the tribal governments of their people and have formed new inter-tribal and pan-Indian organizations.

In New York City members of the Puerto Rican community are assuming an important role in the city's political life. Many mainland Puerto Ricans express the hope that New York City will become genuinely bilingual with Spanish and English spoken by the majority of residents.

In this new political period, these developments within non-English-speaking communities are of particular interest to the student of language. The demands for bilingual instruction in these communities keep increasing. For some, these plans for education in both the mother tongue and English is a totally new concept. For others, the demand is for the rebuilding of former educational systems, such as the Spanish-American schools in the Southwest or the Cherokee academies.

At the same time, in the barrios, the colonias, the reservations, and the ghettos, the schools are being criticized as alien institutions, and the evidence supporting that notion is substantial.

Figures compiled by Barrett in the Southwest on the plight of the Mexican-American student in the Southwest show that in 1960 the median for school years completed by Spanish surname individuals of both sexes 14 years of age and over was: 9.0 years in California; 8.6 in Colorado; 8.4 in New Mexico; 7.9 in Arizona and 6.1 in Texas. (It is interesting to note that the income of the Spanish-Americans, though universally low, shows a relatively higher pattern in California than in Texas, where school achievement was lowest.)

In New York City, while one out of every four pupils in the elementary schools is of Puerto Rican birth or parentage, Puerto Ricans have less formal education than any other identifiable ethnic group in the city. In 1960 about 87 percent of all Puerto Ricans over 25 in the city had never completed high school. In 1963, of nearly 21,000 academic diplomas granted in New York City, only 331 went to Puerto Ricans.

The statistics relating to the education of Indian children in this country are even more dismal. As late as 20 years ago, less than half of all school-age Navajo children were in school. The 1960 census figures show that 10 percent of all Indians over 14 years of age have had no formal schooling at all: nearly 60 percent have less than an eighth-grade education and 50 percent of all Indian school children drop out before finishing high school. While a handful of bilingual education programs was initiated in the 1950s in the Southwest, the campaign for bilingual education did not become widespread until the 1960s when increasing pressure was placed on legislators at the city, state and federal levels to enact bilingual education measures. Support for these new bilingual education programs was not limited to spokesmen from the non-English-speaking communities. In 1966, for example, the NEA-Tuscon survey group, a broad committee of Anglo and Spanish-speaking educators, made a strong recommendation in favor of bilingual education.

In 1967 bills were introduced in Congress to amend the Elementary and Secondary Education Act of 1965 to provide for bilingual education programs. Hearings were held in the summer of 1967 in the Southwest by Senator Yarborough and in the East by Senator Robert Kennedy of New York. The testimony at these hearings by representatives from Mexican-American and Puerto Rican groups expressed the great need for bilingual and bicultural programs, and reflected both the increasing demands in the Spanish-speaking communities for large-scale bilingual programs and the strong and united support of these groups for federal subsidy for bilingual education.

The amendment, known as the Bilingual Education Act, was passed as Title VII to the ESEA of 1965, effective as of July 1, 1968 and administered by the United States Office of Education. According to the draft of the guidelines for Title VII, it is "Designed to meet specific education needs of children 3 to 18 years of age who have limited English-speaking ability and come from environments where the dominant language is other than English . . . Title VII funds are available for exemplary pilot or demonstration projects in bilingual and bicultural education in a wide variety of settings. These projects should demonstrate how the education program can be improved by the use of bilingual education." In line with this mandate, it would be well for those who are designing bilingual programs to note the recommendations contained in Professor C. S. Knowlton's report on "Spanish-American Schools in the 1960's." Knowlton argues that the instructional use of Spanish language in classrooms in New York City, Los Angeles and the many smaller cities and towns, was not sufficient in itself to improve the education of these children; that a new curriculum must be devised with *cultural* as well as *language* requirements.

Bilingual education thus is proposed as a more humane and enriched school experience for the non-English-speaking child, a means toward the development of a harmonious and positive self-image. Another argument for bilingual progress stresses the pedagogical soundness of teaching young children basic subjects in their own tongue. But while many of the arguments put forth for bilingual education are supported by common sense and the testimony of those who have experienced the effects of having to give up their mother tongue to become educated in an English-speaking system, the relevant research is scant and is likely to remain so for some time. Given present limitations in the social sciences, a research validation of the complex interaction of language with the individual in his many roles presents a task of formidable difficulty.

On the other hand, the claims for the pedagogical soundness of a bilingual approach in educating the child who is not a speaker of the national language are based on constantly accruing research evidence. A number of foreign educational institutions, drawing upon the experience of other polylingual nations, are for the first time taking a serious look at the potential of bilingual education. In addition, some limited experimentation has begun in the United States as well.

One carefully evaluated bilingual demonstration project is the Iloilo experiment, begun in 1948 in the Philippines. An experimental group of children were taught reading, arithmetic and social studies in Hiligaynon, their local vernacular, in the first and second grades. In the third grade they were switched to instruction in English. Within six weeks their performance in all tested subjects, including oral English, surpassed that of a control group who had received all instruction in English from the first grade on.

Another bilingual experimental program produced similarly effective results in Sweden. A group of children received an initial ten weeks of reading instruction in Pitean, the local dialect. They were then switched to instruction in literary Swedish. The results showed that the Pitean-instructed group learned to read more rapidly than a control group of Pitean speakers taught from the outset in literary Swedish. By the end of the first year, the experimental group had surpassed the control group in all language arts skills in literary Swedish.

In Chiapa, Mexico, an experimental group of children were taught to read in their native Indian languages. When the children had mastered their Indian primers, they entered first grade where all subsequent instruction was carried out in the national language, Spanish. Test data on reading skills *in Spanish* revealed that those Indian children who had first been taught to read in their native tongues read Spanish better and with greater comprehension than their peers who have been instructed only in Spanish.

Closer to home is a noteworthy bilingual program being carried out at the Coral Way School in Miami, Florida. This program includes both Spanish-speaking and English-speaking children, and has as its teaching goal the total mastery of both languages for all children. The evaluation data now available, covering a three-year period, indicate that while the children are not yet as fluent in their second language as their first, they learn equally well in either. In addition, the results demonstrate the bilingual curriculum is as effective as the standard curriculum in all academic subjects.

Another United States bilingual program in San Antonio, Texas, is achieving similar results. An experimental group of children of Spanish-speaking background, instructed in both Spanish and English during their first grade in school were able at the end of the year to read, speak and write in both languages. The children scored better on tests measuring cognitive growth, communication skills and social and emotional adjustment, than did their control peers who were taught solely in English. Tests administered at the end of the second year of their bilingual instruction indicate similar results.

These findings are of particular interest at a time when psychologists are probing the role of language in the intellectual development of children. We are witnessing a shift away from a preoccupation with the accumulation of information as the focus of learning to an emphasis upon basic processes. Consequently one of the great benefits of bilingual instruction of young children may be in helping them to develop the use of language for problem-solving in their native language. Once they have learned the value of words for memory and thought, they can apply this functional knowledge of language to the acquisition of a second language. The second language may then serve to extend the child's intellectual skills.

Some groups of bilingual children have been found to achieve better than their monolingual peers, in spite of long held beliefs to the contrary. In a study of ten-year-old French Canadian children in Montreal, bilingual children scored significantly higher on intelligence tests than monolingual children. According to the authors, balanced bilinguals (i.e., children with mastery of both languages) had the advantage over their monolingual peers of a language asset, a greater ability in concept formation, and a greater cognitive flexibility. The investigators concluded that "the bilinguals appear to have a more diversified set of mental abilities than the monolinguals."

Thus while some conceive of bilingual education as an efficient approach to the acquisition of the national language and culture by non-English-speaking children, others hold to the view that bilingualism can only be successful as a mutually developed and mutually experienced process of learning and teaching, involving both majority and minority communities. We subscribe to the latter.

DAVID L. KIRP

Race, Class, and the Limits of Schooling

The factors involved in the issues of equal treatment and discrimination are partly racial and ethnic prejudices. But in an even more fundamental sense, these are interlinked with social class. Most sociologists view American society as stratified in either three tiers (affluent, middle, poverty) or five tiers (upper, upper-middle, lower-middle, upper-working, lower-working). In either scheme, blacks, Puerto Ricans, Indians, and Mexican-Americans occupy the bottom stratum of society in disproportionately large numbers. In

David L. Kirp, "Race, Class, and the Limits of Schooling," *The Urban Review,* a publication of the Center for Urban Education, vol. 4, no. 3 (May 1970), pp. 10–13. Reprinted by permission.

the article which follows, David Kirp examines some of the ramifications of race and social class.

It is a traditional American belief that all citizens have an equal educational opportunity. As Tocqueville noted well over a century ago, "America . . . exhibits in her new social state an extraordinary phenomenon. Men are seen on a greater equality in point of future and intellect, or, in other words, more equal in their strength, than in any other country of the world, or in any age of which history has preserved the remembrance." Even when he was writing, Tocqueville misstated the case, for the common school was by no means a universal phenomenon, and a growing elite, far better educated than the Jacksonian common man, was being trained at a handful of American and European universities. More important, Tocqueville equated equality with likeness, assuming "equal strength" to be the crucial issue, rather than equal opportunity to test out whatever one's strength was.[1]

Americans have seldom worried about the connotations of 'equality'. We believed, particularly after the Supreme Court's "separate but equal" decision, that equality did not demand that blacks and whites be schooled together, as long as their separate schools provided the same calibre of instruction. For 50 years we rejected the notion that compulsory separation inevitably stamped the white school as superior and the black as inferior. That tidy view was cast aside only in 1954, when the Supreme Court held compelled segregation to be unconstitutional.

The Court's decision in *Brown v. Board of Education of Topeka* was couched in terms of equality. "Education is perhaps the most important function of state and local governments. . . . In these days, it is doubtful that any child may reasonably be expected to succeed in life if he is denied the opportunity of education. Such an opportunity . . . is a right which must be available to all on equal terms." The Court made clear that "equal terms" did not countenance separate facilities even if they were purportedly equal. But if equal facilities would not suffice, what would? Was racial integration the sole criterion for equality? Was the Court, in citing evidence of the psychological harm caused by segregation, indicating that integration was an educational necessity, or was it suggesting that compulsory segregation was constitutionally repugnant, whatever its educational implications? In couching its decree in "equal protection" language, was the Court demonstrating willingness to approve any schooling scheme which did not separate blacks and whites, or was the Court reserving a right to consider outcomes—

the effects of schooling—in determining whether equality of educational opportunity existed? The *Brown* opinion did not clearly confront these issues, and for the next decade they went undecided and even unnoticed. *Brown* was tested out at countless southern schoolhouse doors; indeed, resisting the *Brown* mandate became part of the southern way of life and a tactic for political survival. Its bearing on the northern school situation was largely unexplored. The North's school problems, it was felt, were not fundamentally constitutional but financial; greater fiscal support of city schools could make meaningful equality a reality there.

The Coleman Report (*Equality of Educational Opportunity*) shattered those notions. It was anticipated, when the report was commissioned in 1964, that its extensive survey of American public education would reveal massive differences in the quality of school facilities in predominantly black and predominantly white schools, and that it would attach the blame for racially different school outcomes to these differences. The report's conclusions, however, were quite different: relatively little variation in facilities was reported (this was in part due to the nature of the survey), and those that were found seemed to have little impact on the outcomes of schooling. Nor did the number of students in a classroom, or even the extent of teacher experience and training, seem to matter greatly. Two factors emerged as crucial for success in school: the family and social class background of the schoolchild, and the school's social class composition—the "educational backgrounds and aspirations of the other students in the school."

The Coleman Report described; it did not prescribe. Yet from it many professionals in education saw a way of restructuring the schools to make equal those factors that really affect school success, a way to compel effective equal opportunity. For the professionals, the Coleman Report provided a useful basis for urging heterogeneous schools: not only was it morally right for poor children and rich children to go to school together, it was also directly relevant to the quality of education that both received. The Court's language in *Brown* v. *Board of Education* was broad; it might well be extended to make such social class mixing a constitutional requirement. After all, how could the Court *not* insist upon a view of equality that would assure generally better public education for *all* children, that would uphold the promise of an equal opportunity for an equal outcome? Lyndon Johnson's famous Howard University address made reference to this understanding of equality. "We seek not just freedom but opportunity. We seek not just legal equality but human ability. Not just equality as a right or a theory, but equality as a fact and equality as a result. To this end equal opportunity is essential, but not enough, not enough." Two years later the United States Civil Rights Commission Report, *Racial Isolation in the Public Schools,* described the range of techniques—busing, Princeton Plans, educational parks—that could translate the need for social heterogeneity into reality. The triumph of rational, professional solutions, efficient solutions with perceivably beneficial implications for the schoolchildren affected by them, seemed almost at hand.

That triumph has not come to pass, and only now can one wonder whether it would have been a triumph at all. The reasons for the rejection of the professional's solution are not wholly irrational. From the first, serious questions were raised (by economists Sam Bowles and Henry Levin, among others) concerning the adequacy of Coleman's data, and the propriety of the statistical analysis employed in examining those data. These challenges had two noteworthy effects: they revealed that the massive data collected were susceptible to differing interpretations, none of which was necessarily 'true', and they robbed the Coleman Report of any aura of omniscience, rendering it vulnerable to less scholarly criticism.

Significant doubts were also raised concerning the importance of the kind of educational success that Coleman measured. *Equality of Educational Opportunity* equated success with performance on standardized achievement tests. In terms of eligibility for higher education and for jobs, such an equation is readily defensible; for available evidence indicates that achievement test performance bears directly upon traditional conceptions of success. Yet such a measure tacitly promotes schooling and job holding, traditional American values, as the values most worth stressing in schools. It ignores more subtle kinds of personal success—questions of identity, of a sense of control over one's self and one's environment, of self-esteem—and these other factors have in recent years been regarded as increasingly important.

Furthermore, population shifts (which accelerated during the 1960s) made it less likely that racially and socially mixed schooling of the kind and magnitude that the Coleman Report supported could ever be achieved in the big northern cities. Negroes were moving in large numbers into these cities, while even larger numbers of middle class whites were fleeing to suburbia. Distances between city and suburb, as well as the durability of school district boundaries, strongly discouraged attempts to bring together children from the two camps.

The Coleman Report was written at a time when laymen more

readily accepted the wisdom of professional educators. Those professionals assumed that rational, disinterested discourse on education,
carried on between themselves, was possible and right, that in fact the
professional was capable of making fundamental educational policy
choices. They attempted to reach the most efficient resolution—the best
education for the most children at the least cost—and in so doing saw
education as an end in itself, quite removed from politics. The professional educators supported proposals that would bring together small
school districts, because of supposed economies of scale that would
accompany such centralization and, more important, because only large
school districts could engage in the kind of social engineering that
seemed appropriate. This professional planning ignored a dimension
of equal educational opportunity that, finally, could not be ignored; the
equal right to make decisions shaping the course of public education;
an equal chance to exercise control.[2]

The beginnings of an understanding of 'control' can perhaps best
be had by examining the problems encountered by Norwalk, Connecticut, a suburb of New York City. In the early 1960s, an enlightened
school board, concluding that the then prevailing de facto school segregation was morally wrong and educationally damaging, determined to
change the situation. The school board's first thought was to bus children
both into and out of the black ghetto, but fear of white community resistance led the board to a different remedy: it would end de facto segregation by phasing out the ghetto schools. All schools in Norwalk would
be integrated; none would have fewer than 8 percent nor more than
28 percent black students; black students would be bused out of the
ghetto and into the white schools; white children would continue to go
to neighborhood schools. The plan received initial approval of all segments of the community. In 1968, however, as the last ghetto elementary
school was about to be closed, the local chapter of CORE protested.
When the school board ignored the protest, CORE sued the board, seeking to prevent it from closing the ghetto school. In its lawsuit, CORE
called at first for the reopening of black neighborhood schools, arguing
that if whites were entitled to neighborhood schools, blacks were equally
entitled; subsequently CORE modified the suit to insist upon cross-
busing, arguing (again on equal protection grounds) that if black children were to be bused to white schools, then white children should be
bused to black schools.

The Norwalk case posed numerous dilemmas for the court.[3] How
does a court decide this kind of question: does it defer to the wisdom

of the board of education, the body charged with the responsibility of education policymaking, or does it reject the board's claims to expertise? What sorts of evidence does the court consider in reaching its decision: does it rely on Coleman's findings? Does it order that the neighborhood be polled, to determine what kind of schooling the residents want? Does it set educational guidelines, and thus thrust itself for the next decade into the schooling business in Norwalk? Which is the community whose interest it bears foremost in mind: the black neighborhood, the Norwalk community, some broader community? Norwalk poses, on a comparatively manageable scale, the critical questions to be raised concerning community control. What does community control mean? Does it make political sense? Does it make pedagogical sense?

While the language of 'community control' is often used interchangeably with 'school decentralization', the two concepts differ basically. Advocates of decentralization seek structural adjustments in the system which would delegate more bureaucratic and decision making responsibility to local administrators. The decentralization supporters propose important bureaucratic restructuring, intended to make the system more efficient. Unlike supporters of community control, they do not advocate vesting significant power in assemblies of community representatives. Their model is not the town meeting-run community school but the essentially autocratic, and historically successful, parochial and independent school.[4]

Even among those who would vest the power to make decisions concerning the running of schools in the community itself, there are serious disagreements. Does the community 'participate' in those decisions, does it 'have a say' (how important a 'say' is rarely specified) or does it exercise final decision-making power? Over what kinds of decisions does the community exercise that power? Curriculum? Teacher selection? Budget—spending *and* raising money for the schools? What 'community' controls the schools? The parents? The residents? The activists? The children themselves? Put another way, how are the conflicting interests of these different communities, each of which feels that it has a legitimate interest in the outcome of public education, reconciled?[5]

The arguments made in support of 'decentralization/control' also differ widely. The administrative decentralists argue that current difficulties are in large part caused by a school system structured so poorly that, as David Rogers has most recently pointed out in his study of the New York City schools, little effective decision making is carried on at *any* level.[6] If this description of the inadequacies in the education decision-making process is accepted, then the remedy is not to take powers away from the central governing agency and give those powers to local schools, but to redefine power and responsibility in such a way that it can be exercised effectively at both the central and the local level.

Those who support greater community involvement in education decision making argue quite differently. They indict the schools for failing to reach whole segments of the population, for imprisoning rather than instructing school children (*Death at an Early Age*, the title of Jonathan Kozol's book, suggests a metaphor more ominous than imprisonment), for creating a permanent underclass, unaware of its potential and doomed to repeat the careers of its fathers. The increasing number of dropouts is no longer thought to represent personal failure or social class differences, but rather is considered symptomatic of the system's breakdown. Given such a breakdown, advocates of control argue that they can do no worse in running schools; indeed, that their more intimate knowledge of the children and their problems will enable them to do far better.

A second level or argument reaches to *Equality of Educational Opportunity* for 'scientific' support. The support that was the basis for that report included several questions designed to measure 'fate-control', the degree to which children feel that their own efforts, and not fate, determine the course of their lives. The responses indicated a striking correlation between an individual's sense of fate control and his performance in schools. Supporters of community control have relied on this finding; they argue that community-controlled schools will give black students a sense that they can reconquer their surrendered identity, that this sense will in turn enable them to succeed more regularly in what was formerly viewed as a hostile and ego-defeating school environment.[7]

Control advocates also see community-run schools as a way of forcing the white establishment to take their demands seriously; in this light, the community school becomes a power base in a very traditional sense, a mode of politicizing the black community as well as a source of jobs and patronage.[8] This desire to acquire political muscle is felt also in efforts to control other social service enterprises, notably public housing projects, Model Cities programs, and, as Daniel Moynihan has recently reminded us, the War on Poverty.[9]

Community control has become so fashionable that it seems heretical to suggest reservations.[10] Yet reservations, both political and pedagogical persist. To those who desire a set of neutral principles by which to evaluate the propriety of public policymaking, community control in Ocean Hill-Brownsville raises the spectre of a more unsettling possibility of community control in Alabama. That objection, however, is hardly overwhelming if one is willing to make distinctions between very different situations; indeed, if broad constitutional limits are accepted as to what community-controlled schools may do (communities must promote socially and racially integrated schools), neutral principles may be possible.

More important doubts can be raised concerning the political astuteness of the argument for control. How does a community control its own schools? Can a single community exert significant power over the textbook publishers, whose materials are faithfully relied upon? Or will the district somehow find the money to free numbers of teachers from teaching, enabling them to write their own curricula? How will the community identify, and attract, sympathetic teachers? (Or will sympathy be gauged solely by skin color?) Once hired, how will the schools judge their performance, to assure that the teachers remain in sympathy with the community's felt needs? How can these schools reconcile their judgments of teachers' competence with the union's demands for teacher security and with procedures that guarantee teachers' rights to due process? How can a community-run school, necessarily dependent on outside sources for adequate funding, make its own budget decisions? How, in other words, can it acquire fiscal independence from the government bureaucrats and from the foundation bureaucrats? These questions suggest the inevitability of important and little discussed compromises between the desire for community control on the one hand and the necessity for accountability to those who give financial sustenance to the exercise of control on the other.[11]

As long as schools, and not tenants councils or poverty agencies, are to be the mechanism for community power, the *pedagogical* consequences of community control, its effect on children, must be decisive. Schools are not entirely or even primarily political entities; they define their task as one of educating children (and occasionally grownups), and their success or failure will be measured by how well they accomplish this task.[12] Control advocates propose massive (and probably costly) changes in the education system, and offer few assurances that such changes will positively affect the quality of education that children receive. Is it not self-evident that slackness in the superintendent's office bears on (or causes) disasters in the classroom.

To those who continue to believe in the importance of racial and class mixing in the schools, community control, as described by its advocates, will have decidedly negative consequences. Adherents of community control, particularly in New York, tend to define their communities ethnically or racially, an attitude that in fact, reflects an actual condition. Even if, for example, the Ocean Hill-Brownsville district was interested in integrating its schools, it would first have to widen its definition of community. Until that happens, such districts can only hope to create separate but better schools. However, judging from programs tried up to now, there is little reason to be optimistic about realizing such hopes.

In few areas has integration been tried and found wanting, as control advocates claim; it would be more correct to say that it has seldom been honestly tried. School systems have often been able to beat back efforts at real integration and only in rare instances (Berkeley, for instance) have plans which promoted systemwide integration been put into effect. The distinction is crucial, for community-controlled schools, insofar as they harden neighborhoods against each other, make race or class integration unlikely at any time. Community-controlled schools might have been thought of differently, so that (for example) the restructuring of the New York metropolitan area's school districts led to the creation of an upper East Side-East Harlem district or, more radically a Bronx-Westchester or a Queens-Nassau district. Such a redistricting would permit educational options (and alternative notions of community control) to be worked out. The power to redistrict in that fashion rests with the same state legislature that has been struggling to restructure New York City's school districts, yet no thought of exercising that power has been voiced.

Many of the parents in those communities that seek to control the schools view education in much the same way as did Horace Mann a century ago, as "the great equalizer of the condition of men—the balance-wheel of the social machinery." They hope that a restructured school system will generate in their children the faith that success in school will be reflected in later successes, in their jobs and in their personal lives.[13] Yet there is little objective reason to believe that such faith will be rewarded, that the centuries of despair and distrust will be offset in the nation at large by reports of a beacon elementary school here, a handful of Harvard black *magnas* there; to arouse those hopes, without seriously preparing to fulfill them, is to perpetrate the cruelest (and even revolution-sustaining) of social hoaxes. "Our industrial troubles arise . . .

because a whole section of the people feels itself to be disinherited, to be living and working outside the pale of privilege and opportunity." That comment by R. H. Tawney, made 40 years ago with reference to England, applies equally well to the American condition. The existing inequalities of opportunity (in education as well as elsewhere in the larger community) and the social crises that these inequalities create—these, and not the lesser debate between community schools and educational parks, or some such, are the central matters to which all concerned, professionals *and* communities, need to address themselves.

NOTES AND REFERENCES

1. That assumption was reaffirmed a half-century later by Georgia Populist Tom Watson. "Close no entrance to the poorest, the weakest, the humblest. Say to ambition everywhere, 'the field is clear, the contest fair; come, and win your share if you can.'"
2. Charles Hamilton offers an advocate's appraisal of the decline of the professional in "Race and Education: A Search for Legitimacy," *Harvard Educational Review,* fall 1968.
3. Few of these dilemmas were in fact resolved by the district court decision, which upheld the busing of only black students as a "rational" distinction between those neighborhoods which were appropriate and those which were inappropriate for schools. The opinion seems unlikely to influence greatly future decisions concerning the issues; it is dubious constitutional law at best.
4. See Irving Kristol, "Decentralization for What?" in *The Public Interest,* spring 1968.
5. 'Community' may be defined in terms of identifiable groups within particular area (parents, residents, activists, etc.) It also, and more typically, has a geographical connotation (neighborhood, city, state, nation, etc.) Each of *these* communities has a stake in the outcomes of public education, and therefore feels that it should also have a say in the 'control' of that education.
6. David Rogers, *110 Livingston Street: Politics and Bureaucracy in the New York City School System.* New York: Random House, 1968.
7. The Coleman Report data do not appear to support this reading. Coleman found that students in integrated schools, while having a lower estimate of their relative capabilities than students in segregated schools, were less convinced that fate and not personal ability controlled their destinies. They were, in short, able to perceive their chances more realistically—and, as Thomas Pettigrew has suggested, able to work to improve their own self-assessments—than were students in segregated schools.
8. See Glazer and Moynihan, *Beyond the Melting Pot* (1963), which describes similar political forays by other New York City minority groups.
9. Daniel Moynihan, *Maximum Feasible Misunderstanding: Community Action in the War on Poverty* (1969).
10. Even programs for keeping the school open past 3:00 p.m. for special courses taught by professionals for children and their parents are described as 'community school' programs.
11. "Reconnection for Learning," popularly known as the Bundy Report,

specifies some of these compromises. The report talks about the need to "vest educational authority in communities throughout the city" yet its implementing plan gives the mayor power to select five of eleven members of the community school board, and more importantly gives him final fiscal control over the schools; the plan also limits the freedom of local boards by requiring them to conform to state teacher certification and curriculum standards.

12. I am not insisting upon any measure of effectiveness except a negative one; schools are not effective if they serve solely to politicize communities, and a measurement of schools' success in political terms is not a complete one.

13. This faith in the efficacy of education is apparently shared by the children of the ghetto. A survey of juveniles arrested in the 1967 Detroit riots asserted that children believed that education—more so than nonviolent resistance, violent action, legislation, and persuasion and example—enables Negroes to "get their rights"; that "the only way to get what you want" is to "get a good education," not to fight for it, to take it, to get a good job, or "you can't (get what you want)." R. Komisaruk and C. Pearson, "Children of the Detroit Riots," *Journal of Urban Law,* summer 1967.

GLENN SMITH

Schools and the American Dilemma over Social Class

Several of the preceding articles indicate schools exist partly to ensure perpetuation of the status quo. Do schools maintain a privileged position for the affluent, upper levels of society? If so, how do they do so while advocating equality? What techniques do schools employ?

All societies have some degree of social differentiation, but the existence of social stratification presents a peculiar dilemma for Americans. On the one hand, it is a deeply ingrained and easily recognized phenomenon which seems operationally "right," but on the other it contradicts a cherished tradition and self-image of egalitarianism. Does not our Declaration of Independence assert the equality of all men? Have not oppressed people from many "corrupt" countries flocked here to the bastion of freedom and opportunity? Have we not fought wars to abolish slavery, make the world safe for democracy and stop totalitarian aggression? And have not European observers since Alexis de Tocqueville (1832), told us that people in America "in their social state" exhibit "a greater equality in point of fortune and intellect . . . than in any country of the world, or in any age of which history has preserved the remembrance?"[1]

The reconciliation of these mutually contradictory traditions is accomplished in America by a form of Orwellian "doublethink"—holding simultaneously two opinions which cancel each other out, knowing them to be contradictory, yet believing in both of them. This involves forgetting whatever it is necessary to forget, then drawing it back into memory again at the moment when it is needed, and then promptly forgetting it again, all the while achieving the supreme subtlety of applying the same process to the process itself.

The basic premise on which social doublethink rests is that in America, unlike other countries, everyone begins with an equal chance but that differing abilities and effort produce a hierarchy of rewards. The logical inference from this starting point is that those who enjoy enviable social positions earned them in a fair contest and are therefore entitled to the accompanying benefits. Conversely, anyone who does not occupy the stratum he would like in the social structure has only himself to blame. It is extremely important that most people accept this as fundamental truth, for if most Americans believed their place in the social hierarchy derived primarily from accident of birth, the privileged would be uneasy, and the dispossessed angry. Yet it is equally necessary that it *not* be true, i.e., if birthright did not play an important part, parents in the upper reaches of society would be highly distraught, for many of their children would be displaced by those from below. As Warner and others note: "Most American parents believe that the best measure of their success in this life, and a good indication of their deserts in the future life, are to be found in the rise or fall of their children in the social scale."[2] To leave such an important dimension of life to genetic roulette would be unthinkable, so mechanisms must be found to guarantee the social status quo while appearing to ensure equal opportunity. We are therefore under a deep but largely unconscious compulsion to hold tenaciously to opposite poles of a contradiction.

WHERE DO SCHOOLS FIT?

There are many social institutions and mechanisms which help guarantee social stratification, but the single most effective tool of the twentieth century for keeping the social order intact while appearing to offer equal opportunity is the educational system. School "is primarily a skirmishing ground over which our children fight the preliminary rounds of the class battle in which some of them will take more serious part when they grow up," say David Frost and Anthony Jay of British schools.[3] In America, we regard schools as not merely a skirmishing ground, but the battlefield itself. We acknowledge this in our strident propaganda against dropping out of school. The amount of schooling one has, we constantly tell our flagging pupils, is an important determinant of adult social class level. A more accurate statement, however, would be that one's social class background determines in large measure how much and what kind of schooling he will receive, for the battle is rigged from the start and most of the winners are predetermined.

HOW SCHOOLS MAINTAIN THE SOCIAL STATUS QUO

The reader should keep in mind during the following discussion that a complex interweave of factors operates in schools to guarantee that the academically brilliant sheep will be separated from their brothers, the academically dull goats, along socially acceptable lines. To isolate one factor from the others does violence to the subtlety of the system, but such separation is necessary for analytical purposes.

Marks, testing, and guidance counselors

Any analysis of schools must include, and probably should begin with, an understanding of the system of rewards and punishments known as marks. These are now so basic to the institutions comprising our educational system that few teachers, administrators, parents, or for that matter pupils can really imagine a school without them. But it has not always been this way, and knowledge of the history of when and how the schools changed is helpful in understanding what marks do today.

Until the last quarter of the nineteenth century, elementary schools were not usually graded by level (first, second, third grade, etc.), and few schools of any type, including colleges, utilized an A, B, C, D, F mark or its equivalent. Neither marks nor graded primary classes were essential because most children of lower social class parents went to a "common" school only a short time—just long enough to learn some arithmetic and acquire basic literacy—before dropping out to go to work. Children whose parents had the money (i.e., upper class and

Table 1. Extent of school participation, 1870–1970

	Percentage of 17-year-olds graduating from high school	Percentage of 18–21-year-olds in higher education
1870	2.0	1.68
1880	2.5	2.72
1890	3.5	3.04
1900	6.4	4.01
1910	8.8	5.12
1920	16.8	8.09
1930	29.0	12.42
1940	50.8	15.68
1950	59.0	29.88
1960	65.1	34.86
1970 (proj.)	80.7	40.00

SOURCE: U.S. Bureau of the Census, *Historical Statistics of the United States: Colonial Times to 1957* (Washington, D.C.: Government Printing Office, 1965), p. A-7; *Statistical Abstract of the United States, 1969.* 90th ed. (Washington, D.C.: Government Printing Office, 1969), pp. 121–124.

many middle class parents) went on to academies—privately supported secondary schools—and often on to college. These latter two groups, however, were quite small (2.0 percent and 1.68 percent, respectively, of the people of high school and college ages in 1870); and any child who could afford to spend the required number of years in school and who behaved himself reasonably well could expect to graduate. For the person who could not afford much schooling, but who wished to better himself socially, there remained only to grasp one of the theoretically numerous possibilities for making money in an age of early industrial development and individual enterprise.

As the country industrialized after the Civil War, these conditions changed. Jobs which children had held either disappeared or were taken by adults. Women, who had always stayed home, entered the labor force. The expansive possibilities associated with an open frontier diminished as the free land disappeared. Life became more specialized, complex, interdependent, and anonymous.

During the same time, schooling changed in important ways, too. An ever-growing proportion of the population spent longer periods of time in schools: tax-supported high schools replaced the private academies; elementary schools became sequentially structured with one level following another; and all types of schools turned increasingly to a "scientific" marking system, most commonly A, B, C, D, F. In short, the school became the universal church of a secular society in which heaven was replaced by material affluence and the Lamb's Book of Life by permanent record cards, which reflected the level of purgatory to which each sinner was assigned.

The adoption of a marking system per se was probably less important than was the "standardized" testing base on which it rested, for while marks indicated the degree of success or failure, they did not assign responsibility. In a society where merit alone was supposed to be the basis for success and rewards, it was very important that as few people as possible leave school blaming their failure on the whims of teachers. This was especially so since teachers were themselves overwhelmingly from one social class (lower-middle) in a school system which purported to serve all social classes equally. While it would be naive to suggest that ability testing grew up as a direct response to the unconscious desire to maintain social inequality, almost certainly the scientific testing movement would not have been so popular in schools had it not performed this function. Schools seized upon standardized testing because it appeared both objective and scientific—merely describing the unavoidable nature of reality—and at the same time ensured that the "better" classes would remain in control. It met the doublethink test.

The testing movement, on which so much that is important in American schools rests, started in France around the turn of the century. Alfred Binet, at the request of the French government, developed an instrument for predicting which children were most likely to fail in school. To do this, he made two basic assumptions: 1) that success and failure in life are indicated by one's relative position in the social structure; 2) that if one asks children questions based upon knowledge which is both common and basic to people who are "successful," those who know the most right answers at the youngest age are most likely to succeed, and conversely the more years a person spends acquiring this "basic" information, the less likely he is to be successful. Binet expressed his prediction of success, or mark of "intelligence," as an IQ (intelligence quotient) score, the distribution of which in any "normal" population he assumed would approximate a bell-shaped curve.

A group of psychologists at Stanford University modified Binet's work for American use, and the resulting Stanford-Binet intelligence test has been widely employed in our schools since the end of World War I. Virtually all children have taken this or a similar test very early in their school careers, and the results have been the basis for assigning

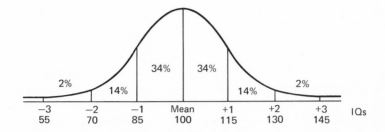

Figure 1. Normal distribution curve with standard deviations and WISC IQ's.

marks—"intelligent" children, if they work to capacity, should receive high marks; "dull" children, even if working to capacity, should not receive very many top marks. And other things follow from a child's marks: the kind of work given in school, teacher expectations for the child and, indirectly, the child's expectations for himself, and the important process of "guidance." The impact of all this on the child's later social class level deserves further treatment, but first a closer look at the nature of the tests themselves is in order.

It is readily apparent from the assumptions Binet made, and which have been implicit in virtually all intelligence or ability tests since, that the very concept "intelligence" is social-class loaded. In other words, the tests predict future success and failure in terms of present success and failure as measured against upper and upper-middle class norms. The Stanford-Binet itself furnishes an excellent example of how these tests discriminate along social class lines. One part of the test, which can be given to children as young as two or three years old, is a series of eighteen pictures of "common" objects which the tester holds up one at a time and asks the child to identify. All are items which all children are supposed to have had an equal chance to know. One of the eighteen is a cream pitcher of the sort which is used to pour milk or cream into coffee or tea at the table. The child receives credit for a correct answer if he says either "creamer," "cream pitcher," or "ewer." Any other response, no matter how imaginative, is wrong. Obviously a child who grows up in a home where a cream pitcher is used and referred to by one of these three names (i.e., an upper class or upper-middle class home) stands a much better chance of being rated a good success prospect than a child whose family pours milk into the coffee out of a carton (i.e., a working-class family).

Although the Stanford-Binet has been replaced by the Wechsler Intelligence Scale for Children (WISC) as the most widely-used sorting device in schools, it is still used extensively for young children. And none of the replacements of the Stanford-Binet is substantially less social-class loaded. Even Joseph L. French's Pictoral Test of Intelligence, published in 1964 and generally conceded to be a very reliable test, is so biased that children of professionally and technically employed parents score 25 percent higher than children of unskilled working class parents.[4] Even the most "pro-test" psychologists now generally concede that there is sufficient culture-loading in even the best of the widely used tests to account for a difference of 15 to 30 IQ points between the average scores of people in the highest social class level of American society and those in the lowest. While this may mean that no more than one-fifth to one-fourth of a person's "intelligence" is environmentally (as opposed to genetically) determined, it is enough to make all the difference in school and in later life. The difference between an IQ of 95 and one of 125 is the difference in becoming a policeman and a university or corporation president.

Although tests are the base upon which much of the social class differentiation takes place in schools, several other factors contribute refinements. Indeed, without these, the test results would be largely meaningless. Among them are tracking (ability grouping), teachers' attitudes and self-fulfilling prophecy.

Ability grouping. One of the most frequent uses to which the results of standardized tests are put is to divide a school population into groups according to test results. The theory behind this practice is very attractive. It removes the potential embarrassment felt by "dull" children who often do not know the right answers when in the presence of "bright" children who do know. Additionally, the "dulls" do not hold up the "brights" by constantly asking for explanations which the faster children do not need. Such separation is what has almost always been implied in America when educators talked about "providing for individual differences." Taken at face value, ability grouping appears to be a humane practice aimed solely at helping children learn better; however, it performs other tasks which are far more important and less benign. In other words it possesses the qualities required of any credible mythology, that of combining obvious and attractive truth with subtle falsehood.

The real function of "ability" grouping is to separate children according to social class background without appearing to do so. In this way schools which theoretically treat everyone equally serve the children of different social classes in different ways.

A further note of explanation is perhaps in order for those not intimately familiar with the actual operations of schools. If grouping rested on test results alone, social discrimination would be successfully achieved generally, but there would be glaring individual exceptions because tests, like mortuary tables, predict for groups, not individuals. For this reason school people enter a teacher-administrator "judgment" factor for group placement purposes. This permits a quiet adjustment in case a child's score seems seriously out of line with his background and behavior patterns. Thus, if the daughter of a physician makes a low score and is put into a lower social class group, her parents will often complain and the principal will usually concur that she would really be happier and do better work if she were "with her friends." Or if the son of one of the local "river rats" should happen to score high on the test, he would stand a good chance of being moved to one of the lower groups because "he is disruptive in class, runs with a rough crowd, and has a bad attitude." But if the child of lower class parents scores well and shows that he is eager to assimilate the values, attitudes, and associational patterns for those above him in the social scale—i.e., if he is *upward mobile*—he will likely stay in one of the higher "ability" groups. In this way, the school keeps the social stratification intact, but selects a minority for upward mobility. One must keep in mind that social class stratification does not imply the kind of rigidity characteristic of *caste* societies, those in which almost no social movement is possible. The chance for upward mobility acts as a safety valve, attracting the support and talents of the most ambitious and aggressive people in society.

Self-fulfilling prophecy. The practice of ability grouping has been criticized by some educational philosophers and sociologists since its inception in the 1920s. But only recently have researchers discovered that children tend to perform according to teachers' expectations and that these are significantly influenced by the ability group into which children have been placed. Robert Rosenthal and others in several experiments have found that not only is school performance affected by teacher expectation but also that IQ scores change significantly and that the changes appear to be cumulative. If this is true during the short period of six to eight months that the experiments occupied, consider how important twelve years of teacher expectations will be in a child's life.

Neighborhood schools

Another aspect of the American school system which reinforces inequality is the time-honored concept of the neighborhood school. This is the practice of requiring a child to go to a school in his own immediate community, a widely followed practice defended on the basis that it is both productive of community spirit and beneficial to the child. In actual fact, this practice means that children in cities tend to go to school only with other children of their own social class since housing patterns and school subdistrict boundaries tend to follow social class lines. The blackboard jungle and ghetto schools which have become commonplace in American cities are one result of this practice. When one realizes that working class schools are controlled by upper-middle class boards of education—boards of education consist overwhelmingly of physicians, lawyers, dentists, and industrialists—and are operated by upward-mobile lower-middle class teachers, the incidence of school vandalism, truancy, and dropout in these schools is hardly surprising. Money is unequally distributed among schools in such a system with the general result that middle class schools receive the newest buildings, equipment, and text material, and the most extensively prepared teachers.

The outcome of the American school system, seen in social class terms, is a major reinforcement of the class system. Children of working class parents enter school at a disadvantage, a disadvantage which is reinforced throughout their school careers. In the 1960s one-fourth of American fourth, fifth, and sixth graders received Ds or Fs, and 50 percent more received Cs. As psychiatrist William Glasser points out, a C to most people is less than a satisfactory grade and is cause for internalizing a feeling of failure.[5] A disproportionate share of low marks goes to working class children, while middle class children receive the bulk of the As and Bs. A typical Midwestern city in the mid-1960s reported that 69 percent of the fourth graders in an upper-middle class neighborhood school received As and Bs while only 6 percent in a lower-working class school received those marks. By the time the students have reached college age, the school system has done its social class selection very effectively. In 1965, approximately 85 percent of children

Table 2.

Percentage of students from each social class who entered college in 1965.

	Male	Female
upper and upper-middle	90	80
lower-middle	62	45
upper-working	35	24
lower-working	8	4

SOURCE: Robert J. Havighurst and Bernice L. Neugarten, *Society and Education,* 3rd ed. (Boston: Allyn and Bacon, Inc., 1967), p. 98.

from upper and upper-middle class homes entered higher education, whereas only 6 percent of those from lower-working class families began a collegiate career.

Nor is this the end of selection. The higher a student's social class background, the more likely he is to attend an expensive, prestigious Ivy League or liberal arts college or major state university. The lower a student's social class origins, the greater the likelihood he will attend a relatively low-prestige state college or municipal university.[6] Furthermore, social scientists have repeatedly found that the higher one's socioeconomic status the more likely he is to finish any kind of college once he begins. The old process of teacher expectations, self-concept, and parental expectations combines with the high cost of tuition to "cool out" the lower class children in higher education. The entire process is carried out, in the words of Christopher Jencks, "in a low-key way which gives the student at least the illusion of making his own choices."[7] Were this not the case, he goes on, "the rejects would feel that their ambitions had been blocked out by a particular identifiable group, namely the academicians, who judge them inadequate and they might mobilize politically to alter the system."[8]

This, then, is the hidden dimension of the official mythology of the American school system. The belief that it is equally open to all, that every child has a chance to go as high and as far as his native talents will permit is as false as it is popular. It is institutionalized doublethink on a supremely effective scale. The unpalatable truth is that American schools are no more egalitarian than those of the Scandinavian countries, Britain, or the USSR. They merely appear to be.[9]

The problem of doublethink in American education cannot be solved simply by damning standardized testing, for the test makers have devised the kinds of instruments which schools have requested. Nor does a blanket condemnation of the school system achieve anything, since we have the kinds of schools that the dominant forces in our social order have wanted. The question for teachers—indeed for all Americans—is whether we can afford the luxury of a social class system based upon wide disparity in wealth, prestige, power, and influence—whether a social class system based upon scarcity can successfully be maintained in a society characterized by over-abundance. Put differently, does a class system appropriate to an industrializing society, with its emphasis on differentiated status, pay, and styles according to one's job fit a post-industrial society which is automating most jobs into oblivion? And finally, is a school system unconsciously designed to preserve such a social class system desirable? At the very least, teachers and parents must decide whether it makes any sense to try to force all children to stay for twelve years or longer in a school system designed to eliminate most of them at the end of half that time.

The real question is whether this society can or should continue unaltered. The problem is as deep as the roots of Western civilization. Whatever the answer, the time is past when those connected with schools can permit themselves the easy response of unconsciously settling on the side of blind conservatism. Teachers must consciously face up to the doublethink demands made upon them by their society, or be unwitting tools of the vested interests of the past.

NOTES

1. Alexis de Tocqueville, *Democracy in America.* Edited and abridged by Richard D. Heffner (New York: Mentor Books, 1956), p. 54.

2. W. Lloyd Warner, *et al., Who Shall Be Educated? The Challenge of Unequal Opportunities* (New York: Harper & Row, Publishers, 1944), p. 49.

3. David Frost and Anthony Jay, *The English* (New York: Avon Books, 1968), p. 33.

4. Joseph L. French, *Pictoral Test of Intelligence Manual* (Boston: Houghton Mifflin Company, 1964), p. 16.

5. William Glasser, *Schools Without Failure* (New York: Harper & Row, Publishers, 1961).

6. Seventy-five percent of students in Ivy League schools are from upper and upper-middle class backgrounds, and only 5 percent are from working class homes; at typical state colleges, 20 percent of the students are from the top two classes and 30 percent from working class homes. Robert J. Havighurst and Bernice L. Neugarten, *Society and Education,* 3rd ed. (Boston: Allyn & Bacon, Inc., 1967), p. 107.

7. For every 100 fifth graders in 1959–60, 97 entered the ninth grade, 85 the eleventh, and 72 graduated from high school in 1967. Forty of these entered

college, and twenty will receive degrees in 1971. Of the twenty, more than eight will be upper or upper-middle class, about six will be lower-middle class, about five will be upper-working class, and less than one will be from lower-working class parents.

8. Christopher Jencks, "Social Stratification and Higher Education," *Harvard Educational Review*, vol. 38, no. 2 (Spring 1968), pp. 284–285.

9. See, for example, Robert J. Havighurst, "Education, Social Mobility, and Social Change in Four Societies," *International Review of Education*, vol. 4 (1958), pp. 167–183.

GERALD E. LEVY
Acute Teachers

In view of Glenn Smith's charges that schools are operated in such a way that people from the groups at the bottom of the social heap tend to stay there, one must ask: What happens to the many young, idealistic, well intentioned teachers who are hired each year? Why have they not wrought a quiet revolution? This essay by sociologist Gerald Levy describes some teachers hired by "Midway School"—a typical ghetto school. In case the reader supposes that the other half of Midway's teaching force—those not described below—are more effective, the author speaks in even more discouraging terms of them.

About half of Midway's staff are acute teachers, most of whom are products of an emergency summer program of college-level courses designed to alleviate the acute shortage of teachers in ghetto schools. Open to anyone with a college degree, the emergency program is paid for by the city and guarantees the untrained recruit a job in the fall. In exchange, the acute recruit has to sign a statement pledging to teach for a year.

The "open recruitment" of teachers attracts a mixed bag of applicants whose motives, interests, and ages are determined by a variety of factors not necessarily directly related to teaching.

Among the recruits who finally received positions at Midway, ten can be described as wishing to pursue a teaching career. Eight of them

From *Ghetto School* by Gerald E. Levy, Copyright © 1970 by Western Publishing Company, Inc., reprinted by permission of The Bobbs-Merrill Company, Inc.

are women who have just graduated from college. Two are mothers in their forties whose children have grown up and who wish to begin or return to a teaching career. Some of these more career-minded teachers actually want to teach in a ghetto school.

The rest of the acute teachers are primarily motivated by their desire not to be drafted. They enrolled in the emergency summer program because it offered them the opportunity to avoid the war in Vietnam. Several afternoon sessions of the training program were devoted entirely to convincing the 1000 or more draft-age men that their draft deferments would be forthcoming upon completion of their training and assignment to a school.

The vast majority of acute teachers are just out of college, graduate schools, and previous jobs which did not offer them protection from the war. Thus, young aspiring lawyers, accountants, businessmen, and graduate students in psychology, sociology, political science, and history comprise a major block of teachers at Midway. After being in the school for a short time, these teachers come to feel that they are doing a form of alternate service not too different from their fantasies about Vietnam. They often joke about the advantages and disadvantages of the two alternatives. In view of their experience with the children, the war imagery can take on a reality which an outsider could not imagine to be appropriate to a school. After particularly bad days in the classroom, these acute teachers congregate and compare their difficulties with the children. The teacher having the most difficulty with his class is soothed with the comment, "At least it's not as bad as Vietnam."

In spite of their questionable motives for coming to Midway and the forced or tentative nature of their commitment, many acute teachers would like to do a good job. In their own and others' eyes, they would like to be successful. Many want good references for future jobs. Almost all would like to feel that they were earning their pay.

THE AMELIORATIVE IMPULSE

Acute teachers initially express no public disdain for Black or Puerto Rican children. Indeed, many acute teachers pride themselves on their liberal and progressive politics, their opposition to the war in Vietnam, and their support of the War on Poverty and other ameliorative programs. Some of the graduate students see themselves as budding college professors, intellectuals, and social critics. A few have read Paul Goodman and would like to change the school system. Several have been active in the civil rights movement and would like to continue their civil rights activities as teachers. A few have had jobs in welfare, social work, and poverty programs. These latter are less optimistic about achieving their political goals in the school.

When the acute teachers arrive at Midway, their basic sympathies are with the children and the parents. They would like to "reach out to" or "make it" with the children whom they view as "disadvantaged" individuals to be "helped" through "sensitive and creative teaching." But these humanistic intentions and sympathies are not, in most instances, based on personal experience with ghetto inhabitants. Acute teachers have learned about the ghetto from newspapers, magazines, TV, movies, and books. Their sympathies have been cultivated in suburbs and universities which are totally divorced from the objects of the sympathy. They assume they can successfully apply their suburban and academic morality to Midway School.

THE RHETORIC OF ORIENTATION

Before being assigned to a school, these good-intentioned acute teachers are given a brief orientation in the district office by the district superintendent:

> We have called this meeting to accomplish three goals. We would like to tell you what our district is like. We would like to assign you to a school which is closest to your home. And we want to personally welcome you to the district. District 7 has eighteen elementary schools, four junior high schools and two high schools. It encompasses the Rogers Park and Randolph Park areas. In this district we have a very active community and school board which is interested in only one thing—good schools and good teachers. We have in District 7 the support of the community. Now the principals in District 7 do not think that they are God's answer to education. They are down to earth, accessible, and want to do everything in their power to help you new teachers to have a satisfying and successful experience.
>
> Now we do have problems in our schools. However you will be happy to teach in this district. You will not be afraid to come to any school in this district. There has not been any picketing. We are happy that the community is behind us. So now that we have cleared up any misconceptions you might have about the district, we can turn to more technical matters.
>
> First of all, I have to tell you something that may disturb many of

you. Those of you who are from the high school part of the emergency summer training program, I have to tell you that you will be teaching elementary school. There are just no vacancies in the secondary schools and we only have vacancies in the elementary schools. Now if you can get some secondary school outside the district to request you I will release you. But if for any other reason you wish to change to another district I will not release you. Now I know that many of our high school people who are young men will take the assignment be- cause of the draft. I will not go further into this.

The superintendent conveys to the acute teachers that problems which occur in the district are not occurring, and reminds them of the conse- quences of refusing the assignment.

Upon being assigned to Midway, acute teachers are informed by chronic teachers that almost everything they were told by Superin- tendent Stratton and his assistant Golden is the opposite of what actually exists in the school. Chronic teachers say that "the school is in a state of complete chaos," that "Dobson doesn't do anything but sit in his office," that "all Morton and Ryley do is tell the teachers to meet dead- lines and send them notes when they don't," and that "Mrs. Jackson wants to fire all of the white Jewish teachers" and "take over the school":

> The administration will attempt to hide and gloss over a lot of prob- lems in the school, but you will find out soon enough how difficult the children will be and what you will have to do to survive.

Interspersed between these conversations with chronic teachers are formal orientation conferences with the administration:

> *Morton:* Now I'm just going to say a few important things until the principal comes in. School will be on three different sessions because the new wing is not completed. Now one of the most important things in getting started is the establishment of routines for the children and for yourself. Now you're going to have problem children—children who will give you trouble. The minute you have a problem you can't expect us to immediately do something about it. But you can keep a file on him, an anecdotal record, and if patterns emerge, we'll even- tually take care of it. Now of course the instructors in the universities say "be creative with the children," "work with them," "love them." But this cannot be accomplished without routines and we expect you to concentrate on this aspect.

(Dobson is introduced)

Dobson: You constitute almost half of our present staff and we have the job of making you into teachers. It takes anywhere from three to five years to become a teacher. Some make it in less. Your first year of teaching will be the most difficult job you will have in your life. Plan books are to be submitted every two weeks. Sometimes they will have comments on them. Sometimes they will have few or none. We will read them carefully or casually, depending on the individual involved or the situation. The purpose of the plan book is to see that you have a plan and cover the curriculum so that you know what you are doing. The children will do everything in their power to confuse you, take advantage of you, obstruct your teaching until you are firm with them—until you let them know that you know what you are doing. We have one guidance counselor and referral is made to her through the supervisors. But remember you are responsible for classroom discipline. The more you have to call a supervisor for help, the less efficient you are in classroom control. You are to use anything and everything to maintain classroom control except physical violence. First of all, it's against the law. Also, parents are sensitive to any physical violence and children will sometimes tell their parents. No matter what a parent tells you, even if she says, "Give him a good beating," never lay a hand on a child in anger because there can be repercussions. It's all right to put your arm around a child if you have established rapport with him or if it is an appropriate situation for touching him— putting your arm around him in a friendly way.

Even stronger is the chronic teacher's stress on the overriding necessity for control.

A lot of new teachers, well, they want to be very idealistic—want to be a buddy to the kids—have a nice relaxed atmosphere in the classroom. Well, if you do that the kids will destroy you. You've got to be firm at the beginning, keep them busy, organize the routines. Don't take any nonsense. Then, after a while you can accomplish something and let up later. But if you start off on the wrong track, it will take you maybe a whole year to control the class. The first few weeks, if you accomplish nothing but control, you are doing a job.

Thus, the acute teacher is advised that his inability to control the children will be taken as evidence of his inadequacy as a teacher. The teacher who loses control becomes dependent on other teachers and administrators to regain it. But other teachers resent having to "stop whatever they are doing" to help a teacher "break up a fight," "remove a child from a classroom," "take a disruptive child to the office," or "quiet down a class." The teacher who relies heavily on other teachers and administrators for the solution of his problems with children gets a reputation for incompetence. He is thought to be "not doing a job." All his humanitarian dreams, liberal ideas, and sympathetic inclinations are redefined as the basis of failure. His commitment to becoming competent, to being self-sufficient in his work, to working for his pay, and to his self-image as a white-collar professional is threatened by the prospect that those teaching methods demanded of him will be inconsistent with his personal morality.

The practical education of the acute teacher begins when he observes at first hand how children are treated at Midway. He sees them being marched around the hallways. In a *controlled* classroom, they sit in their seats with their hands folded, go to the blackboard, clean up the floor, get their coats, put them away, clean the erasers, sharpen pencils, line up straight, two by two. The typical teacher gives commands in a stentorian voice. Often he shouts them. The volume of the commands increases in relation to the degree that they are not being followed. When commands and shouts do not work, he uses the hand or the stick. He "knocks heads." To the acute teacher it looks like what he had imagined boot camp might be like.

The military techniques and the methods of violence that he observes conflict with the moral codes of his own academic and suburban past. He views them as ethically and aesthetically repugnant. The acute teacher finds himself in the position of being expected to participate in activities for which he would immediately condemn himself as well as others. Nevertheless he must face the practical problem of teaching the children. The children severely test his ability to hold to his previous values.

THE EFFORT TO BARGAIN WITH THE CHILDREN

In spite of the warning and example of administrators and chronic teachers, an acute teacher is likely to attempt a soft line with the children. He may greet his class informally, not demand that they keep a perfectly straight line to the classroom, and not try immediately to establish rigid routines. He allows the children drinks of water and trips to the bathroom. He does not immediately clamp down when the children attempt to talk to each other, leave their seats, or leave the classroom. He may even look the other way when he observes children eating in class. He initiates a policy in keeping with his liberal ideology that enables him to sustain his feelings of moral superiority over the chronic teachers.

He may assume that if given a certain amount of leeway, the children will recognize his partiality toward them. He hopes that the children will reciprocate by appreciating his humanitarian efforts. The teacher's easy-going approach is an indirect plea to the children for exemption from the battle over control.

THE ACUTE TEACHER IS DESTROYED

The children do not take up the bargain on his terms. Seeing that the teacher is not concerned with a straight line, the children dispense with the line. If he fails to clamp down on talking, eating, and moving around, the children talk, eat, move, and leave the classroom as much as possible. Children see the liberal policy not as an invitation to participate in a well-mannered civilized classroom, but as an opportunity to realize objectives of their own. The acute teacher is at first not aware that the children may have their own objectives.

Still the acute teacher's liberalism is conditional on the children's empathy toward his problem. He expects the children to be as sensitive to his problem as he feels he is to their problem. He reacts angrily to their lack of appreciation and unwillingness to uphold their end of the bargain. He feels personally betrayed and begins to shout at the children, demanding that they keep quiet, stay in their seats, and stop eating. The demands are ineffective, for he had granted these freedoms previously. So the teacher must begin to threaten. He threatens to send a child to the principal's office, write a letter home to his mother, or have him suspended. He may chase a child around the room, pound his fist on the table or threaten to hit him. With each betrayal of the teacher's sense of decency and fairness, he depends more and more on the very "indecent" techniques he previously condemned.

But the shouting and threatening fail to pacify the children. For they are cognizant of the teacher's inexperience. They are furthermore aware that his permissive policy has been an experiment. The children distinguish between acute and chronic teachers' use of techniques. The shouts and threats are not part of a disciplinary plan but merely an emotional response to the situation. Thus, the children regard attempts at control as a loss of control. They experience the loss of control as a higher form of victory than the freedom to eat, talk, or move around.

The more the teacher screams at the children, pounds his fist on the table, and chases them around the room, the greater their delight in the victory.

The children are delighted because they are invulnerable. The teacher is making all sorts of threats he has no intention of carrying out. They are extremely sensitive to the discrepancy between threats and action. The discrepancy is established by calling a series of bluffs. The rebel leader tests the teacher to see how far he can go without being punished. If the teacher backs down the rebel leader ups the ante. The called bluff and the upped ante define for the less courageous children the level on which they can safely pursue their disobedience. If the rebel leader screams at the teacher and gets away with it, the other children feel they can talk to each other without consequence. If he runs around the room, they get out of their seats and walk around. If he starts a fight, they run around the room. Soon all the children, even those who are usually obedient, start leaving their seats, getting drinks, talking, screaming, fighting, eating—anything that is at least one degree less extreme than the rebel leader's activity.

Finally, all commands are useless. The teacher gives orders knowing they are not going to be obeyed. The children know that he acknowledges his impotence. Each escalation in shouting, stamping, and pounding is seen by the children as a further admission of impotence. It takes ever more extreme measures to get a response from them because they immediately become accustomed to the current level of escalation as the norm. The more the teacher escalates, the more he establishes his impotence.

The teacher's awareness of his impotence finally precipitates a desperate act. After shouting at the children with no apparent results or just staring at them for a few minutes, he suddenly grabs a child and makes an example of him in front of the class by dragging him across the room, twisting his arm, grabbing him on the back of the neck, or hitting him on the shoulder or face. He may even drag him out of the room to an administrator's office and deposit him there.

Control in the classrooms of some acute teachers breaks down to the point where the teacher feels like a cop in a ghetto riot. Fights break out. Books, spitballs, thumbtacks, paper airplanes, paper clips, food, and chairs fly across the room. Occasionally, children consciously caricature a riot. They stage elaborate fights, organize group chanting, and sing dirty songs for the teachers' benefit. Regardless of the intensity of the disruption, the children never lose sight of the teacher's response. Their delight in their activity is directly proportional to his desperation.

In the process of losing control, frenzied teachers lose all perspective. Their faces get red and puffed. Their clothing is rumpled and covered with chalk dust. At times, classes and teachers become completely hysterical. In the midst of the hysteria, a teacher may beg the children for a few minutes of peace. Another may try a number of things in rapid succession, hoping that one of them will work. First he screams at the children. Then he makes a joke. Then he appeals to their guilt. Then he begs again. Some are driven to tears. Finally he makes an example of someone. The more hysterical the teacher becomes the more desperately random his behavior.

The children's energy and staying power is limitless. With each hysterical outburst the children appear more confident in their disobedience and intent on their rebellion. Very rapidly the acute teacher is physically and emotionally exhausted.

The acute teacher responds to his loss of control with feelings of personal inadequacy and unworthiness. Among men, these feelings border on anxiety about their masculinity. They begin to compare themselves unfavorably to the chronic male teachers who strut around the school. Among certain teachers the initial experience with the children is destructive to the point where previous successes, financial, academic, occupational, and erotic, temporarily lose their salience. They talk about their inability to sleep nights worrying about what the children are going to do to them the following day. Their experience in Midway School causes deep personal fear, even terror.

The sense of being destroyed is accompanied by an awareness that they are reneging on their intentions to be human with the children and their desire to be a respectable professional. The anger felt toward the children for not allowing them to live out their liberal ideas and be a good teacher is complicated by an awareness of using "chronic techniques." At different points for different teachers a sharp battle line is eventually drawn between themselves and the children.

For the teacher, the crucial issue is then defined as who is going to be destroyed. One put it tightly, "It's them or us." Reluctantly, the teacher then must admit that he is beginning to brutalize the children. If brutalization of the children (and himself) is seen as the only basis for survival and guilt is the only possible response to his brutalizing, the acute teacher is destroyed.

In actual fact twenty-one of the thirty-five acute teachers were "destroyed." In educational circles outside of Midway School the term "being destroyed" is defined as "failure" because the teacher becomes "personally involved" and is unable to control his class. The phrase "being destroyed" conforms to usage at Midway School where everyone knows personally many examples of teachers who were driven to the verge of madness before they began to give up the teaching methods which they hoped would be consistent with their ethical and moral standards. Under ordinary circumstances some of these teachers would have quit their jobs and left Midway. But as devastating as their experience is, Midway as a way of life is thought to be a better alternative than Vietnam. They wish to avoid Vietnam for the same ideological reasons that they hope to avoid the methods of the chronic teachers. Thus when their own teaching methods don't work, and they feel destroyed, the acute teachers react as if they had been sent to Vietnam and look for any means to survive.

CLOSING RANKS WITH THE CHRONIC TEACHERS

Previous to their initial encounter with the children, chronic teachers were objects of moral indignation for acute teachers. Initial observations of chronic teachers at work confirmed their preconceptions about the quality of teachers in ghetto schools. But now, contact with the children has made it difficult for acute teachers to sustain an unambivalently critical attitude toward those teachers whose advice and warnings about their relationships to the children have turned out to be so accurate.

Teachers who, a few days earlier, criticized and condemned the "immoral" activity of the chronic teachers, actively seek their advice. Desperate acute teachers buttonhole well-known chronic teachers in the teachers' lunchroom, the halls, and the general office, to seek information as to how they can gain control and prevent their own destruction. Chronic teachers are generous and explicit with their advice. They view the interest in their techniques as a further indication of their competence, and a vindication of their position toward the children.

Acute teachers seek the ear of other acute teachers who they hope will not moralize about their behavior with the children. To his relief the acute teacher discovers that many others are having similar problems. Whenever the opportunity arises, acute teachers congregate in the lunchroom, the office, the halls, and outside their classrooms to relieve each other of their burdens.

The mutual confessions often become contests. The object is to determine who is having the greatest difficulty with the children. Teachers claim that they have been more totally destroyed and have taken more drastic counter-measures than any other teacher. Through competitive confessions the acute teachers exempt each other from any moral accountability for their actions with the children. Add to this the advice-seeking from chronic teachers, and the acute teacher has taken the first hesitant steps toward a redefinition of his *modus operandi* in the school.

Once the acute teacher realizes the impracticality and self-destructive effects of his ethical standards, the emphasis of his activity rapidly shifts from attempting to maintain the standards to developing a method by which he can survive. Only when experience forces the acute teacher to loosen the moral inhibitions of his past can he hope to attain the "experience" necessary to becoming a "competent" teacher. Having learned that control is synonymous with education and now being willing to try anything to establish control, he has adopted the very moral psychology he would have needed to survive in Vietnam.

CHARLES R. KNIKER

The Search for Equal Educational Opportunities

Since the 1954 U. S. Supreme Court decision that racially separate schools are illegal, there have been numerous approaches to "desegregate" or "integrate" schools. The following article analyzes the major approaches so far employed to end racially different treatment by schools.

On a spring day in 1954, the United States Supreme Court decreed that a Negro, Linda Brown of Topeka, Kansas, had the right to attend a white school. In its decision, based on psychological evidence as well as legal precedents, the Court insisted that a dual school system was inherently unequal. Writing for the Court, Chief Justice Earl Warren called on the states to provide equal educational opportunity for all students, "with all deliberate speed."

Since 1954, numerous plans have been proposed to alleviate the sufferings in racially imbalanced school districts. The claims at times have been grandiose and the evaluation of the remedies' effectiveness confusing. This article surveys some of the more publicized programs. Each remedy's assumptions and goals are discussed first, followed by one or more examples. A tentative assessment of each program's success concludes the description.

Four types of remedies have been advocated:

1. compensatory education plans;
2. school desegregation strategies;
3. teacher education programs;
4. the community control option.

This essay concentrates on the first two types of remedies. Most government programs and civil rights organizations have focused their attention on the first two strategies.[1] The third option, teacher training, is described briefly because of its relatively small size and recent beginning. Examples of some community control programs are described in Part 4 of this text. More specific evaluation of many programs surveyed here can be found in Meyer Weinberg (eds.), *Desegregation Research: An Appraisal.*[2]

Although the four remedies are not given "equal time" (or space), it is important to ascertain some basic similarities and differences of the programs. The first three operate within current political structures. Only community control seeks extensive redistribution of power over school policies, most frequently from central school boards and administrators to local parent organizations. Compensatory education plans and school desegregation remedies are directly concerned with changing student attitudes and behavior. The former stresses changing student perceptions of himself; the latter concentrates on changes in school environment. Teacher preparation programs appear to be saying that changes in teacher selection and training may produce more dramatic changes in the school climate than programs that emphasize student changes.

We cannot forget that most programs mentioned here are still adolescents. To predict their outcome is as difficult and meaningless as forecasting how our young nephews and nieces will turn out. Yet, one phenomenon has proved strikingly consistent about these programs. Most efforts show students improve markedly during their first years, only to "tail off" as they leave the program. Psychologists label this tendency the Hawthorne Effect. Experimental subjects overreact to their chosen status, and their "ego trips" distort the realistic aid the program may have given them. Longitudinal studies are needed to learn whether many of these remedies really do contribute to the search for more equal educational opportunity.

COMPENSATORY EDUCATION

Compensatory education plans begin by assuming the causes of racial isolation are deep-seated in America, and that integration is not likely to occur in the immediate future. Reminiscent of Booker T. Washington of Tuskegee Institute, proponents of compensatory education urge that academically successful blacks who gain responsible jobs will break down neighborhood segregation patterns more rapidly than national or state fair-housing laws will. Therefore, these plans tolerate segregation patterns.

Second, the compensatory plans concentrate upon individual student skills. Typically, they single out the child who has problems in reading, speech, and vision. Increasing efforts are being made to identify social skills the disadvantaged children may lack, as well as attitudes that may hinder their progress in school. Whatever the skill involved, the essential task is to select individuals with problems and provide them with intensive remedial help.

Finally, as Sloan Wayland of Columbia University Teachers College has noted, compensatory remedies are permeated with a quantitative air. "Start the child in school earlier, keep him in more and more months of the year; expect him to learn more and more in wider and wider areas of his experience, under a teacher who has had more and more training, who is assisted by more and more specialists."[3]

Examples of Compensatory Education Plans

1. *Remedial programs* are the most common form of compensatory education. As *Racial Isolation in the Public Schools* notes, this strategy incorporates such factors as the reduction of the number of students per teacher, provision of extra help to students during and after

school, counseling, and use of special teaching materials designed to improve basic skills.[4] Ninety percent of the counties in the United States qualified for remedial funds when Congress passed the Elementary and Secondary Education Act of 1965.

One highly controversial example of remedial instruction is found in the More Effective Schools program sponsored by the United Federation of Teachers in New York City. MES called for drastic reductions in class size and a vigorous pre-school program. There were only to be fifteen pupils in pre-kindergarten rooms, twenty in kindergarten, fifteen in first grade, and no more than twenty-two in grades 3–6. In their contract with the city, the union pressed for numerous staff specialists to complement the teachers' staff. Each MES location, for example, was to have four or five assistant principals, and a community relations teacher was to be responsible for teacher-parent problems and to follow up on cases of absence by students.[5]

Numerous studies were done on MES students. Columnist Joseph Alsop became an ardent supporter of the program. The Center for Urban Education, a regional U. S. Office of Education research bureau, conducted several studies which did support the conclusion that a more positive attitude toward schooling was the prime outcome of the MES program. On the other hand, critics noted that some studies indicated virtually no academic gains by participating students who reached fourth grade, compared with other fourth-graders who had not participated in MES.[6]

Under the Elementary and Secondary Education Act of 1965, the federal government has spent a billion dollars a year for remedial programs. Recently the U. S. Office of Education published a report of such efforts during the 1967–1968 school year. The USOE found that wealthier school districts were receiving higher amounts per pupil than the poorer school districts. The report said of Title I's compensatory reading program: "Pupils taking part in compensatory reading programs were not progressing fast enough to allow them to catch up to non-participating pupils."[7]

2. Another avenue toward equal educational opportunity is the *cultural enrichment program*. Frequently found in the middle-class and affluent schools in the past, it has only recently been offered extensively to poor children. The pupils are taken to museums, theaters, other schools, and perhaps are entertained in their own school building by guest artists.

In 1956 the Higher Horizons program began in New York City,

incorporating many of the facets suggested above, plus training teachers to have more positive attitudes toward student performance. Initial studies of the program suggested a major breakthrough had been made. However, a study completed five years after Higher Horizons had begun found no significant differences in school performance and educational goals between students who had and those who had not attended Horizon schools.[8]

3. A third compensatory remedy plan is the *curricular-extracurricular* program. Some forms of this option focus on the student's self-image, and others seek to improve the parental attitude toward school. The central finding of the 1966 Coleman Report[9] supports this type of program. The study of 600,000 school children concluded that a student's self-esteem, built upon family and peer influence especially, had a strong correlation with success or failure in school.

Most typical of the curricular programs has been the black history movement. Some schools with large black populations have both required and elective black studies courses. Some have incorporated black studies in the social science area.[10] Another movement is instruction in the early grades in a language familiar to certain ethnic groups—American Indian and Puerto Rican children, for example.[11] Early evidence from studies done with Spanish-speaking children seems to indicate that beginning school in Spanish, their "home" language, enhances rather than retards school performance. The black history program is so new that it is nearly impossible to evaluate its impact.

One of the most extensive extracurricular programs beamed at parental involvement in school activities has been the Banneker Project in operation in St. Louis. The project started in 1957–1958 and by 1965–1966 involved twenty-three schools with black majority student populations. To build parental support of the schools, teachers made home visits and established programs and events at school sites. Like the Higher Horizons program, the students' initial reading scores indicated significant gains after the program was introduced. Evaluation of the program in 1966, however, suggested that the improvements were not permanent.[13]

More recently, parental involvement or extracurricular plans have attempted to employ parents in the schools, most commonly as teacher aides. In some cities, parents also serve on advisory boards. A program of this nature, now widely copied, was first tried in Tucson, Arizona. By having the parents in school to witness day-to-day routines and interact with teachers, it is hoped the parents can aid others in the community to build a more positive image of the school. In some cities, the teacher aides are assigned to Operation Headstart classes or classes made up of Headstart graduates. In Des Moines, Iowa, this plan is called Operation Follow Through.[14]

4. The last type of compensatory program is the *pre-school strategy*, which usually stresses verbal and social skills. Not unlike the remedial plans in most respects, it underscores the goal of building the student's self-esteem. Of course, its distinction is in its efforts toward preparing pre-schoolers to succeed once they begin in school.

The most prominent example of this program is Operation Head-start, first tried in Waukegan, Illinois. In some cities the program had to be administered through political channels, thus gaining some adverse publicity in its early stages. Under the motto, "Do Something Now," the program was expected to show immediate results. Studies done on the effectiveness of Headstart have not pleased some impatient observers. Generally, both critics and supporters note that disadvantaged children have gained verbal skills and appear near the national norms on school readiness tests for first grade.[15] The controversial Westinghouse study on "The Impact of Head Start" found, however, that the summer Headstart programs accomplished far too little to be worth the investment.[16] Most authorities conclude that the program appears to offer a great beginning, but it has not carried through sufficiently in later grades to hold gains made by students.

Conclusion

Compensatory plans, when used as a sole remedy to promote equal educational opportunity, seem ineffective. This is even more definite in areas of racial and socio-economic isolation. Dr. Thomas Pettigrew, professor of social psychology at Harvard University, summarized the position of many experts when he said, "All of the evidence we have available would strongly suggest that compensatory education in segregated both race and class wise situations, is in effect, wasted money."[17]

SCHOOL DESEGREGATION PLANS

Unlike compensatory education, school desegregation plans begin with the assumption that immediate efforts at racial mixing are essential for success in schooling. Advocates of this philosophy point to evidence in the *Racial Isolation* study and the Coleman Report for support. Some civil rights leaders have objected, since it implies blacks are less intelligent than whites and can only improve when mixed. In a provocative article, "Is Integration Necessary?" former CORE leader Floyd McKissick pointed out that blacks have never been in school systems they truly control, but if such a situation did exist, he felt academic advancements would compare with white student performance levels.[18]

Desegregation plans underscore group practices rather than individual programs. Virtually all remedies in this category are flooded with group terminology: moving this *class* of students, merging two *districts*, exchanging *groups* of grade levels.

Whereas compensatory plans concentrate on skills, this type of remedy usually implies that new facilities, improved curricula, and experimental media equipment will more likely encourage improvement in learning.

While the compensatory remedies emphasized the quantitative "more," school desegregation plans stress movement. Many of the plans necessitate logistical planning, whether for busing or encouraging students to sign up for special electives at integrated schools.

Despite these differences, the two strategies have one significant bond. Both maintain the power decisions—hiring and firing of teachers and budgetary allotments—in the hands of a central school board. Whether Boston or New York City or Des Moines, most school boards and bureaucracies are dominated by white upper-middle class membership.[19]

Examples of School Desegregation Plans

1. Theoretically, the simplest and cheapest way to provide racially balanced schools is to redraw the boundary lines to counter population shifts or additions. Such an idea has not worked well in the largest urban centers. New York City, for example, made one hundred changes between 1959 and 1963 and was not able to keep abreast of the rapid white exodus and the influx of blacks and Puerto Ricans.[20] Also, some school districts such as South Holland, Illinois, were accused of racial gerrymandering when they realigned student populations.

2. Another plan which involves a minimum amount of travel for students would be a *site selection* concept. As the need for new buildings arises, could they not be placed at locations that would ensure maximum integration? Smaller cities have been more successful than large cities

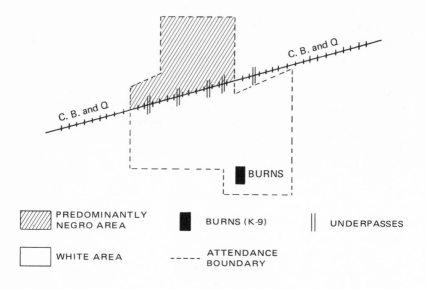

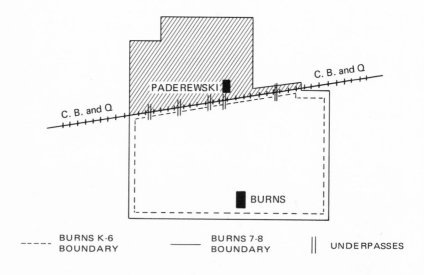

Figure 1. Burns Elementary School boundary before (top) and after (bottom) opening of Paderewski Elementary School in Chicago, Ill.

in doing this. Much depends upon the desires of the local school board, too. In Chicago, a new school was needed to meet the student enrollment increase of a black-white neighborhood. As Figure 1 indicates, the school actually built encouraged racial imbalance when it opened.[21]

3. One school desegregation option, *school pairing,* seems to work well in small cities. Frequently called the "Princeton Plan" because it was first tried in that New Jersey community, it merges two neighborhood schools into sister schools. Under this plan in some communities, one administrator is responsible for both buildings. The redistributing of the students is based on grade level rather than proximity to one school, as illustrated in Figure 2.[22]

4. *Open enrollment,* unlike the proposals just considered, involves much greater movement by students. Usually parents are given the choice of sending their children to any school in the system. For whites who believe in multiracial school environments and blacks who wish to escape decaying buildings, this plan provides hope. It also offers the possibility of relieving some overcrowded classrooms and filling underutilized buildings.

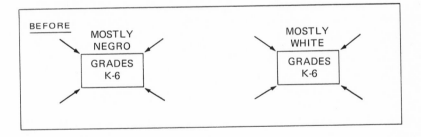

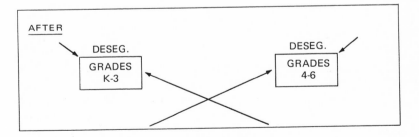

Figure 2. Pairing. Before pairing, students enroll according to each school's attendance area. After pairing, students of both attendance areas enroll in the two schools according to grade.

In practice, several problems have emerged. In 1965–1966 Boston adopted open enrollment. Despite the aid of a parents' organization and a plan called "Operation Exodus," the strategy failed, largely because parents had to bear the burden of transportation costs. New York City learned that such a plan increased segregation because open enrollment was frequently selected by the few white parents in some predominantly black areas.[23] Some school systems now correct this flaw by allowing transfers only if they improve the racial balance. For example, a white child in a 50 percent white school would not be allowed to go to a 75 percent white school. The most serious charge against the plan is that it rarely changes the situation of black majority schools in the inner city.

A variation of open enrollment is called "freedom of choice." Some Southern strategists believe that if they can convince the courts that each parent in their districts has the freedom to choose his child's school, the school system could not be found guilty of discrimination and segregation. So far, the courts have consistently denied this argument. In Houston, Texas, for example, the school board advertised freedom of choice but added certain guidelines. Children were re-enrolled in the same school they attended before freedom of choice was declared in effect. The board declared that if a brother or sister of an applicant had previously attended a school, he would be admitted rather than an applicant who had no previous contact with the school.[24] Through such policies as these, the courts felt true freedom of choice was not guaranteed.

Open enrollment works best when school administrators actively publicize and fully finance the program. Rochester, New York, seems to have a successful program. In 1969 Waterloo, Iowa, initiated Project Bridgeway. It sought to create a two-way street by moving 200 black students from a 100 percent black elementary school and replace those students with white students. Via the media, the community was alerted to new programs to be instituted at Grant Elementary—team teaching, a nongraded curriculum, special resources, and such. Eventually, the goal of 200 students was obtained from twenty-seven other schools in the system and three parochial schools.[25]

5. A similar plan is called *school closing.* As is frequently the case, minority group members attend schools which are the oldest and in the worst state of repair.[26] By closing such a school and distributing the students to other schools, some measure of racial balance can be achieved. Figure 3 illustrates what occurred in Syracuse, New York. Englewood Cliffs, New Jersey, and Berkeley, California, as well as several cities in

Florida, have tried this approach. Generally, the program appears to work.[27]

6. The school desegregation plan which has provoked the greatest discussion has been forced busing. One wonders why a mobile society can become so frightened by yellow vehicles that now bus half of the school children in the country every day. Obviously, most people grow upset when they envision their children in a strange neighborhood, or feel their children will be harmed academically by the addition of disadvantaged youngsters. Busing has usually been promoted on grounds that it relieves overcrowded schools and aids racial understanding. The evidence from several studies on the performance levels of both students who are bused and students at the receiving schools indicate that the interaction apparently helped the former gain in scores and in no way diminished the performance levels of the latter.[28]

Recently some school districts, such as Austin, Texas, have sought to comply with court-ordered integration by busing *all* students for a portion of the day. Generally the courts have considered such plans in violation of the spirit of integration.

As columnist Joseph Alsop has pointed out, however, the major deficiency in busing programs is that they are too limited in scope.[29] In Hartford, Connecticut, for example, only 1 percent of students who could have been bused were, in fact, bused. Since school systems are not noted for overbuilding, it is hard to imagine there will ever be extensive openings in receiving schools.

7. The *magnet school-supplementary center concept* found favor with President Nixon, probably because of its voluntary characteristics.[30] The essential aspect of this option is that it is part-time, and it is based on inducing students to choose attendance at schools that offer special programs.

The magnet strategy is typically a high school phenomenon. Certain schools in a system are designated as specialist schools. One school may offer advanced science classes, another computer programming, a third commerce and secretarial programs. The student attracted to a special program may attend a neighborhood high school in the morning, then go to a second high school in the afternoon. In Los Angeles, about 25 percent of the 13,000 students involved up to 1970 were provided busing for this program.[31]

There are limitations. In Oklahoma City, Frederick Douglass High School was designated the science center. White students who arrived at the predominantly black school came fifteen minutes after the other

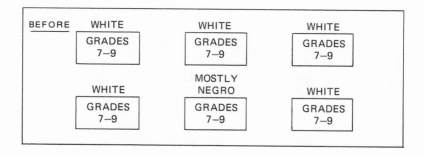

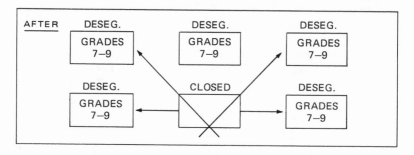

Figure 3. School closing. The predominantly Negro junior high school is closed and the students are bused to other schools.

students were in class and left five minutes before the others were dismissed from school. In addition, incoming students were kept in a separate classroom.[32]

The supplementary center experience is usually done with elementary-level children. Classes from the school system are brought to a central building which houses special facilities such as art displays, film libraries, and theaters. In Cleveland, about 300 students a day attend a center. In Mt. Vernon, New York, it has been estimated that some 6,000 elementary students spend 40 percent of their time in the Children's Academy. Students from various schools are mixed at the Academy.

As *Racial Isolation* concluded, most of these magnet or cluster schools were able to receive only a small number of students, and the voluntary nature of the program prevented much opportunity for integration contacts.

8. The *educational complex* plan has minimal student movement in the early years of school, but movement increases as students leave

elementary schools for intermediate schools and then high schools. This remedy has been promoted by the Center for Urban Education based in New York City.

When first proposed, the complex was based on the sociological and political realities that few parents wish to have their children transported long distances in a city during the children's early years, and that taxpayers would not vote for construction of numerous new buildings.

The program calls for each child to attend his neighborhood elementary school for four years. The second four years would be spent in a school drawing from several diverse neighborhoods. High school presumably would encompass more group representations. A feature of such a plan would be the pooling of teaching and administrative resources of the participating schools.[33]

If New York's "4–4–4" format is indicative of this program, the outlook is dim. A brand new intermediate school, I.S. 201, was erected in Harlem. It was supposed to attract white students from Queens. It never did. The demographic patterns in our large cities suggest that minority groups are effectively isolated for the pre-high school years.

9. The grandest (in scale anyway) school desegregation remedy is the *educational park,* or campus plan. In the late 1960s, some thirty communities considered erecting totally new campuses which would concentrate educational efforts at central locations. Some smaller communities were speaking about parks to accommodate 10,000 students. Larger systems speak of student populations from 15,000 to 25,000.

Such larger campuses would bring together children from many neighborhoods and presumably would break down racial walls as well as socioeconomic barriers. Some sites are as large as thirty acres. The projections include taking over land masses such as former military bases, or building over highways or filling in rivers next to cities. Sociologist Robert Havighurst of the University of Chicago has stated that the fallacy of many such plans is that they still do not include a broad enough spectrum of socioeconomic groups. For financial as well as social reasons, Havighurst advocates a new type of school district, one which would consolidate inner-city schools with suburban plants. Thus, a typical district would be pie-shaped, with its point in the city and its broad base in the affluent, suburban zone.

Those opposing the park concept immediately suggested that the size would inhibit integration. They argue that most individuals and

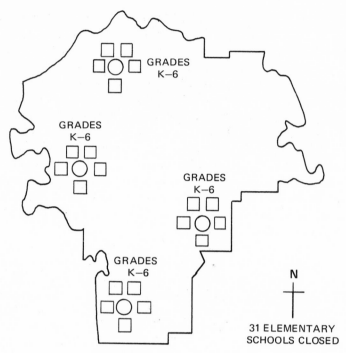

Figure 4. Syracuse campus plan.

possibly even minority groups would not be blended together for meaningful relationships. Some also object to mixing pre-schoolers with high school students. To counter these arguments, most of the plans break down school units into grade-level areas. As Figure 4 indicates, several pods, each housing several hundred students, may be joined by a central-library-commons-auditorium. Perhaps one such unit would be pre-schoolers or grades 1–3.

East Orange, New Jersey, and Hartford, Connecticut, plan parks which would enroll all children at one site. Berkeley, New York City, and Pittsburgh envisioned several locations. At this writing, Pittsburgh has shelved their plans. Some cities had purchased land and were beginning construction. However, none is operative now. One serious problem, of course, is time. East Orange contemplated it would take twelve to fifteen years to finish their campus. In the current climate of financial conservatism about school expenditures, one wonders how many other plans will be halted.

Conclusion

Compared with compensatory programs, school desegregation remedies seem to have enjoyed more success since 1954. Small cities, as a rule, seem to have made more progress than large cities in overcoming the problems of racial isolation.

Yet no one can forget that today there is more segregation than in 1954. Although southern schools have responded to the challenge to integrate, *de facto* segregation in the North has offset gains made in the South.

Overall, results of both programs seem far from satisfactory. With many desegregation plans, the chief flaw appears to be that most schemes are brought into operation too late, or they involve far too few people.

TEACHER EDUCATION PROGRAMS

Teacher education programs turn the emphasis to the instructor instead of the student. Advocates say that having new equipment or placing students in new buildings will not solve what may be "communication" problems. To ensure that students may succeed in school, the school system must provide teachers that are sympathetic to the various cultural backgrounds of their charges.

In one 1965 survey of teacher education programs, less than 10 percent indicated they were attempting to provide special instruction for teachers who planned on going into urban education. It would be impossible to list programs that have come and gone for teacher preparation, but one may say it is doubtful that more than 20 percent of teacher preparation institutions have provided significant programs for urban teachers.

Examples of teacher education programs

1. *Consortium* training appears to be a wave of the future. One such program is CUTE (Cooperative Urban Teacher Education), which began in Kansas City, Missouri, in 1966. Thirteen liberal arts colleges in Missouri and Kansas, together with representatives of the federal Mid-Continent Regional Educational Laboratory, developed guidelines for instructing student teachers in the Kansas City area. Students spend

sixteen weeks at the Laboratory, and under the direction of experienced educational leaders and knowledgeable city experts, they learn about city life and conditions in their community and schools. Seminars are a frequent learning structure. One of the reservations about the program is that it still is small, with approximately twenty-five students per semester.[35]

2. *Residents in Training* programs are a second variety of teacher education. The idea is to encourage more people from ghetto areas to go into teaching. Some of these programs recognize that the talents of these individuals should not be shut off until they have completed college training, and so programs such as C.O.P. (Federal Career Opportunities Program) pay residents from inner-city locations to work in schools part-time and to go to school as students part-time. The academic goal would be a bachelor's degree in education.

Conclusion

Like the other programs, this appears far too small to make a major impact in the near future. Interviews with people in the programs reveal that many participants believe their training is valuable and will contribute to their success later on.

THE SEARCH GOES ON

The evidence presented here clearly indicates that America has not provided and does not now provide equal educational opportunity for all its students. Perhaps the negative cast placed on results of the programs described is due to the fact that we expected these proposals to deliver change in too short a time, and we have not provided participants with enough help.

Just as one is ready to give up, however, it appears that some programs do offer the possibility for nudging the nation closer to equal opportunity. At this point, however, no single remedy could be described as a major avenue for success.

NOTES

1. U. S. Commission on Civil Rights, *Racial Isolation in the Public Schools,* Vol. I (Washington, D.C.: U. S. Government Printing Office, 1967), pp. 115–183. Much of the outline of this article comes from this source. The

evidence presented in that major study has been condensed for student interest reasons.

2. Meyer Weinberg (ed.), *Desegregation Research: An Appraisal,* 2nd edition (Bloomington, Indiana: Phi Delta Kappa, 1970), 460 pp.

3. Sloan Wayland, "Old Problems, New Faces, and New Standards," in *Racial Isolation, op. cit.,* p. 115.

4. *Racial Isolation, op. cit.,* p. 116.

5. Anonymous, "The Controversy Over the More Effective Schools: A Special Supplement," *The Urban Review,* vol. 2, no. 6 (May 1968), pp. 15–34.

6. For a lively exchange between Alsop and MES critics, read Roger R. Woock (ed.), *Education and the Urban Crisis* (Scranton, Pennsylvania: International Textbook Company, 1970), pp. 216–234. See especially Robert Schwartz, Thomas Pettigrew, and Marshall Smith, "Fake Panaceas for Ghetto Education," pp. 216–222; and Joseph Alsop, "Ghetto Education," pp. 223–234.

7. U. S. Office of Education, *Education of the Disadvantaged: An Evaluative Report, Title I, Elementary and Secondary Education Act of 1965* (Washing, D.C.: U. S. Government Printing Office, 1970). Reaction was from Des Moines *Register,* September 7, 1970.

8. *Racial Isolation, op. cit.,* pp. 124–125.

9. U. S. Office of Education, *Equality of Educational Opportunity* (Washington, D.C.: U. S. Government Printing Office, 1966), 737 pp.

10. *U. S. News and World Report,* "Black History as Schools Teach It," November 4, 1968, pp. 68ff.

11. *The Center Forum,* vol. 4, no. 1 (September 1969). The whole issue is devoted to the subject of bilingualism.

12. *Ibid.*

13. *Racial Isolation, op. cit.,* pp. 12–122.

14. Des Moines Public School System, *Annual Report 1969–70,* copyright September, 1970, by Des Moines, Iowa, Public Schools.

15. John F. Cawley, Will H. Burrow, and Henry A. Goodstein, "Performance of Head Start and Non-Head Start Participants at First Grade," *Journal of Negro Education,* vol. 39, no. 2 (Spring 1970), pp. 130–131.

16. Victor G. Cicirelli, *et al., The Impact of Head Start: An Evaluation of the Effects of Head Start on Children's Cognitive and Affective Development,* the report of a study undertaken by Westinghouse Learning Corporation and Ohio University under contract B89-4536 dated June 20, 1968, with the Office of Economic Opportunity (Washington, D.C.: Office of Economic Opportunity, June 12, 1969). The preliminary report was issued in April 1969.

17. Testimony of Dr. Thomas Pettigrew before the Select Committee on Equal Educational Opportunity of the U. S. Senate, May 13, 1970. His remarks appear on pp. 745–767 of the Committee report.

18. Floyd McKissick, "A Communication: Is Integration Necessary?" *The New Republic,* December 3, 1966, pp. 33–36.

19. David Rogers, *110 Livingstone Street* (New York: Random House, 1968), describes the New York City system; and Peter Schrag, *Village School Downtown* (Boston: Beacon Press, 1967), details the Boston school system.

20. *Racial Isolation, op. cit.,* p. 150.

21. Figures 1–4 come from *Racial Isolation, op. cit.* This one is from p. 48.

22. *Ibid.,* p. 141.

23. *Ibid.,* pp. 147, 148.

24. *Ibid.,* p. 66.

25. Interview with Dr. George W. Hohl, former Superintendent of Schools, Waterloo, Iowa.

26. Alvin Tofler (ed.), *The Schoolhouse in the City* (New York: Fred-

erick A. Praeger, 1968), especially Ben E. Graves, "The Decaying Schoolhouse," pp. 61–66.

27. *Racial Isolation, op. cit.,* p. 144.

28. *Ibid.,* pp. 131–137.

29. Joseph Alsop, "Ghetto Education," in Woock, *op. cit.,* pp. 228–229.

30. The Nixon education address delivered on March 24, 1970, specifically mentioned the supplementary centers as a promising remedy for racial integration goals.

31. Los Angeles City Schools, APEX Report (Area Program for Enrichment Exchange), published by the Los Angeles City Schools in August, 1970.

32. Report by Barry Jones, Iowa State University student and resident of Oklahoma City, citing reports of the Oklahoma City School Board.

33. *Racial Isolation, op. cit.,* pp. 166–167.

34. *Ibid.,* pp. 168ff.

35. Mid-Continent Regional Educational Laboratory, "Innovation in the Inner City," a monograph published by McREL in January 1969.

THOMAS F. PETTIGREW

Equal Educational Opportunity Testimony

In 1970 the U. S. Senate appointed a select committee under the chairmanship of Walter F. Mondale to investigate the question of equal educational opportunity. The committee heard testimony from many expert witnesses, including Dr. Thomas Pettigrew, a social psychologist who is among the leading academic exponents of "educational parks" as a solution to racial and social class discrimination in schools. The following excerpts from his testimony give some data on the extent of inequality in present schools, as well as giving Professor Pettigrew's suggestions for change.

Senator Mondale: Dr. Pettigrew, we are delighted to have you with us today, and you may proceed as you wish.

Dr. Pettigrew: Thank you. I appreciate the opportunity to testify before your committee today. One of the essential components of equal educational opportunity for the United States is racial and social class

Hearings, U. S. Senate Select Committee on Equal Educational Opportunity, 91st Congress, 2nd Session. Part 2 (Washington: U. S. Government Printing Office, 1970), excerpted from pp. 743–801.

integration of our nation's public schools. The relevant social science research, in my opinion, forces this conclusion upon us. Racially isolated schools contribute to increased racial prejudice and disharmony in our country; they deter the academic achievement of minority children; and they fail to prepare America's youth for the interracial world of the future.

Let me add at the onset that these same considerations appear to be true for social class as well as race and ethnicity. The findings of a large array of different studies, including the Coleman report on equal educational opportunity, demonstrate convincingly that schools with significant numbers of middle class children have significant benefits for less advantaged children regardless of race. Put bluntly, children of all backgrounds tend to do better in schools with a predominantly middle class milieu; and this trend is especially true in the later grades where the full force of peer group influence is felt. . . .

I should also like at the onset to draw a sharp distinction between truly integrated facilities and merely desegregated ones. A desegregated school refers only to its racial composition. And it may be a fine school, a bad one, perhaps a facility so racked with conflict that it provides poor educational opportunities for both its white and black pupils. Desegregation, then, is the mere mix of bodies without reference to the quality of the interracial interaction. While it is a prerequisite for integration it does not in itself guarantee equal educational opportunity. By contrast an integrated school refers to an integrated interracial facility which boasts a climate of interracial acceptance.

A vast body of social science research shows that interracial acceptance is most easily generated in any institution, educational or otherwise, when the two groups share equal status and work for common goals. In addition, competition for the goals should not occur between the groups, and the intergroup contact needs the support of authorities and law. I firmly believe that effectively designed federal legislation can encourage the establishment throughout our country of not just desegregated schools but truly beneficial integrated schools.

You have heard in previous testimony about the demonstrated improvement in minority achievement in integrated schools. Consequently I would like to stress this morning the other main benefits of integrated education. I believe that social research strongly indicates that integrated schools are one of the chief mechanisms our society has so far devised for the amelioration of racial prejudice. It is sometimes patronizingly asserted that integrated schools are something to be accomplished for black children. I wish to stress that integrated education is in my view, as a social psychologist and race relations specialist, an essential for all children. Indeed, in these unsettling times of conflict, I believe it is not an exaggeration to maintain that integrated education is an essential for the future viability and harmony of our country.

Allow me to describe the results of just one of the research studies I have in mind when I make these sweeping statements. In 1966, the U. S. Commission on Civil Rights, as a part of its broader study of racial isolation of the public schools (1967), a study in which I participated, interviewed representative samples of white and black adults in northern and western cities. Black adults who themselves attended integrated schools as children have more positive racial attitudes and more often send their children to integrated schools than comparable black adults who attended only segregated schools as children. They are typically making more money and are more frequently in white collar occupations than previously segregated blacks of comparable origins. Similarly white adults who experienced as children integrated schooling differ from comparable whites in their greater willingness to reside in an interracial neighborhood, to have their children attend interracial schools and to have black friends. For both black and white adults, then, integrated education did in fact prepare its products for interracial living as adults.

Once the desperate national need for truly integrated public education is recognized, the current status of the racial composition of our schools can be viewed as alarming. If one chooses the extreme definition of segregated schools consisting of 90 to 100 percent black students, then two-thirds of all black first graders now in public schools and one-half of all black twelfth graders in public schools are segregated in America today. If one chooses the more realistic definition of a segregated school as being a majority black school, then seven-eighths of all black first graders in public schools and two-thirds of all black twelfth graders in public schools are segregated in America today. Note that segregation of black children is most severe at the elementary grades, which considerable research has shown to be the most important of all for integrated education. White children are even more segregated. Four-fifths of both white first graders and twelfth graders in public schools are found in 90 to 100 percent white institutions.

Actually the problem we face is even more severe than these drab data indicate. Public schools in the United States are rapidly becoming less, not more, heterogeneous both in terms of race and social class.

There is more racial segregation in public education today, than there was in May 1954 at the time of the U. S. Supreme Court ruling against de jure public school segregation. This means to me that the great majority of American children are not receiving the training that is required for a racially harmonious America of the future.

The problem . . . is most intense in the large central city, such as Washington, D. C. There are four basic reasons why central city segregation of schools has reached such enormous proportions:

1. The antimetropolitan manner in which our school districts are drawn and operated. We have uneconomically divided public education into more than 25,000 separate and inefficient districts. We have over 75 school districts in metropolitan Boston alone, 17 in metropolitan Denver, and an incredible 96 in metropolitan Detroit.

2. The growing racial and class divisions between central cities and their suburbs combine with our multiple districting to furnish the single biggest factor behind urban school segregation. Over 80 percent of all black metropolitan residents live in central cities, while over half of white metropolitan residents live in suburbs. And present housing trends do not erode this pattern. Thus, even if we did not have school segregation within districts, we would still face a national problem of school segregation across districts. But of course we also face a major problem of intradistrict educational separation.

3. One seldom recognized contribution to this pattern is the depletion of the central city's pool of middle class white children by large parochial and private school systems. Thus three-fifths of the school-aged white children of Philadelphia and two-fifths of the school-aged white children of St. Louis and Boston do not attend the public schools. This pattern not only makes the public school student composition unrepresentative as to race and religion, but as to social class as well; for private schools disproportionately select off the invaluable resource of middle-class children.

4. Only fourth do we come to the most publicized reason for central city segregation—the cynical and willful planning by school systems to achieve maximum race and class segregation. In this regard I would like to observe that the prevalence and persistence of conscious effort to segregate throughout this country has put the concept of de facto school segregation in questionable repute among racial specialists. In every instance of which I am aware

where the history of central city's pattern of public school segregation has been studied in depth, governmental action in the terms of the Fourteenth Amendment has been uncovered. Unlike blatant state laws requiring segregated schools that characterized for many years my native South, school segregation in northern central cities has repeatedly been found to be the result of school board actions, real estate zoninig, urban renewal, and highway decisions, et cetera. Consequently, I am naturally skeptical about any federal policy that is based on a rigid distinction between so called de facto and de jure school desegregation. I believe that governmental decisions created our present pattern of separate schools and can now reverse this pattern. If I may be allowed a terrible pun, what the law giveth, the law can take away.

In small cities and towns, the remedies for educational segregation are well known: districtwide redrawing of school lines within a district, the pairing of adjacent schools, careful placement of new schools, the alteration of feeder patterns and the conversion of more schools into districtwide specialized institutions. But these techniques for smaller localities are mere palliatives at best and counterproductive at worst for the large central city situations; but remedies are available for the New Yorks and Portlands and Washingtons. They become apparent as soon as we recall the causes of central city segregation which I have just listed. That is why we must take metropolitan measures which cut across central city and suburban lines. We must facilitate cooperation between public and private school systems. And needless to say, we must end conscious policies of segregation when they come in obvious or subtle forms of de jure separation.

A metropolitan perspective is essential. Pessimists often regard the racial integration of schools as impossible because of the growing concentrations of black Americans in central cities. But as soon as we adopt a metropolitan perspective the dimensions of the problem are abruptly altered. Black Americans constitute only 11 percent of our national population and only about 14 percent of our metropolitan population. I am not advocating metropolitan consolidation of school districts, but rather a new level of cooperation between the central city and its suburbs. Until now we have discouraged such cooperation by shaping our state and federal support of public education almost entirely in terms of single and isolated districts. To me, this policy has unwittingly strengthened the roots of the inefficient educational structure that is failing us. While not diminishing local prerogatives, a policy of state and federal funding that places strong incentives for cooperation between our 25,000 school districts would be an important step forward both for equal educational opportunity and the efficient use of public funds.

It is also obvious that integrated schools of the future in metropolitan areas must draw from wide attendance areas so as to be less dependent on shifting and segregated residential patterns. This will require what has come to be the most controversial aspect of integration: busing. So first let me direct a few remarks concerning this issue. . . .

First, there is no solid evidence of which I am aware which indicates that busing is harmful to children. Indeed, I fervently hope that it is not harmful, for almost half of all schoolchildren are bused in the United States each school day, and school buses are estimated to travel each year . . . approximately two million miles. If it is harmful then we have harmed American schoolchildren in great numbers since the invention of the bus. Second, busing is not an educational technique, it is only a means to an end. To regard it as a direct technique of public education is like saying that your occupation is commuting.

Obviously, you commute in order to reach your employment and a long and tiresome trip is only compensated by employment which you value. Consequently, the question in education is not busing per se but whether the bus ride in a particular instance allows your child to receive a better education five miles away than he can receive at the so-called neighborhood school at the end of the block. In short, I agree with Professor Kenneth Clark who argues that it is what is at the end of the line that counts.

I believe that several designs can meet these integration criteria and offer such attractive schools that parents and children will want to be bused to them. Allow me to close my statement by considering one of these designs as illustrative. And I am not suggesting, urging this as the only way to do it, but only as illustrative, and that is the metropolitan educational park. Ringing our major cities with educational parks each of which serves both inner city and suburban students, offers one basic plan. . . . Each park would be located on neutral turf in an inner ring suburb or just inside the central city boundary. And it would be so placed that the same spoke of the mass transit system could bring both outer ring suburban children into the park and inner city children out of it.

The attendance area of each park would ideally cut out a metropolitan pie slice containing a minimum of 12,000 to 15,000 public school students, with the thin end of the slice in the more dense central city and the thick end in the more sparse suburbs. And they could be placed on "neutral turf" so that we might have American schools, rather than black schools or white schools, where the other race is merely a guest in the school. That is not the only way to do it, obviously, but I am thinking of a campus design. You might think of two or three different high schools, eight or ten junior highs, and fifteen to twenty separate elementary schools and on a hundred-acre or more plot. . . . One of the advantages of the park is that you could determine mix, and here it would be relatively independent of the residential segregation by class and race. Two, the advantages of the neutral turf is obvious. Three, lower capital costs. Educational economists estimate that we would save 15 to 20 percent in capital building funds to build a park in the fashion I am describing at once, rather than the same capacity on the single site model. A fourth advantage is lower operating costs. It would not be much lower, because you would have increased transportation costs, but it would be lower enough so to pay for the transportation with a little left over. I am not advocating saving money, but freeing money to do things in public schools now that we are unable to afford at the present time. Five, I believe parks have an advantage, like all new institutions, of making it easier to maximize innovations. I am not thinking of Orwellian electronic equipment, but social considerations, ways of teaching students, and that park makes it easier to have tie-ins with parochial systems and private systems that would be constitutional and, I believe, tie-ins with universities, and if you are interested in that, I would like to go into that in the discussion. Finally you could have status-generating facilities, better facilities, in other words, that attract middle class parents to send their children there, and not just white middle class parents, but black middle class parents, too. I am thinking of Olympic swimming pools and so forth.

Summing up, the advantages are a cost efficiency, more individualized instruction possible, wider course offerings, special facilities, and coordination with universities and parochial schools. All of these advantages of a well designed metropolitan park are features that I think parents white and black, would welcome in the schools of tomorrow. This is critical, I think, because integration efforts of the past have seldom come as an intrinsic part of a larger package promising an across-the-board improvement for all children.

In addition to the natural resistance to change, four major objections have been raised to the park concept. One, the excessive capital cost; and two, the phasing out of existing schools as they exist in central cities and suburbs; three, the problem of impersonalization in large complexes, which we might call the Kafka problem; and four, the loss of neighborhood and involvement in the school. Each of these is a serious objection and deserves comment, and I would like to make brief statements about each. . . .

The kind of park I am describing does not exist today anywhere in the United States, though there are many educators in the United States that have thought long and hard about such parks and from whom I borrow the idea. It is not my idea. Why don't we have them? Basically, because of the very expensive initial capital cost is why we don't have them; and it would take, I am sure, federal inducements to bring them about. Second, the phasing out of present single-site facilities and obviously, parks would be phased in. We are coming into a period—we are not in it yet—but then in a few years, when enrollments in public schools begin to take another fairly steep increase as they did in the 1950s and early 1960. It will not be as steep as it was in the 1950s, but it will be steeper than what we have been having in the late 1960s. So this will fill schoolrooms anyway. Second, there are many schools which need replacing, particularly old central cities like Boston, where the median school, or the typical school, was built about 1910. You could close the Boston schools and there would be nothing greatly lost. Finally, even with some fairly modern facilities, there is a great need for community centers in some of these areas into which schools might be converted.

One problem which made me cool to the educational park idea myself was the problem you might call the Kafka problem—the impersonalization. I believe Kafka is already here in public education, and the problem is what to do with this now, not to fight off something that has not come. For instance, Los Angeles High School is larger right now than Harvard College, one unit. I think, if designed right, and of course with no ingenuity at all you could design a living hell of an educational park. What I am talking about, of course, is a carefully designed one. A carefully designed one, I believe, could turn the clock back on Kafka. That is, get back to smaller units of schools, as it becomes economically feasible to build smaller units. If you look at almost any school system, and ask the school system, "What is your newest plant?" say on the elementary level, and ask "What is the capacity for the new elementary school you just built?" They will tell you 800 or 1,000. Ask them what is the capacity of the previous elementary school they built. They will say 600 and the one before that, 400. Kafka has been coming in creeping proportions anyway, for hard economic reasons. We are increasingly forced to build bigger and bigger units. I believe a well designed metropolitan park could actually reverse this trend and build smaller units back to 400 or 500, for instance, capacity for elementary schools. We could fight the impersonalization of the large complex problem.

Finally, the often stated criticism of loss of community involvement. I feel toward this like I do about the Kafka problem a little bit. That is, I believe we have already lost involvement in many public schools, and we are talking about how to again capture it back. We lost it for single-site schools, and not the parks. Again, I believe this would be a critical planning issue, and that a well planned park could involve parents better than we manage to involve them now in single-site schools. For instance, we could afford facilities in advance of what we are able to afford now in public education at no greater expense that would attract parental use nights and weekends in a way single-site schools do not attract today. Many other ideas have been proposed that would make this loss of community ties not a reality for a well-planned park.

In summary, then, those who say that there is nothing we can do about the educational segregation of our major cities are fortunately wrong. This is not to say that desegregation progress will be easy or even that we will do what is necessary to achieve that progress, but it is to say that the potential can be done for a significant number of urban Americans, white and black.

CHARLES & ARLENE SILBERMAN

Equal Educational
Opportunity Testimony

*Two other witnesses at the Senate hearings were Charles and
Arlene Silberman. They had recently finished leading a team conducting a three-and-a-half-year investigation of American schools.
Mr. Silberman has since reported many of the group's findings in*
Crisis in the Classroom *(New York: Random House, 1970), and
Mrs. Silberman has written a number of magazine articles which
also describe their conclusions. Their testimony was, therefore,
based upon a very contemporary acquaintance with schools all
over America. Additionally, Mr. Silberman previously conducted an
investigation of racism in America,* Crisis in Black and White *(New
York: Random House, 1964). Their commentary is an appropriate
conclusion to Part 3, even though some of it transcends the issues
of inequality and could fit logically at several other places in this
book.*

Mr. Silberman. "What the best and wisest parent wants for his own
child," a great American educator once wrote, "that must the community
want for all of its children. Any other idea for our schools is narrow and
unlovely; acted upon, it destroys our democracy."

Our democracy is not destroyed, but it is in danger. Not the least
of the reasons is the fact that the community has not wanted for all its
children what the best and wisest parent wants for his own child. As a
result, the public schools are failing dismally in what has always been
regarded as one of their primary tasks. What has distinguished public
education in the United States from education elsewhere, in fact, has
been precisely the expectation that the public schools would create a
sense of unity and national purpose in a society that otherwise might be
racked by ethnic, religious, and racial conflict. As Horace Mann, generally acknowledged to be the father of the common school, observed a
century and a quarter ago, "Education, beyond all other devices of

Hearings, U. S. Senate Select Committee on Equal Educational Opportunity,
91st Congress, 2nd Session. Part 1A (Washington: U. S. Government Printing
Office, 1970), excerpted from pp. 201–239.

human origin, is the great equalizer of the conditions of man—the balance wheel of the social machinery." Never have we needed the schools
to play this role more than now; never has their failure to do so been
more ominous for American democracy. If the United States is to fulfill
its promise of becoming a truly just and humane society, the schools will
have to do an incomparably better job than they are now doing of educating youngsters from minority and lower class homes—Negro Americans, Puerto Rican Americans, Mexican Americans, American Indians,
and poor whites in particular, and of educating all children in general.

    If the committee is to understand the current crisis, however, it
must understand that the failure is not new; it is one the United States
has tolerated for a century or more. The public schools have never
done much of a job of educating youngsters from immigrant or native
lower class homes. While it would be difficult to exaggerate the importance of the wide acceptance and belief in the goal of equal educational
opportunity, that goal has never been realized. On the contrary, we
have greatly romanticized the role the schools have played in stimulating
social and economic mobility for immigrant and poor native-born students. There have been some notable exceptions; but for the ethnic
groups who comprised the bulk of the immigration of the middle and
late nineteenth and early twentieth centuries, education was not an
important means of mobility. Education did not become important to
these groups until after they had achieved middle class status.

    Why, then, the current crisis? There are two reasons. The first is
that education is vastly more important today than it used to be, which
means that the schools' failure matters very much more now than it
used to. . . . The other . . . is that parents of minority youngsters now
recognize the importance of education. Earlier minority groups were
more or less indifferent, and sometimes hostile, to the schools, which
appeared to threaten the solidarity of the group, which they valued
above mobility. Today Negro parents, and increasingly Mexican American, Puerto Rican, and American Indian parents are eager for their
children to have the means of mobility and they are angry at the schools'
failure to provide it.

    What must be understood, however, is the fact that the defects
and failures of the schools which educate Negro and other minority
youngsters are, in good measure, simply an exaggerated version of what
is wrong with schools everywhere. "The most deadly of all possible
sins," Erik Erikson suggests, "is the mutilation of a child's spirit." It is
not possible to spend any prolonged period visiting public school class-

rooms, as I have done, without being appalled by the mutilation visible everywhere, in the most prosperous suburbs as well as the most poverty-stricken urban and rural slums: mutilation of spontaneity, of joy in learning, of pleasure in creating, of a sense of self. *The public schools are the kind of institution one cannot really dislike until one gets to know them well* [emphasis added]. Because adults take the schools so much for granted, they fail to appreciate what grim, joyless places most American schools are, how oppressive and petty are the rules by which they are governed, how intellectually sterile and esthetically barren the atmosphere, what an appalling lack of civility obtains on the part of teachers and principals, what contempt they unconsciously display for children as children. I assure you I had not realized this until I began spending day after day, week after week, sitting in public classrooms.

And it need not be! What my studies have demonstrated, beyond any doubt, is that public schools can be organized to facilitate joy in learning and intellectual and esthetic expression and to develop character—in the rural and urban slums no less than in the prosperous suburbs. This is no utopian hope; there are models now in existence that can be followed. The most exciting elementary schools in the United States are to be found in the state of North Dakota—in hamlets like Starkweather and Edmore, with populations of 250 and 400, as well as in cities like Grand Forks, Fargo, and Minto—where, with assistance from the U. S. Office of Education, the University of North Dakota is collaborating with the state department of education to revamp completely the way in which schools are organized and run, and thereby to overcome the unequal educational opportunity which this state has been providing its almost entirely white student population. Unequal opportunity due to the fact that children in that state were scoring well below the national achievement. But there are models to be found, too, in New York City's Harlem; in the black ghettos of Philadelphia; in Tucson, Arizona, in schools serving a predominantly Mexican American population; in Portland, Oregon, in a high school serving a predominantly white working class and lower-middle class neighborhood; and in many other parts of the country.

In short, the public school system can be reformed. What makes change possible, moreover, is that what is mostly wrong with the schools is not due to venality, or indifference, or stupidity, but to mindlessness. What distinguishes my criticism of the public schools from that of a number of other critics, I believe, is at least in part my appreciation of the difficult and sometimes heroic role which teachers play. To be sure, teaching has its share of sadists and clods, of insecure and angry men and women who hate their students for their openness, their exuberance, their color, or their affluence. But the great majority of teachers, principals, and superintendents are decent, intelligent, and caring people who try to do their best, by their lights. If they make a botch of it, and an uncomfortably large number do, it is because it simply never occurs to more than a handful of them to ask why they are doing what they are doing—to think seriously or deeply about the purpose or consequences of education.

It is fashionable, I know, to disparage talk about educational purpose or educational philosophy. To talk about purpose, however, is in no way to be abstract or theoretical. On the contrary, educational purpose or philosophy is exemplified and transmitted in the way schools are organized and run. Education is inescapably a moral as well as intellectual and esthetic enterprise. What educators . . . must recognize is that how teachers teach, and how they act, may be more important than what they teach; the way we do things, that is to say, shapes values more directly and more effectively than the way we talk about them. Children are taught a host of lessons about values, ethics, morality, character and conduct every day of the week, less by the content of the curriculum than by the way schools are organized, the way teachers and parents behave, the way they talk to children and to each other, the kinds of behavior they approve or reward and the kinds they disapprove or punish. . . . Students are taught lessons about the worth and individual humanity of children who belong to different ethnic, racial, and religious groups by the ways in which schools deal with these groups— whether, for example, schools segregate students by race or whether they bring them together in integrated common schools. Indeed, segregated schools teach a lesson about the worth and humanity of black children, and of white children as well—that is far more powerful and far more lasting than all the civic classes, salutes to the flag, and recitals of the Pledge of Allegiance put together.

Thus, I agree completely with the argument which Dr. Kenneth Clark put before this committee last week, namely, that racial segregation is at least as damaging to white children as it is to black children. I do not mean to disparage the evidence that integration raises the academic achievement of black children. What makes integration crucial to this nation's future, however, is not so much what it does to raise academic achievement as what it contributes to the creation of a humane, decent, and united society. That is what the public school's major purpose must be. . . .

Senator Dominick. Mr. Silberman, . . . The thing that this committee is concerned with is the question of what should be done about minority groups. It is generally known, and is perhaps implicit in your statement that the majority of the people on welfare today are white, not black. Mr. Coleman, in his testimony before us Monday, indicated that his investigation of the comparative schools, found that the significant difference in schools was caused by the different backgrounds of the children rather than by tangible classroom variables such as teacher-student ratios or student-classroom ratios. Do you agree that the economic background is the determining factor in education?

Mr. Silberman. I agree, Senator Dominick, that in terms of the things which Professor Coleman measured, the critical factor is not what he called the quality of the school or the inputs into the school, but rather the nature of the student body and the nature of the home environment from which the child comes. What must be recognized and realized, I think, is that Professor Coleman, given the exigencies of time, measured only what could be very easily measured in quantitative terms, which was to say the dollar expenditure per pupil, the number of books in the library, the average size of class, things of that sort. And he found that the results were not related to these kinds of inputs. There is a large body of other research in England and in this country which reports the same kind of findings.

But these are not the critically important differences. The important differences are qualitative, not quantitative. I don't have at my fingertips the average expenditure per pupil in the schools in North Dakota that I am talking about. I am sure they are considerably less than in most of the prosperous suburbs in the East. But what distinguishes those schools is not the size of the class, not the number of books in the library, it is the warm human atmosphere which makes it possible for teachers to deal with each child as an individual rather than standing in front of the classroom trying to teach an entire class as a group. The critical variables have to do with things that are very hard to measure quantitatively.

. . .

Senator Hughes. . . . How can we have a great majority of principals and teachers who want to do their best and then have a system that can be so openly indicted?

Mr. Silberman. Because teachers are victimized by the system of education that we now have every bit as much as the children. Teachers work in surroundings that almost no one else would tolerate. They punch timeclocks like factory workers. They have no privacy. Their conditions are debilitating, to say the least. What is most crucial, however, is that the schools operate on an assumption of distrust. And the most crucial factor is the traditional technique of what some educators disparagingly call "the chalk and talk method," which is to say education in which the teacher stands at the front of the room as a source of all wisdom, all authority, and attempts to teach all children simultaneously, the same thing for the same length of time.

Studies of classroom dialogue, the verbal interaction between students and teachers, indicate that teachers talk anywhere between 60 or 80 percent of the time. All of the children together talk the remainder of the time, and they are talking almost invariably as a response to a question. Given this sort of structure, we define a problem of discipline and control. . . . If the teacher tries to alter this approach, he or she is immediately struck down because the principal way in which a teacher's competence is judged in most school systems is by the degree of control he exercises over the class. So long as the class is quiet, the teacher will never hear a complaint. If there is any noise or movement, regardless of whether that reflects intellectual excitement, the teacher will be criticized. One illustrative example of this, and I will stop. In one school that I know, a sixth-grade science teacher, particularly interested in science, discovered that one of his students was the son of a local butcher. So he acquired from the father the respiratory system from a cow and the next day he had the entire class gathered around him. He had his jacket off, his shirtsleeves rolled up, his hands deep in the respiratory system showing the youngsters how the heart worked and pumped blood to the rest of the body. They were just extraordinarily excited. When he went down to the office for lunch and looked in his mail box, there was a note for him from the superintendent of schools, and the note, to paraphrase—I have a precise quotation in my book—read:

> I looked in your class this morning. Teachers are not supposed to have their jackets removed. If for any reason their jacket must be removed, their shirtsleeves certainly should not be rolled up.

Well, that teacher got the message. . . . And when . . . the structure is changed so that teachers can develop their own creativity, so that they are treated and regarded as professionals with something to contribute on their own, the ordinary average classroom teacher performs in an entirely different way. It is the system in which they are encased that produces the behavior. If you change the way in which schools are organized, you get a very different kind of teacher behavior.

Senator Brooke. Mr. Silberman, you stated that you agreed with Dr. Kenneth Clark that racial segregation in public schools is equally damaging to white children as to black. What are the damages specifically to white children? Mrs. Silberman, would you like to answer that?

Mrs. Silberman. I think the main damage is that white children pick up quite unconsciously a sense of superiority, of their own superiority, which they carry with them all the days of their years unless they then have another experience.

Senator Brooke. Do you distinguish any difference between the damage done to black children and damage done to Puerto Rican children or Indian children?

Mrs. Silberman. A difference in damage? No.

Mr. Silberman. It is hard for me to answer, because I am, I think, more familiar as a result of my earlier work with the damage that has been done to black children in this country than with the damage done to Mexican Americans or American Indians. I suspect that the damage to black children is greater, but that in no way suggests that the damage done to other minorities is not so profound as to be a matter of great concern.

Senator Brooke. What would be the difference, then, specifically? Give me one example of the difference of the damage to Mexican Americans and the damage to a black child.

Mr. Silberman. I think the difference is that racial prejudice runs very much deeper in American life and in western life than ethnic prejudice. Our whole language is suffused with imagery. If we keep someone out of the club, we blackball him. Black is the color we use for funerals. The white lie is the permissible lie, the black lie the unpermissible lie. And this imagery is so deeply rooted in our language and our consciousness, the heritage of slavery, segregation, discrimination is so great, that racial prejudice is almost in the air we breathe. I don't believe that it is possible for any white person to grow up in this country free from prejudice, free from a sense of superiority. I think it is possible for whites to overcome that, to come to grips with their own feelings. It is because this sense of racial superiority and difference is so deeply imbedded in our life and in our institutions and our language that I feel racial segregation is more damaging than ethnic segregation. But I want to emphasize that I am not trying to minimize the damage done to

Mexican Americans or Puerto Rican or American Indian children, but simply to suggest that the damage is even greater because of the peculiar circumstances of our own history.

Senator Brooke. It is a question of degree in that regard?

Mr. Silberman. Yes, sir.

. . .

Senator Brooke. You referred in your statement to petty and depressing rules by which our schools were governed. What are you referring to specifically? What sort of rules are you referring to?

Mrs. Silberman. They sound almost too silly to bring before you. I think of one school, for instance, where children must carry their books on their left arm and when the principal was pressed for reasons as to why this rule existed, he was flustered primarily because he really hadn't thought about it much and it exists because it exists. Finally, he said, "That way, they can hold the banister on the stairway and prevent accidents." And I said, "Have there been very many accidents in the other schools where this rule does not obtain?" He had no answer.

I think of another school I visited, which was a junior high school, an eighth-grade class. As the bell rang, these youngsters, some of whom were a strapping 6 feet, 4 inches, had to line up in single file before they could leave the room. When I was interviewing the principal of this particular school, I asked if he could explain that rule to me, as it would be of interest. He said, "Haven't you noticed how narrow our halls are?" I said, "I really hadn't. I noticed as soon as the youngsters left the classroom they dispersed into the hall immediately." His reply was, "Oh? Well, we will have to put more monitors in the hall then, won't we?" So it is things of this ilk that have nothing to do with purpose.

. . .

Senator Randolph. . . . You have said, "The present school system is one that there is a mutilation of opportunity." Would you explain that to me more fully?

Mr. Silberman. I mean that in a twofold sense, sir. In terms of the schooling for all children, there is, as I indicated, a mutilation of the spirit, of joy in learning, and in discovering. The premium in most schools is on conformity, on getting the right grade, on getting the right answer. School becomes for the child a kind of game of trying to dope out what it is that the teacher wants to know, what is the "right an-swer"—right in the sense of what the teacher wants, which tends to stifle initiative, independent inquiry. . . . Now, the process is far more serious for minority children because it is compounded by a set of sometimes conscious and sometimes unconscious attitudes of prejudice, lowered expectations.

To give you one example of what destroys the spirit of a black student, a youngster I know, a high school junior, was terribly eager to go to college. When he talked to his guidance counselor, the response was, "What? You go to college? Don't make me laugh." When he was insistent, she suggested a few of the poorer southern Negro colleges. His record was poor. He had moved to the community in which I live as a youngster of 10 or 12 from Birmingham, Alabama, and he had not yet made up the deficits. But we knew him. He was a friend of my oldest son, was around the house a good bit, and he struck us as not simply highly motivated, but as having a combination of motivation and articulateness which suggested that there was more here than the grades were reflecting. So we helped get him into an "Upward Bound" program at a local college which was federally financed. As a result, after just the first summer in that program, his grades shot from Fs and Ds to Bs and Cs. By the end of the spring of the following year, he was show-ing so much promise that the "Upward Bound" officials recommended him for another partially federally financed program, a transitional year program.

There were 500 applicants for this program at Yale; 60 were accepted. He was one of them. When he went to his guidance counselor to ask that the transcript be sent to Yale, she said, "What, you go to Yale? That is crazy. Don't make me laugh." He was accepted. When he came to tell her, she looked up from her papers and said, "Oh," and went back to shuffling her papers. Several weeks later the superin-tendent of schools heard about it and made a big thing of it in the local newspaper, and when some local civil rights leaders were meeting with the education officials to express some complaints, the answer was, "Look at this youngster, we got him to Yale, that shows what we are doing for him."

After the year at Yale, he is now a student and freshman at one of the finest liberal arts colleges in the country. . . . [But] this some-times conscious, sometimes completely unconscious prejudice . . . [usually] prevents black youngsters from having the opportunity to learn. Prejudice, and lowered expectations; the other chilling phrase is, "They are doing as well as can be expected." This destroys the opportunity for an education.

. . .

Senator Dominick. . . . I want to ask you about the so-called school park system, where everybody from the city will go to, say, maybe three schools within the city. . . .

Mr. Silberman. . . . The school park has struck me from the very beginning as a kind of fuzzy liberal "pie in the sky." There may be some operating somewhere. I don't know of any that are. They do in a sense involve a postponement of a solution until the whole process of urban renewal, condemnation of land, agreement on site, construction and so on takes place. I don't think we can afford to wait that long. More to the point, the size or nature of the building, it seems to me, is the least important aspect of the school. I have seen superb schools in ninety-year-old buildings. I have seen dreadful schools in brand-new buildings. So it is what goes on inside that is crucial, and the advocacy of the educational parks haven't addressed themselves to that question. In terms of your first question, I share Professor Coleman's conviction that integration will raise academic achievement, that it does so, not through the impact of race but through the impact of social class. But I regard that as only a very partial statement of what is required.

. . .

Senator Brooke. There is an increasing number of blacks, very respectable body of blacks, who are favoring more and more black schools, black-controlled schools. How do you view this—I won't call it a phenomenon—but how do you view this suggestion?

Mr. Silberman. I view it as a quite natural and almost inevitable response to the failure of the courts, the state and local governments, and federal government to enforce the Supreme Court's mandate of 1954. Having waited sixteen years for the law to be enforced, I think it is understandable that there is some skepticism as to whether it will be, and some attempt, therefore, to search for the solution.

Senator Brooke. Do you think this is a main reason why the blacks are advocating black-controlled schools?

Mr. Silberman. I think this is the major factor that is responsible. I think there are other important factors as well. A search for black identity. Attempt to develop pride in self after all of the centuries of humiliation is a terribly important part of it. But certainly in New York City it was the failure to integrate that first produced the phenomenon. It has then taken on a rationale of its own in terms of pride of identity, in terms of responsiveness of the schools. . . .

In the high school in my own community, Mt. Vernon, New York, which is roughly 40 percent black, 60 percent white, the black proportion has been rising quite rapidly. Five years ago there were severe disorders. There were guards posted all over the school. A new superintendent came in and persuaded the principal to retire, appointed a new principal, who on the first day of school that September announced to the assembled students that he had removed the guards because he trusted the students to maintain order themselves. He managed to convey to the students two things: One, that he liked them and trusted them, that he had empathy for them; and secondly, that he was not any pushover, that he had removed the guards because he wanted to give them a chance to maintain order, that he hoped he would not have to restore them. He also took great pains to establish close relations with the black students who had some kind of leadership among the student body and with the white students who were leaders and asked them to report immediately to him any incidents of racial slurs and tension, so he could try to deal with them.

That school of 3,000 students, which had had to have guards all over the place, had no guards and had no disorder the entire year. And in the spring, when a local radio station ran an annual contest for the most popular high school principal, this man was elected, although this was his first year at the school. The students could send in as many votes as they wanted. Each vote was a 3 x 5 file card with the name. They sent in, with 3,000 students, something like 2.5 million votes, so he was elected the most popular principal in the metropolitan area.

Senator Randolph. How many votes?

Mr. Silberman. 2.5 million. They spent their entire spring vacation going around to every stationery store in town getting contributions of file cards and getting each student to fill out as many as he possibly could. This was the degree of rapport and trust that he had established in a racially very tense community where there had been demonstrations and threats.

He is no longer there. He left in part because of opposition from school board members who wanted much more repressive schools. Two and a half years later he received an offer for superintendency and he left. The school is now chaos. There are guards all over again. There are drugs being sold and used all over the school. There have been firebombings and there have been all sorts of disorders. . . . I think what is crucial is that the whole atmosphere has changed because the administration of the school now takes a very different approach.

I have two examples of what happens under the present system.

In one instance a black student on crutches walked the entire corridor. This is an enormous building. It is a two-story plant with now 4,000 students and it covers a huge acreage. He walked the entire length on crutches. An assistant principal told him there was a school regulation, which no one had ever heard of and to anyone's knowledge had never been enforced before, that students had to walk on the right side of the hall, and so ordered him to go all the way back to the end of the corridor and come back on the right side because he had been on the left side.

Another youngster whom I know came to our house one morning. He had been suspended from school. He came to us because his mother was about to enter the hospital for major surgery and had extremely high blood pressure and he didn't want to upset her. He had been suspended because he was accused of sexually molesting a white girl when she passed his table in the cafeteria. He happened to have been sitting with one of my sons at lunch. I went over to the school to see the deputy principal. He told me, "Oh, there was no question, the girl had witnesses." I asked, "Why didn't you call the boy's witnesses? One of them happened to have been one of my sons." He said, "Well, we knew we didn't have to because she told us he had whispered obscenities in her ear when she had been boarding the school bus the end of school a month before." In point of fact, the boy was on the wrestling team and so he didn't take the school bus home. The incident could not have happened. Moreover, the parents of the girl seemed to have been mentally unbalanced. A few nights before, they had disrupted a public meeting I attended a number of times to constantly report that their daughter was always being molested. When I said to the deputy principal, "You know that these parents are paranoid or something," he confessed to me that he had suspended the boy to get these parents "off his back." The girl, as he put it, was "a floosey," but he said that she was constantly making accusations, that the last time this happened he had not suspended anyone and the parents had gone to the school board, which had reprimanded him for not acting.

The result is that a boy who had been an A and B student is now getting D and F. This kind of incident occurs in that school over and over again. The result is an atmosphere of distrust and hate that builds up, rather than trust and understanding, and of a breakdown in order which brings more repression, which brings more striking back, which brings more repression, and the cycle just perpetuates itself. And the school board seems to have learned nothing from the earlier experience with the principal, who was able to put the responsibility on the students. . . .

Chairman. Thank you very much. You have given several persuasive examples of how our schools stifle incentive and impose rules upon children which appear to interfere with learning, enthusiasm, self-respect, and all of the rest. A similar indictment was made by . . . others. Is it your testimony that these examples are symptomatic of our entire system more than they are bizarre exceptions which could be used possibly to prove something that doesn't exist as a general matter?

Mr. Silberman. No, sir, I believe they are systematic. I have given some strong examples. They are by no means atypical. They essentially stem from the fact that the schools are not organized to facilitate learning. They are organized to facilitate order, and the result is a whole set of rules and an insistence on silence and lack of motion that we adults find impossible to observe. I would suggest that, as an exercise, the members of this committee attempt to spend an entire day in school and attempt to sit as still and as silently as the students are required to do; you would discover that it would be impossible for them really to do so and they would begin to wonder how children could do it.

· · ·

Chairman. What emphasis would you place on early childhood days?

Mr. Silberman. That is a very difficult question to answer. I think I would perhaps place less emphasis than is now being placed on it.

Chairman. You mean in terms of rhetoric?

Mr. Silberman. In terms of rhetoric. My own views have changed over the last several years, but it seems to me that the experience of a substantial number of programs indicates that the gains that are achieved in preschool programs wash out quite rapidly in the schools unless the schools themselves are changed.

Chairman. Is that an indictment of the early childhood efforts?

Mr. Silberman. It is an indictment of the schools, but there is an implicit assumption in the early childhood approach—in the whole emphasis on early childhood education—that the problem is the child and not the school. The reason minority and lower class children fail is that they enter schools lacking certain cognitive and affective skills that middle class children have. I advanced the same argument myself a number of years ago and the solution is to change the child to fit the school. My own studies and my own evaluation of the preschool programs suggests that we might be wiser to put our money into changing the schools to fit the child rather than changing the children to fit the schools.

Chairman. We have talked a good deal about the educational philosophy and direction of schools. Could you in response to my final question put what you have said in the context of the significance of an integrated school system?

. . .

Mr. Silberman. I think to try to put the question of integration and equal educational opportunity in the context of my remarks would be to really emphasize the fact that education is inescapably a moral enterprise. Schools teach values, as I indicated in my testimony, more by the way in which they are organized, the way in which teachers behave, the way they talk to children, the kind of behavior they reward, the kind of behavior they punish, than by the curriculum. If our objective is to be to develop students who will be human beings, who not only will have a sense of self and the ability to learn, but a respect for the integrity of other people, this would be an enormous step toward the creation of the human society. *The greatest problem facing American education is not to increase its efficiency, it is to change it so it can contribute to a human society. . . .* [emphasis added]. This cannot happen unless the schools are transformed. What I am saying is that merely desegregation in the sense of the physical rearrangement of children will have some important effect on raising academic achievement. To have an important effect on creating humane, decent, respective individuals, the schools themselves will have to change, and this is what I have tried to address myself to. It is not either/or. If I have to choose between integration or no integration, I would say, yes, let's integrate. I am not saying don't do that. I am saying let's not stop there. Let us go up further as part of a larger process.

Mrs. Silberman. There is a thought that occurs to me in terms of this business of equal opportunity to education and changing the schools and how do you find a format that links it all together. If you integrate the schools as they now exist, what you are going to come up with too often is "tracking," which is what is happening; and the next step is that most of the kids who come out of all-black schools and who are perhaps lower class kids are going to be in one track and the upper-middle class are going to be in another track, and they don't get to know each other anyway and the lesson that white youngsters may learn from that kind of integration is that black youngsters are dumb. So to continue the format that we have may teach some lessons that nobody wants taught. Therefore, integration needs a new kind of arrangement in the schools in order to give the message that we would wish.

Chairman. That is the essential point, and we have heard the same message from other witnesses, who testified about integrated efforts in which Mexican Americans were involved. It was their opinion that poorly planned integration was little better than none. . . . So when we talk about integration, we always have to talk about an environment which will foster stable, constructive integration.

We are most grateful to you for being with us today.

part 4

"Free public schools are the cornerstone of our social, economic, and political structure and are of utmost significance in development of our moral, ethical, spiritual, and cultural values. . . . The public school system is not expendable. Any movement that would diminish this vital asset will be opposed by the Association."
—National Education Association resolution, 1969

"What is the realistic meaning of alternatives 'within the system,' if the system is the primary vehicle of state control? . . . School cannot at once both socialize to the values of the oppressor and toil for the liberation and the potency of the oppressed. If the innovation is profound, it is subversive. If it is subversive, it is incompatible with the prime responsibility of the public school."
—Jonathan Kozol

Directions
schools explore

Following the Revolutionary War, American nationalists liked to call the fledgling country the "Great Experiment." The title seemed to fit the democratic social system and the restless spirit of its settlers. Experimentation was also a mark of the nation's efforts at schooling.

Throughout the country's development, there have been many individuals and groups who chose to explore alternative paths to educate their children. It is ironic today that public education is so often assumed to be the American way, for as Part 1 intimated, the near monopoly of public schooling is a recent phenomenon.

On every major rung of the educational ladder, private instructional models preceded public forms. The Congregational Church instituted Harvard, the first college. Before the first public high school in Boston in 1821, private academies for boys and seminaries for girls had operated for years. Before elementary school patterns crystallized, young children had been exposed to dame schools in New England, Sunday schools in the Midwest, and charity schools in the Middle Atlantic states.

Historians of education have minimized the growth of non-public schools. Their accounts applauded the growth of and the improvement in public schools following the Civil War. To bolster their case that the American mainstream supported universal education, historians mustered a variety of examples: the courts' approval of community tax support (Kalamazoo, Michigan, 1874), improved teacher training and certification programs (such as the Normal school movement), development of textbooks to replace such haphazard teaching tools as the Montgomery Ward catalog, and more orderly administration of school programs (the introduction of the Carnegie unit, to measure a student's exposure to a subject area).

But while public schools were becoming the dominant pattern for the majority of American youth, the non-public school has also grown rapidly. It was during the 1880s and 1890s that Roman Catholics and German Lutherans began parochial systems of instruction. Private "progressive" nurseries grew alongside the kindergartens. Adult study clubs, such as the Chautauqua Literary and Scientific Circle, enrolled millions. In 1890 approximately 40 percent of the high school students in the country were in non-public schools.

Also, non-public schools have grown steadily since World War I. Ninety-five percent of all Jewish day schools now in existence were founded after 1930. More than 80 percent of today's Baptist, Presbyterian, and Episcopal schools originated during that same period. Although Roman Catholic school enrollments are declining dramatically, some new forms of schooling being tried may offset the loss. Currently about 12 percent of the nation's students in elementary and secondary schools are not attending a public school.

In 1971 the U. S. Supreme Court ruled that the states of Rhode Island and Pennsylvania had violated the first amendment clause which prohibits the "establishment of a religion" when they reimbursed the salaries of parochial school teachers of secular subjects with public tax monies. Many newspaper accounts and academic scholars predicted this decision would hasten the end of the Roman Catholic system and perhaps most other efforts at private schooling.

When one considers that 435,000 Catholic students who attended parochial school last year will attend public school this year, the case for the decline and disappearance of non-public school appears strong. However, legislators of other states, like Rhode Island and Pennsylvania, will face shortly, if they have not done so already, the fact that this movement places a tremendous burden on the taxpayer. One can predict more efforts to strengthen the non-public system.

Further, the Roman Catholic decline will be partially offset by schooling efforts of "new" groups. For a variety of reasons—belief that the public school curriculum is too secular, desire for racial isolation, support of a more humanistic pedagogical approach—non-public schools are springing up in every part of America. The sponsors of such schools include Episcopalians, Southern Presbyterians, Jewish synagogues, fundamentalist sects, Black Panthers, White Citizens' Councils, and Summerhill-type groups.

The story of America's educational experiments may be viewed as a profile of changing national values. Frequently the school has been modeled after another institution in the culture. In colonial times school was usually patterned after a church fellowship. Early twentieth century educators liked to think of the school as a factory. More recently, schools have been likened to motels or franchise outlets, providing a standardized diet for a mobile nation. We may ask now: What are schools modeled after today? What should be the model for tomorrow?

The reader will note that the chapter title omits the words "new" and "alternatives." The omissions are deliberate. These historical notes may aid the reader in posing another basic question: Are the directions taken significantly different from experiments in the past?

The order of the readings should invite another type of question. It is obvious that the directions being explored vary considerably. Have the major goals of schooling been altered? Have new power alignments behind school policy been changed?

The readings are divided into three groups. The first group, containing six articles, explains programs which *recast* some segment of the school program—the location of schools, for example—but which do not fundamentally alter the present structure. The next two articles are based on experiments which *reform* some aspect of the power structure, such as school financing. The last two selections argue for radically altering the goals and shape of the dominant technological model of schools today.

RICHARD MARTIN

Anything Goes

In the following article, a Wall Street Journal *reporter describes "informal" elementary classes in North Dakota—the kinds of classes mentioned approvingly in the Silbermans' testimony in Part 3. The reader will note that, despite worries by some critics, schoolrooms are not really being turned over to children. There is more flexibility and more stress on making learning fun, but children still must go to school and may only choose from the options the school makes available. Children may not decide whether or not they want to learn math, science, spelling, reading, and writing. They may decide on what order to do so and have more choice in the media they employ. The school, however, retains ultimate control of and responsibility for what occurs.*

Minto, N.D.—The fifth-grade classroom in this tiny, windswept farm community worries the principal, horrifies other teachers, infuriates the janitors and stuns parents.

It's a scene of near chaos. Desks are scattered. Melon-crate book-

Richard Martin, "Anything Goes: More Educators Endorse Informal Classrooms as Spur to Initiative," *Wall Street Journal*, vol. 51, no. 34 (December 1, 1970). Reprinted by permission.

cases overflow with wood scraps, encyclopedias, games, puzzles and magazines. A rabbit, a hamster and two white rats are caged amid the clutter. There's an aquarium, too, and chicken eggs are hatching in a homemade incubator. Giggles punctuate the constant hum of conversation, and most of the 20 pupils seem to be in motion most of the time. Some sprawl on the floor reading, writing and painting. At one point, two boys are playing chess. Two others, who have crawled inside a crude cardboard hut, are working math exercises.

A lot of people say this is no way to run a classroom. But growing numbers of educators are just as strongly convinced that it is an ideal setting for developing the initiative, creativity and critical thought processes individuals need to cope with the increasing complexity of life in a fast changing society. Schools should be set up to bring out the most in each child, whatever his talents and regardless of his intelligence, not just to maintain order and stuff heads with facts, these educators contend.

MR. SILBERMAN'S VIEWS

In his new book, "Crisis in the Classroom," which is based on a three-year $300,000 study commissioned by the Carnegie Corp. of New York, Charles E. Silberman urges a remodeling of elementary school classrooms along less rigid lines as part of a vast reordering of U.S. education aimed at producing "a more humane society." The author, a Fortune editor and former Columbia University professor, says North Dakota's informal classrooms "are in many ways more exciting, and certainly more innovative, than anything one can find in the Scarsdales, Winnetkas, Shaker Heights and Palo Altos of the United States."

The informal classroom isn't a North Dakota phenomenon, by any means. Such classrooms are widespread in England and have cropped up in scores of U.S. cities in recent years. At least one other state, Vermont, is considering introducing "informal" classrooms on a statewide scale. In contrast to the usual snail's pace of educational change, the concept has swept across this frozen farm state like a January blizzard.

In many ways, North Dakota is ideally suited to its unaccustomed role as a test model for educational innovation. "If we can't do it here, it can't be done anywhere," says Kenneth Underwood, Fargo's superintendent of schools. "Our classes are relatively small, and, compared to much of the rest of the country, we just don't have any financial or social problems here. There's no racial strife, and we don't have to negotiate with unions for every minute of our teachers' time."

MOVE ASIDE, TEACHER

Thus, schools scattered throughout the state are creating informal classrooms like Minto's, shoving desks, lesson plans and even teachers out of the way to give youngsters plenty of room to satisfy their natural curiosity and eagerness to learn.

The driving force behind the drive to bring informal classrooms to the state comes from a radically different kind of teachers' college, the New School of Behavioral Studies in Education. A small experimental unit of the University of North Dakota in Grand Forks, the New School has scrapped conventional college methods of teacher training and has knocked down the traditional barriers between teachers college campuses and the public school classrooms.

The New School opened two and a half years ago to a barrage of criticism. Its plans to promote educational changes were opposed by many faculty members of the university's big, 87-year-old college of education. The New School was attacked by members of the state's John Birch Society, and some state and local school administrators were hostile to its goals.

But since then the opposition has faded fast.

This year 34 of the state's 375 school districts are participating in the program, up from 13 in the 1968–69 school year. Currently about 10 percent of the 74,000 children in North Dakota's 593 elementary schools are attending informal classrooms, which cost no more to set up and operate than normal classrooms. "It's quite a thing for this to take off as fast as it has when you consider how many programs of a demonstration nature never succeed in moving off dead center," says Kiaran Dooley, director of state and Federal programs for the State Department of Public Instruction in Bismark.

FANS AND SKEPTICS

So far, the New School has sent 150 new teachers out into classrooms and has "retrained" another 210 experienced ones. It tries to send its graduates into schools in groups of two or three so that they can give each other help and moral support. Making a changeover from a traditional to an informal classroom is usually a complicated, painful process, and the difficulty is often increased by the skepticism, and occasional hostility, of some principals and veteran teachers.

Vernon J. Schreiner, Minto's elementary school principal, is one of the skeptics. "The fifth-graders are enjoying school all right, but I'm not sure how much they're learning," he says. "I don't think math and grammar are getting enough emphasis. And I wonder how they'll adjust to a traditional sixth-grade classroom next year."

In Grand Forks, Doris Onstad, who got a master's degree at the New School and transformed her first-grade classroom last year after 15 years of traditional teaching, recalls: "I was so excited and so eager, and the other teachers just laughed at me. It hurt." Peggy Wambolt, a sixth-grade teacher in Fargo with six years' experience, says: "The other teachers still look at me sideways sometimes, but I think that more and more I'm being accepted. They come and visit now. They still say my room's a mess, but with 28 different things going on it has to be."

Mrs. Wambolt, in her second year of informal teaching, is usually in her classroom from 8:30 a.m. to 6 or 7 p.m. "I just can't keep ahead of these kids. I can never seem to have enough work ready for them," she says. In Grand Forks, Roger Graham, with nine years' experience teaching fifth-graders and sixth-graders, says the informal class "is much more demanding of my time and effort. I go home just shot. But there's a much more rewarding, very personal relationship between teacher and students than I ever had before."

Keeping a classroom from sliding over the thin line between freedom and chaos adds to the strains on a teacher for at least the first year of informal teaching. "Few kids learn to read by happenstance, and you have to be sure they do learn," says Neil Hensrud, one of three New School faculty members who spend much time visiting classrooms in the state to encourage and advise. "Some framework must exist for kids to work within. The teacher can't just turn the classroom over to them."

The idea is to provide lots of options that will get children actively involved in learning but that will let them set their own priorities. Instead of being a prime source of frustrating defeats, "classrooms need to be places where children can test their ideas, find their strengths and share what they learn with others, so they can feel they are worthwhile persons," says Sharon Melancon, who teaches a combined class of third- and fourth-graders in Fargo.

"Children basically want to learn and are interested in finding out about the world because it is just so very interesting," says Mrs. Melancon, who is in her second year of informal teaching after eight years in conventional schools. "Common sense tells us that a certain portion of the day needs to be spent by young children mastering the basic skills in math, reading and writing. But these activities can be made more interesting by tying them in with the interests of the child."

For example, a story about children who built a clubhouse prompted her class to try building one, too. Her pupils drew plans, using their own measurements, arithmetic and geometry. They listened to tape recorded lessons on handling tools. A group then went to a lumberyard and got some old wood, and the class built a small playhouse on the schoolground. They wrote stories, poems, songs and letters telling of their experiences. Small groups studied such related topics as termites, Indian homes, the homebuilding industry, skyscrapers, trees and the evolution of tools.

Some parents, nevertheless, worry that their children are having too much fun in informal classrooms to be learning as much as they should. Hank Yagelowich, a chemist in Grand Forks, frets that his son "is getting short-changed" in his informal first-grade class. "It's fine if you can combine educational value and fun, but there's some stuff that you just have to grind out," he believes. "Educators today are too concerned with gimmicks."

No two informal classrooms are alike, but most share a number of common characteristics. There is emphasis on ingenuity and improvisation. Mimeographed math exercises sometimes contain no instructions; figuring out what to do is part of the exercise. First-grade reading materials often consist mostly of story books and stories the children themselves have made up and dictated to an adult.

Frogs, fish, snakes, birds and animals are standard equipment. Cast-off sofas and battered easy chairs are common, along with rugs, pillows and cushions to make the floors more comfortable. There are gasoline engines, electric motors and an incredible variety of puzzles and games to take apart and manipulate.

A favorite piece of equipment is a $3.25 microscope made of a chunk of wood, two knobs, a piece of mirror and a cheap plastic lens. It can be dropped without harm "and the kids love them," says Leonard Marks, who teaches science at the New School. "They're always bringing stuff in to look at and by playing with one of these they can learn a lot more about how lenses work than they could from an expensive microscope that has to be put away and locked up most of the time."

Mr. Marks shows teachers how to make cheap, durable cardboard rocking chairs, tables, playhouses, study carrels and other furniture and how to build a variety of classroom equipment, including games and puzzles, for only 10 percent to 20 percent of the cost of buying similar commercial products.

"Listening stations" equipped with tape recorders, phonographs and many sets of earphones, are usually present, too. Principals say the extra cost of projectors is offset by savings on workbooks and texts, since teachers want only two or three copies of a textbook, instead of one for every pupil.

One unusual aspect of an informal classroom is the presence of parents—reading to children and listening to them read, telling about their own travels and interesting experiences and helping out with a multitude of more mundane chores. Parents also chaperone groups of two to four youngsters on field trips for research projects they are pursuing on their own. Teams of Fargo sixth-graders, for example, recently visited a medical center for a study of arthritis, called on a bank for research on the history of money and interviewed a snowmobile maker about possible harmful effects of his product on the local ecology and wildlife.

"Parents today are involved in the schools less than they used to be and less than they want to be; too many teachers haven't wanted them around," says Vito Perrone, director of the New School. He crisscrossed the state talking to 10,000 parents in homes and schools in the New School's first year of operation, and he credits their involvement in the program with much of its growth.

"Once they see what we're doing, parents tend to become very supportive," he says. "But many have been supportive from the beginning. All the time principals and superintendents were telling me that parents would never accept the changes we wanted to make that first year the parents were telling me they sounded great."

Parents in towns throughout the state have held evening workshops where New School faculty members talk about the program's methods and goals, field questions and let parents play with the puzzles and equipment their children use in class. One workshop last month drew 100 parents to the school in Milnor, which has a population of only 658.

Mr. Perrone frequently attends such gatherings. "Most college deans would rather make a speech to a state convention or a civic club, but Perrone will drive across the state at the drop of a hat to talk to parents," says Sheldon Schmidt, a New School professor. "He's very persuasive," adds Mr. Schmidt. "I saw him operate on a state official once. He ended up with a grant and the guy's support and at the outset of the meeting the official was determined not to give him either."

Some skeptics are being converted. "I can see some distinct benefits to an informal classroom, even though I can't swallow the whole package," says Mr. Schreiner, the skeptical Minto principal. "Just having them here has put a certain amount of pressure on the rest of us to change, to individualize our other classrooms more." George W. Starcher, president of the University of North Dakota, says the program "has really shaken up education in this state, and the thing that delights me is seeing these old superintendents changing their ways and seeing other colleges and school administrators beginning to imitate New School programs."

There are other measures of success, too. Tentative findings of tests aimed at comparing learning gains in both informal and traditional classes "indicate that what we're doing does help the kids," Charles Nielson, a New School testing specialist, says cautiously. "We're certain that at the very least kids aren't doing any worse," he adds. . . .

DRPA STAFF MEMBER

A School Without Walls

At the secondary level, too, are innovative programs. Philadelphia's Parkway School, and similar schools in a few other cities, are unique in using the museums, businesses, and parks as classrooms to stimulate learning. But there are serious questions: Are "schools without walls" a model for change, or do they merely offer an escape for a handful of students while legitimizing the regular schools for most students? Can any city accommodate tens of thousands of students outside the confines of schools? If one of the purposes of schools, as critics allege, is keeping children off the streets, would any community support such a program on a full-scale basis?

It's the only high school in the country that has a biology department with a collection of two million insects from all parts of the world, an art museum containing 100,000 master works ranging from medieval to modern, a library that houses nearly a million volumes.

The school is Philadelphia's Parkway Program, an experimental attempt by educators to bring the community and students together to breathe new life into a suffocating urban educational system. It is called "a school without walls" because it has no building that can be identified as the traditional schoolhouse.

Parkway's classrooms surround the two-mile length of the 12-lane, tree-shaded Benjamin Franklin Parkway. Soon they are expected to dot other parts of the city. One area under consideration is the historic Independence Hall section overlooking the waterfront.

Anchoring the western end of the Parkway, is the impressive Museum of Art. On the banks of the Schuylkill River, the museum's U-shaped building of Greco-Roman architecture covers 10 acres of ground. Within its walls, students can absorb the styles of Van Eyck, Cezanne, Picasso, Rubens and Renoir. And a short distance away is the Rodin Museum.

At the other end of the Parkway lies the heart of center city Philadelphia. It is here that Parkway students have been able to see the operations of government and business first hand. "The city is learning from our kids," says Cy Swartz, a Parkway teacher in evaluating the success of the school since it began operation in February. "Many of them have made positive impressions on the people they've come in contact with. A significant part of the program is to help society understand our adolescents—these youngsters feel so cut off in so many ways."

The city itself offers a classroom filled with sights and sounds no four walls could contain. "We've gone to Penn Fruit, the Greyhound Bus Terminal and City Hall for some of our subjects," said a young art teacher. And one sunny morning she took her students over to Rittenhouse Square, where the annual flower show was in full bloom. The young artists busily began working to capture the colorful swirl of babies, balloons and blossoms.

Between the art museum and city hall are a number of the school's other classrooms: the library, the county court house, the Academy of Natural Sciences, the Franklin Institute and the Moore College of Art.

Aside from the fact that these places contain facilities that no other school could afford to match, there is another practical reason for operating this kind of setup: The taxpayers did not have to spend $15 million on a new school building. "We're a bargain!" chuckles John Bremer, the director of Parkway School. But he sees Parkway as more than a way to save dollars. "I just don't think what we have been offering in our schools meets the needs of a sizable percentage of students."

Bremer's office, as well as the school headquarters, is at 1801 Market Street. The second floor quarters provide space for administrative offices and room for students to store their books and papers in da-glo decorated lockers.

The walls of the community room are festooned with the eclectic selection of prints from Rembrandt to Picasso. Movement up and down the narrow stairs is constant and the noise level fluctuates from a low buzz of conversation to loud punctuations of students and teachers greeting each other.

Casual. On the surface that's the word to describe Parkway. Dress ranges from conventional to mod for both teachers and pupils. Students may address teachers by their given names. "I had to get used to hearing myself called by my first name for the first couple of class meetings," recalls Jay Galambos, an Insurance Company of North America training specialist who teaches basic insurance to Parkway students.

Galambos is one of several specialists on the faculty who have been donated by their companies. He taught for several years in a sub-urban school district before joining INA. "Having lived and worked in that kind of situation, I had never been exposed to the nitty-gritty of urban life. These are sophisticated kids and every time they hear talk, they want the truth."

Open. That's another word to describe Parkway. Students are able to attend the school's free-wheeling Friday faculty meetings. They take place around a long table in the school's headquarters and are attended by the "regular" teachers on the faculty. The staff numbers nine full-time, fully certified teachers and 13 university interns who work along with the instructors in class and tutorial programs. The teachers like Galambos, contributed by business and institutions, help reduce the student-teacher ratio to two to one.

Although there is the air of casualness surrounding Parkway, Bremer insists that it is a tightly structured program. "The structure is just different from the type of school we're used to. Our students spend more time studying than their counterparts in regular high schools." The school day lasts from nine to five for many Parkway youngsters. And a special class on television techniques held with an instructor from Channel 29 takes place on Saturday morning.

In order for Parkway to offer courses in such things as television and insurance, it depends upon the business community of Philadelphia. "We now have more offers of help (from business) than we can use," says Bremer. "And I think all educators should welcome the chance of help from business."

Smith, Kline & French Laboratories is another of the companies that is helping Parkway. In a bright, walnut-paneled room at the company offices on Spring Garden Street, a psychology class discussed drug abuse. Al Strack of SK&F's research and development department parried some of the verbal thrusts made by the group:

"Eighty percent of the kids taking drugs really dig it," one commented. "Kids know what they're getting into."

"Every heroin user says he can handle it," Strack replied. "Ask the kids at Synanon. People who use drugs are people in trouble."

The discussion spilled into overtime as several students continued the conversation with Strack after the class was dismissed.

Students studying law enforcement have the benefit of Harvey Steinberg's experience as an assistant district attorney. A law graduate of the University of Pennsylvania, he too is a former teacher.

One of his class sessions was held in a courtroom at the city juvenile court. First they heard the case of a youthful runaway and another about a gang incident. After the hearings ended, the group stayed in the courtroom to talk about the cases and about law in general. The next session was to meet in City Hall, where they would hold their own mock trial, a case of aggravated assault upon a police officer. "I thought it was going to be a murder case," said one disappointed member of the class.

Budding engineers and scientists are able to take classes at the Franklin Institute. The Institute itself is a pioneer in public education. After it was founded in 1824, it provided free education to the young men of Philadelphia. This led to the establishment of the city's first public high school.

As one group toured a section of the Institute, they learned the principles of electricity. As one girl shyly laid her hand on a shiny metal sphere her hair literally stood on end. This group will be qualified ham radio operators by the time they finish their course.

Other courses offer the students unique experience that they would never find in the traditional classroom. A Spanish class is held in the home of a Philadelphia Spanish-speaking family. The film-making group assembles twice a week in the Board of Education's film media center in South Philadelphia. The anthropology class meets at the Philadelphia Zoo. All in all, there are more than 90 specialized courses offered.

The student body at Parkway School is probably the most heterogeneous collection of personality types and IQs to invade any school, according to one faculty member. One reason is that they come from all parts of the city—and a few from the suburbs. More than 2000 applied for the 120 places available to city students. Selection was made by dividing the applicants into eight districts and drawing 15 names from each area out of a hat. The remaining 20 were chosen from a special lottery involving the suburbs.

The students come from academically tough schools such as Central and Girls High, from large ethnically mixed metropolitan junior and senior high schools, from the white, middle class neighborhoods in Northeast Philadelphia, the Negro neighborhoods of North Philadelphia and from the Italian and Irish sections of South Philadelphia.

Most, like the student from a large city high school, are pleased with the program. "The school I came from was just too crowded. When we took tests or handed in homework, we put a number after our name. At Parkway, I know just about everybody and they know me."

A fellow student agrees. "At the junior high school I used to go to I was in ninth grade. Here, I'm a student."

The teachers share the students' enthusiasm. One commented: "When a parent notices a dramatic improvement in a child's personality in just three months, that's fantastic! Something must be happening." Not only are the students being affected, but the teachers are too: "I'm certainly not the same person I was six months ago," stated another young teacher.

Parkway's ungraded classes combine youngsters in all four high school levels. Pennsylvania state law requires courses in mathematics and English but most offerings selected by the students are the ones they want to take—and this cuts across all grade lines.

The students not only came to Parkway from different cultural backgrounds, their academic records are equally mixed. Some were "A" students under the old system; some were barely surviving. "But I don't care either way," says Bremer. "Whatever their record was, we can provide them with a better framework in which to learn." An informal (what other kind) survey of Parkway students indicates that roughly one-third would have dropped out of school eventually.

The tutorial program provides students who are scattered throughout the city with an identifiable group and regular contact with the school. During sessions, which number 15 students, teachers can determine if a child needs special help in areas like math and language skills.

Bremer and the other teachers are optimistic about the potential growth of Parkway. He hopes to have other units set up throughout the city. He says that half of the present students want to continue with courses during the summer and he expects enrollment to reach 700 by the end of the upcoming academic year. This means that expansion will be necessary.

Two sites are under definite consideration. One is near the Philadelphia College of Art on Broad Street, five blocks south of City Hall. And the other is in the historic area along the Delaware River near Independence Hall.

The program has been funded by a $100,000 grant from the Ford Foundation and Bremer's salary is paid by federal money. But, the Parkway School will be included in the Board of Education's capital budget for next year. "All we're asking for is the $680 per student that is now being spent by the Board. We're still going to have to depend on Philadelphia's businesses and institutions because if they withdrew their support, we couldn't operate. As long as we can show them that they get some profit from the program—and some fun out of it—that support will continue."

It's not unusual that Philadelphia should be the place where one of the most innovative experiments in education is taking place. For it is here that one of the first organized programs for public education in the U. S. was put into practice, in 1818.

CENTER STAFF

Store Front Learning Center in Boston

One of the frustrations of people who dislike schools is the difficulty of changing them from within. This is especially true of ghetto school situations, where parents are usually politically impotent. A group of disenchanted citizens in Boston have established

Reprinted by permission of the Storefront Learning Center, 90 West Brookline Street, Boston, Massachusetts.

a *supplementary "storefront" learning center. The promotional description which follows gives some clues about what interests children and some techniques for improving school and neighborhood relations. But does it offer really new dimensions in schooling? On a practical level, can enough money be found to sustain more than a few "storefronts" on a long-term basis?*

NOVEMBER 1969

Boston's South End is an area bruised and aching from the problems that assault our nation's inner cities. Nearly every block is scarred with burnt-down houses, stubby trees, vacant lots which—the junkyards of today—could be the playgrounds of tomorrow. The smashed-in windows of deserted warehouses are boarded up sometimes, most often not, and the glass which shatters in the back alleys below sparkles for the old people (there are many of them here) and the children (there are many of them, too) who come there to linger or to play because they have no other place. Living conditions in the South End are invariably over-crowded, usually substandard. The unemployment rate is high. Drug abuse, prostitution, muggings, common events here which provide promotions for police, and copy for journalists, force the children who grow up in these streets to be daily witnesses. They have no choice.

The South End/Roxbury Crossing area is distinguished from the rest of Roxbury both because of the racial heterogeneity of the neighborhood (predominantly black and Spanish-speaking, Chinese, white, gypsies, and many other ethnic groups are represented, too), and because of the relative residential instability of the population. A large percentage of the inhabitants of the South End are recent arrivals from southern states and from Puerto Rico. Though economically deprived and architecturally humiliated, by urban renewal projects no less than by exploitative landlords and vandals, the South End is rich in its multiplicity of human resources and strengths, and in the desire of many of its residents to save themselves and their children.

For people have been taking notice over the past few years. Community action councils and settlement houses, legal assistance projects and housing services are side by side with the rubbish-strewn yards and the skeletons of burnt-down houses. Residents are vocal and active in recognizing their needs and shaping their community. But there are *many* needs, and children especially make theirs known: that they need a place to learn, a place to talk, a place to play. Inherently creative, children will use the materials at hand: lacking a tree, they will use a fire-escape; lacking a playground they will use the street; lacking a school which gives them lessons in relevance and health, they will learn the lessons of the street, lessons of cynicism and despair, to the ultimate destruction of their own spirit and that of the community around them. They plead for less oppressive instruction.

Often, no one is listening.

The pleas of the children reached responsive ears this time. It was in the summer of 1968 that a small group of black and white people first defined the need, proposed the structure, and sought the funds to establish a nonstructured learning center in Boston's South End ghetto. It was in September 1968 that this Learning Center first opened, operating at that time out of a small storefront office on Tremont Street: hence the name, which has stuck, even after the cramped quarters were abandoned for the spaciousness of an empty warehouse three blocks away, obtained virtually rent-free from the city of Boston.

The Store Front Learning Center came where it was needed. Located on West Brookline Street, between Tremont and Washington Streets, it is in a highly accessible, main-thoroughfare location of the South End, convenient both to foot traffic and public transportation, the most common modes of travel for its youthful and mobile visitors. But its accessibility is more than geographic: it is accessible, too, because its structure, both within and without, is shaped in response to the needs of the community. It is easily approachable. It was designed that way.

A child, exploring the city streets, would have no fears of approaching the Store Front Learning Center. It looks like the kind of place he'd want to go into. Bright drawings enliven the old brick wall, the words "Store Front Learning Center," hand-lettered, suggest the contents—but it's after all, an old warehouse now housing wares of a different nature, and it looks like it's been in the neighborhood a long time and belongs there. That warehouse now houses an exciting atmosphere, abundant in both human and material resources—books, films, tapes, typewriters, magazines, science and art materials. Children who are reluctant before the doors of formal institutions, whose interest wanes in the labyrinth of filling-out-applications-and-completing-forms, whose inerests are something other than being confined, at a pre-scheduled time, to a predetermined body of material, will be put off by none of these. The Learning Center is not a high-powered tutorial program nor an official structured "nursery," not a recreation center nor a pre-college briefing center equipped with social workers or guidance counselors. It is a place where learning is available, where a child, propelled by his own interests, may stop by without announcement and select from the continuing smorgasbord of intellectual excitements, the particular area that interests him most. It's a kind of street-school, a wide-opening learning center that a child can get to easily and to which he wants to return.

The old furniture warehouse has become a "learning warehouse" an atmosphere in which the dynamics of learning have replaced the pedagogy and passivity of teaching. The people who started the Learning Center—the parents, volunteers, college students, and staff members who work there—the children who come there to investigate—are giving a new and spirited definition to learning. The Store Front Learning Center was constructed on an assumption of trust in a child's ability to be self-propelled, on a belief that a child's motivation is self-generating and self-renewing, if presented with interesting materials in an atmosphere that promotes and stimulates independent inquiry, without pressure, threat, or manipulation. The premise was that, under ideal circumstances, people will learn if there is an ample and exciting variety of intriguing intellectual stimuli placed before them. This premise, which inspired the founders of the Learning Center, was well founded.

The children are not the only ones who learn at the Learning Center. They may have been the first. Natural detectives, children are alert to the clues that portend a good thing, they are quick to scout it out. Parents come because they're interested in their children's interests. Teachers come, too, inspired by a variety of motives. And here's the other learning that the Learning Center is able to foster, and here's its uniqueness: the atmosphere that allows the children to inquire, to be curious and follow the directions in which their curiosity leads them (whether it's reading a paperback from the library of 7000, especially selected because of high relevance to the black, inner-city child's experience, or fiddling with the lights and batteries of a science project)—this is the atmosphere, too, in which parents and teachers are drawn together, and this is the place which makes possible the involvement of all those concerned with education in Boston to come together; victims of one educational experience, they are now witnesses of another and, freed of the traditional barriers, are able to meet on a kind of neutral ground.

The intention of the Store Front Learning Center was not to place itself in competition with the Boston public schools, but to supplement the school experience, by providing an educational resource center for the teachers, future teachers, parents, and neighborhood children all under the same roof, in an effort to hit head-on at the number one problem of the northern ghetto: fear, distrust and enmity between black parents and white teachers. The manner in which community parents and classroom teachers are brought together in an atmosphere of interesting and intriguing educational materials in which the the children are involved is disarming: habitual fears and racial and class hostilities may be temporarily forgotten. It is this overriding factor of fear and hostility which must be dealt with prior to any problems of pedagogy, prior to any issues of curriculum. The Learning Center does this, by exploiting the new materials—the books and games and film and puzzles —as a device for drawing in the classroom teachers.

We know why the children come, and why the parents come. But what makes the teachers come? How do they hear of the Learning Center and why do they keep coming? In some cases, the children have been the couriers of the new experience. By bringing back to their regular classroom some of the books and materials from the Learning Center they have made explicit recommendations. Some teachers have acted on this and been drawn in out of curiosity. In other cases, the parent-directors of the Learning Center have gone directly to local school principals and have invited them to send their teachers down to work with them. The response of the principals has been good, and teachers have subsequently come down in greater numbers. A third method of communication has been the direct personal approach, on the part of the parent-directors, to teachers known to be already sympathetic to the black community, urging them in turn to approach some of their less sympathetic fellow-teachers. For it is, after all, an old story for civil rights-oriented educational programs to pull in hip and imaginative young teachers, while leaving 95 percent of the children back at school with the patient, ordinary, un-radical and un-hip teachers who make up the ordinary inner-city faculty. It is these teachers the Learning Center must reach, to achieve its full success. The apparent emphasis at the Learning Center on educational materials and styles establishes an atmosphere that is politically lowtoned, ostensibly a safe atmosphere for the kind of teachers who have consistently steered clear of activism and who wouldn't join the picket lines, thus bringing them together with teen-agers and parents from the black community on a basis of easy intimacy and of unhurried conversation of the sort which commonly leads to the development of unexpected loyalties.

The clearest evidence of the fact that teachers regard the Learning

Center as a valuable experience both for themselves and for their students is the fact that they *use* it, in a variety of ways. In some cases, teachers request—and receive—lists of book-titles, game-companies, and curriculum materials recommended by the Learning Center; in some cases, they take materials with them back into the public classrooms. In other cases, a teacher may bring her entire class over to the Center during school time, to participate in the creative activities available there. Class visits are so popular now that the Learning Center, because of spatial limitations, invites teachers to sign up for visits on a priority basis. The classroom can accommodate up to forty or fifty children in a given block of time, and the Learning Center encourages the teachers to plan visits to last approximately two hours. From past experience, it has become apparent that children profit most from a series of successive visits.

When a class comes to the Learning Center, there is a short preliminary talk to introduce them to the different activities in which they may participate. Then the class dissolves, forming smaller interest groups in which children may work in the area most appealing to them. There are many possibilities: language arts (reading, typing stories, dramatic work with puppets), arts and crafts (painting, clay work, printing, making musical instruments), math (attribute blocks, Cuisenaire rods, various math games), science (work with batteries and bulbs, the Visible Man). In addition, black studies, Latin American studies, and a bilingual program have been designed to meet the needs of the urban child, focusing on a multilevel and wide age group. For Puerto Rican children, there are lessons and classroom assignments in Spanish and lessons in Spanish for teachers.

For the teacher, there is a wealth of material on urban education and the direct assistance and enthusiasm of some of the leading educators in the country who serve the Learning Center on a consulting basis. Tuesday evening seminars, organized by parents and aimed at local teachers, feature community leaders and educators, and serve to draw parents, teachers, and older students, militants and moderates together, with growing attendance.

Everyone learns at the Learning Center: the child, the parent, the present urban teacher. The future teacher has a place there, too. The educational environment created at the Learning Center may serve as a laboratory which answers the pleas of the students and faculty of educational schools alike, for more concrete and specific forms of training in ghetto situations and with ghetto residents present, providing the same challenges, though without the same professional risks and without the same areas of psychological insecurity which are likely to be encountered later on in classroom situations. In the first year of its existence, forty student-teachers from Harvard, Tufts, Boston University, and Wheelock came in to the Learning Center. Their work there was supervised and coordinated by two parents. Several of the students received course-credit for the work they did at the Learning Center; most attended seminars and workshops on community concerns which were sponsored and directed by the Learning Center. Many of these students have now entered public classrooms in Boston and in other core-area school systems, bringing with them both the professional expertise and the humanizing loyalties gained from their experience. Again this September we began work with three new teams of teachers-in-training from Harvard, Boston University, and the University of Massachusetts in Boston. Their presence defines another aim of the Learning Center—to establish itself as a laboratory environment in which students preparing to become teachers may obtain on-the-spot experience and in which experienced teachers obtain retraining of a sort not generally available within the classroom of a school of education. The goal of the program is to encourage and develop a group of teachers who will be deeply acquainted with community people and with community training in new approaches and techniques suitable to the public classrooms. Training involves particular emphasis on essential skills (reading, math, social studies), as well as on an overall humanizing, redirection of teacher outlook and of professional behavior. Ultimate emphasis is given to the preparation of the teacher as a change-agent, an individual who, once trained and sent out into the public system, will be able to convey to others a contagious sense of enthusiasm for the attitudes, techniques and areas of special skill acquired during the period of the Learning Center Training.

In addition to the aforementioned materials and activities available at the Learning Center, there is a parent-run preschool playroom (five mornings a week) for twenty neighborhood children, an art workshop for "drop-in" after school hours, a tutoring project, and quiet evening study time. The Center is open five days a week, from nine in the morning until eight at night. In the Art Workshop, children become artists along with an adult; they learn through the dynamics of participation, not the passivity of instruction. A once-a-week photography workshop is also available.

Who were the people who made the decision to build an educational center on a broken and forgotten street, a venture that grew in a single year from a pioneer three-person project into a complex educational facility with a trained staff of twenty-five?

They were people—parents and teachers, many from the South End community—who had been around Boston a long time, who knew the children and who knew the Boston school system. They had in common their concern for these children and their belief in them, and the Store Front Learning Center was a structure dedicated to this belief. They were people who had been founders and are now Trustees of the New School for Children in Roxbury, a black community venture in education which had met exciting and unanticipated success; but they were people who felt, despite this success, a sense of incompletion in the area of maximum possible service and commitment to the surrounding neighborhood. Thus the Learning Center was conceived.

The Learning Center is a nonprofit corporation with a Trustee Board of five members, of whom three are community parents, one is an attorney and one is an educator. The Board delegates responsibility to the Learning Center staff, which consists of a director, Mrs. Edward Burns (with the ultimate responsibility for the entire program and personnel); an associate director, Mrs. Eugene Washington (coordination of university and student ties); two co-directors of the educational program, Mr. Charlie Tyson and Mrs. Sandra Fenton (both former teachers); a director of community relations, Mrs. Joyce Johnson; and two co-directors of the preschoolers' playroom, Mrs. Loretta Roach (a community parent) and Barbara Kibler (a former teacher who doubles as the afternoon art workshop director). These staff leaders are assisted by teacher's aides from New Careers, Neighborhood Youth Corps, Commonwealth Service Corps, college work-study students, and volunteers.

Jonathan Kozol, one of the founders of the center and its constant consultant, has served as a link to the curriculum agencies and to various specialists in the universities and suburban schools. These specialists have, in turn, trained our staff and student-teachers in a series of math, science, and reading workshops, with the help of donations of books from publishers and games and materials from manufacturers and business.

Another kind of consultation is also available to the Learning Center through the many links our Board of Sponsors offers. Among our sponsors are community and education leaders such as Luther Seabrook (Highland Park Free School), Ellen Jackson (Operation

Exodus), Melvin King (New Urban League), Kenneth Brown (United South End Settlements), James Breeden (United Front), Thomas Atkins (Boston City Council), Noam Chomsky (professor and writer), Robert Coles (child psychiatrist and author), Howard Zinn (professor and writer) and John Holt (educator and author).

The staff of the Learning Center have also been engaged in extensive meetings with Alic Casey (the District Superintendent), Evans Clinchy (Planning Center), Neil Sullivan (Commissioner of Education), Ray Dethy of Northeastern, George Thomas and Dean Sizer of Harvard Graduate School of Education, and Chancellor Broderick of the University of Massachusetts, and foresees a good likelihood that the Learning Center will achieve sufficient recognition as a satellite service to public schools and as a training-lab for teachers, during the course of the next two years, to find its ultimate financial support through the federal, state, and local agencies concerned with public schooling. The staff, however, believe that three years represents the minimal period of time in which this could be effected.

What, then is the Store Front Learning Center? A place where children—and those concerned about them—can come together, in an atmosphere free of politics or pressure, to learn. While the children learn from the Cuisenaire rods and logic games and drawing, their parents and their teachers can learn from this mutual confrontation. Such humanizing centers on neutral territory are gravely needed if public education is to be redirected to meet the needs of the urban child. The Learning Center makes this possible. It is unique for, while faithful to its belief in the children that inspired it and the community which it serves, the Learning Center is also recognized as a program with more than local significance because of this impact-value in seeking to make its influence felt upon the public school classroom. The Store Front Learning Center, which began with a $5000 grant from the Committee of the Permanent Charities, long outgrew its storefront; not surprisingly, it has also outgrown its present three floors in the old warehouse. Another floor in the building or in the neighborhood, at least, to use for seminars, staff resource material, a teacher-training library, and discussion sessions is an immediate requirement. Copying equipment is also badly needed.

STEPHEN ARONS

The Joker in Private School Aid

*The preceding article describes one kind of private schooling ven-
ture. Private schools have long been significant in America and
may challenge the public near-monopoly in the future. The following article goes beyond the usual description of the financial plight
of non-public schools and summarizes court decisions and state
measures which provide funds for them. The author also questions
whether the way private schools have been funded has curbed the
diversity which should be their chief characteristic.*

In the past two years—overnight as legislatures count time—at least six
states have passed laws providing substantial general aid to private
schools, and similar bills are pending in half a dozen other states. This
new concern by state legislatures for non-public education is a response
to a well-organized Catholic lobby and to simple arithmetic: By supporting in part the education of children in non-public schools, nine-tenths
of which are operated by the Roman Catholic Church, they can avoid
supporting in full the education of the same children in public schools.
The Supreme Court this term will review two lower-court decisions on
comprehensive state aid to non-public schools: *Lemon vs. Kurtzman* and
DiCenso vs. Robinson. Both of the decisions are being tested for their
constitutionality on First Amendment grounds because they provide
for the purchase by the state of "secular" educational services for children in private schools.

It is by no means clear how the Supreme Court will resolve these
conflicting decisions. The financial impact its decision will have on the
public school treasury is obvious. The impact of the Court's views on
separation of church and state is a subject of great speculation and
abundant brief writing, but the profound effects that rejection or approval of these particular laws will have on the entire course of American education, and in particular on its desperately needed reform, has
been almost totally ignored.

It isn't hard to see why many of the people opposed to these laws have focused so closely on the First Amendment issue and its underlying principle of insulating the political process from religious factionalism. It is, after all, the fact that this insulation has worn thin that has made the statutes possible. Preserving the "wall" between church and state is indeed a basic problem. But purchase-of-secular-services agreements have educational consequences that are perhaps even more important.

Ideally, these laws might prove a powerful force for equalization of educational opportunity, for stimulation of wide experimentation in both public and non-public schools, and for development of new schools that will provide greater diversity in education. But it appears that their effect will be just the opposite.

Under the scheme provided for in the Pennsylvania and Rhode Island legislation, the state purchases, by contract with a non-public school and its employees, secular education for students in such schools. The contract usually calls for payment of part of the salary of certain lay teachers and for texts and other teaching materials, as well as for the costs of standardized testing. The secularity and public purposes of these services is thought to be insured by limiting the instruction performed to that done by teachers of such courses as physical science, mathematics, or foreign languages. It is argued that these courses by their very nature cannot be tainted with religious doctrine.

In deriving this theory of what constitutes secular education from the church-state decisions of the past twenty-five years, it appears that questions of education policy were furthest from the minds of the drafters of these laws. In fact, one could take a much grimmer view, for aside from preserving the existing private schools, the effect of these laws will likely be to preserve or make worse the already intolerable inequities and inadequacies of public schools, while restricting the capacity of the public, especially the poor and the minority groups, to find alternatives.

This conclusion is substantiated by a review not only of the Pennsylvania and Rhode Island laws being tested but also of those passed in Connecticut, Ohio, and Michigan, and of those pending in several other states. From the point of view of education reform, seven specific criteria are useful in evaluating this legislation: 1) the level of aid provided; 2) the degree to which the aid equalizes the purchasing power of rich and poor; 3) the degree to which the legislation would encourage uniformity rather than diversity of education programs; 4) the amount of due process available to recipients of aid who believe they have been unfairly treated; 5) the extent to which the parents would be made cognizant that they had a choice among schools; 6) the amount of information about these schools that would be available to parents; and 7) the restrictions on racial discrimination in school admissions.

No state under these new aid laws pays enough to cover the cost of operating a private school. Rhode Island's law pays 15 percent of a teacher's salary. Pennsylvania pays "reasonable cost" of certain teachers' salaries but reduces that amount to a prorata share in the inevitable event that legitimate requests exceed legislative appropriations. Michigan begins by paying "not more than 50 percent" of the salaries of certified lay teachers, and the story is basically the same in Ohio and Connecticut. The low level of aid is hardly an unexpected discovery, since it is the purpose of this aid to maintain but not replace current private expenditures for education, and inasmuch as the secular education theory holds that the First Amendment can be satisfied if only part of the education in non-public schools is paid for.

The result of providing only incremental aid is that only a few existing alternatives to public education can survive—those with dependable access to private financing—which is to say those serving the wealthy and institutions supported by religious organizations. The poor and middle-class who do not desire religious education and cannot afford to supplement the small amount of state aid must fall back on the public schools, which will consequently become more segregated. The black community schools and the free schools serving mixed socioeconomic and racial groups will be squeezed out. The result is free choice for those with access to private wealth and compulsory miseducation for the rest.

Nor is there any prospect for the disappearance of this bias in the long run. The economic and political leverage of the affluent and the supporters of church schools, which led to the laws in the first place, will be maintained because the aid continues the existence of their schools. The poor and the middle-class in general, lacking any basic economic or political franchise for education, find no place to take hold. State education budgets will be fought out between those who have a vested interest in increased expenditures for public schools and those who have a vested interest in limiting public school financing, while maintaining a modest level of aid to private schools.

Some of the existing state laws attempt to minimize these problems by devising aid formulas designed to put the poor in a somewhat better bargaining position. Connecticut, for instance, increases its 20 percent contribution to a teacher's salary to 50 percent if the school enrolls one-third disadvantaged children, and to 60 percent if it enrolls two-thirds disadvantaged children. While this provides an inducement to private schools to include disadvantaged children, it does not change the fundamental bargaining position of poor parents, because they must still depend on money provided by either higher-income parents or the church to subsidize their children's education.

Pennsylvania approaches the equalization of economic power for all parents by providing for payment of actual cost of teacher salaries. This does not prevent the private school from increasing tuition to the point where the poor are priced out of the market, but it does at least make it possible for the poor or middle-class to go to a school without much outside financing. Nevertheless, this possibility is largely a chimera because the law's prorata sharing provision means that only a fraction of the actual cost of salaries will be paid. Thus, neither the Connecticut plan, which also honors first those claims based on the presence of disadvantaged children, nor Pennsylvania's, with its prorated half-promise to pay all instructional costs, really provides independence and effective choice to all parents. Rhode Island's statute, which provides a flat reimbursement of only 15 percent of teachers' salaries, is even worse on this score. Even those states, such as Illinois and Wisconsin, that are considering per capita grants instead of purchase of secular services fail to equalize substantially the bargaining power of all parents.

Diversity is also forestalled by state-imposed restrictions on how money can be spent. Some of these restrictions, of course, are designed to get around First Amendment problems by limiting the aid to subjects thought to be free of religious content or overtones. But such specific restrictions also apply to secular schools—though they needn't—with the result that the absolute minimum is done to encourage secular alternatives to existing systems. In fact, this merely hints at the legislatures' policy of discouraging diversity wherever possible. Ohio is the most blatant example. There, the aid law 1) requires that private school teachers must hold state certificates; 2) permits the state superintendent to review courses, teacher and student evaluations, and test scores; 3) prohibits the use of services, materials, or programs not available in the public schools; and 4) states that education in non-public schools "shall not exceed in cost or *quality*" that offered in the public schools (emphasis added).

Not all the statutes are so considerate of the sensibilities of the public school bureaucracy or so overtly anti-competitive, but it is common to find provisions in the aid laws requiring teacher certification, satisfactory performance on standardized testing, state approval of texts and teaching materials, and general equivalency with the public school curriculum, not to mention compliance with building and health codes and narrowly conceived attendance requirements. The degree to which the states feel free to call the tune is already out of proportion to the amounts they are willing to pay the piper. While there is only enough aid to sustain established private schools, there is enough regulation to hamper the development of most experimental schools.

Although failure to comply with these requirements can result in termination or denial of aid, only the Connecticut statute provides for notice of such state action and hearing procedures through which a school can argue its case. Nor do those states that set minimum standards guarantee that schools meeting those standards will receive a fair share of the available aid. Pennsylvania, in addition to several vague regulations, grants the state superintendent of public instruction authority to "establish rules and regulations pertaining" to payment. The opportunities for arbitrary treatment at the hands of state officials are apparent, particularly when one considers the heterodox and even radical stance taken by many alternative schools. The absence of significant procedural due process, in four of the five laws in other states, is not reassuring.

The formulas for the purchase of secular services dilute the effectiveness of parent choice even among private schools receiving aid. In most cases, the teacher or school receives the aid directly, regardless of the number or type of children in the school or class, and the money would continue to come in even if a large number of parents abandoned the school. The school would, of course, lose the tuition these parents were paying. While the connection between parent choice and economic survival is not severed, it is substantially weakened.

The new aid laws also deny parents the means to influence the policies of the schools they choose for their children, and none of the laws provides for informing parents of the nature of the alternatives open to them. Systematic dissemination of basic information is essential to a consumer or democratic political system, but, aside from the guarantee that schools meet dubious state standards, these laws have not seen fit to encourage informed choice. In addition to the other bars to diversity, none of the plans makes any provision for aiding or encouraging the start of new schools, for instance, through technical assistance or low-cost loans. Indeed, the Connecticut purchase-of-services law requires that a school either be in operation prior to the passage of the act or file a statement of intent to operate as a school *three* years before applying for aid.

The consequences of these bills—their failure to support adequately secular, non-elitist schools, their failure to ·equalize the bargaining position of the poor and middle-class, their failure to foster competition and diversity, and their failure to provide for significant influence by parents—tend simply to extend and reproduce all the failures of the public schools. They are indeed unfortunate consequences, but one further consequence of these laws is intolerable: the lack of effective barriers to prevent racial discrimination.

Almost all require a certificate of compliance with Title VI of the Civil Rights Act of 1964, but certificates are easy to sign, and only Connecticut provides for any enforcement procedure. It is reasonable to assume that at some point the Supreme Court will extend Fourteenth Amendment safeguards against racial discrimination to schools receiving this comprehensive state aid. But this could mean nothing more than that the whole tedious process that started with the public schools in 1954 must be gone through again with private schools. In light of this and the obvious enforcement problems engendered by a large number of independent schools, it is quite likely that because of the absence of specific standards and grievance procedures, the overall effect of these bills will be the further segregation of public schools, an effect that might reasonably be considered de jure segregation because of the method of its accomplishment. During the recent trial of a Connecticut suit challenging the state's purchase-of-services plan, considerable evidence of these segregation problems was presented.

These disastrous purchase-of-secular-services plans seem to have gained political support in part because no alternative way of aiding non-public schools has been regarded as feasible. However, a recent study commissioned by the Office of Economic Opportunity demonstrates that an education voucher plan is not only a feasible alternative but that for the poor, for minority groups, for educational pluralism, and for the general health of American education vouchers would be preferable.

The report to OEO recommends an experiment of five to eight years in duration. Parents of school-age children in the experimental area would receive vouchers approximately equal to the average per-pupil expenditures public schools had previously maintained. For parents of educationally disadvantaged children the value of the voucher would be increased, perhaps to as high as twice the basic amount. Students could attend any approved school, whether operated by a public or private authority. Regulations of approved schools would remain about as they are now, securing a minimum basic education but placing no premium on uniformity. Admissions to oversubscribed schools would be conducted by lot for 50 percent of the places, with the school choosing the other 50 percent, provided it did not discriminate on the basis of race. Systematic information about schools would be collected and published by a local Education Voucher Agency (EVA) that would administer the entire experiment.

The proposed experimental voucher plan seeks to meet each of the objections raised in discussing purchase of secular services. It does not divide the electorate into those favoring increased public school funds and those seeking to divert public funds to private schools, because every child's education is paid for by voucher, regardless of which school he attends. The level of support is adequate to meet all operational costs of running a school, eliminating the need to rely upon private funding with its inherently discriminatory effects. Aid is delivered per capita and is skewed in favor of the poor and working classes, providing significant bargaining power to those in low-income brackets and incentives to schools to enroll disadvantaged children. Diversity is aided by relying for education standards on the state minimums that already govern a wide range of private schools. Furthermore, since the insulation of church and state is accomplished by creating a system that, similar to the one in the GI Bill, substitutes the individual for the state in deciding which schools receive aid, no complex of secularizing regulations is needed. The plan is carefully designed to provide school data sufficient to allow an informed choice by parents. Finally, the lottery provisions and the provision of free transportation for students provide a reliable protection against racial discrimination.

Although the Court will not be passing upon any form of vouchers in *Lemon* and *DiCenso*, the comparison is certainly instructive on educational, economic, and racial issues. The purchase-of-secular-services legislation that the court will be testing this fall responds to two needs: saving the public treasury from the expense of educating erstwhile parochial school students, and avoiding the constraints of the First Amendment's church-state provisions. But this particular form of meeting these needs only creates further problems. In order to save ourselves a few dollars, we will hamstring an incipient educational reform movement based on educational and cultural diversity and racial and economic equality. To prevent an entanglement of church and state, we will create a bureaucracy and a set of regulations that will hamper the education experiments we must have if we are to find out how best to dismantle the schooling monolith we are locked into. The narrowness of the concerns expressed by those who favor or oppose these bills will be partly to blame.

In this context, it makes little sense to rely, politically or constitutionally, solely on arguments based on separation of church and state. The most important question is not whether private schools should receive aid—it seems clear that one way or another they will—but whether a way can be found to provide that aid and simultaneously advance the reform of our whole system of education. The recent flurry of discussion about tuition vouchers at least represents an attempt to view these problems together and come up with a comprehensive solution to all of them. If the Court finds the purchase-of-services theory unconstitutional, it is likely that the energy behind those laws will be put into some form of voucher plan that makes the parent the determinant of which schools will be aided. If the Court finds the present aid plans acceptable, there will be a rush of state legislation duplicating these plans all over the country, and one promising means of converting the financial crisis in private education into a force for broad educational reform will have been lost.

TIM PARSONS

The Community School Movement

The community control movement, alluded to in the preceding unit, is described in more detail in the following article. While community control—if it were actually implemented with attending power shifts—looks good as a reform possibility, the fact is that it has not yet been tried very extensively. Will it be? Will the groups who now have power relinquish their favored positions?

Tim Parsons, "The Community School Movement," *Community Issues,* Institute for Community Studies, Queens College, New York, vol. 2, no. 6 (December 1970). Excerpts reprinted by permission.

Although the basic idea of local control and individual responsibility is central to the American ideal, massive corporations, unions and governmental units have taken us far from the individual entrepreneur, craftsman and one room school house. Increasing numbers of poor people, as well as disaffected middle class youth, are struggling to alter large impersonal American institutions or establish alternative structures.[1]

The 30 community controlled school projects described here are almost all located in predominantly low income, minority group communities. They are distinguished from the middle class free schools in that the thrust has come from people who traditionally have lacked both significant control and options in the formal education they or their children engage in. This thrust has evolved in three basic structures: 1) quasi-independent community school or programs within public school systems, 2) independent community schools, and 3) minority controlled existing state school districts. Although the independent community schools are non-public in their source of funding, all are "public" in the sense that they are generally open to all children on a first-come, first-served basis without a required tuition screening out the poorest children.

What is a community-controlled school?

In brief, a community-controlled school is a school in which parents, students or residents who form a self-defined "community" previously lacking control exert extensive decision-making power over the policies of the school or schools serving that community. Some explanations are needed:

Community. "Community" is the crucial word which separates this new form of school from most instances of "local control." Living within large "local" districts are many groups of people who have lost or never had any significant control over and responsibility for the local public school. The size of the self-defined "community" can vary widely from a large area with a connection by name and a sense of shared needs—such as Harlem or Watts—to a small group of parents living on one block or students attending one high school.[2]

Controversy has frequently arisen over the question of who speaks for "the community." Early stages in the formation of a project may center on outspoken self-appointed leaders who demonstrate the greatest concern for basic change in the schools.[3] Most of the projects described in this report have then evolved toward community or parent elections of a board.

Control. To exercise control is to have the power to make decisions which will govern significant aspects of the schools' operations. *None* of the projects in this report have *total* control, just as local districts in this country do not exert total control. Publicly supported projects confront the potential of a higher level veto, review or even takeover[4] as well as state laws setting minimum standards and restricting or prescribing certain actions. Independent community schools may be limited by shortage of funds, local fire and building codes and state laws setting minimum certification or other standards for non-public schools.

Many of the community or parent groups in public sub-systems are so limited in their powers that their projects are best described as "efforts" for community control. They are included in this report more because of their commitment to gaining greater control than their actual wielding of power at present. They can be distinguished from most "advisory committees" in their unwillingness to accept most professional staff decisions or high level vetoes which are contrary to community interests. They have and frequently take recourse to direct pressure, legal or political action to oppose an unpopular decision imposed on them.

Major areas in which decision-making powers may be exerted include hiring and firing of staff, planning or approval of program and curriculum, granting of contracts for construction, maintenance and repairs, determination of size and allocation of a budget. Some or most of these powers may be delegated to the staff *by parents* under the principle of community control. However, this should not be confused with cases of bureaucratic "decentralization" in which powers are assigned *directly* to professionals at a local level by a central board or superintendent.

School. A number of the projects described here contain more than a single school (a complex, federation, district or sub-system); other projects are programs encompassing some grades or classrooms within a school (the Follow Through parent-implemented programs). Because of these varying structures, the terms "projects," "programs," "school" or "schools" are alternately used in describing the projects.

Another term used increasingly by schools which are or are attempting to become community-controlled is "community school." Some confusion arises from this due to the earlier usage of "community school" to designate schools in which many programs serving diverse community interests are included.[5] Although community-controlled schools also tend to develop a variety of programs serving the community, the distinguishing feature of all "community schools" described in this report is the increased decision-making powers exercised by parents and community.

A SUMMARY OF OBSERVATIONS

Each community school has its own unique history, curriculum, and structure. Yet, there are a number of clear generalizations which emerge from an overview of the thirty projects.

Observations of community school curricula

1. Parents Support Innovative Approaches. Many educators fear that low income parents will choose repressive, traditional classroom approaches and shun new, more effective methods for learning. It is often true that militant and community residents attack educators for "experimenting with our kids."

The great amount of innovation present in the schools described in this study strongly indicates that parents want new approaches when *they* are in the position of choosing them and are assured the power to alter the programs if they find that their children are being hurt by them. Experimentation-innovation is often viewed as manipulation when exerted by professional educators not accountable to parents. The same militants who are the usual opponents of this "manipulation" when externally controlled are often the activist board members of the community schools who have chosen to implement innovative programs "to help our children learn."

2. Parents choose a great variety of innovative approaches, often based on a newly emerging view of their children as learners and a new philosophy of education. Most approaches are individualized. Parents have selected a wide variety of innovative approaches. Some accent development of skills, some stress personal-social development; most combine both areas. Generally, all efforts lead to greater individualized learning. This has centered on the use of more personnel, particularly community residents, rather than a stress on machines and technology.

Many parents deeply involved in setting directions of schools are developing a new view of their children as reflected in a child-oriented philosophy of education. This is especially evident in small community schools where an active dialogue occurs between young parents and young staff with new ideas based on a new vision of the world. Though not a single vision, it contains the common strains of cooperation before competition, sharing above consuming, and personal and small group communication rather than bureaucratic procedures and structures. Not as unstructured as many free schools, these community schools have nevertheless moved far from traditional public school programs.

3. *The curriculum bias is toward open classrooms or the Leicestershire approach.* Within the variety of innovative approaches to classroom organization and curriculum, the most widely adopted or borrowed from model is the Leicestershire approach developed in British infant schools. More recently educators have begun to use the term "open classroom" or "open education" for this and similar approaches which stress allowing the individual child to explore his own interests and best paths to learning by choosing among a variety of activities. Classes usually are vertically grouped; that is, each classroom includes children of at least two or three different age levels. Classes often follow an "integrated day" format; that is, the child chooses what subject he wishes to pursue at what time of the day or day of the week. Lectures on one subject or skill are eliminated; even small teacher-organized group work tends to disappear in favor of individual projects or student-initiated cooperative projects.

The majority of the independent community schools follow variations of the "open classroom" approach; a half-dozen of the publicly supported projects include classrooms experimenting with similar approaches.

4. *The most extensive classroom changes are evident in the smaller projects/schools.* Basic departures from the traditional lecture-teaching, rote-learning structured total class activities are evident in nearly every classroom of the small independent community schools and projects involving less than approximately five hundred children. Traditional classrooms and teachers, though diminishing in numbers, still constitute the majority in the larger districts in which control by parents is quite limited in decision-making power and/or funds.

Observations of community involvement and integration

1. Parent and community involvement is much more extensive in community schools. The small projects and schools have a significantly higher percentage of their parents deeply involved. The contrast between the typical public school and community schools generally increases greatly as the community schools or projects decrease in size. Though approximately the same number of parents may be active with the various programs, this means a much higher *percentage* of parents involved in the small programs. A great variety of ways in which parents can participate has been developed in community schools. (For examples, see especially the East Harlem Block Schools sketch in Chapter IV.)

2. Community-controlled schools utilize community resources, especially personnel, much more extensively than most inner-city schools. Not only have these projects been the leaders in hiring greater numbers of personnel who live in the immediate community (who are often parents) but also they have used these employees in a great variety of roles. Not restricted to the traditional role of an aide who patrols the halls and lunchroom or does the teacher's clerical work, these community people make home visits, raise funds, act as full teaching assistants or partners in the classrooms, and sometimes as regular teachers. Great stress has been placed on training and new career opportunities as well as natural partnerships with or supervision by professionals. Again the smaller independent schools and Follow-Through projects have generally utilized community personnel more extensively, considering their size, than the larger districts.

3. More integration of staff and/or student bodies is found in community controlled schools than in regular public schools. Where no integration of student bodies is possible in either community or regular schools, the community boards are generally receptive to integration. Widespread efforts to select black administrators for those projects and schools serving predominantly black students have led to some conclusions and fears which are not supported by reality. Community boards have generally selected their leaders with a strong view toward providing the students with a success model from their own race. Yet most of the independent community schools which are located in areas where public schools are totally segregated have moderately integrated (a rate averaging about 80:20) student bodies. Their faculties usually include nearly equal representation from minority and majority groups. Public community school projects also generally have integrated staffs, selected according to ability and willingness to work with parents and community residents. The many white union teachers who left the Ocean Hill-Brownsville and IS 201 demonstration districts in New York City were mostly replaced by white teachers. Although parents in newly won positions of control in community schools or districts do not want to relinquish this control to white control—via bureaucracy or an influx of white parents—many indicate their openness to adding white students.

Other observations:

1. Professional educators hired by parents often experience a basic change in attitude: A chance for parent-professional partnership. Many teachers and administrators who have been interviewed by parent personnel committees praise the depth and perceptiveness of the questions asked by parents. They often compare these interviews with those conducted by harried or facile professional administrators who have no direct stake in the children's education. In contrast to the large New York City demonstration districts where teachers were initially inherited rather than hired by the community boards, teachers hired by parent boards often speak of a new respect for parents.

Though they must prove they can work with parents and tenure often is not guaranteed, professionals in small community schools generally have greater rather than less power to implement new ideas in their classrooms. Because of this, community schools may be the best path to the situation in which both parents and teachers feel increased control over their lives and jobs. A real parent-professional partnership has already emerged in some community schools.

2. Bureaucratic demands and power struggles are generally a continuing problem for publicly funded projects. One consistent exception is the Follow Through Program. The most widely known struggles have faced the three locally funded demonstration districts in New York City. However, even efforts designed to avoid traditional educational bureaucracy by creating a new state district (CCED in Massachusetts) or a federally funded model district (Anacostia in Washington, D.C.) have faced many bureaucratic obstacles. Consistently escaping the damning criticism is the Follow Through program funded by the Office of Economic Opportunity and administered by the Office of Education. A rare group of administrators of this program has been able to fund independent community schools and "parent-implemented" projects within public systems without imposing the usually crippling red tape. Their main expectation has been that the parents have significant powers in designing and controlling the program. Although a few criticisms are heard of the standardized evaluations administered to children in each project, most local projects praise the administration of Follow Through and contrast it with other publicly funded programs. Follow Through provides a model for those seeking to use federal funds to promote true local participation and control rather than further centralization. It is an answer to those federal legislators and administrators who pretend to support "local control" by advocating block grants of federal funds to the states, knowing that the state bureaucracies are usually less supportive than the federal bureaucracy of innovation and the needs of low income communities.

3. *In most inner city areas, alternative institutions outside the regular public systems are the only place where basic change occurs.* Small independent community schools, no matter how successful, are ignored by most public school educators because they involve only a small percentage of the many children of low income families enrolled in schools. However, such a small proportion of inner city public school children are "successfully educated," even by the public schools' own standards, that the number of children presently enrolled in independent community schools in New York, Boston and Milwaukee are already quite significant. Though improvement is evident in some publicly-funded community control efforts, progress is severely limited by bureaucratic opposition and the ever-present difficulties created for parents and professionals alike who attempt to function within large systems. Small scale community schools within public systems are likely to be successful only where an unusual amount of control is relinquished to or captured by parents. School systems where this is likely to occur appear to be rare.

The consistent superiority of independent community schools in the areas of parent involvement, student attitudes toward learning, and use of community resources suggests that public aid to community schools or a parent voucher system is the most promising direction for most cities.

An observation in need of more research

Achievement in community schools is equal or superior to public schools with similar student populations. The strengths of many community schools are not measurable by traditional tests. Although early reports from the few schools which utilize achievement tests are positive, it is certainly much too early to reach a conclusion. The danger, in fact, is that foundations and the Congress will want firm results too quickly and in the traditional form of test scores. The rapid turnover of "unsuccessful" experiments in American schools is probably due more to the fact that we don't allow them to establish themselves before evaluating them than it is due to shortcomings in the new idea. Trial time is particularly important for community schools in which the governance of the school and the relationship between parents and professionals is radically altered. There is always an extended "shake-down" period in any new school, whether controlled by parents, professionals or both.

Reports of decreased vandalism, eagerness to learn, improved attendance and an elimination of pupil suspensions are more significant measures at this early time than achievement scores. In the long run, the child's and his family's feeling of control over their own lives is certainly vital in this increasingly complex world. Academic skills are only one element helpful in maintaining a sense of control. The actual daily practice of sharing in the control of one's own life, schools and other institutions is at least as significant.

AN EXAMPLE OF A QUASI-INDEPENDENT COMMUNITY SCHOOL WITHIN THE PUBLIC SCHOOL SYSTEM: GREELEY

Greeley, Colorado provides a different setting for a parent-implementation model. A city of 44,000 located in a prosperous farming area 55 miles north of Denver, Greeley contains a sizeable low income Mexican-American sub-community.

Since Greeley had unsuccessfully applied for Follow Through projects through normal channels, school officials welcomed the prospect of being specially funded. Misunderstanding the thrust of parent-implementation, however, Greeley had already drawn up a fairly detailed proposal by the time the first Follow Through consultants (led by Tony Ward, then Director of the East Harlem Block Schools) arrived in August, 1968. Explaining that parent-implementation meant parent planning *from the beginning,* the consultants proceeded to visit most of the forty families to be included (another 40 children are added each year) and organize a parent meeting. After an explicit description of the potential powers of the parents and a brief description of some parent-controlled schools, the consultants left the parents alone to set their own priorities and directions. It was made clear that the money from

Follow Through (30,000 dollars in 1968–69) would be available for their children's education only if the parents organized and reached decisions about its expenditure. Parents selected an eight member (later reduced to seven) interim Board, selected a local school staff member to be director and set times for future meetings. Within a few weeks they had also hired a kindergarten teacher, family contact worker and class-room aide.

Their rapid action was somewhat surprising—and partly regretted. The Director, hardly known to the parents and not sympathetic with parent-control, was asked to resign by the Board ten months later. Board members point out that "this first year was a hard struggle and the Board learned from their mistakes. There was a great turn-over of Board members but things kept moving."[6] In the summer of 1969 they decided to hire a new Director; they selected a Mexican-American who was referred with the help of the local school district. The new Director came into the program vaguely aware of Follow Through but learned rapidly.

Predominantly Mexican-American, the students are being taught in both English and Spanish at the kindergarten level. Instead of keeping most Follow Through children together (as in the kindergarten in 1968–69), the parents have chosen to integrate their eighty children into the three first grade and two kindergarten classes. For the 1969–70 school year the Parent Board selected additional aides, a Spanish teacher, and a Follow Through classroom teacher. The parents also selected a "model sponsor" or general curriculum approach which is to be developed in the Greeley classrooms with the help of David Weikart from Michigan. The selection of this particular approach was made after visiting other schools and seeing presentations of other possible curricula.

Each Board member has a personal notebook which contains past meeting minutes, major reports and resolutions, as well as federal Follow Through or other regulations which may affect their operation and control of the Greeley program. Full parent control of federal Follow Through funds has been unquestioned. The Title I Director and other local school officials coordinate with the parents in planning the expenditure of Title I and local funds.

AN EXAMPLE OF AN INDEPENDENT COMMUNITY SCHOOL: EAST HARLEM BLOCK SCHOOLS

When a higher authority has ultimate control over the bulk of a school's funds (as is always true of the public sub-systems described in Chapter

III), community decision-making can always be limited. However, the advantages of establishing schools totally independent of public authorities are balanced by the frustrations of securing adequate and flexible funding. Without exception, the major problem facing independent parent and community schools is funding.

Parents are clearly the crucial element in the East Harlem Block Schools. Although visitors are also impressed by the competent professional staff, the *parents* founded the schools, hired all staff and are always present in the schools—as volunteers, visitors, staff, etc. Located in a predominantly Puerto Rican area of East Harlem, the two pre-schools and one elementary school enroll approximately 150 Puerto Ricans, blacks, and Italians.

Extensive parent involvement

A core of parents at the Block Schools are fully aware that the three schools wouldn't exist without their work and initiative. All parents have ready access to all phases of the Schools' operations—a sharp contrast to New York City Public Schools. They may choose their level of involvement: 1) merely gathering information about the school and their child in regular monthly class meetings (attended by about half the parents each month) or through the frequent visits and phone contacts of the teachers; 2) taking on responsibility as an assistant teacher or parent coordinator or as a volunteer in fund raising, classrooms, or painting and maintenance; 3) becoming policymakers on the parent Board of Directors or the three Schools' personnel committees; or 4) acting as advocates of the Schools and their philosophy with local and national groups.

It is fascinating to find a high degree of decentralization of power within a complex of schools with a total enrollment of one hundred fifty. A sixteen-member Board of Directors (all parents) sets general policy, hires a general program director and directors for each of the three schools. Personnel committees in each school interview and hire all teachers and other staff from among those candidates recruited and screened by each school director. Although the bylaws provide for election of Board members by the parents of each classroom, in actuality most committee and Board members are selected by a volunteer and consensus process. If more than one person wishes to serve, the Board is enlarged.

Both the Board and personnel committees retain full power to fire staff. Many parents have first discovered through this committee work that they instinctively know much about what makes a good teacher for their child. Other more experienced parents help them put their concerns into words and questions. Professional teachers interviewed by these committees frequently report that the parents' questions are much more probing and perceptive than those of professional educators.

Volunteering for a personnel committee is frequently the first step to more extensive involvement. After parents gain self-confidence in a group and learn more about the school and education, they often wish to spread their ideas to others. A list of parents acting as *advocates* for the Block Schools is extensive:[7]

> . . . a parent coordinator to speak at Bank Street College; a Board member to attend the conference of the Federation of Protestant Welfare Agencies; several parents to attend the U.S. Office of Education's Follow Through planning conference in Washington; several parents to negotiate with the Division of Day Care; two parents to meet with the Carnegie Foundation; parents to visit other schools; parents to join the City-wide Committee for Day Care; Board members to meet with the Human Resources Administration; representatives to attend the Community Council on Poverty meetings; several parents hired by the U.S. Office of Education as consultants to community-controlled programs in Colorado and Arizona; the list goes on and on.

History

For a group of low income parents in East Harlem the hope of creating their own school was almost unthinkable—until 1965. Then some parents, mostly Spanish-speaking, from two blocks in East Harlem learned that the Anti-Poverty Program had funds which could be used to start their own nursery school. After some lengthy discussions about their desires for such a school and employment of an interim director, the parents asked Tony Ward to become Director of the school. A resident of the block, Mr. Ward had moved to East Harlem and set up a tutorial project after completing college.

Unwilling to send their children to inadequate neighborhood public schools, in 1967 some of the parents agreed to open an elementary school as well. Located in a storefront and church, the elementary school has expanded a grade each year and in 1970–71 is due to extend through the fourth grade.

Curriculum

The Schools' founding parents did not begin with a specific educational philosophy. They knew that they wanted the best possible staff and teachers; they wanted their children to learn actively, to enjoy school, and to be treated with warmth and respect. The current open classroom philosophy has evolved through experimenting with alternatives and a dialogue with their professional staff. The Parent Board once hired a Montessori teacher and later two teachers who conducted a Summerhill style classroom. The first was rejected as too structured; the latter as too unstructured.

Most classrooms are now a mix of concern for individual learning and social development, using some of the materials and techniques of the British Infant Schools and Schools for the Future. Teachers are concerned with providing children a choice among a variety of activities and alternative paths to acquire necessary skills. Written and verbal reports about a child's strengths, needs and progress replace formal grades. For the elementary school students, a highlight of the year is the week spent living on a farm. Many field trips (averaging more than one a week for each child) throughout the year extend this effort to learn from the environment. Although less stress has been put on Puerto Rican culture or history than might be expected, the Spanish-speaking assistant teachers are always present to support children who haven't yet learned English.

Staff

The Board has selected a young administrative and teaching staff. Almost all are in their twenties. The Board dismisses staff which fail to meet their high standards. Teachers have been dismissed despite support for them from the Director. Believing in continuing staff accountability, the Board does not grant tenure to any of its staff. Although there is moderate staff turnover, continuity has always been provided by those who remain. The parents who are assistant teachers and parent coordinators also tend to remain with the Schools for a number of years. These paid full-time assistants work as full partners to the certified teachers, carrying out similar teaching functions. Teachers and assistants meet daily to plan the next day's schedule and exchange observations about the children.

Block Schools' teachers with prior experience in public schools often speak of a completely different feeling toward parents. Their respect for parents begins with the first interview in which parents decide whether they'll have a job. It is continually reinforced through the partnership on staff and supportive parent meetings and activities.

Parent board

The Parent Board of Directors is generally content to delegate administrative and curricular matters to the staff. The Board determines long
range plans and policy. It regularly reviews proposals and budgets drawn
up by the staff. It constantly evaluates and monitors the Schools' operation.

The Board usually operates in a quiet, friendly and deliberate manner. There have never been controversies which divided the Puerto
Rican, black and Italian parents along racial lines (though the Puerto
Ricans, a majority in the neighborhood, clearly have the major share in
controlling the Schools). Cooperation among parents has grown over
the five years as they have spent time together in school and social
activities.

The Board admits neighborhood children to the Schools on a first-
come, first-served basis (except that first preference goes to siblings of
those presently enrolled). City Day Care regulations place limits on
the family income of pre-schoolers, who pay a small tuition on a sliding
scale. The token tuition for elementary school children (two dollars a
week) is often left uncollected.

Funding

The two pre-schools operated on OEO Community Action Program
grants until 1968. Then the Block Schools negotiated with the New
York City Division of Day Care for continued support. Though the
parents agreed to accept Day Care funding, they are in a continuous
state of negotiation because the Division of Day Care is not accustomed
to dealing directly with the concerns of parents in control of a school.
Specifically, the parents objected to the arbitrary assignment of two caseworkers who were insensitive, patronizing and didn't speak Spanish.
Though the parents succeeded in having acceptable caseworkers assigned, they are still tied to eligibility requirements which require offensive interviews regarding financial status of families. The personal
nature of case records kept in public files is a similar concern. The
parents also feel that not all parents should be forced to work in order
to qualify for the Schools' services. They feel that there is greater value
in their 10 hours-a-day pre-schools than merely babysitting service. The
Schools find that inadequate funding and traditional day care guidelines

obstruct innovation as well as the achievement of the Parent Board's basic educational and community development goals.

The elementary school is funded by a variety of small foundation grants, contributions from individuals, and a Follow Through grant. An advisory board of well-to-do New Yorkers helps secure some funds. Mailings to a list of regular donors usually raises about 8000 dollars a year. These sources allow much greater flexibility of operation than in the two publicly funded day care centers. The Director contrasts the smooth very successful operation of the elementary school with the struggle to maintain high morale in the day care centers. Rarely is there enough money in the elementary school's account to meet more than the current payroll. Dedicated staff members have frequently continued to work without pay—on faith that the money will be raised.

Changing public institutions

The Block Schools' pressure on the Division of Day Care has helped alter the interpretation of some guidelines as well as the Division's attitude toward funding of other parent-controlled day care groups. Appointed to the Board of Directors of the New York City Day Care Council, the Borough President's Advisory Committee on Day Care, the Board of Directors of the Day Care Assistance Fund and the Mayor's Task Force for Early Childhood Development, representatives of the Block Schools put many hours of work into developing alternatives to present policies and programs.

The Block Schools have proven to be a training ground for parents and staff to gain the skills necessary to change other public institutions. In addition to their activities in day care, some parents have increased their activity with local public school parents associations attended by their older children, and two parents ran for the local school board in District 4.

The Parent Board has set an internal goal of extending the elementary school to the eighth grade. Meanwhile as the pioneer in their field they are responsive to other parent groups wishing help in establishing independent community schools.

AN EXAMPLE OF A MINORITY CONTROLLED STATE SCHOOL DISTRICT: INKSTER SCHOOL DISTRICT, INKSTER, MICHIGAN

The racial exclusionist policy of all-white Dearborn, Michigan, is well known. Less publicized is its effect on the adjacent community of Inkster and the Inkster School District (which encloses a slightly different area than the city of Inkster).

Programs limited by state funding structure

Both Inkster and Dearborn are Detroit suburbs with largely working class residents. However, Inkster lacks the tremendous automobile plants which provide millions of property tax dollars to exclusive Dearborn. The Inkster School District is eighty percent black, mostly residing in homes valued from eight to twelve thousand dollars. The District levies one of the highest tax rates (which also is based on an extremely high rate of evaluation) in the state of Michigan. Nevertheless, Inkster has been unable to open a new Junior High School completed in 1968 with funds from a special two million dollar bond issue because of its low property tax base. It does not raise sufficient funds for it to be staffed and maintained. Meanwhile, the overcrowded conditions in the system's one junior high school and six elementary schools become more critical.

In 1969, the District joined with Detroit in a legal suit seeking a redistribution of state funds so that each Michigan school district would receive support according to need, or at a minimum, as much money per pupil as in richer communities with higher tax bases. As measured in dollars and the choices that sufficient funds allow, local power and control is still lacking despite the locally elected School Board in Inkster. Most Board decisions are determined by financial crises rather than by choosing among major alternative paths of action.

Despite the shortage of local funds the Superintendent has been able to develop an elaborate kindergarten program through a Title III, E.S.E.A. grant. Stressing language development through language labs and small classes, the quality of the program has attracted a twenty percent white enrollment for this centralized, "integrated" program. At upper grade levels, most white children are sent to parochial schools.

Community review committees

As in most school districts, community participation occurs primarily through contacting friends who are members of the School Board and by ad hoc citizen pressure groups. In an effort to broaden direct community involvement in schools beyond the elected Board of seven, a former Superintendent instituted a system of special review committees. Including community residents, representatives of parents associations, teachers, and Board members, the committees review candidates for major administrative positions and make recommendations on major new programs or construction. Their findings are presented to the Superintendent and Board for final action. The present Superintendent was selected through this procedure.

More radical steps toward broad based community control are unlikely to occur soon in Inkster due to a very strong teachers union (predominantly black) and a black superintendent who stresses the importance of the professional in decision-making.

NOTES

1. It is no mere coincidence that many middle class youth, alienated by their own mass production schools and mass society, are among the strongest advocates of community control. It is striking to compare the rapid spread of small community schools or districts, free schools and communes with the acceleration in development of conglomerates by the established business community, the development of the consolidated "superagencies" in government, and the continued interest in metropolitanism among political theorists in universities. A polarization among Americans on the issue of size and responsiveness of institutions versus efficiency is central to growing support of alternative institutions as expressions of a burgeoning "counter-culture."

2. The definition of community for these projects is sometimes made by or negotiated with an external power which sets ground rules for the schools. The danger of artificially forming a district in an area which lacks a sense of community is best exemplified by the Two Bridges District in New York City (see Chapter III).

3. Often resistant professionals, parents and community residents have chosen to examine the motivation of these self-appointed leaders rather than weigh the merits of their proposals.

4. As exercised in Florida in the Spring of 1970 by Governor Claude Kirk.

5. Mainly initiated by the Mott Foundation of Flint, Michigan, these "community schools" have often been criticized by community-control advocates for the patronizing manner in which the programs *serving* the community are planned, controlled and implemented by professionals. Community advisory committees usually have little or no power in staff selection or program design.

6. This was written by Billie C. Martinez (Chairman), Marge Feurt (Co-Chairman) and Marge Shepherd in response to the author's original draft of this sketch. May, 1970.

7. Included in "Philosophy" by Dorothy Stoneman. (Director, East Harlem Block Schools), New York: 1970, p. 4.

JOHN OLIVER WILSON

Performance Contracting:
An Experiment in Accountability

*A potentially significant direction for private enterprise in school-
ing is the performance contract movement. Advocates see this as
a significant breakthrough in learning techniques, especially for the
disadvantaged. Using computer-assisted instruction coupled with
incentive rewards (green stamps, transistors, and toys), these programs have developed convinced followers and skeptical opponents. John Wilson, a man who likes public contracting, explains
the basic components of such a system and describes three situations where performance contracting is being tried. Serious questions, however, remain: Do the programs work, or is this seductive
gadgetry that "teaches for the test?" And, if they do work, are there
unacceptable side effects from having experts programming and
manipulating the learner? Does performance contracting help the
school do more efficiently what Jerry Farber (in Part 1) charges the
schools with now—robbing the learner of his sense of self determination?*

Over the years there have been many efforts to improve the education
of underachievers. These efforts have emphasized the provision of more
funds, additional books and tutors, summer study programs, smaller
class sizes, and counseling, with the hope that a greater flow of resources
into the schools would guarantee better education. Recent evaluations,
in particular the now famous report of Dr. James Coleman, have indicated that per pupil expenditures are not the primary factor in determining the child's progress in school. In spite of this, we have continued
to pour millions upon millions of dollars into our public schools while
underachievers continue to lag behind their successful classmates.

Thus, there was excitement in the winter of 1970 when educators
and government officials heard rumors that a new project in Texarkana
was doubling previous achievement levels of some children.

John Oliver Wilson, "Performance Contracting: An Experiment in Accountability," *Instructor*, © June/July 1971, Instructor Publications, Inc., pp. 21–26.
Used by permission.

Apparently this result was being achieved through something called performance contracting. Its elements are relatively simple:

• A contractor signs an agreement to improve students' performance in certain basic skills by set amounts.
• The contractor is paid according to his success in bringing students' performance up to prespecified levels. If he succeeds, he makes a profit. If he fails, he isn't paid.
• Within guidelines established by the school board, the contractor is free to use whatever instructional techniques, incentive systems, and aids he feels can be most effective.

The Texarkana project, funded under Title VIII of the Elementary and Secondary Education Act, was intended primarily as a program for preventing dropouts. The contractor, a private firm, removed students from their normal classrooms and conducted the program in mobile units. Teachers were aided by paraprofessionals and a broad range of teaching machines and other audiovisual devices. The curriculum was highly individualized. These features in themselves were not revolutionary. What was more unusual about Texarkana was the contractor's use of material rewards to trigger the children's learning process and the teachers' instructional efforts. It was hoped these material rewards later could be replaced with intrinsic incentives.

The children were offered such rewards as trading stamps (which they could use for gifts) and free time during the class period (which they could use to read magazines, listen to records, or engage in other recreational activities). Incentives to teachers included stock in the company.

The contractor was paid only to the extent that he was successful in improving students' scores on standardized reading and math tests.

Staff members from the Office of Economic Opportunity who visited Texarkana saw great promise in performance contracting as a means to help children achieve satisfactory results. But they also realized that results of this one program did not prove its value. A much broader, clearly defined, and carefully evaluated experience was necessary before it could be confidently stated that performance contracting could help children learn. Thus the Office of Economic Opportunity decided to mount a nationwide experiment to provide the information that school boards should have before deciding whether to enter into performance contracting.

THE EXPERIMENT

The experiment was launched in August and September, 1970, in 18 school districts with six private firms—Singer/Graflex, Quality Education Development, Westinghouse, Plan Education Centers, Alpha Learning Systems, and Learning Foundations. Every major geographical area and every major racial and ethnic minority are included. Students in the experiment are Puerto Rican, Mexican-American, black, white, Eskimo, and Indian. All were carefully selected; the majority were at least two grade levels below norm.

In each location, two sets of levels are involved—first through third, seventh through ninth. About one hundred students per grade per site have been receiving instruction for about an hour daily each in reading and in math for the school year.

Because the primary purpose of the experiment is to compare the impact of performance-contracting education with the impact of normal education received by underachieving children, a similar group of students in traditional classrooms was selected and tested. These children, who attend nearby schools, are matched closely with the children in the experimental program. Since students in the experimental schools but not in the experimental program are exposed to rub-off or transfer effects, they were felt to be a less than ideal control group. However, they have been included as a special comparison group to provide an opportunity to examine the transfer effect itself.

In addition, several of the selected schools already had some type of remedial reading or math program—specialized teachers, tutors, or teaching machines. Students in these classes make up a special program group, and their performance, whenever possible, will be compared to that of students in all other groups.

Altogether, more than 27,000 children are participating in the experiment. About 10,800 are in the programs offered by the private firms; 11,880 in the control group; 2,700 in the comparison group; and 1,000 in special programs. An additional 1,080 pupils are part of a contract between two districts and their teachers' groups.

One contractor, Education Turnkey Systems, Inc., is providing management support for the schools. This support is necessary because of the newness of performance contracting and the rigorous reporting and program documentation needed for evaluation. Another contractor, the Battelle Memorial Institute, independent of all other experiment participants, is administering pre- and post-tests to experimental and control students, analyzing the differences between the scores of the two groups and collecting and analyzing other data needed for a thorough evaluation.

The six private firms were selected for the variety of their approaches to performance contracting. For example: Plan Education Centers uses few audiovisual aids and offers few incentives to students or teachers. This contractor relies heavily on programmed texts and existing instructional materials, believing that incentives are intrinsic to the system. Learning Foundations, on the other hand, relies strongly on teaching machines and other devices, and, for both students and teachers, emphasizes incentives that gradually change from extrinsic and tangible to intrinsic and attitudinal.

To gauge the extent and nature of performance contracting capabilities and to avoid "teaching to the tests," an elaborate evaluation structure has been devised. First, the test of reading and math achievement being used to determine the contractors' pay is randomly selected from three standardized tests. Part of the payment is also determined by the performance of students on criterion-referenced tests, used to measure the attainment of interim performance objectives. Finally, a separate and broad standardized test is being used for OEO's evaluation purposes.

To guarantee the reliability of the test scores, four safeguards have been incorporated in the evaluation:

- Companies do not know which form of the standardized test is being used. Company personnel are not involved in administering or scoring the tests.
- Because companies might inadvertently use material that contains test items, however, the management-support contractor is conducting a curriculum audit on a spot basis to remove any test items from the classroom curriculum.
- Retention tests will be given during the 1971–72 school year to determine whether gains have been made because of "cramming" or "teaching to the tests," or whether the students have actually learned under the firm's instruction.
- The final safeguard is the strict penalty for "teaching to the tests." If it is determined that this has occurred, the Office of Economic Opportunity has the authority to terminate the contract and require the contractor to return all funds paid so far.

As a result of this careful design, the Office of Economic Opportunity hopes to learn what kind of results can be expected from a variety of students from a variety of backgrounds. It is hoped that the results of this experiment will be replicable across the country. Because of the use of a variety of control and comparison groups, the Office of Economic Opportunity may discover what levels of skill improvement can be credited to performance contracting and which might have occurred during the traditional learning process. Rigorous accounting procedures will give reliable estimates of cost/effectiveness ratios. And, finally, a great deal will have been learned about the problems of administering, implementing, and negotiating performance contracts.

If OEO learns that performance contracting does not produce significant gains in achievement levels, that it is impossible to administer, or that its cost/effectiveness ratios make it impractical, obviously it will have to attempt to devise different methods. If performance contracting proves successful, educators and government officials will have important knowledge on how to educate disadvantaged children.

Potential advantages of performance contracting

Obviously it is hoped that performance contracting will improve basic reading and math skills, skills needed to master virtually every other subject children will confront in school. But performance contracting seems to have the potential for effecting other improvements as well.

Better overall performance. This method forces a school system to decide what it wants to accomplish, how accomplishment will be measured, and how it will be rewarded. Thus the decision-making process revolving around consideration of a performance contract may well result in more clearly defined goals for teachers and administrators. And, because performance contracting emphasizes the performance of individual children rather than class norms, this decision-making process should help to focus attention on the needs of those lagging farthest behind.

Accountability. The proponents of performance contracting say it shifts the emphasis from what is done, how it is done, and how much is expended, to what is learned. Because it is premised on precise standards of contractor performance, it gives school boards precise indices of what that performance costs, an invaluable tool for their decision-making process. At the same time, it guarantees to taxpayers that they will not have to pay for programs that don't work.

Dropout prevention. There is some evidence that children drop out of school (among other reasons) because their academic performance is poor. Thus, if achievement can be improved, children may be encouraged to stay in school. (This theory would appear to be substantiated by the Texarkana experience.)

Integration. A major barrier to school integration is the fear of white parents that their children's achievement will be adversely affected when placed in classrooms with underachieving nonwhite children. Thus there is the possibility that if performance contracting can produce quantum increases in the achievement levels of nonwhite children prior to integration, white parents may be less opposed to integration.

Individualization of instruction. Performance contracting may offer a cost/effective vehicle for introducing individualized instruction in the less affluent inner-city school.

Potential disadvantages of performance contracting

Critics have charged it will:

Take control over the educational process away from the public. It would appear that quite the reverse might happen, since the heart of the system is the contract between the elected school board and the contractor. The board sets the standards, devises measurement tools, and certifies that measurement takes place.

Help big business establish an educational monopoly. Again, it would seem that performance contracting may have the reverse effect. Ten companies bid on the original Texarkana project; at least fifty have bid on more recent contracting projects.

Result in distrust among teachers, who will be unwilling to share successful teaching techniques. Initial experiences indicate that greater, rather than less, teacher cooperation results. In several instances, teachers are pooling incentive pay to purchase new instructional materials. Contracts also can be written to provide incentives to teachers as a group, instead of individuals.

Encourage cheating and "teaching to the tests." This apparently did happen in Texarkana, but extensive safeguards to prevent test result contamination have been built into the experiment. It is too early to state whether this problem can be eliminated.

Place too much pressure on students, forcing them to become overly competitive. This problem has also been considered in the OEO experiment. It should be noted, however, that the classroom has always been a competitive place. In performance contracting, the student competes only against himself.

Two additional issues must also be considered—testing procedures and school board capability to negotiate performance contracting. The adequacy, fairness, and reliability of normal testing procedures remain one of the greatest concerns of both advocates and critics of performance contracting. The OEO is working with this problem by supplementing standardized tests with various other indices of success, including criterion-referenced tests. But more attention needs to be given this critical issue.

Of equal concern is the inexperience of school boards in negotiating performance contracts. Unless they can build the legal, contract, and negotiating staffs necessary to a successful operational program, the concept will falter even before it can be implemented.

THREE REPORTS OF PERFORMANCE CONTRACTING NOW IN ACTION

Project IMPACT—Duval County, Florida

Major features: IMPACT (Instruction and Management Practices to Aid Classroom Teaching); funded by Duval County School Board and Title I; involves 300 first graders in three Jacksonville schools; excluded were students with an IQ below 75; participants attend "Maximum Achievement Centers" during the day; teachers come from existing faculties, selected for willingness to participate and capacity for innovation; proposal written by school system, private contractors bid on basis of that proposal; program emphasizes learning by discovery and is developmental rather than remedial; Phase I began February 1, ends in June, Phase II will run from September 1971 to June 1972, Phase III from September 1972 to June 1973; no incentives being used.
Contractor: Learning Research Associates.
Contract objectives: Raise IQs of elementary pupils and increase thinking, reading, writing, math, social studies, and science skills; determine cost/effectiveness of such instruction; improve teaching skills and use of professional resources.
Auditor: Educational Testing Service.

Anita Garner, principal of Jacksonville Beach Elementary, one project school, says the classroom teacher is the key to this program.

"Teachers involved in IMPACT are enthusiastic because care

was taken to select those whose approach to teaching was compatible with the open education techniques we wanted to employ.

"At the beginning of the program we 'discarded' all of our textbook series and began to use *Words in Color, Algebricks, The Taba Social Studies Curriculum,* and *Science: A Process Approach.* For three weeks immediately preceding February 1, project teachers were engaged in full-time in-service training with consultants. For each subject area, they examined the inquiry process and learned how to apply it in the classroom. They also became familiar with the materials I mentioned and observed classroom demonstrations. They worked long hours during those three weeks preparing themselves for a new kind of teaching."

We asked IMPACT teacher Sarah Thomas, Garden City Elementary, how she and her students adjusted to the program that began at midyear.

"After a couple of weeks I think we began to feel quite comfortable with the inquiry approach. It took time for the students to adjust to asking, probing, and discovering instead of our telling them what is to be learned. They used to rely on us for praise or verbal reinforcement—now they are beginning to realize that the self-satisfaction that comes from grasping a concept is the real reward in learning.

"Using this very individualized approach, I find I'm a more patient and understanding teacher. I feel I've been able to develop closer relationships with my students."

Pam Riechmann is a first-year teacher who agreed to sign a three-year contract in order to take part in the program at Jacksonville Beach. She's very optimistic about what can be achieved during the next two years.

"Perhaps this program runs smoothly for me because this is the first year I've taught—I didn't have any patterns established or habits to break. Teaching on such an individualized basis seems natural to me because I've never had to teach thirty children at once."

Are incentives to motivate children a part of IMPACT?

"No—we don't give the kids candy, toys, and rewards if that's what you mean. You see, our classroom is such a fantastic place to be that it's incentive enough just being there. The worst punishment you can give a child is to make him leave. Our room is a warm, congenial learning environment. We already have a variety of wonderful materials and anything else we need is furnished by the company. All we have to do is ask."

Bernice Scott, who is director of the program's planning and design, talked about how student progress will be evaluated.

"We'll measure pupil performance with standardized achievement tests and criterion-referenced tests which are specifically constructed to measure a student's mastery of the program's objectives."

At the end of Phase I, judgment of LRA's success will be based on a variety of criteria, and payment made according to prearranged percentages. Fifty percent is based on the reading and math performance of project pupils as compared with a random sample of other Title I pupils. Thus, unless the IMPACT pupils do at least as well as the random sample, the contractor will be denied half of the payment.

Twenty-five percent is based on IMPACT pupils' performance on criterion-referenced tests. Based on individual pupil performance, the amount paid to LRA will be prorated so that achievement of less than 40 percent will result in no payment at all.

Twenty percent of LRA's earnings is based on performance in reading, math, social studies, and science over and above normal expectations. This 20 percent is broken down further as follows: 40 percent for reading, with a gain of .5 grade level, as measured by the SAT, required for payment to begin, 40 percent for math under the same conditions as for reading, and 20 percent for social studies and science with evaluation based on scores on Part 1 of the Stanford Early School Achievement Test. The remaining 5 percent of the contract price will be paid to LRA based on gains in IQ scores.

How does the community feel about Project IMPACT?

Mrs. Garner says articles and features which appeared in the local press, and TV specials, did a lot to tell the public what IMPACT was all about. "From the beginning of the project, we've involved the community—we've held several informational meetings and open houses. Some parents have even been able to sit in on the teacher-training sessions. We send home a newsletter once a month which keeps them up-to-date. We also encourage them to visit the classroom. Parents who think that this type of learning atmosphere is too unstructured or too permissive begin to understand the inquiry method when they see it in action."

Incentives Only—Mesa, Arizona

Major features: OEO-funded; involves one junior high and three elementary schools and an equal number of control schools; offers remedial work in math and reading for 100 students per grade in grades one through three and seven through nine; involves use of incentives to increase reading and math skills of selected disadvantaged students who show low achievement; no outside private contractor; carried out by regular teachers, using regular methods of instruction in their own classrooms; project participants selected on basis of low income and low achievement; students not aware of experimental grouping; began in November, ends in May; incentives for both students and teachers; all students in project classes receive incentives even though not all are part of testing group.

Contractor: Mesa School District and Mesa Education Association.

Contract objective: To determine if the use of student and teacher incentives can accelerate mastery of basic skills by disadvantaged students.

Evaluator: Battelle Memorial Institute.

Doug Barnard, director of the "Incentives Only" program, explains the way it works, as follows.

"We began this project with the assumption that, for the average child, a report card and teacher praise is all that is needed for incentive. We believe that the economically deprived child must be rewarded more frequently and in different ways."

Designated experimental schools were presented with an overview of the project task. Each faculty voted to be a part of the project or to be excluded. No students were transferred, bused, or homogeneously grouped for the study. In all schools, normal classroom teaching methods and materials are being utilized. Project classes remain basically as they were when the school year began—the addition of incentives is the only difference. Some classrooms of thirty students may contain only seven or eight designated as project students, but in such cases, all students receive incentives.

Don Blair, principal of Lehi Elementary, one of the participating schools, says:

"Our teachers establish with each student a set of goals to be achieved. When students reach the goals, they are rewarded. Our incentives program corresponds with the student's level of achievement. It consists of immediate rewards, such as candy and small toys, and delayed rewards, such as time to use educational games, watch movies, and go on field trips. Each teacher tailors a reward system to fit the personality of the child involved."

Lois Williams, who teaches a first-grade class at Lehi School, is happy to be involved in the project.

"It requires a very individualized approach which is very different from the traditional teaching methods you learn in college—it's challenging but gratifying when you see the results."

How does she feel about the reward system?

"I use the incentives in two ways: to reward scholastic achieve-ment and to modify behavior. Because of the rewards I think the students are more motivated, and I've noticed fewer discipline problems. Let's face it, children will clean up their desks faster if they know they'll get a piece of candy when the job is done. Giving little but meaningful rewards seems to make the school day go along much more smoothly now."

How lasting are the effects of the incentives?

"This is a question parents ask—we began with small material rewards which we are slowly replacing with social incentives such as group activities. Of course, our ultimate objective is to make gaining knowledge the incentive for learning."

Mrs. Audrey Young, a second-grade teacher at Jefferson School, was opposed to the program at first.

"I didn't like the idea of giving tangible rewards—it seemed that praise and the satisfaction of understanding should provide enough in-centive for achievement. Now I view the program more objectively—it works very well for some children. For others, I've had to find different ways of 'turning them on' to learning. The teacher must be very per-ceptive—he must sense what will motivate a child and how much pres-sure he can take. Rewards must be given for real mastery of a skill, real accomplishment of a goal—not just the appearance of having accom-plished it."

Do students get used to being rewarded for what they do?

"One of my little boys took a story home to read. His mother said she'd love to hear it. The little boy replied 'OK, but what are you going to give me for it?'

"We try to explain to children that receiving rewards for achieve-ment is a little arrangement we've made just to use in school—most children understand this."

How have parents reacted to the Mesa project?

"Favorably, for the most part," says Mr. Blair. "The Mesa School District has always made it a point to work closely with the community and this project is no exception. We held briefings, wrote newsletters, and had extensive coverage in local newspapers and on television. No parents have requested that their child be removed from the project thus far. Many have been impressed with the results they see—kids actually say they like school and attendance has improved."

The program's teacher incentives are given in June if project stu-dents gain more than one grade level over their pretested achievement.

Incentives are of four types: a cash salary supplement, cash for hiring aides, cash for purchasing additional materials, and released time for planning. At this writing, each school would decide what to do with the money it receives.

Teachers at Jefferson School are thinking about using the money to buy materials for the school but the Lehi School faculty favors giving each teacher a salary bonus for each project student who shows a grade-level gain.

What will happen next year when the funds are gone? Mrs. Williams feels no teacher could afford to personally sponsor a program of this nature, but she's convinced rewards work and she plans to purchase small items with her own money and make use of intangible incentives such as free time for games and play.

Dr. Barnard says that the results in June will determine whether a similar program will continue.

"We're simply asking ourselves, 'Will a child who knows he'll receive candy or a toy for a successfully completed task work harder than a student rewarded only by praise and a good grade?' The incentives approach may not work for all students, but if it proves to be a way of reaching some, then educators should consider it."

Reaching Potential Dropouts Early—Dallas, Texas

Major features: OEO-funded; remedial education experiment in raising achievement levels of disadvantaged children in math and reading; involves six hundred students from grades one through three in one elementary school, and seven through nine in one junior high; an equal number of schools and students in control group; contract held with private firm but local teachers are used; contractor, not teacher, held accountable for student achievement; released-time incentives for students, cash-bonus incentive for teachers; teaching done in ALACs (Accelerated Learning Achievement Centers), made from regular classrooms which were air-conditioned, carpeted, and redecorated; began August 1970.

Objectives: To identify potential dropouts at an early stage of academic development and design an academic program that will interest them in academic achievement and improve their basic math and reading skills.

Contractor: Quality Education Development, Inc., taking educational responsibility; Education Turnkey Systems, Inc., providing management support.

Evaluator: Battelle Memorial Institute.

With the exception of first graders, participating students were recommended by former teachers as being students lacking the desire or the ability to achieve," explains Donald Waldrip, Assistant Superintendent of the Dallas Independent School District. "Their measured IQs had to be 70 or over and they had to be at least two years below their appropriate grade level in reading. This data was provided by standardized tests. All project students also had to be from the group classed as 'disadvantaged' by Title I guidelines.

"First-grade participants were selected differently. Forty-six of the total one hundred students were designated on the basis of readiness tests obtained at the kindergarten level, and the remaining fifty-four students were chosen at random from entering first-grade students. All first graders would have been chosen on the basis of kindergarten data, had enough of them been able to attend kindergarten.

"Low-achieving, disadvantaged children make up the control group and one hundred similarly selected students serve as replacements for project students.

"Pre- and postachievement tests and interim performance criterion-referenced tests, supplied and administered to both control and experimental groups, will serve as data sources for comparative analyses."

Each ALAC houses one teacher, one aide, and twenty-five students per hour. A recent visitor to the ALACs in the H. S. Thompson Elementary School describes them this way.

"Four classrooms open to a hall which is separated from the rest of the school by colorful dividers. The walls of the ALAC are brightly painted—several gaily colored designs hang from the ceiling and delightful student art is displayed on both sides of the hall. Going from a regular classroom into the ALAC hall may startle the casual passerby. The contrast shows the effect a bit of paint, a little money, and some rearranging can have on the educational environment of an old building."

The program is totally individualized. Teachers stress letting every student progress at his own rate. In reading, students begin with i/t/a and change to traditional orthography when they are ready. In arithmetic, unit tests provide the information on which teachers base individual prescriptions. Small-group instruction, one-to-one tutoring, and individual work with both hardware and software are common sights in the ALACs.

Lois Palfrey, a reading teacher at Anderson Junior High, feels that students who haven't learned to read before are doing so now because in the individualized program they aren't experiencing failure.

"I have some of the students who were doing poorly in my language arts class last year—their progress is amazing. Since the materials match their level, they don't become frustrated and quit."

The Dallas project offers no tangible incentives to students for academic achievement as several other projects do. Instead, successful completion of work is rewarded with time to spend in a special area stocked with records, tapes, books, and educational games.

Teachers involved in the program receive a salary bonus 14 percent above the regular salary schedule. The bonus is not tied to pupil gains. Instead, it is paid for the extra duty involved (work at night and an occasional weekend).

For the contractor, however, payment is received on a different basis.

"Unless the students achieve at least a 1.4 grade-level increase, we do not give the companies one cent," says Mr. Waldrip. "The company absorbs the cost of teacher salaries and equipment."

When the project began it had both supporters and opponents. A member of the Classroom Teachers of Dallas questions using business methods in teaching. "Business has a materialistic approach," he said. "The contracts are a new scheme by businessmen to sell more of their products—a way to market more machines and prepackaged materials."

A committee of classroom teachers is studying the present program, and the local administrators' organization has recently contracted with the school district to manage their own guaranteed performance program. It's still too early to draw definite conclusions about what's going on in Dallas, but school authorities describe themselves as "cautiously optimistic."

ERIC WENTWORTH

Plan Test of Competition by Schools

One proposal for breaking the monopoly of public schools is the "voucher" system. The reader may recall from the Gallup poll in Part 2 that Americans are about evenly divided over the desirability of such an approach. Several questions surround the use of vouchers or "edu-credit." Would schools advertise? Would curriculum become more daring? Would teacher tenure go? Should vouchers be confined to schooling, or could education come in a different institution or in no institution? Is this not the kind of tool bigots will welcome?

Washington, D.C.—The Office of Economic Opportunity (OEO), despite awesome obstacles, is cautiously going forward with plans for a multi-million-dollar test of what could be this century's boldest venture in school reform: educational vouchers.

The idea is to introduce competition into the American public school system. Parents would receive a voucher for every school age child equal in value to that child's per capita share of the public school system's budget. They could "spend" the voucher as tuition not only at the neighborhood public school but at some other public school or at any participating private or parochial school.

PROPOSED EXPERIMENT

The proposed experiment has already aroused louder, broader opposition than backers first expected. Moreover, continuing study of its feasibility is turning up a host of practical problems. Early hopes of launching the project next fall have waned.

Still, OEO officials expect to hand out small grants soon to several school systems willing to look into their own potentials as the test site. Current candidates include Gary, Ind., Seattle, Wash., San Francisco, San Diego and Alum Rock (in San Jose), Calif.

Eric Wentworth, "Plan Test of Competition by Schools," *The Washington Post*, December 26, 1970. © The Washington Post. Reprinted by permission.

OEO wants to launch the test in elementary schools of a city school district, or part of a district, which has social, economic and racial variety plus private as well as public schools. If it finds a good prospect, it will invest a substantial sum in detailed planning before the final go-ahead.

In theory, educational vouchers seem simple enough. Advocates, among them economist Milton Friedman, claim that vouchers create a buyer's market, cracking the public school monopoly and giving ghetto parents in particular—whose vouchers would carry an added subsidy—a choice at last in their offspring's education.

Especially radical is the idea that individual public schools would compete not only with private schools but with each other for pupils and, thus for voucher income to finance their programs.

RIVALRY ADDS

Such rivalry for prestige and funds, proponents believe, would lead to replacing public schools' traditionally unappetizing educational fare with a tasty and nourishing smorgasbord of classroom innovations which rich and poor alike could share.

OEO planners contend that the regulated voucher system they have in mind should meet the main objections raised by critics. They are relying largely on proposed controls developed with OEO funding by education critic Christopher S. Jencks and his colleagues at the Center for the Study of Public Policy in Cambridge, Mass.

Nevertheless, a broad array of special-interest groups has charged that vouchers could induce racial segregation, widen the gap between rich and poor, violate separation of church and state, subject parents to "hucksterism," and threaten already-strained public school treasuries.

The National Education Association and American Federation of Teachers are leading a coalition of 17 nationwide school and church groups asking Congress to investigate vouchers. Their request may be met when OEO authorizations come up for renewal next year.

Further hurdles would follow. OEO planners want the experiment to run at least five years and expect to spend as much as $6 million annually in federal support. But Congress normally votes money one year at a time, which means the project would start without assured funding for its full duration.

TEST SITE SOUGHT

If OEO can find a test site, the state government would have to back the venture and pass "enabling" legislation. The requirement of state legislation would also give voucher critics another crack at scuttling the project. Foes of the voucher venture can be expected to attack at the local level, too.

Milwaukee school Supt. Richard P. Gousha reported opposition in his community to the school board's surrendering authority to the "educational voucher agency"—linchpin of the OEO scheme. While voucher planners say this agency could simply be the existing school board, they much prefer a body with broader—perhaps wholly separate— representation.

Their plans call for this new local agency to designate those schools that can participate in the project. The agency would require each participating school, public and private, to disclose detailed information about its budget, educational goals and resources.

AGENCY IS BANK

The voucher agency would also have to determine which children were eligible, because of poverty or other special needs, for voucher subsidies. Finally, the agency would serve as the "bank" where individual schools would turn in the vouchers they receive from entering students for cash or credit.

For the public school system, using vouchers could entail a major overhaul of budgeting and bookkeeping.

Voucher planners trust the principals would use this authority to try bold innovations and give their schools more individual character. But Jencks for one concedes that some, wary of controversy, might stick to bland conformity.

The planners also recognize that parental free choice can only work in a community where total enrollment capacity exceeds the number of pupils. Thus OEO hopes to provide some sort of federal aid to help launch or enlarge non-public schools.

Board Chairman Allen Calvin of Behavioral Research Laboratories has pledged that his educational systems company will start a school for at least 200 pupils wherever the voucher project takes root.

However, other private educators could be leery of new investments without assurance that over-all federal funding would continue to
keep the project afloat.

PRIVATE RELUCTANCE

Private schools may also be reluctant to take part because of the regulations designed to prevent abuses feared by critics.

The antipoverty planners' immediate challenge is just getting the
project off the ground. None of the school systems interested in feasibility studies has committed itself to going any further. Much will
depend on how much local support they can find.

OEO recognizes the project can succeed only with widespread
community backing. Both the federal planners and Jenck's Cambridge
team have been trying hard to explain their safeguards against racial
bias and other abuses. Unregulated vouchers, backers agree, would be
a "disaster."

ESTELLE FUCHS

The Free Schools of Denmark

*Denmark has found a practical way of allowing parents to start
alternative schools. The following article explains how tax money
is allocated, what provisions must be met, and what happens if
schools fail. If it works for Danes, can it work for Americans?*

Denmark is a country long acclaimed for its achievements in education.
It has had worldwide influence through its extensive programs in vocational and adult education. But more important, Denmark presents for
a democratic state a model of public education that is flexible in the
use of alternative types of public schools, many of them organized and
controlled by parents. It is through their system of Free Schools (*Fri-*

skoler) that the Danes have shown how a modern nation can establish standards of education required for national life and the protection of the young, while at the same time provide for the freedom of parents with special religious, ethnic, economic, or pedagogic interests to oversee and direct the education of their children with minimal interference by the government.

In the United States, a state-controlled education system has come to mean that parents who are dissatisfied with the education provided for their children must either move to areas where school systems are more compatible with their interests, turn to private, non-publicly supported schooling, or exert pressure for internal reform. However, only those in the upper socioeconomic brackets are able to exercise the first two of these options. The very poor and the non-white are limited in their choice of residence, and since the federal and state governments do not subsidize tuition for private elementary education, the costs are prohibitive for those with low incomes.

Although local control over schools is deeply rooted in American tradition, to move in the direction of direct parental control of publicly supported city schools contrasts sharply with present inner-city school organizational patterns. It also conflicts with trends toward national assessments and national standards which are imposed on the lower schools by such forces as the universities and nationally standardized examinations, presumably in keeping with the needs of a technologically oriented, mobile, urban nation.

Denmark, however, has a fairly centralized educational system with national standards, but it also makes provision for publicly financed schooling outside the state system. Parents are accorded the right to arrange for the schooling or tutorial instruction of their children, including the right to organize, staff, and supervise the schools their children attend. Moreover, the government provides considerable financial and organizational assistance to these private schools. The state-run public schools retain no monopoly over the education of the young, although the government retains the right to establish standards in curriculum and sanitation in the independent schools.

The roots of this system go back to the beginning of compulsory school attendance in Denmark in 1814. Provision was made then to permit parents to employ alternative education for their children in the form of tutoring or schools separate from the state schools (a principle not firmly established in the United States until 1925 by the Supreme Court decision in *Pierce vs. The Society of Sisters*). In Denmark, two major influences helped establish and maintain the tradition during the nineteenth century. One was that the state religion (Evangelical Lutheran) was taught in the public schools, and those who found such instruction unsatisfactory (because of dissident viewpoints or because they practiced other religions) sought alternative educational forms as a guarantee of their religious liberty.

The other significant factor was the independent school established by Kristen Kold along the lines suggested by N. F. S. Grundtvig. Though deeply religious and a clergyman himself, Grundtvig opposed compulsory education and especially compulsory religious education. In language curiously like that used by the more adamant of present-day critics of American schools, he attacked some of the schools of his time as "schools for death" and "scholastic houses of correction." Extolling folk culture and humanitarianism, he had a deep, lasting influence on all Danish life. The independent school established by Kold, in which the pedagogical emphasis was upon oral presentation, discussions and singing, and in which rote learning and drill were absent, was soon copied by parents all over Denmark.

The Grundtvig-Kold influence is important because it affirmed the pattern of establishing schools outside the national system. It also helped affirm the deeply rooted resistance to compulsory education so that even today, Denmark, while providing abundant free educational opportunity through the university level, compels school attendance only between the ages of seven and fourteen.

At present, all schools in Denmark, whether state or Free Schools, follow a similar organizational pattern, although there are major differences in matters of religious training, language usage, pedagogical methodology, and educational aims. The system is composed of three departments: the primary school (grades one through seven), the lower secondary school (grades eight through ten), and the higher secondary school (grades eleven through thirteen). More than 500,000 children in both state and Free Schools attend the Primary School Division, the only compulsory division in the system. Upon graduation from the seventh grade or at age fourteen, children may exercise the option of leaving school. Those who choose to remain move in two separate streams, one leading to the academically oriented Real School (*Realskole*), the Higher Secondary School (*Gymnasium*), and eventually the universities, and the other to voluntary classes with a vocational emphasis.

Existing parallel to the regular state system, there are more than

175 Free Schools offering primary schooling. The largest number, 114, are *Grundtvig-Koldske Friskoler,* operating in the direct tradition of the two educators and practicing the pedagogical and religious principles espoused by them. There are nineteen Catholic private schools, one Jewish school, and twenty-eight German schools.

Despite the liberal financing and government cooperation in the formation of independent schools, they are used by only 7 percent of the children of compulsory school attendance age. The right to educate children at home, outside of any school, is also provided by law, but few parents use this prerogative.

Of the Danish population that does take advantage of the right to use Free Schools, the majority clearly represents those who wish a particular religious education for their children other than that provided in the state schools. Seventh-Day Adventists, Catholics, Jews, and Grundtvigians are among these. The German-speaking ethnic minority also maintains its own schools, and in these the German language is used as a medium of instruction.

Another group chooses the Free Schools for the purpose of insuring a traditional university-oriented education, and at times this group includes upper-class as well as upwardly mobile middle-class people who wish their children to travel in socially prestigious circles. The Zahles Gymnasieskole in Copenhagen is one such school, maintaining high academic standards and attended at times by members of the Danish royal family. Although its doors are now open to children from all segments of the population, the Zahles school retains its prestigious reputation and is characterized by a relaxed yet formal aura of a college preparatory institution.

More recently, those espousing the educational philosophy of John Dewey and influenced by A. S. Neill's Summerhill have founded the Little Schools (*Lille Skole*). Here the educational milieu tends to be fairly permissive and informal, with a heavy emphasis on creativity in the arts and a stress on the development of cooperation and humanitarianism. These schools are based on the principles that pupils must be allowed a great deal of democratic freedom, that the students ought to play as active a role in the educational process and the running of the school as the teacher, that creativity be emphasized, and that parents play an active role in the daily workings of the school.

Laws governing the organization, funding, and regulation of the Free Schools are administered by the Ministry of Education, which must be kept informed concerning location, headmaster, and attendance at each school. Free Schools can be founded by organizations, individuals, or groups of parents, the latter receiving more liberal benefits.

Children are protected because the schools are held accountable for the quality of their instruction and facilities. If, upon inspection, the instruction is found to be not as good as that received in the ordinary schools, a report is made to the appropriate local school board officials, and if the situation is not corrected within a year, the Ministry of Education decides whether the school should be allowed to continue to function. In general, instruction is required to be at least as good as in the public schools in the basic subjects of Danish and arithmetic. In all other matters the school is free to pursue its particular interests.

Inspectors are chosen by the Ministry of Education. Interestingly enough, however, many schools are given the right to select their own inspector—generally a professional with views sympathetic to the aims of the particular school—who will act in a sense as a citizen notary to certify that the requirements of the state laws governing education are being fulfilled. Permission to choose an inspector is generally granted to schools owned by a circle of parents. That the school may choose its own inspector does not appear strange to the Danes, who argue that his role is to insure that the state requirements are met, not to pass judgment on the school. Since the school meets the religious, pedagogic, or ethnic interests of the parents of the children involved, it ought to be inspected by someone neither antagonistic toward nor unfamiliar with its purposes and style. There are few cases of disapproval of an inspector chosen by groups of parents.

The financial assistance given the Free Schools consists of funds for staff, for children, and for buildings. Schools become eligible for assistance in various ways. A private school, i.e., one owned by an individual or a group such as a church, becomes eligible after it has been in existence three years. In keeping with the more liberal provisions for parents, self-owned institutions and schools run by groups of parents become eligible even sooner, and such a school can receive funds even if it enrolls as few as ten pupils. The Ministry of Education can include in this number children ranging from preschool classes through the tenth grade. The liberality of this provision becomes evident when it is remembered that public education in Denmark becomes available ordinarily only at age seven and is compulsory only through age fourteen, or the seventh grade.

The government provides salaries for the staff members of the

Free Schools at a rate equivalent to 85 percent of the salaries paid public school teachers and headmasters. In many cases, the Free School teachers have smaller pupil loads than those carried by teachers in the public schools, but they are paid on the basis of number of lessons taught rather than on pupil registration. The pupil-teacher ratio is restricted, however, by the fact that the schools must pay the additional 15 percent of a teacher's salary, and few institutions have enough money to allow for more than one teacher per ten pupils. Usually, as in all Danish schools, the headmaster also teaches.

In addition to funds for salaries, the state provides 50 percent of the money it would cost the government to keep the child in a regular public school and provides the same services, such as free milk, to the children. Application forms for funds for staff and children are simple, requiring only the names of teachers, lessons taught, names of pupils, attendance records, and certification by an inspector that state requirements are being met.

The Free Schools also receive aid from the government to establish school buildings. State loans are made and paid for at 4 percent interest, and the state retains mortgage rights to the buildings. There is no time limit set on repayment of the loan, and the loan cannot be recalled as long as conditions under the law are met and the property used as a school. Loans for three-quarters of the costs of additional buildings, improvements, expansion, furniture, capital investment, educational materials, and modernization can also be obtained when schools formerly owned by individuals or organizations other than parents are reorganized into self-owned institutions.

Despite the legal incentives, the actual founding of a Free School requires a great deal of motivation, commitment, organization, and some financial ability. The Lille Skole de Mezasvej in Elsinore illustrates how such a school is founded. Dissatisfied with the public schools for reasons that included large classes, curtailed academic programs for the children, and annoyance that their concern as parents branded them as troublemakers by school authorities, some twenty-nine parents banded together to organize a Little School. They found a building, borrowed money from the banks, and assumed responsibility for the loan. These founding parents then bought wood and paint, and within a few months converted a former hotel to a pleasant, cheerful, sprawling school. The responsibility for paying the loan passes on to each new group of parents. It took four months before government money was forthcoming, but the parents were able to keep the school going until the full financial benefits under the Free Schooling law became available. The founding of the school required an initial investment of about $72 per child.

The vast majority of the Danish population uses the state public schools primarily because they are generally of excellent quality in teaching, physical structure, and opportunity for children. The modest fees associated with Free Schools do not account for their use by only 7 percent of the population. In this fairly homogeneous nation, with no extremely sharp class differences, the public schools do not present barriers to some children to achievement in the larger society, nor does the teaching within the schools clash markedly with the beliefs and wishes of most parents.

The Free Schools are not without criticism. The Danes are so proud of their modern public school system that many question, for example, the implication of snobbery by those using special preparatory schools. They raise questions of the propriety of the state supporting teachers' salaries at lower pupil-teacher ratios in the Free Schools. Also, they question the propriety of seeking solutions to educational controversy outside of a public school system deemed good for all. The Little Schools particularly are the targets of those who disapprove of permissive education, and who also view the humanistically oriented, protective, and intimate environments provided in these schools as a return to an archaic educational form unrealistic in the preparation of people for modern society.

On the other hand, Danish tradition holds the highest respect for the right of the parent to oversee the education of his child. Essentially a tolerant people, most Danes view the Free Schools with favor, seeing in them a protection of personal religious and political liberty. The Little School advocates see their schools as protection against bureaucratic encroachment by the state through its schools, and as protection against mass fabrication of people without regard to individuality. Like many advocates of American private schooling, some Danes defend the Free Schools because their freedom to innovate and experiment is seen as a stimulus to the public schools. The existence of these schools is regarded as helping to guarantee the quality of public education, because they act as competitors in a situation where the public schools have no monopoly and, therefore, have to maintain excellence.

A significant effect of the existence of the Free Schools is that they remove much conflict from the public schools. Any dissident minority, with minimum expense and with government cooperation, can leave the system and establish its own school. The result of this is that when Danes discuss educational problems, they tend to stress professional, pedagogical concerns or the matter of finance. They rarely discuss the kinds of problems that are considered important in the United States, such as school-community conflict or teacher-administrator difficulties. A striking characteristic of Free Schools is the general coincidence of goals on the part of parents, teachers, and administrators, and the harmonious relations among these groups. Certainly, were a serious disagreement to develop, there would be no point in retaining a child in the school; when serious difficulty arises in public schools, there are alternatives available. Parental control in the Free Schools, through the hiring of a headmaster and the approval of the hiring and firing of teachers, does not appear threatening to school staffs whose pedagogical and philosophical bents coincide with those of the parents.

Since all *Friskoler* are required by law to provide education in Danish, there does not appear at present to be serious concern over the bicultural education received by minority groups. While there are complaints about the *Friskoler* laws, the major ones are that the government does not provide enough financial help, and that it ought to provide 100 percent of the funds for teachers' salaries, fully equivalent funding for the children, and more money for supplies. Efforts to remove public support for *Friskoler* are likely to be met by serious opposition from conservative traditionalism as well as progressive elements.

Does the Danish experience with Free Schools have relevance to problems facing education in America? There are, of course, basic differences between the two nations that preclude any easy or direct modeling of one system upon the other. One major difference is the fact that in Denmark the Evangelical Lutheran state religion is taught in the public schools. From the very beginning of compulsory education in that country, the existence and support of schools outside the state system was viewed as a guarantee of religious liberty. On the other hand, in the United States, the separation of church and state is seen as essential to religious liberty, and the public support of any educational system that includes religious instruction traditionally has been viewed as a danger to the democratic system. Although this view has been modified by the "child-benefit" theory of aid to education, it remains a strong current in American educational thought.

Another basic difference is that Denmark, despite its German-speaking ethnic minority and several religious minorities, is a fairly homogeneous nation and does not face a race problem. The United States, on the other hand, not only has racial heterogeneity, but includes a multiplicity of ethnic and religious minorities and larger economic class differences. Public, compulsory education was long seen as essential for the accomplishment of the homogenization of Americanization of immigrants whose differences were viewed as threatening to national unity. Although at present the schools are no longer educating many immigrants and the recognition is growing that cultural differences are deeply entrenched in American life and ought to be valued, the traditional belief that the public school somehow acts as a unifying force has not disappeared.

Still a third difference is that the Danes, although they may sometimes question the snobbery of certain upper-class schools or the separation of some intellectual groups from the public schools, do not see in the Free Schools a threat to their democratic way of life. In this country, on the other hand, the private school system, where it has been supported occasionally by state governments, has been seen to operate either as an intrusion upon the principle of separation of church and state or, more recently, as an effort to circumvent integration. Thus, state-supported private schools tend to be viewed as potentially anti-democratic.

Yet, the fact remains that affluent Americans have far greater choice concerning the education of their children than do the poor of America's inner cities. Those who are confined to the ghettos either by race or poverty or a combination of both are completely dependent upon a public school system that is compulsory and monopolistic, and which is increasingly viewed as intrusive. Pious talk concerning the democratic nature of the public school system does not change the fact that for many it is unsatisfactory, and that social and economic class has a great deal to do with the educational choices open to a family. Movement to the suburbs or into private schools are not choices readily available to the urban poor. At present a major alternative open to this group, when consciously dissatisfied with the schools, is to engage in social protest, a phenomenon American inner-city school systems have seen develop in recent years.

At first, much of this social protest centered on the eradication of de jure and de facto school segregation. More recent efforts have concentrated on decentralization of school systems and the substitution of local community control. It would appear that even if public school districts were under the direct control of local parent and community groups, this form of organization would not preclude the disaffection of some groups from what would remain essentially a monopolistic, compulsory educational system. As the experience of community control in New York has shown, such programs run the risk of being stillborn, strangled not only by the opposition of conservative forces supporting the traditional system, but also by internal factional dispute.

A publicly supported system that allows for alternative forms of school organization does give the promise of meeting special minority needs, whether they be a desire to rear children via Montessori or Summerhill pedagogy or instruction in Swahili, ballet, or Amish traditions, without disruption of the work of the larger public system. That this would then tend to remove from the school its most militant critics and leaders of needed reform has been observed in Denmark. Yet, there is wide agreement on the difficulty of effecting change within the large bureaucratic systems that our schools have become, and what is often forgotten is that alternatives outside the system are already used by those able to afford them. The provision of alternatives to larger numbers of people opens the possibility of creative use of talent and the implementation of reforms presently inhibited by the organizational needs of schools as they are presently constituted. Should the alternative of publicly funded private schooling be made available, funding short of 100 percent is likely to facilitate the acceleration of the flight of the upwardly mobile and middle class out of the public system. For alternatives to be truly universal, they must be free and include the provision of supplies, buildings, and funds for staff.

For those who fear the fragmentation of the public education system, the Danish experience supports the view that alternative forms of schooling do not mean the inevitable demise of the state-run public schools. On the contrary, vigorous support for public education and the maintenance of high standards draws the allegiance of the vast majority of the population.

An advantage of a system with publicly supported alternatives is that freedom from the monolithic compulsion by huge bureaucratic organizations may free the public schools of debilitating conflict. But perhaps the most important advantage is that permitting concerned groups of parents and community organizations to set up schools for segments of the population that find the present system unsatisfactory may unleash creative potential and make possible an educational renaissance.

A. S. NEILL

I Hate My School—
Can I Come to Summerhill?

What kinds of school experiences might parents want for their children if economic barricades to starting independent schools were removed? Some educators, parents, and students are now calling for "free" schools—a more radical alternative to traditional schooling than "open classroom" or "school-without-walls" models suggest. What is meant by the term free school? Usually the expression designates a school where students have relatively more power, and hence freedom, than in typical schools. How much freedom do students have? How much should they have? Is there a danger of anarchy and license?

By far the most famous free school in existence today is Summerhill, a fifty-year-old, private boarding school in Leiston, England. While there is no proof that it is the best free school in the world, some knowledge of it has become very useful for anyone seriously interested in alternative styles of schooling, because it is so much better known than any other. Thousands of visitors from all over the world have inspected the school since 1960 (on a typical Saturday there will be from ten to fifty visitors). Many schools have tried or are trying to copy at least some of the ideas used at Summerhill (see Appendix B), and over 600 college and university courses are now requiring the book Summerhill: A Radical Approach to Child Rearing *by A. S. Neill as part of their reading. What is the school like and what does its founder believe? A few basic facts about Neill and the school will help the readers understand the basis for Neill's comments in the article which follows.*

Alexander Sutherland Neill founded New School in 1921 in Dresden, Germany. Two years later he moved his school to Sonntagberg, Austria, and a short time later to Lyme Regis, England, where he adopted the name Summerhill. In 1926 he located in Leiston, England, where the school has remained, except for a few years during World War II when he moved to Scotland. The school

A. S. Neill, "I Hate My School—Can I Come to Summerhill?" Reprinted from *Psychology Today* Magazine, March, 1968. Copyright © Communications/Research/Machines, Inc.

The editors wish to thank Mr. Ralph Gross, founder and director of Medieval University in Des Moines, Iowa, for assistance in locating information about Summerhill.

is in many ways a reflection of Neill's unhappy childhood, which grew out of Scottish Calvinism, a stern schoolmaster father and a somewhat indulgent but socially upward-mobile mother. Neill did not do well in school himself, finding it impossible to study effectively subjects which did not interest him. He did, however, graduate from the University of Edinburgh though he did not enter until he was twenty-five after he tired of being a low-level primary school teacher.*

    In founding Summerhill, Neill intended to minimize the negative influence he had felt as a child. To do this, he tried to avoid external authority and morality as much as possible by allowing each child to form his own judgments in matters which affected only him, and having the whole group rather than the headmaster or faculty make policy and arbitrate disputes for the community. This is accomplished in weekly parliamentary meetings. The school has consisted at any one time of twenty-five to seventy-five pupils, aged five to sixteen, and usually under ten staff members. Neill admits his direct democracy would not work without a good proportion of older pupils. Classes consist of the usual school subjects, including arts and crafts, but class attendance has always been left to individual choice. No pupil need ever to go to class unless he wants to. Swearing and masturbation are not frowned upon—a fact which has led some critics to classify the school as one of the "goddamn and fornication at five" variety —but sexual intercourse, while approved of in theory, has been discouraged in practice for fear the school would be closed.

    For many years Summerhill attracted mostly "problem" children, and Neill spent a great deal of time giving private lessons (P. L.'s)—psychoanalytic sessions—to liars, bedwetters, thieves, and pyromaniacs, and children suffering from rejection and repression. He himself underwent analysis for many years, first with Homer Lane and finally with Wilhelm Reich, so that much of what he has written deals with personality difficulties and especially with sexual repression. After the popularity of the book Summerhill, he has had a waiting list of children so that his student population no longer consists overwhelming of children with difficulties. They do, however, still come almost exclusively from middle class families, because of the tuition cost ($720 to $1440 per year).

    The following article, written when Neill was eighty-four, reflects half a century of free school experience by one of the world's best known radical (Neill's own designation) schoolmen.

Just over 20 years ago I had two books published in New York, *The Problem Teacher* and *The Problem Family.* So far as I could make out each issue sold a few hundred copies and the rest were sold as remainders

---

* The best detailed biographical treatment of Neill is in Robert Skidelsky, *English Progressive Schools* (Baltimore: Penguin Books, 1969).

at a few dimes each. The press notices I got were either luke-warm or hostile. One called the books old hat. "We have lived through this in the States and there is nothing new for us." Twenty years later the book *Summerhill* became a best seller in the States. Why? I have no idea. I like to think that the U.S.A. has come up to date rather than that I have gone out of date. I do not know why I get so large a mail from the U.S.A. It is mostly from young people and in the seven years since the book was published I can recall only two hostile letters. Many are from school children. "Can I come to Summerhill? I hate my school. It is all pressurization. The teachers make every lesson dull and dead and originality is frowned upon." Oddly enough, although our British education is all wrong, I never get letters from home children.

The mystery to me is this: Why has America become conscious that its education is not good enough? Why now and not 20 years ago? Surely the schools have not changed all that much. But is it a case of a change of society? Is society sicker than it was a couple of decades ago? I fancy that that is the deep reason. In all countries youth is rebelling. Alas, too often rebelling against all that does not matter. The hippies, the flower merchants show their protests, not against war, not against race discrimination, not against the stupid learning we call education; no, all the challenge is the right to wear long hair and leather jackets and blue jeans. That is the impression I get in this country, but from what I hear and read about America the young, especially in the universities, are challenging real evils—the insane dollar values, the dead uniformity of the people who have been molded and indoctrinated so much that they are automatic slaves to any ideas thrown out by the press and the TV screens. In Britain I think that the average TV program is geared to a nation of 10-year-olds. Our B.B.C. refused to put on *The War Game* because it told of the horrors of an atomic war and it might upset the nice folks who want to think that God is in his Heaven and all is right with the world. The young feel that they have been cheated by the old, lied to, castrated by their parents and teachers. They no longer accept glib answers—in Vietnam we are saving the world from Communism; in South Africa we are preserving the God-given rights of the superior whites; in the U.S.A. we are battling to preserve the white civilization. It is significant that all these reasons involve hate and war and possibly ultimate death to humanity. Youth sees a world full of savagery. Hitler's six million Jews paved the way for a world that accepted torture and death as almost commonplace factors in our modern life. In short, the world is very very sick, and youth

feels it but, alas, cannot do much about it. Summerhill's good friend
Joan Baez, recently in prison, has no power over the hate merchants;
all she can do is to march in protest and then be carted to prison. It is
the helplessness of youth that so often brings despair.

In this American *Stimmung* the book *Summerhill* was launched
in 1960. It caught on because it was voicing what so many of the young
had felt but had not intellectualized, had not made conscious. For its
theme was freedom—real freedom, not the sham thing so often called
democracy. Freedom for all to grow at their own pace; freedom from
all indoctrination, religious, political, moral; freedom for children to live
in their own community, making their own social laws. To many a
youth Summerhill became synonymous with Paradise. I hasten to say
that it isn't—*Gott set dank!* Most of the rebellion stems from home, from
what Wilhelm Reich called the compulsive family, the family that
strangles youth, fears youth, often hates youth. From my mail I am led
to believe that the American family is more dangerous than the British
one. I never get the sort of letter I had two days ago from New York.
"I am 17 and I am allowed no freedom at all. I have to be in at certain
hours and if I am late my father hits me. I hate my parents." A girl of
a middle-class family. I have had scores of similar letters. A boy of 15
writes, "I hate school and cannot concentrate on my work and my parents bully me all the time because they say that I must go to college
and get a good job." I have no idea how much truth is in Vance
Packard's *The Status Seekers* but even if a 10th is true it gives a terrible
picture of American civilization. A Cadillac-civilization with its sequel,
dope and drugs and misery for those who cannot accept the god of cars
and furs and wealth.

This looks like an attack on a country by an outsider and it may
well be resented by some readers, but I do not mean it as an attack; it is
a case of trying to think aloud the answer to the question: Why did the
Summerhill book catch on in the U.S.A.? At home we have our own
miseries and troubles. The growing race hate due to the immigration
from Jamaica. The futility of a culture that dwells on bingo and football
crowds, on infantile TV programs; a culture that gives the cheap sensa-
tional press millions of readers while the more cultured papers—*The
New Statesman,* the *Observer,* the *Sunday Times*—too often struggle
to keep themselves alive. World sickness is not confined to North America. Russia has its teen-age gangsters also.

One reason why Summerhill appealed to the U.S.A. may be that
it is, so to say, anti-education. The great American educationists, Dewey,

Kilpatrick and their kind, were mostly pre-Freudian in their outlook. They kept linking education to learning, and today in all countries educational journals concentrate on the learning process. I escaped that trap. I was and I am ill-versed on what the educationists did. I never read Rousseau or Pestalozzi or Froebel; what I read in Montessori I did not like, partly because it made play the mate of learning. Learning what? Summerhill is not a seat of learning; it is a seat of living. We are not so proud of David who became a professor of mathematics as we are of Jimmy who was hateful and antisocial and is now a warm-hearted engineer with much charity and love to give out. Summerhill puts learning in its own place. I have more than once written that if the emotions are free the intellect will look after itself. What a waste it all is! Sixty years ago I could read some Latin and Greek. Today I can't decipher the Latin words on a tombstone. Our schools teach children to read Shakespeare and Hardy and Tennyson and when they leave school the vast majority never read anything better than a crime story. For my part I'd abolish nearly every school subject, making geography and history matters for the school library, and quadratic equations a luxury for the few boys and girls who loved maths. Abolish exams and my school will have only creative teachers—art, music, drama, handwork, etc.

Every man has a bee in his bonnet. It was comforting to read in Erich Fromm that Freud had to be in the station an hour before his train was due. My original bee was psychology. In the 1920s my home was Vienna and my associates the psychoanalysts. Like all young fools I thought that Utopia was just 'round the corner. Make the unconscious conscious and you have a world full of love and fellowship with no hate. I grew out of that phase but did retain the belief that education must primarily deal with the emotions. Working for many years with problem children made my belief stronger. I saw that the aim of all education must be to produce happy, balanced, pro-life children, and I knew that all the exams and books in a million classrooms could not do a thing to make children balanced. A B.A. could be a hopeless neurotic—I am an M.A. myself. A professor could remain at the age of 10 emotionally. What the emotional level of the British Cabinet or the American Pentagon is is anyone's guess; my own guess is a low one. Today in any school anywhere it is the head that is educated; every exam paper proves the point.

Now one cannot flee from reality. I could not say to prospective parents, "Exams and school subjects are not education and I refuse to teach the ordinary school subjects." That is what the Americans would call flunking out, and, by the way, I get too many letters from students in the U.S.A. saying, "I can't go on with my college career. The teaching is too dull; I am flunking out. I want to be a child psychologist." I answer that they won't let one be a child psychologist unless one accepts their qualification demands. I wrote to the last man who had flunked out, "If you haven't the guts to walk through the muck heaps, how can you ever except to smell the roses you value so much?"

I do not find this flunking-out element in old Summerhill pupils. One of my first pupils spent two years standing at a mechanical belt in a car factory. He is now a successful engineer with his own business. His brother who wanted to be a doctor had to pass an exam in Latin. In just over a year he passed the matriculation exam in Latin. "I hated the stuff but it was in my way and I had to master it." That was over 40 years ago when students did not as a rule flunk out. I do not think that youth has become defeatist; rather it is that society has reached a point of futility and cheapness and danger where youth, frustrated by the mundane standard of success, simply gives up in despair. "Make Love not War" is a most appropriate motto for youth even if youth feels it is a hopeless cry, and it is a hopeless cry; the hate men who make wars force youth to die for country but when the young demand freedom to have a sex life, holy hypocritical hands are held up in horror. Youth is free to die but not to live and love.

I fear I am rambling, not sticking to the point. My consolation—too many who stick to the point make it a blunt one. I ramble because I am trying to evaluate Summerhill as a factor in the sick world, really asking what value freedom has for youth. One is naturally apt to think that one's geese are swans; one tends to forget or ignore the outside world, so that when a lecturer in education in an American college wrote and told me that over 70 percent of his students thought that Summerhill was all wrong it came as a shock. I had repressed the idea that when the young are conditioned and indoctrinated from cradle days, it is almost impossible for them to break away, to challenge. Few can stand alone without a supporting crowd behind them. "The strongest man is he who stands most alone." Ibsen.

I like to think that freedom helps one to stand outside the maddening crowd. Symbolically one sees differences. The conventional suburban office-goer with his striped trousers and his neat tie and his neater mind on one side. On the other, the creator, the artist to whom exterior things mean but little. Compare the tailoring of L. B. J. with that of a film director or a Picasso. Symbols, but characteristic. Put it this way: Summerhill gets hundreds of visitors but I do not think that any visitor ever notices that my staff never wear ties. Summerhill hasn't got to the Old-School-Tie stage. But one cannot carry such phantasying too far; my old friend Bertrand Russell wears a tie, and no one would claim that he is a crowd man.

I think that one aspect of Summerhill is that it, rightly or wrongly, gives pupils an anti-crowd psychology. I could not imagine any old pupil following a Hitler or for that matter a Kennedy or a Reagan. This sounds incongruous because the chief feature of Summerhill is the self-government, the making of laws by one and all from the age of five to 84. Pupils become ego-conscious and at the same time community-conscious. Bill can do what he likes all day long as long as he does not interfere with the freedom of anyone else; he can sleep all day if he wants to but he is not allowed to play a trumpet when others want to talk or sleep. It is as near democracy as one can get; every child is a member of parliament able to speak "in the house." No doubt because this democracy is real and honest our old pupils cannot tolerate the sham we name politics. Because politicians have to rely on votes nearly every urgent reform is delayed for two generations. In England an M.P. has—say—a predominantly Catholic constituency or a Baptist one. How can he act honestly when faced with some reform—a bill to abolish punishment for homosexuality, a much-needed reform of the divorce and abortion laws? Was any great man a politician? Any Darwin, any Freud, any Einstein, any Beethoven? Was any big man ever a crowd-compeller, a demagogue?

When children are free they become wonderfully sincere. They cannot act a part; they cannot stand up in the presence of a school inspector because they will not countenance insincerity and make-believe. Tact forces them to make minor adaptations as it does with you and me. I dutifully doff my hat to a lady although I realize that it is a meaningless, even dishonest, gesture, hiding the fact that in a patriarchal society a woman is inferior in status, in pay, in power. To tell a social white lie is often a necessity but to live a lie is something that free people cannot do. And my pupils feel that to be a member of a crowd must involve living a lie.

This crowd psychology angle is important. It is at the root of the sickness of the world. A neighboring country insults your flag and many thousands of young men die for the honor and glory of their fatherland. National hatreds everywhere, Greek v. Turkey; Israel v.

Arabs; Rhodesian white v. Black. And it is not only the nationalism crowd. Our football grounds are full of irrational, partisan hate and violence. Gang warfare is not confined to Chicago. Yet in a way violence is minor. It is the violence that a crowd inflicts on its members that frightens, the violence of intimidating, of molding. A school uniform means: We are members of a crowd, a crowd that will not tolerate opposition. We must all dress alike, think alike, act alike. For the great law of any crowd is: Thou shalt conform. The world is sick because its crowds are sick.

Education therefore should aim at abolishing crowd psychology. It can do this only by allowing the individual to face life and its choices freely. Such an education cannot lead to egocentricity and utter selfishness, not if the individual is free within the confines of the social order, an order made by himself. The slogan "All the way with L. B. J." shows the iniquity of the crowd, a system that makes crowd members sheep who can feel the most elementary emotions without having the intellectual capacity to connect such emotions with reason. Today our schools educate the head and leave the emotions to the crowd-compellers—the press, the radio, the TV, the churches, the commercial exploiters with their lying advertisements. Our pop heroes and film stars have become our leading schoolmasters, dealing with real emotions. What teacher in what school could have a few hundred hysterical females screaming their heads off when he appeared?

The danger today is undeveloped emotion, perverted emotion, infantile emotion. Millions scream in Britain every Saturday afternoon when their favorite football teams take the field. If the evening paper had a front page in big lettering "Atom War Very Near," most of the spectators would turn to the back page to see the latest scores. Crowd emotions are not touched by news of starvation in India or China. It is this same unattached unrealized emotion that makes the crowd numb to any realization of a likely atomic war. Crowd emotion is not shocked by our inhuman and un-Christlike treatment of criminals in prison; it does not even realize that the inhumanity is there. And none of us is guiltless. I do not cut down my tobacco and give the savings to the starving nations. We are all in the trap and only the more aware of us try to find a way out. My own way is Summerhill or rather the idea behind Summerhill, the belief that man is originally good, that, for reasons no one so far knows, man kills his own life and the lives of his children by harsh and anti-life laws and morals and taboos. It is so easy to cry, "Man is a sinner and he must be redeemed by religion" or what not. God and the Devil were comfortable explanations of good and evil. One thing I think Summerhill has proved is that man does not need to become a "sinner," that man does not naturally hate and kill. The crowd in Summerhill is a humane one. In 47 years I have never seen a jury punish a child for stealing; all it demanded was that the value of the theft be paid back. When children are free they are not cruel. Freedom and aggression do not go together. I have known a few children who were reared with self-regulation, that is, without fear and outside discipline and imposed morality. They seem to have much less aggression than most children have, suggesting to me that the Freudians with their emphasis on aggression must have studied the wrong children.

Even in Summerhill, where very few pupils were self-regulated, there is a peacefulness, a minimum of criticism, a tolerance that is quite uncommon. When a Negress pupil came from the States not even the youngest child seemed to notice her color. Our TV showed white faces full of hatred when black pupils were being stoned in the Deep South. This is alarming. We can condition children to hate and kill by giving them a hate environment. But we can also give them another sort of environment—were I a Christian I'd call it a love-your-neighbor environment. But then, what is a Christian? Catholics and Protestants beat children in home and school—didn't Jesus say suffer the little children? The Christians see that they suffer, all right. But to narrow the life negation to religion is wrong. A humanist can hate life and children; he can be as anti-sex as any Calvinist.

Summerhill has not answered many questions, the biggest one being: Why does humanity kill the life of children, why does it take more easily to hate than to love? Why did jackboot Fascism conquer a nation of 60 million?

One answer to the question of world sickness is sex repression. Make sex a sin and you get perversions, crime, hates, wars. Approve of children's sex as the Trobriand Islanders did under a matriarchal system and a Malinowski will fail to find any trace of sex crime or homosexuality before the missionaries came and segregated the sexes. Wilhelm Reich, to me the greatest psychologist since Freud, dwelt on the necessity for a full natural orgastic life as a cure for the sickness of an anti-life society. Then came the new American Interpersonal Relationship school of Sullivan and Horney, with long case histories of patients who seemed to have no sex at all. I have a book on problem children written by an Adlerian; I failed to find the word sex in it. And in all this divergence of views on sex, what can one believe? One can make the guess that the torturers of German Jews were sex perverts, but can one safely conclude that the men in the Pentagon are Hawks because of their sex repressions?

I have gone through many phases in the last 50 years, the most exciting my long friendship with Homer Lane and then with Reich. Now, at 84, I simply do not know the truth about sex. Is a teacher who canes a boy's bottom a repressed homosexual or a sadist or simply a man who has never been conscious of what he is doing? I ask because my father in his village school tawsed children with a leather strap and when I became a teacher I automatically did likewise without ever once wondering if it were good or bad. Looking back now I see that one motive was fear, fear of losing one's dignity, one's power; fear that any slackness would lead to anarchy. I cannot see anything sexual in my tawsing.

Summerhill society is a sex-approving society. Every child soon learns that there is no moral feeling about masturbation or nudism or sex-play. But every adolescent is conscious of the fact that if approval meant the sharing of bedrooms by adolescents the school would be closed by the Establishment. One old boy once said to me: "The fear of closing the school if pregnancies occurred gave us a new form of sex repression." The difficulty was and is this: How far can a school go in being pro-sex in an anti-sex society? Not very far, I fear. Yet one factor is of moment; the pupils are conscious of our attitude of approval. They have had no indoctrination about sin or shame, no moralizing from Mrs. Grundy. Their free attitude shows itself in minor ways. In our local cinema a film showed a chamber pot. The audience went into fits of obscene laughter but our pupils did not even smile; one or two asked me later why the people laughed. Free children cannot be shocked—by cruelty, yes, but by sex, never.

Summerhill products are often said to be quiet, unaggressive, tolerant citizens, and I wonder how much their rational attitude on sex has to do with their calmness of life. They prove that censorship is the product of a life-hating civilization. I never see our adolescents taking from the school library *Lady Chatterley* or *Fanny Hill*. A girl of 16 said they were boring.

Most of our old pupils are pacific. They do not march with banners against the H-bomb or against racial discrimination. I cannot imagine any of them ever supporting warmongers or religious revivalists or play censors. But how much this has to do with a free attitude to sex I cannot know. Certainly sex is the most repressed of all emotions. Most of us were made anti-sex when in our cradles our hands were taken from our genitals, and it is an arresting thought that the men who have the power to begin a nuclear war are men who were made sex-negative long ago. Anglo-Saxon four-letter words are still taboo in most circles, maybe partly for class reasons; a navvy says fuck while a gentleman says sexual intercourse.

I confess to being muddled about the whole affair of sex. I do not know if we all experienced Reich's perfect orgasm there would be an end to war and crime and hate. *I hae ma doots.* Yet it is true that people who have a pro-sex attitude to life are the ones most likely to be charitable, to be tolerant, to be creative. Those who do not consider themselves sinners do not cast the first stone. For charity I would go to Bertrand Russell rather than to Billy Graham.

Billy naturally leads to religion. Summerhill has no religion. I fancy that very few religionists approve of it. A leading Church of England priest once called it the most religious school in the world, but few parsons would agree with him. It is interesting to note that I have had many letters of approval from Unitarians in the U.S.A. I asked one Unitarian minister what his religion was. Did he believe in God? No, he said. In eternal life? "Good heavens, no. Our religion is giving out love in this life," and I guess that is exactly what the Church of England priest meant. It is our being on the side of the child (Homer Lane's phrase) that has aroused so much antagonism among religionists. The other day a Catholic school inspector told a meeting of Catholics that corporal punishment was practiced much more in their schools than in Protestant ones. "We beat the body to save the soul." In the days of that life-hater John Knox I would have been burned at the stake. The widening interest in the freedom that Summerhill stands for fits in with the lessening belief in religion. Most young people, outside the R.C. faith, have no interest in religion. To them God is dead. God to them was father, molder, punisher, a fearful figure. The gods and fathers were always on the side of the suppressors. In Britain the enemies of youth, those who call for the return of beating with the cat, those who want to censor plays and films and language, those who demand strict punishment for the teen-age delinquents, they are not the young; they are the old, the old who have forgotten their teen-age period.

I am sure that the growing interest in freedom for children coincides with modern youth's rejection of a joyless, repressive religion. A religion that has become perverted. Christ's "love your neighbor as yourself" has become: Okay, so long as he isn't a Jew or a Black. "Let him who is without sin among you cast the first stone" has become: Censor plays and novels and measure bathing costumes. Owing to the threat of universal incineration youth today is possibly more pro-life than it has ever been. Juvenile crime is really at bottom an attempt to find the joy of life killed by morals and discipline and punishment. In the days when Summerhill had many delinquents they went out cured simply because they were free from adult standards of behavior. Religion must be rejected because it tells the young how to live, but it does not need to be religion; I have known humanists who gave their children sex repression; I know agnostics who believe in beating children. Really what one believes does not matter, it is what one is that matters. After all religion is geographical; had I been born in Arabia I'd have had three wives and, alas, no whisky.

There is a comic element in religion even if there isn't a joke in the Bible or the Prayer Book. The true believer must know that Bertrand Russell will roast in hell for eternity while Billy Graham sits at the right hand of God. With Russell to look after, the familiar words "poor Devil" will have a real significance.

What is the outlook for freedom? Will the minority ever take over from the majority? And if it does, will it retain its belief in freedom? Doesn't Ibsen say somewhere that a truth remains a truth for 20 years, then the majority takes it up and it becomes a lie? Summerhill has 64 children who are free from molding: the world has millions of children who have little or no freedom, millions of adults who frankly are sheep. One tragedy of life is that men have followers. Men who remain disciples are always inferiors. The Pharisee who thanked God that he was not as other men may have been a conceited ass but on the other hand he may have got hold of something. There is something wrong when millions who praise the Beatles never heard of Milton or Freud or Cézanne, when millions kill the life of their babies, when thousands of young men die in a battle for they know not what. Anti-life is all around us, and I wish I knew why. I wish I knew why mankind kills what it loves. I do not know the answer; all I know is that when children are free they do not kill life; they do not condemn their fellow men. They do not want to tell others how to live. It is significant that old pupils do not seek jobs where they will boss others; few have gone into business. I used to daydream of one's becoming a tycoon and endowing the school, knowing all the time that he would be so hard-boiled that he would not endow anything.

I am not trying to sell Summerhill. I am trying to say that the cure for the sickness of man does not lie in politics or religion or humanism; nay, the cure is freedom for children to be themselves. Like many others I once thought that the Russian Revolution would bring Utopia to youth, for it began with freedom for children, self-government in the schools. Then, according to Reich, the psychologists took charge and youth became sacrificed to political anti-life, so that today communism has no connection with individual freedom to grow naturally. Indeed I often wonder why the Americans are so scared of communism. Both systems believe in the terror of the bomb; both discipline and castrate children; both believe that education means subjects and exams and acquired knowledge. The only difference I can see is who takes the profit? The Russian Revolution proved that the sickness of the world cannot be cured by politics.

The only answer that I can think of is freedom for children, individual freedom, social freedom, sexual freedom as in a small way practiced in Summerhill.

I said that I thought Wilhelm Reich the greatest psychologist since Freud. His diagnosis of man's sickness is deep and wise. Man flees from natural sex by armoring himself against joy in life, stiffening his body, fearing any signs of genitality, changing good emotions into "emotional plague," in short, becoming anti-life, hence wars and many diseases and child-beating. Even if one accepts Reich's diagnosis the question arises: What can be done about it? How can we prevent folks from becoming anti-sex and anti-life? Analysis of any school is not the answer. What effect on humanity have all the case histories ever published? Do all the things Melanie Klein found in babies have any bearing on the education of children? So far psychology has been a matter of diagnosing without any salient suggestions for a cure. Ah, yes, some cases of cures of individual neurotics, but the cure for a sick world, none. A Scientologist has just told me that he could cure any problem child in my school in 10 days.

Are we all fakers? Self-deluders? Do the hundreds of books on psychology published every year have any effect at all? I am inclined to say none, but I am biased, for I cannot read a book on psychology now.

The psychologists have narrowed the science—or is it an art? The doctors have limited psychology to the consulting room and the rich and those with time to spare. How many psychoanalysts have opened schools? A few—Anna Freud, Susan Isaacs, e.g., but the main body of Freudians has done nothing in the way of prophylaxis. The Summerhill Society of New York issues a list of schools claiming to have self-regulation and self-government. Some may be excellent but, as I have not seen any of them, I cannot give an opinion pro or anti. I do not think that they belong to any special schools of psychology and I sincerely hope that they don't. I am sure that the list does not contain the name of the school that claimed to be Summerhillian and washed out a boy's mouth with soap and water when he swore.

The future of psychology should lie not in the consulting room or the hospital for neurosis but in the infant bedroom and the infant school. Mr. Brown's phobia of spiders may fascinate his analyst but his phobia is as nothing in a world of millions of half-alive children.

To return to Summerhill, it went through the stages of the Century—the faith in analysis, the futile attempt to find the original trauma in a young thief. I read them all—Freud, Jung, Adler, Rank, Stekel, Reich—and got more and more confused by their psychological jargon. I never learned the meaning of words like manic-depression, compulsive neurosis, hysteria, etc. Never knew how specialists could draw the line between one and another. Oh, so many were brilliant in their diagnosis and treatment, but in the end what did one learn? And today I feel as confused about the Interpersonal Relationship folks, for, if men like Stekel seemed to overemphasize sex, they seem to denigrate it altogether. So I left schools of thought and concentrated on Summerhill, forgetting theory and avoiding words like complex. "Everyone is right in some way," Reich used to say, the corollary being that everyone is wrong in some way.

Let us face the truth, that we are all little men, even the greatest among us. We do not know how and why the super Rolls Royce, the human body, ticks. We know nothing about life and how it began, nor can we account for the universe. We do not know why Brown dies of cancer and his brother of diabetes. In the psychological realm we cannot account for a Bach or a Milton or a Hitler. We know little about heredity or the origins of love and hate. A doctor does not know what causes a headache. So that we should be wary of panaceas of all kinds —Zen Buddhism, Scientology, Theosophy, psychoanalysis, Moral Rearmament, and a few score of other isms and ologies. We must go on enquiring, searching for the truth, but if we follow a creed, if we label ourselves Freudian or Reichian or Hubbardian or any other ian we have stopped growing, stopped enquiring; we become "yes" men. It worries me to hear of schools in the U.S.A. that call themselves Summerhills. One should take from others what one feels is good. No one should accept any creed, religious or political or psychological. I got much from Homer Lane; later I got much from Reich. But in both men were views that I could not accept, and thus I escaped discipline. If a teacher claims that Summerhill inspired him, good, I wish him luck, but if a school claims to be a new Summerhill I fear it will fail. There is a pioneer in each of us, an explorer, a visionary. As in sport we pay others to play the game for us, so in pioneering; we find it easy to look for a leader and be content to be a humble follower of Billy Graham, Sigmund Freud, Barry Goldwater, Karl Marx. Fans are arrested creators, arrested pioneers. And the big question is: in a world in which the vast majority are fans, how can a few independent people set about "curing" the Establishment?

We must remember that the Establishment has the ultimate power. A bureaucratic Ministry of Education could close my school on material grounds alone: not enough lavatories, not enough cubic feet per child in a bedroom. But, to be fair, the Ministry has not interfered with me in the 44 years Summerhill has been in England. But now that the National Union of Teachers and many Labor M.P.s demand the closing of all private schools, pioneering in education is going to have a bad time. Had there been no private schools there could not have been a Summerhill; the State, the Establishment will allow new methods of teaching history or maths but it is unlikely to tolerate new methods of living in a school. Really I should vote Tory, for the Tories will not lightly give up their Etons and Harrows, and as long as we have the public schools ilke Rugby the smaller private schools will be protected. Alas, the private school is I fear doomed by lack of finance alone. Summerhill would have died seven years ago had not the publication of *Summerhill* in the U.S.A. brought a flood of American pupils. Today people in England do not have the money to support private schools. Those who do, select the established schools, the public schools and the big co-ed schools with their well-equipped libraries, labs, etc. Parents, like teachers, still look on education as learning in all countries East and West. Educational journals seldom mention the child or freedom or creation. When I write a letter about the teaching of English I get quite a few replies, but when I write an article on the psychology of the child no teacher answers.

I want to claim that Summerhill has for 47 years demanded that character is of more moment than the ability to learn subjects. I have never denigrated learning; all I have done is to put it in its second or 10th place. But what effect the school has had on education I cannot judge. Some say that the permissiveness of some schools stems from Summerhill. Who can know? I like to think that it isn't Summerhill, that it is the Zeitgeist, the longing of youth for freedom. Maybe some History of Education in the year 2000 will have a footnote about a school called Summerfield run by a mad Scot called S. A. Neale. Sorry I won't be there to laugh at the footnote.

EMMANUEL BERNSTEIN

What Does a Summerhill Old School Tie Look Like?

All claims aside, what impact does Summerhill actually have upon people who go there? What are ex-Summerhillians really like? How do they relate to the world after having all that freedom? A typical reaction to the Summerhill idea is "That's very fine for a while, but what happens to those poor kids when they try to get jobs or go on to school?" Through interviews with former Summerhill students, Emmanuel Bernstein obtained some answers which are reported below.

One day in 1965 I walked down the tree-arched driveway leading to Summerhill School. A boy shot by me on a bicycle. I passed fields where other children roamed freely, climbing trees or nailing together private shacks. Next to a sunny corner of the main building stood an old sofa, its stuffing sticking through the worn cover. There in the morning sunlight sat a small girl of eight who, with deep concentration, was picking out more of the stuffing.

I had come to England to see Summerhill School and to meet some former students [see "Can I Come to Summerhill? I Hate My School," A. S. Neill, *Psychology Today*, May]. I hoped, through interviews with former students, to answer some of the recurrent questions I have had ever since I read A. S. Neill's book, *Summerhill*. In this school, children were never required to do anything they did not wish to do. And they were allowed to do almost anything they wished

Emmanuel Bernstein, "What Does a Summerhill Old School Tie Look Like?" *Psychology Today*, vol. 2 (October 1968), pp. 37–41+. Copyright 1968. Reprinted by permission.

as long as they did not infringe on the rights of others. No one was required to attend any classes.

And so I wondered. Given such freedom, could children ever accept the responsibilities and limits of society? Could the products of such a permissive atmosphere adjust to the realities of life: a job, marriage, parenthood? Could they learn to cope with the authority of a traditional school?

Filled with such questions, I entered the large, vacant hall of the main building. I was shocked to find a series of bulletin boards filled with page after page of single-spaced, typed rules—with accompanying penalties. One 15-year-old boy told me: "There are more rules in a free school than anywhere else, even though we make them all for ourselves."

It was an interesting day. At one point I wandered into a tiny room where teenagers were playing pianos, guitars and harmonicas while seven- and eight-year-olds leaned against chairs and stared into space, apparently intoxicated by the music. Several of their contemporaries, who sat in overstuffed chairs, amused themselves by tipping each other over.

One girl of eight was dancing the twist with another girl, her face aglow with laughter. Someone whispered in her ear. She stopped dancing, her eyes filled with tears. Her parents had arrived to take her home —a week early. Several children quickly surrounded her, trying to give comfort. Earlier this girl had told me of her activities at the school: music, dancing, writing, reading, acting and painting—and of her boyfriend.

But for others the outlook did not seem so optimistic. Summerhill could be lonely. One group of teen-age boys told me they were bored; their lives had become centered around their tape recorders. There was the dark, thin boy with horn-rimmed glasses, who stared blankly out of a window. And the sad little red-haired girl alone on the front steps.

In the evening I attended the weekly meeting, where children air all personal and school problems, make new rules and abolish old ones. The hall was filled with 75 children, sitting 10 deep on the floor, up the stairway, filling every inch of space. A. S. Neill's tall, stooped figure waded slowly through his children. Occasionally he took a large pipe from his mouth to exchange a word or two. The loud talking stopped as Neill took his place on a chipped, green kitchen chair.

A boy of 12 opened the meeting. Arguments began about bedtime hours. There were complaints from a group of teen-aged boys who said they felt like "zoo animals on display" for visitors. This was discussed in relation to the practice of one enterprising group that charged a shilling apiece to see their rooms. A committee to investigate stealing was abolished; perhaps 10 new rules were established; and just as many were liquidated or revised, all by "ayes" and "nayes."

Later I asked Neill what happened to the children after they left the school. "They go into the arts," he replied. When asked if there was a "Summerhill personality," he said that his students came out well-balanced and sincere.

Back in London, I began my follow-up study in earnest. Officers of the Summerhill Society gave me a few names and these persons gave me more. There are no follow-up school records. I bought an old motor scooter and a large map of the London area and began visiting the household of one former student after another. By the end of the summer, I had seen 50 Summerhill products.

Because the interview took the form of an informal discussion, the study is a subjective one. I gave no tests of any kind. But I was able to find out how former students feel about their experience at the school and just what had become of 50 children who attended Summerhill.

Most interviews lasted about four hours and took place in the homes of these former Summerhill students. I talked to 29 men and 21 women, from 16 to 49 years of age. The median age was 23. The average numer of years spent at Summerhill was 4.3; the median was seven years. (Children may enter Summerhill as early as six and they usually leave before they are 17. No one "graduates" from Summerhill.) Most of the group had attended the school within the last 20 years, though their entrance years ranged from 1924 to 1963.

In the following weeks my initial impressions were strengthened. Some students found Summerhill ideal, but it failed to meet the needs of others.

If there is a quality that could be said to make up the Summerhill personality, it would have to be *tolerance*. This characteristic was mentioned spontaneously by 24 of the former students as most typical of a Summerhillian. Their definition of tolerance was accepting people as they are, without regard to race, religion or other label. Twelve mentioned *sincerity* as the outstanding characteristic of a Summerhillian.

My analysis showed that 10 former students—according to both their own feelings and my observation—had benefited most. They felt strongly that Summerhill had given them confidence, maturity, and had enabled them to find a fulfilling way of life. One felt the school had helped him to break away from an overdomineering mother and to think for himself. Another former student, who recalled having been a bully at Summerhill, said, "It got the hate out of me, somehow." Others said typically: "It helped me to grow out of the need to play continuously," and "It led me to explore and be curious about things." Three stressed that the school had given them a healthy attitude toward sex.

These 10 who had nothing but praise for Summerhill talked of the free environment that helped them develop into more complete personalities through following their natural bent. They were highly communicative people who usually had definite ideas and direction before they came to Summerhill. The average age of this group was 27.

On the opposite side, seven felt that Summerhill had been harmful. They charged that the school had not helped them to grow, but instead had led them to find more difficulty in life than they might otherwise have experienced. Most of these complained of the de-emphasis on academic subjects and the lack of good teachers. Most complained of the lack of protection against bullies. One said, "It made me lose the little self-confidence I had." Another, "I think it gave me the habit of not following through, giving up too easily." These were the more dependent, shy people—both before and after their Summerhill experience. The average age of this group was 26.

Thus, the gregarious, aggressive people seemed to benefit the most, while the school seemed to have a negative effect on the more withdrawn, quiet ones. There were a few exceptions: occasionally Summerhill triumphed by suggesting to some shy pupil the pleasant rewards of becoming gregarious.

Perhaps the most striking finding of this study came out of interviews with the six who left before they were 12 and returned to traditional schools. A shorter stay seemed more beneficial than the completion of schooling at Summerhill. These children had spent at least three years at Summerhill. All but one were enthusiastic about how the school had helped them. Five felt that there were no adjustment problems to the ordinary local schools and were enthusiastic about having learning presented in an organized way. Although usually "behind," they were easily able to catch up to the other children, learning the required academic skills within the first year.

Typical of this group was Connie, now a 27-year-old housewife, who left Summerhill because of the financial difficulties of her parents.

When asked about her adjustment to the regular state school, she replied:

> I loved the way learning was presented! It was something new and fresh! And, you know, it was strange; I couldn't understand why all the other children stopped working when the teacher left the room.

To Connie, the teacher was an instrument for learning. When I talked to Connie's mother, she told me how surprised the teachers and head-master were, for Connie "soaked up knowledge like a sponge."

The single exception to the record of successful adjustment by this group was, interestingly, Connie's brother, Henry, who attended Summerhill from the time he was seven until he was 12. He was the only person I encountered who ever ran away from Summerhill. Nor did he adjust to the local school.

Henry, a thin, shy 24-year-old, said he was immobilized by the sudden rigid discipline when he left Summerhill and tended to stay in the background, afraid to ask questions. He was difficult to talk to; his mother was in the room, and she always answered for him, even interrupting him when he did start to speak. Henry felt he had lost two years when he entered the regular school and that only sheer effort and determination had brought him to his first year of postgraduate physics at London University.

When I compared the statements of the eight who entered Summerhill *after* their twelfth birthday, I discovered that the four who stayed the least number of years claimed to have benefited most. Two who stayed for one year felt that Summerhill enabled them to find themselves, as did the two who remained at the school for two years. All but one of those who entered as teen-agers and stayed three or more years had been in continuous personal and vocational difficulty since leaving Summerhill.

A country doctor who entered the school in 1925 when he was 13, easily passed his examinations for university entrance when he was 16. He summed up his feelings about Summerhill:

> "The freedom was a wonderful thing," he told me. "It was a good experience for me. But I must say there was very little direction from adults. I taught myself what I knew I should know."

Jane, a housewife who married another Summerhill student, left a strict girls' boarding school when she was 12 to enter Neill's school.

"I feel Summerhill saved my life," she said. "I was a nervous child and probably ready for a nervous breakdown . . . Naturally I went wild with the new freedom at first, playing outdoors continually and never opening a book, but I gradually settled down within a few months. For the first time in my life, I was enjoying comfortable, matter-of-fact relationships with boys."

Those who attended Summerhill the longest appeared most likely to have difficulty and tenacious adjustment problems. Of the 14 who spent over 10 years at Summerhill, five felt they had "fairly severe" problems adjusting to society for at least a year after they left. Four still were definitely unsettled and having personal and job problems. They were in their mid-20s.

Yet half of the 14 had little or no trouble adjusting and considered themselves adjusted at present. My observations confirmed this. Most of these ex-students were in their 30s or 40s.

When the replies of the other ex-students were added to this group, I found four additional students who complained of fairly severe adjustment problems lasting more than a year; six who had minor problems that were resolved in less than a year; eight who said either their adjustment to the world was easier because they attended Summerhill, or denied any problem at all. In addition, 20 were not sure how their life at Summerhill had affected their later adjustment to society.

A lawyer who spent the years between six and 16 as a Summerhillian said he had no adjustment problem at all. When he thought about his years at the school, he recalled the happy times at Summerhill and went on to say that "some never wanted to leave that little paradise."

The son of Corky Corkhill, one of the few teachers unanimously acclaimed by his former students, grew up at Summerhill. He said that he had rarely attended classes, but instead spent his time taking Neill's car apart and working with his hands. After he left Summerhill in 1939 when he was 17, he served a three-year apprenticeship in skilled metal work. He worked for the same company until three years ago, when he opened his own highly profitable repair business.

A young man of 20 who spent 10 years at Summerhill told me that procrastination was an attitude easily picked up at Summerhill. "You know," he said. "I think one can stay at Summerhill too long. It was easy to be led astray by new students who did little or no studying."
He did point out that his entire group passed the 11+ exam with above average grades. This crucial examination decides an English child's future; he cannot enter a university unless he passes.

When the positive remarks among the 50 former students were tabulated, five items were mentioned more than any others. Leading the list of benefits were a healthy attitude toward sex and relationships with the opposite sex; a natural confidence and ease with authority figures; and a natural development, in line with personal interests and abilities. Close behind was the feeling that Summerhill helps in growing out of the need to play continuously and makes it possible to settle comfortably into more serious pursuits. The tabulation showed the belief of former students that their Summerhill experience had helped them to understand their own children better and to raise them in a wholesome way.

Most of the former students I interviewed seemed able to cope with authority effectively. This ability to handle authority continued into adulthood. At the age of 24, one Summerhillian was promoted to a junior-executive position despite his lack of college education. The president of the company told him: "You're the only one on this staff who is not afraid to tell me what you're thinking and how you really feel about things."

The majority of Summerhillians had only one major complaint against the school: the lack of academic opportunity and inspiration, coupled with a dearth of inspired teachers. This was stressed by 26 of the students interviewed. I discovered that the school attracted a variety of teachers. Some padded about in sandals, growing long beards, content when the children cut class. Others ran about the school grounds, plucking children from trees and trying to lure them to their lessons. One former student told me that when he first learned to read and write it was in German—because he liked the German teacher so well.

In spite of the complaints that Summerhill was academically weak, 10 of the 50 former students interviewed had passed university entrance examinations. Four of the 10 felt they had lost two or more years cramming to pass. Eight had graduated from universities.

An electrical engineer who had spent eight years at Summerhill told me: "Summerhill is good for children up to about the age of 10. After that it's too weak academically."

Although Neill has stated that his former students left Summerhill to go into the arts, less than 20 percent of those I interviewed could be placed in this category. There was a Sadler-Wells dancer with top billing who learned his first ballet steps and Nijinskilike leaps at Summerhill. There was a young musician who played his piano and composed. And there were two artists, an interior decorator and a writer.

But there were two truck drivers, an apprentice bricklayer, two sales-men, a radio technician and a construction worker as well. There was a noted zoologist who has pioneered in research on the Nigerian snail-disease problem. Six were housewives. Two teen-agers were unemployed, although one of them found a job driving a taxi the week of his inter-view [*see* chart].

Occupations of Summerhillians

HOUSEWIFE (6)	RECEPTIONIST
SECRETARY (3)	BUILDER
STUDENT, UNIVERSITY (2)	RECREATION WORKER
ARTIST (2)	ELECTRICAL ENGINEER
SALES CLERK (2)	STUDENT, PREPARATORY SCHOOL
PHYSICIAN (2)	CONSTRUCTION WORKER
BOOKKEEPER-SECRETARY (2)	BUSINESS ADMINISTRATION
SALESMAN (2)	INTERIOR DECORATOR
TRUCK DRIVER (2)	SHOPKEEPER
LAWYER (2)	CATERER
TEACHER (2)	INSTRUMENT REPAIRER
RADIO TECHNICIAN	DANCER
CABINET MAKER	APPRENTICE BRICKLAYER
UNIVERSITY PROFESSOR	ODD-JOBS
TAXI DRIVER	SPEECH-THERAPIST
ZOOLOGIST	PUBLISHER/WRITER
MUSICIAN	UNEMPLOYED (1)

Although three of the 11 couples interviewed had been divorced, most seemed happily married. Two of the divorced group had remarried, apparently with success.

Without exception, former Summerhillians were raising their own children in a self-directive way. Their interrelationship was warm; the children appeared happy and spontaneous. I found a free and easy kind of relationship in most Summerhill homes.

Of the 11 former students who had become parents, all but one felt that their children were unafraid of them. Most of the parents had conflicting feelings about discipline, and all but two had felt guilty at some time when punishing their children. (This is rather typical of *all* parents.) None of the parents customarily used corporal punishment, although three mentioned an occasional situation when permissiveness had led to physical punishment.

> "I believe in giving as much freedom as possible," said one mother, "but I have had great conflicts. For example, I don't believe in hitting children, but I have lost my temper and 'poshed' them a bit or yelled. Then I felt terribly guilty afterwards."

Only three of the parents had sent their own children to Summerhill. Two others said they would seriously consider sending their children at a later time. Most of these parents offered a belief in freedom as their reason for sending their children to the school, as had most of their own parents.

Those three Summerhillians who had entered their own children in Summerhill had removed them before they reached the age of 13. The removals were almost wholly due to the conviction that not enough emphasis was placed upon academic learning and that Summerhill lacked fine teachers and good equipment.

One second-generation Summerhillian who had spent three years at the school was now preparing to study law. "I hardly opened a book at Summerhill, especially at first," he told me. "Guess I learned to hate learning at the strict ordinary school and that's why Dad sent me to Summerhill."

At the end of his third year at Summerhill, he decided himself to go back to the regular school in his neighborhood. His reason was simple: "I was ready to learn."

Of the six parents who did not plan to send their children to Summerhill, five felt that children should be with their parents. Three of these said they enjoyed their own children too much to send them away.

The 11-year-old daughter of one former student told me: "I go to a Quaker boarding school. I don't think Summerhill would have agreed with *me*. It sounds a little too loose and unorganized.

The ages of the parents among the group of former students ranged from 25 to 49. The average age was 33. Their children were as young as two and as old as 21. The average age of these 14 children was eight.

Upon completing the five weeks of interviews, my feelings were mainly positive. Almost all the former students were working, raising responsive children, enjoying life.

Yet I felt that something was lacking in Summerhill's completely free approach. Neill has said that the goal of good education should be *happiness*. And he has said that happiness is *interest*. It seemed to me that this is where Summerhill's philosophy could be improved. A child cannot be interested in anything until he succeeds. Then he can find satisfaction in anything—even in arithmetic.

(The Summerhill experiment does not stand alone. Between 1933 and 1941, some 1,500 graduates from 30 experimental schools across the United States were compared in the Aiken study with 1,500 graduates of control schools, carefully matched with the experimental group. Students were matched not only for age, grades and I.Q., but for social and economic status, community size and geographical area.

Three hundred colleges—including the Ivy League's Harvard, Princeton and Yale—accepted students from these experimental, sometimes gradeless schools on the basis of the school's recommendation. Students from the experimental schools did better in college by every measure of academic success: grades, academic honors, participation in activities, orientation toward occupational choice. And researchers found that the more *experimental* his secondary school was, the better the graduate performed in college.)

When, the next fall, I faced my ungraded New England class of seven- to 12-year-olds with reading and emotional problems, I began to apply some of the lessons I learned in England. Don struggled for hours over a single page of arithmetic. When told he did not have to do any arithmetic, he left the workbook in his desk for a month without opening it. Suddenly he began doing 10 to 15 pages of problems each day, racing with another student. In less than two months he had mastered a year's work.

But not all children can handle complete freedom. Frank just wanted to draw. With new confidence, I told him how good his picture was and asked him how high the school building was. He guessed wildly, as he did when I asked him the length of our school room.

Others in the class began wondering, and rulers began to appear from desks. The room was measured. At recess, Frank and a friend climbed down the fire escape to measure the height of the building in yards. Now they had to learn division in order to change the yards to feet.

Frank was told he could draw, but only after the division problem was done. If Neill was observing, he would surely say, "This is certainly not a Summerhill classroom." But if he came back an hour later, he would find Frank busily drawing, his division mastered.

And Jimmy, who wanted to spend all his time on scientific experiments! I ordered him to write up all his experiments, giving the date, the procedure and the results. He struggled, but within a week he began to see the importance of recording what day the mold began to grow in his test tube filled with yeast and sugar, and how it became fuzzy and changed from day to day.

Would Neill say that Jimmy was not self-directed, that he wrote only for *me?* Or would he see a child learning new satisfactions, finding new horizons open? I would hope the latter, for there *is* a middle ground. A compromise with Summerhill, a guided freedom, might bring together the best of both approaches to education.

BIBLIOGRAPHY

The Free Schools of Leicestershire County. *Christian Science Monitor,* May 14, 1966.

Freedom, Not License! A. S. Neill. Hart, 1966.

Summerhill. A. S. Neill. Hart, 1960.

Summerhill After 50 Years. Emmanuel Bernstein in *The New Era,* Vol. 48, no. 2, pages 30–31, 1967.

Teaching Children to Think; Schools for Children. Joseph Featherstone in *New Republic,* August 19, September 2, September 9, 1967.

Thirty Schools Tell Their Story. Wilfred Aiken in *Adventure in American Education,* Vol. 5. Harper, 1943.

part 5

"Only if we understand the school system as the central myth-making ritual of industrial societies can we explain the deep need for it . . . and the inextricable way in which schooling is tied to the self image of contemporary man."
—Ivan Illich

"Our schools are, in a sense, factories in which the raw materials (children) are to be shaped and fashioned into products to meet the various demands of life. The specifications for manufacturing come from the demands of the twentieth-century civilization, and it is the business of the school to build its pupils to the specifications laid down. This demands good tools, specialized machinery, continuous measurement of production to see if it is according to specifications, the elimination of waste in manufacture, and a large variety in output."
—Elwood P. Cubberley

School
of the future

Through all the articles presented in the first four parts runs the assumption—tacit or explicit—that education must be institutionalized and that school is its most logical and legitimate institutional house. Even critics as radical as Jerry Farber do not want to abolish schools, but to reform them—to make decent places of them. Though many authors represented have seen a harlot in the temple, their suggestions deal either with driving her out, reforming her, or with finding out how she got there and stopping others from getting in. The possibility that the temple itself is the problem and that it ought to be abandoned, supplanted, or bypassed has not yet been seriously treated.

The identification of education with schools is so nearly universal that few people now think seriously of the possibility of one without the other. But just as some of the preceding authors suggest that schools do not educate, those which follow hint that education may not require schools, at least not as we have known them. The universal school as a remedy for mass illiteracy is a very recent and perhaps now outmoded concept.

GEORGE B. LEONARD

Visiting Day, 2001 A.D.

In the first of three articles which comprise this epilogue, George Leonard offers a vision of a "learning environment" in the year 2001. One may well ask, however, whether he really breaks with schooling, or even whether the future which he depicts is a desirable one.

Anyone who tries to draw the future in hard lines and vivid hues is a fool. The future will never sit for a portrait. It will come around a corner we never noticed, take us by surprise. And yet, foolishly, I cannot deny a vision born of indignation and hope. George Sand has called indignation at what is wrong in humanity one of the most passionate forms of love. If this is so, hope for something better may be love of a more enduring sort. Kennedy School in Santa Fe, New Mexico, exists not in the blazing immediacy of the twenty-first century, but in the indignation and hope of today. If it should sound like science fiction, do not be misled. Everything there is technically feasible. We don't really have to wait until the year 2001; it is only people, their habits, their organizations that may take so long to move. The alternatives, real alternatives, exist now.

A spring morning, 2001 A.D. It is visiting day, but not in any special sense; every day is visiting day. We are among those parents who frequently drop by Kennedy School when our children are there or even on those rare days when they choose not to attend. We go not through any sense of duty (though I guess that old-fashioned word would apply to what we feel for our children), but out of sheer fascination. In fact, there's a certain amount of kidding among members of our adult learning group about how much time we spend in our children's early-school —"lifting ideas for our own projects."

We catch a glimpse of the school before driving our electric down the ramp and into the underground parking lot. The sight, as always, pleases us—gleaming geodesic domes and translucent tentlike structures scattered randomly among graceful trees; a large grassy playfield encircled with flowers; all of it a testament to the foresight of community planners who set aside the land decades ago. Educators in the great strip cities haven't had it so easy. Some of them have had to build vertically; others are still engaged in lengthy negotiations for enough land for a few trees and flowers.

We walk up a ramp to an entrance. Two postgrads, an eleven-year-old boy and girl, welcome us with hugs and kisses. The girl finds our electronic identification devices on a large board, and we clip them to our clothing. The boy gives each of us a flower—a large orchid-like bloom, orange speckled with deep red, for my wife; a lavender rose for me—the products, we know, of botanical experiments by a group of six- to ten-year-olds. We thank our hosts with another embrace and stroll through a grove of oaks toward the Basics Dome, where we may find our three-year-old, Sally. Even if we knew Sally was somewhere else, we'd probably go there first anyway.

On the way, we pass children of various ages in various states of consciousness. Some are walking aimlessly, alone or in small groups, perhaps toward some destination, perhaps not. Others are running. We notice a group of around seven of the older children with two of the educators in impassioned encounter near one of the biggest trees. Almost in our pathway sits a little girl with long black hair and dark skin—probably of Mexican-Indian extraction. Her enormous black eyes seem to hold a powerful dream, and we tiptoe around her, so as not to disturb her inner voyaging. But she looks up and, for a moment, shares with us something mysterious.

A total of some 800 children between three and ten are enrolled in Kennedy, but on a typical morning only about 600 (around seventy-five of each chronological age) are on the school grounds. Most of the educational environments are in operation from eight in the morning until six in the afternoon. Children can come when and if they please; there's no problem at all if parents wish to take their children on extended trips or simply keep them home for something that's going on there.

While the children are on the school grounds, they are *absolutely* free to go and do *anything* they wish that does not hurt someone else. They are *free learners*. The italics belong to Will Hawthorne, Kennedy's Principal Educator. The free-learning concept has, of course, been accepted for years all over the U.S. Almost every educator gives it lip service, and the overwhelming majority of them follow it to one degree or another. Will, however, lives and breathes it.

"*Everything* starts there," he tells parents. "Until we had the free learner, we really didn't know *anything* about education. The free learner built Kennedy School." Will is a student of educational history and has created several experiential tapes on the development of the concept. "This feisty old radical named A. S. Neill started a place called Summerhill in England in 1924," Will tells parents. "Children were relatively free, but there was no systematic attempt to create learning environments, to find out what human beings really were capable of. There was no real vision of the human potential. Summerhill was mostly a *reaction* to the incredibly inefficient and cruel teaching system of the day. Unfortunately, too, it was tied to the dogma of the then voguish Freudian psychology, with its static and limiting views of the human personality. Still, there was a remarkable interest in Neill's books that reflected a widespread though unfocused hunger for educational reform.

"It was not until the late 1960s and early 1970s that real free-learning schools began springing up here and there, and it was only then that educators could start learning about education. The first such schools were crude affairs. For one thing, the educators of that day found it very difficult to give up the idea of teacher-led classes at certain periods. So—even though the children were ranging freely all over the building—you had someone walking around at given times ringing a bell to announce the beginning of, say, 'math class' for anyone who cared to attend. If the class was made interesting enough—a heroic endeavor under the circumstances—quite a few kids would come. But the enormous *inefficiency* and the *expense* of the 'class and teacher' situation became more and more apparent. Learning environments could be created, it was discovered, for constant operation and full utilization, always available for children and yet always amenable to modification by educators.

"Among the earliest such environments were simple, paper-and-pencil self-instructional programs, mostly in such basic subjects as reading, spelling, figuring and the like. Most of them were terribly linear, unimaginative and single-tracked. But they did their job in demonstrating that the free-learning situation was feasible, even in terms of the strictly limited training offered in that day. Not only that, they freed some teachers to become educators, and these fledgling educators began asking themselves questions on what education was all about. Free learners were there to help give them the answers.

"At around the same time, another development moved in from an entirely different direction. Several large corporations started pushing Computer-Assisted Instruction (CAI). The computer learning programs were at first even more limited and stereotyped than the paper-and-pencil programs. And the learning consoles were mounted, of all places, in 'classrooms.' Children had come to them at certain fixed periods and sit there under the 'guidance' of 'teachers.'

"You know, this is one of the most difficult things for our children to recreate experientially. I mean, the whole business of classrooms and teachers. They can conceptualize it. They've seen the historical films. But, during their history-drama sessions, they rarely can truly get the *feeling* we know existed then. When the child playing teacher forces the children playing students to sit still while teacher gives a long blackboard demonstration, the students find it very hard to get the *feeling* of being bored, distracted, or squirming and hoping for time to pass. Many of them simply go into a relaxed, serene state of semimeditation, enjoying the whole situation immensely. The child serving as history-drama coordinator senses this, naturally enough, and stops the drama amid much laughter and confusion. The fact that children once had to get *permission* to go and urinate is even harder for them to understand.

"Anyhow, the computer and the free school were destined for marriage, and it didn't take them long to get together. By the mid-1970s, most of what was called 'Computer-Assisted Instruction' was being applied in free-learning situations. Immediate economies and efficiencies were realized in terms the Systems Engineering people of the time could understand. The system was, in fact, *too* efficient for the educational goals then envisaged. Children could finish everything too fast and too easily. 'Homework' went right out the window, creating dismay and anxiety, strangely enough, among many parents. The Great National School Debate of the middle and the late 1970s concerned what to do with all the extra time gained by the new mode of learning. The question generally was stated in this fashion: 'What is the province of education?' The answer was simple: 'Everything.'

"During the 1970s, most schools spent a great deal of time with encounter groups for children and educators. These served to educate the emotions and to break down the old protective, defensive patterns of relating. They helped open people to all sorts of capacities they barely realized they had. Gradually the encounter mode became a part of everything the learners did, and it was no longer necessary to set up these groups as such.

"At the same time, educators were finding out that computer-mediated programs could be constructed to encourage uniqueness rather than sameness in learners. In fact, by tying to the ongoing program referents from a memory bank consisting of all the learner's past responses, the learner's distinctness from all other learners could be rapidly increased. Too rapidly, it seemed to some educators.

"The programs still were narrow, concerned with one 'subject' at a time—in other words, they were *programs*. Then, gradually, they evolved into what we now call 'dialogues.' It started when programmers began adding novelty and surprise through what they at first termed 'extraneous material.' For example, material about astronomy would pop up in programs on Eastern philosophy. Soon, they began realizing that what they were adding was by no means extraneous. Far from it, cross-matrix learning increased the central nervous system's capability for making connections, as well as enhancing mastery of any given subject. The early 1980s were fascinated by Cross-Matrix Stimulus and Response (CMSR). Naturally enough, the cross-matrix linkage started out quite teleologically, with the dialoguers seeking 'reasons' for their connections. But 'reasons' were found to be unduly limiting. Random retrieval through a central school computer made it possible to bring material up from the general cultural data bank, from the learner's own past responses and from the discontinuous symbolic storage to create displays that were anything but teleological.

"It was about this time, too, that dialoguers began conceiving the displays not only as learning aids, but as artistic creations in their own right. It occurred to them that the two—art and learning—really were one. That was still in the period when the displays were presented on old-fashioned cathode-ray television screens mounted in front of each learner. The art-and-learning movement was given a tremendous push around 1985, when the hologrammatic-conversion problem was solved for mass production. Laser-type projection created images of unimagined brightness and resolution—*moving* images that seemed to hang in mid-air, in dimensions that somehow outshone reality.

"An even more important development of the 1980s was the application of Ongoing Brain-wave Analysis (OBA) to Computer-Assisted Dialogue (CAD). The experiments of such pioneers as Kamiya and Adey had already shown that it was possible, through computer analysis, to identify the brain-wave patterns not only of certain general states of consciousness but also those associated with effective short-term memory. Certain experimenters began attaching brain-wave sensors to learners' earphones, so that their wave patterns could be fed directly into the computer for ongoing analysis and immediate influence of the dialogue. In this way, the learning process could march along much more swiftly and surely, and the number of overt motor responses —speech or key pressing, for example—required of the learner could be greatly reduced. If the learner was responding neurologically, the dialogue could move on. His general state of consciousness could also influence the dialogue.

"It took a few years for OBA to spread to most of the nation's schools. By that time, of course, musical-rhythmic sound had become a key matrix in CMSR. As the Hindus say, *Nada-Brahma-,* Sound Is God. And with sound responding to a learner's innermost states, a sort of cosmic counterpoint was born. The 1990s were a period of consolidation of the basic techniques, with breathtaking advances in the state of the art not only in Computer-Assisted Dialogue, but in a great number of educational environments."

Will Hawthorne's ebullience turns to caution only when the matter of Direct Brain-wave Manipulation (DBM) comes up. "First of all," he says, "it will be many years before DBM has anywhere near the subtlety and specificity of CAD through the usual sense channels. Then, too, I just don't like the idea of bypassing the senses, the sources of ever-present joy. No, if I have anything to say about it, there won't be any Kennedy children wearing those cumbersome DBM electrode helmets until I've seen a lot more data, especially concerning sensory side effects."

Some parents and children consider Will hopelessly conservative in this matter. But one visit to the Basics Dome explains why he is reluctant to "go inside." My wife and I find our pace quickening as we approach the most active and spectacular learning environment at Kennedy. We go in through one of three tunnel-like entrances and emerge near the center of a great dome lit only by the glow of laser learning displays that completely surround us on the dome's periphery. Sitting or sprawled on cushions scattered on the floor are other parents and older children who have come just for the experience, in addition to the little children waiting their turns at the learning consoles. We settle down and open our senses.

No matter how many times you visit the Basics Dome, its initial effect is literally stunning. It takes a while for the nervous system to begin processing; first, you have to surrender to the overwhelming sensory bombardment that comes from every side. There are, around us, forty learning consoles, at each of which is seated a child between the ages of three and seven, facing outward toward the learning displays. Each child sits at a keyboard, essentially less complex than that of an old-fashioned typewriter, but fitted with a number of shifts so that almost every symbol known to human cultures can be produced. The child's learning display, about ten feet square, is reflected from the hologram-conversion screen that runs all the way around the inner surface of the dome. The image appears to stand out from the screen in sometimes startling colors and dimensions. The screen is slightly elevated above the child's horizontal eye level so that everyone in the dome, by turning all the way around, can view all of the learning displays. Each display joins the one on either side of it, so that the total effect is panoramic. And each has its own set of stereo speakers, joining in a panorama of sound.

There are almost always children waiting for each console. A small electronic tablet on the back of each chair shows the name of the child in the chair and the number of minutes he has left in his learning session. The amount of time allowed for each session varies; it is calculated electronically according to the total number of children waiting in the dome, but it is never less than twenty minutes. Young children entering the dome shop around for consoles that have few or no other children waiting and that have the shortest time to go. The child assures his waiting place simply by touching the tablet with his electronic identification device (EID); a receiver picks up the information and the child's name appears at the bottom of the list on the tablet.

When a child takes the chair to begin learning, another radio receiver senses his presence through his EID and signals the central learning computer to plug in that particular child's learning history. The child puts on his combination earphones and brain-wave sensors, so that OBA can become an element in the dialogue. (Some schools use the brain-wave pattern, much in the manner of a fingerprint, to identify the learner.) Once the computer picks up the child's ongoing brainwaves, it immediately begins reiterating (in drastically foreshortened form) his last learning session. The child watches his most recent lesson reeling by on his display. If he wants to continue where he left off last time, he holds down his "yes" key until the reiteration is finished. If not, he presses "no," and the computer begins searching for other material appropriate to the child's level of learning, material which is flashed onto the display until the child presses "yes." The "select" process generally takes less than two minutes. The dialogue then begins.

At any given time during the dialogue, five variables are at hand:

1. A full bank of the basic, commonly agreed-upon cultural knowledge, arranged in dialogue form. Most children go through the entire basics bank in the four years from age three through age six.
2. Basic material arranged in Cross-Matrix Stimulus and Response form. This material appears at random intervals along with the dialogued material, to provide novelty and surprise and to help the child learn to make those unexpected leaps which are so much a part of discovery.
3. The child's brain-wave pattern, analyzed in terms of general consciousness state and short-term memory strength.
4. The child's overt motor responses as typed on the keyboard or spoken into a directional microphone mounted on the console.
5. Communal Interconnect (CI). This is one of the very latest educational developments. Only a few of the nation's schools have it. Through CI, the material on one learning display sometimes influences and is influenced by the material on nearby displays. This makes the learning process far more communal. It also helps tie together all forty displays into a single learning-art object, enhancing learning and appreciation, not only for the children at the consoles, but for the many spectators in the dome as well.

As soon as our senses become accustomed to the sounds and sights and smells in the dome, we look around for Sally. We are pleased to find her at one of the consoles. We move over to the side of the circle of spectators nearest her.

Sally, we notice on the electronic tablet on her chair, is only five minutes into her learning session. There is a Negro boy, probably six, on her left who is deep into a simple calculus session. On Sally's right, a girl of four or five is dialoguing about primitive cultures. Sally herself, as in her last several sessions, is concerned with simple language skills. It quickly becomes apparent that she has launched into a session on breaking her linguistic set. Standard spelling and syntax are generally learned during the first half of a child's third year of age. During the second half (where Sally is now) an equal or greater amount of time is spent trying out alternate forms. This leads eventually, after the basics are finished, to a key project: almost every child, working with friends, creates an entire new language before leaving Kennedy School.

We watch Sally's display, which now seems to be billowing with pink and lavender clouds. Gradually, the clouds take the shape of some kind of animal's face. Before I can make out what it is, I hear Sally saying "Cat" into her microphone. Almost instantly, a huge, grinning cat's face gathers form and the word "cat" appears at the bottom of the display. Then a written conversation begins between Sally and the Computer-Assisted Dialogue, with the words of each appearing on the display:

> CAD: Can you think of an alternate spelling?
> SALLY [*Typing*]: kat.

On the display, the giant cat face recedes and is transformed into a white Angora cat, surrounded by vibrating, jagged radial lines of many colors. A purring sound comes from the display.

> CAD: How about another?
> SALLY [*Pausing a moment*]: katte.

The purring becomes louder.

> CAD: A cat is a kat is a katte.
> SALLY [*Quickly*]: A katte is a kat is a cat.
> CAD: Copy cat.
> SALLY: Koppy kat.

There is a pause as the cat image gradually fades and the purring mingles with sweeping electronic music coming from the display on the left. As the dialogue goes on there between boy and CAD in the lovely visual symbols of calculus, a spinning wheel fills most of the display. Through its spokes, slender and glistening like the spokes of a bicycle wheel, may be viewed the rush of its motion—across grassy fields, deserts, down winding mountain roads. A ghostly image of the wheel appears on Sally's display, too, along with multicolored, dancing wave forms, related somehow to her brain waves. On the display at the right, an African pygmy with a blowgun stalks an unseen prey through dense jungle as the girl at the console carries on a voice-only dialogue with CAD. Suddenly Sally begins to type again:

SALLY: A cat hiss a kat hiss a katte.
CAD: WILD!!!

Sally's display explodes for a moment with dazzling bursts of color, then becomes the jungle of the girl at the right, in which may be seen the prey of the hunter, a leopard. A tentative, suspenseful drumming echoes back and forth between the two displays. The two girls turn to each other smiling, then Sally quickly starts typing:

SALLY: A tiger is a tigger./ A gunne has a trigger.

A moment after the last letter of Sally's couplet appears on her display, the jungle remains the same, but the leopard becomes a tiger and the pygmy becomes a white hunter of the early twentieth century, carrying a gun. The girl at the right snaps her head around at Sally, smiling, and Sally laughs delightedly.

CAD: Why not "leopard"?
SALLY: "Leopard" doesn't rime with "trigger."
CAD: Okay. How about some alternate spellings for "leopard"?
SALLY: That's easy. Leppurd.

Meanwhile, the girl at the right keeps talking to CAD and suddenly the tiger becomes a leopard, the white hunter, a pygmy again. The pygmy lifts his blowgun and with a sharp, explosive exhalation that echoes through the dome, sends a dart into the air. The display becomes a closeup of the dart coursing in slow motion across the girl's display, across Sally's and into the boy's at the left, disappearing in the hub of the spinning wheel. Another dart arches across the three displays, then another and another, sailing, soaring, starting always from different angles but ending invariably in the center of the boy's spinning wheel.

"Beautiful CI!" I hear my wife exclaim, and I notice that several people are watching the sequence and listening to the rise and fall of the accompanying electronic music. I also see that the flight of the darts is beginning to influence displays even farther along the line. But the boy continues his calculus dialogue and Sally goes on, too:

CAD: "Leppurd" is good, but you don't have to stay with sound correspondence. Would you like to try something farther out?

Sally presses her "yes" key, then pauses before beginning to type:

SALLY: Leap-heart.
CAD: Nice. Do you want to do another?
SALLY: No.

The flying darts begin to fade. Gradually, Sally's display takes on the deep, rich, undulating plum purple that often characterizes the brain's alpha-wave pattern. Some of the gorgeous richness spills over onto the displays at either side. We know her eyes are closed. She is serene. It is one of education's more valuable moments. We, too, are serene. It is easy, in this setting, to share Sally's feeling. We also share the sheer delight of the educators who set up and constantly modify this learning environment. It is a kind of delight that was unknown to lecturers.

When Sally's session is finished, we walk with her out of the Basics Dome. We talk for a while, but soon she sees some of her friends and leaves us. They run off toward the thickest grove of trees to continue an animal game that may take them the rest of the day.

So we stroll from one place to another, looking (but not too strenuously) for Johnny, our nine-year-old. If we were in a hurry to find him, it would be easy enough. We would merely go to the Central Dome and present one of our electronic identification devices to the ongoing scan, then read out Johnny's approximate present location. Every child wears an EID whenever he is on the school grounds, and the central computer continually tabulates how much time he spends in each educational environment. In addition, whenever the child is in dialogue with a CAD, his learning experience is stored in the computer. This allows Kennedy's educators, not only to keep track of each child's educational development with a minimum of effort, but also to evaluate the drawing power and effectiveness of each environment. The first principle of free learning is that if an environment fails to draw or to educate, it is the environment's, not the learner's, fault.

Visiting educators from educationally underdeveloped nations sometimes find it hard to understand that EID tracking serves not to enforce conformity, but just the opposite. In fact, "asymmetry" is highly valued. Will Hawthorne becomes quite excited when a young child resists the enticements of the Basics Dome for a year or two. Such a child may turn out to be so unique that much can be learned from him. And individual uniqueness is itself one of the main goals of the educational process.

Anyway, learning the basics, the commonly agreed-upon cultural stuff, is so sure and easy that there's never any worry about delay in starting it. It seems incredible to today's children that there ever was.

"I still find it hard to believe," Johnny sometimes says, "that people of Grandpa's generation spent *most* of their time in school learning just what the little kids learn in Basics."

'It's really true," my wife tells him. "They learned *much less.* And they did spend almost all their school time working at it."

"*Working?*" Sally asks in amazement.

"Yes. *Really.* And there were all sorts of discussions and arguments about how to do it and every kind of agony you can imagine."

MAX GUNTHER

What's Around the Corner for "Sesame Street"?

Max Gunther's article on "Sesame Street" suggests that television may teach more efficiently than school much of the content school has been supposed to convey. "Sesame Street" is already a start-ling success. But does it mark a general departure from schooling, or is it merely a pleasant supplement? If "Sesame Street" is the wave of the future, what does it portend? Will children stay home longer than they do now? Will they have a choice to watch or not watch? Is TV a new form of schooling, or a break away from schooling?

The president of Ohio Wesleyan University asked the seniors whom they'd like him to invite as commencement speaker this June. They asked for Joan Ganz Cooney, originator of the giggle-and-learn show called *Sesame Street.*

Max Gunther, "What's Around the Corner for 'Sesame Street'?" *TV Guide,* July 10–16, 1971, pp. 20–25. Reprinted with permission from *TV Guide*® Magazine. Copyright © 1971 by Triangle Publications, Inc., Radnor, Pennsylvania.

It is fashionable on campuses these days to grump at virtually any-thing originated by the adult Establishment—particularly anything asso-ciated with the alleged "wasteland" of TV or perpetrated by the Federal Government. And so Mrs. Cooney, who is a 41-year-old adult and who runs a TV show supported largely by federal funds, considers this invitation a significant honor. "The impact of *Sesame Street* has gone beyond anything we dreamed of in the beginning," she says with uncon-cealed delight. "It's being *noticed*."

It is indeed. President Nixon has felt moved to praise it. Con-gressmen have debated it. Educators have variously lauded it and wor-ried about it. College students have solemnly analyzed its qualities as a work of art. Every kid in my neighborhood seems to know who the Cookie Monster is. Though not yet 2 years old, *Sesame Street* has en-joyed what may be the most astonishing success of any show in the whole history of American television. It has ceased to be merely a show. It has become a cause.

Any cause so large and loud deserves investigation, especially when it's supported by one's own tax money. I went around to *Sesame*'s New York headquarters to find out what has been going on. What do the *Sesame* folk feel they've accomplished in the first two years? What have they learned?

Sesame Street began because many people in this country were worried about what happens to poor kids—the so-called "culturally de-prived"—when they start schooling. Having had less intellectual stimula-tion and less exposure to books and magazines than their more affluent classmates, they come into kindergarten or first grade with an often cruel handicap. Letters and numbers that are at least vaguely familiar to the typical middle-class kid may totally baffle a ghetto youngster. He doesn't understand what the teacher is gibbering about, falls further behind, gets frustrated, may end by giving up altogether. The handicap can last for the rest of his life.

The federally funded Head Start program was an early attempt to help kids out of this trap. Head Start youngsters went to summer school before kindergarten. But for various reasons the program didn't suc-ceed as well as everyone had hoped. Other programs were being talked about, but most were only dreams in the minds of their proponents. In Congress, Rep. (now Sen.) John Tunney of California introduced a bill under which federal money would be provided to send all U.S. kids to school at age 3 instead of the traditional 5 or 6. The program would have cost billions of dollars. Congress looked at Tunney's bill, smiled politely and looked the other way.

Then came *Sesame Street*. Joan Cooney, then an obscure producer of documentary films, was talking about preschool education at a dinner party with Lloyd Morrisett of the Carnegie Corporation (a nonprofit foundation). Morrisett suddenly began wondering about TV. Almost every kid in the country, rich or poor, has access to a TV set. TV had long ago proved its stupendous ability to sell toys, deodorants and cake mixes. Couldn't this medium also be used to sell education?

With money raised from the U.S. Office of Education and sundry private sources, Morrisett and Joan Cooney organized the Children's Television Workshop (CTW) as a division of National Educational Television. CTW studied the field for about a year, and in November 1969 went on the air with the first *Sesame Street* broadcast.

Now. How well has it worked?

In terms of money, beautifully. CTW's budget for the past fiscal year (ending June 30) was slightly over $8 million—which compares favorably, to say the least, with the billion-dollar figures associated with other preschool efforts such as Senator Tunney's program and Head Start. It's estimated that over 8 million kids watch the show at least a couple of times a week. In other words, *Sesame Street* costs about a dollar per year per child.

Does the young viewer get his dollar's worth? Some have raised doubts. Cornell psychologist Urie Bronfenbrenner has complained that the show is too sweet—a dream of life such as life never was. There are no racial tensions; nobody ever gets mad; no sharp words are spoken. Bronfenbrenner doubts this will prepare kids for the mean world in which they'll have to make their way.

Some educators have grumbled that this "sugar-coated education" will make kids' and teachers' lives difficult later on, in "real" classrooms. "The pain of a standard education is part of the education," says a Connecticut school principal. "*Sesame Street* makes no demands on the kids. Real school and real life aren't like that. If a problem is troubling you, you can't just switch it off and walk away."

Some of the more mature TV critics in my neighborhood voice other complaints. Kate, age 9, espouses the Bronfenbrenner view. She says the show isn't as funny as the *Roadrunner* "because nobody ever gets crunched." Kate, suffering from a skinned elbow, is obviously aware that real life is violent. Meg, 8, echoes the criticisms of some educators who say *Sesame Street* deals in mere rote memorization. "How can you learn from that silly stuff?" asks Meg. "They show you a lot of letters, but they don't say what you're suppose to *do* with the letters."

But it would probably be safe to say that at least 10 times as many voices have praised the show as have damned it. The Educational Testing Service at Princeton, N.J., tested 943 children before and after they'd watched *Sesame Street* six months. Of the 943, some 731 were considered to be from disadvantaged homes. As the show's supporters had hoped, it turned out that those who watched most often gained the most. In a letter-recognition test, kids who watched the show only occasionally scored eight percent right in the pretest and 14 percent in the posttest six months later. Kids who watched often went from 19 percent to 62 percent.

Other, less formal, tributes have been coming in from all over the country. In Huntington, W. Va., for instance, school officials were so startled by the erudition of the latest kindergarten crop that they launched a survey to find the causes. One question on the survey: "Does your child watch *Sesame Street*?" Most parents said yes.

Meanwhile, responding to both external criticism and internal need, CTW has been changing. Some changes have been purely administrative. CTW has now severed its tie-in with National Educational Television and has become an independent, nonprofit corporation, with Joan Cooney still CTW president and Morrisett chairman of the trustees. The change allows a new flexibility—and also reflects the fact that CTW has grown too big to be anybody else's division. The original staff of about 30 has increased to about 180.

Other changes have been trivial. One of the show's adult characters, Susan, had been portrayed as a housewife but is now a nurse as well. This was in response to a complaint from a women's lib outfit. Women's lib has a thing about housewives.

"We've made a lot of important curriculum changes too," says Dr. Edward Palmer, a psychologist who has been CTW's research chief from the beginning. "We're always changing *Sesame Street* and probably always will. It's an endless experiment—a laboratory on public display."

Palmer's group constantly tests children's reactions to the shows and uses the results to make a continual flow of new recommendations to the production people. In one type of test, for example, Palmer sits kids before a TV set, switches on a *Sesame Street* show and then tries to distract them by flashing pictures on another screen. He wants to know what kinds of video techniques absorb prekindergarteners and what kinds bore them. Some random samplings of Palmer's findings that have influenced the show:

- Children aren't bored by frequent repetitions of a short, lively commercial. In fact, they will remember a letter more surely if it's shown several times in one broadcast than if the same number of repetitions are spaced over a week.
- Little kids don't pay attention for long when adults talk to them directly. But they like to watch what adults *do*.
- Kids are fascinated by "pixilation"—the technique of cutting out frames of a film so as to cause a jerky, speeded-up kind of motion.
- Children remember a jingle or anything else best when they sing or say it along with the TV performer. But 3-year-olds are much more likely to try singing along than are 4-year-olds.

Other changes have had to do with the distribution of CTW's product. The show has slowly but surely spread into new areas where TV sets couldn't receive it before. Some 200 public (nonprofit) stations and 50 commercial stations now carry it. CTW is trying to get more commercial stations to sign up.

There's no money in the deal for a commercial station—not directly, anyhow. CTW won't permit any commercial advertising to be shoehorned into the show; nor may a commercial other than a public-service announcement appear directly before or after *Sesame Street*. But some commercial stations figure *Sesame Street* has a dollar value in that it builds audiences. Kids who watch the show will often stay tuned for the commercially sponsored show that follows—and the station can therefore charge higher time rates for that show, if the ad manager talks fast enough.

In other cases, *Sesame Street* has been able to appear on commercial stations because civic groups or civic-minded companies have bought the time. In Shreveport, La., a parents' group called Citizens for *Sesame Street* was organized to raise the money. In St. Louis, the money was donated by Ralston Purina Co. In Detroit, the money came partly from the school board.

CTW has also had to face some internal money problems. About 40 percent of the past year's budget came from the U.S. Department of Health, Education and Welfare. The remainder came from the Corporation for Public Broadcasting, the Ford and Carnegie Foundations. It's reasonable to guess that the private foundations won't want to go on footing the bill forever. Because of this, and because of ambitious expansion plans now afoot at CTW, it will undoubtedly be necessary to ask HEW—ultimately Congress—for more money. Will Congress pay?

Probably. I talked to Senator Tunney about it. He got into the early-schooling business when his son, raised by Tunney's Dutch wife, flunked a nursery-school admission test because of difficulties with the English language. He thinks all kids should get language and other schooling starting at age 3 and he is still pushing his own program. He doesn't see *Sesame Street* as a substitute for his program because "a TV show demands no response from the youngsters, doesn't help them use their hands or force them to think their way through problems." But he thinks of the show as a valuable "adjunct." His daughter, Arianne, has watched since age 1½. Today, at 3, she knows the whole alphabet.

Would Senator Tunney vote for more *Sesame Street* funds? "Of course I would."

CTW will get some money, though only a fraction of its needs, from several new licensing deals that have been worked out. Western Publishing, Columbia Records, Topper Corporation and others have signed up to produce *Sesame*-oriented books, records and toys. The contracts specify unusually high royalties for CTW, so the manufacturers will make little or no profit. (The profit will be in public relations.)

As for the future, CTW nourishes many dreams. A second show, titled *The Electric Company*, designed mainly to help 7- to 10-year-olds learn to read, will make its debut this fall. This summer the U.S. Department of Labor is underwriting a $600,000 program which it hopes will reach 17,000 preschool children from 14 metropolitan areas. Joan Cooney is mulling over other possible ventures as well—perhaps TV shows aimed at other age groups, perhaps a full-length feature to be shown at neighborhood movie houses.

"I think we've started something big," she says.

"Not nearly as big as it's going to be," says Sen. John Tunney. "People are only beginning to understand what early schooling can accomplish."

IVAN ILLICH

The Alternative to Schooling

*In the final essay of this book, Ivan Illich argues not for the trans-
formation of the school but for breaking up the monopoly schools
now have as social and economic legitimizers. The reader will
perhaps ask whether it is possible to stop regarding schools as the
primary avenue to personal advancement and social acceptability
and start seeing them as one of several sources for acquiring skills.
Illich makes a strong case for disestablishing schools as the "central
myth" of our time.*

For generations we have tried to make the world a better place by providing more and more schooling, but so far the endeavor has failed.
What we have learned instead is that forcing all children to climb an
open-ended education ladder cannot enhance equality but must favor
the individual who starts out earlier, healthier, or better prepared; that
enforced instruction deadens for most people the will for independent
learning; and that knowledge treated as a commodity, delivered in pack-
ages, and accepted as private property once it is acquired, must always
be scarce.

In response, critics of the educational system are now proposing
strong and unorthodox remedies that range from the voucher plan,
which would enable each person to buy the education of his choice on
an open market, to shifting the responsibility for education from the
school to the media and to apprenticeship on the job. Some individuals
foresee that the school will have to be disestablished just as the church
was disestablished all over the world during the last two centuries.
Other reformers propose to replace the universal school with various new
systems that would, they claim, better prepare everybody for life in modern society. These proposals for new educational institutions fall into
three broad categories: the reformation of the classroom within the
school system; the dispersal of free schools throughout society; and the
transformation of all society into one huge classroom. But these three
approaches—the reformed classroom, the free school, and the worldwide

Ivan Illich, "The Alternative to Schooling," *Saturday Review*, June 19, 1971,
pp. 44ff. Copyright 1971 Saturday Review, Inc. Reprinted by permission.

classroom—represent three stages in a proposed escalation of education in which each step threatens more subtle and more pervasive social control than the one it replaces.

I believe that the disestablishment of the school has become inevitable and that this end of an illusion should fill us with hope. But I also believe that the end of the "age of schooling" could usher in the epoch of the global schoolhouse that would be distinguishable only in name from a global madhouse or global prison in which education, correction, and adjustment become synonymous. I therefore believe that the breakdown of the school forces us to look beyond its imminent demise and to face fundamental alternatives in education. Either we can work for fearsome and potent new educational devices that teach about a world which progressively becomes more opaque and forbidding for man, or we can set the conditions for a new era in which technology would be used to make society more simple and transparent, so that all men can once again know the facts and use the tools that shape their lives. In short, we can disestablish schools or we can deschool culture.

In order to see clearly the alternatives we face, we must first distinguish education from schools, which means separating the humanistic intent of the teacher from the impact of the invariant structure of the school. This hidden structure constitutes a course of instruction that stays forever beyond the control of the teacher or of his school board. It conveys indelibly the message that only through schooling can an individual prepare himself for adulthood in society, that what is not taught in school is of little value, and that what is learned outside of school is not worth knowing. I call it the hidden curriculum of schooling, because it constitutes the unalterable framework of the system, within which all changes in the curriculum are made.

The hidden curriculum is always the same regardless of school or place. It requires all children of a certain age to assemble in groups of about thirty, under the authority of a certified teacher, for some 500 or 1,000 or more hours each year. It doesn't matter whether the curriculum is designed to teach the principles of fascism, liberalism, Catholicism, or socialism; or whether the purpose of the school is to produce Soviet or United States citizens, mechanics, or doctors. It makes no difference whether the teacher is authoritarian or permissive, whether he imposes his own creed or teaches students to think for themselves. What is important is that students learn that education is valuable when it is acquired in the school through a graded process of consumption; that the degree of success the individual will enjoy in society depends on the amount of learning he consumes; and that learning *about* the world is more valuable than learning *from* the world.

It must be clearly understood that the hidden curriculum translates learning from an activity into a commodity—for which the school monopolizes the market. In all countries knowledge is regarded as the first necessity for survival, but also as a form of currency more liquid than rubles or dollars. We have become accustomed, through Karl Marx's writings, to speak about the alienation of the worker from his work in a class society. We must now recognize the estrangement of man from his learning when it becomes the product of a service profession and he becomes the consumer.

The more learning an individual consumes, the more "knowledge stock" he acquires. The hidden curriculum therefore defines a new class structure for society within which the large consumers of knowledge—those who have acquired large quantities of knowledge stock—enjoy special privileges, high income, and access to the more powerful tools of production. This kind of knowledge-capitalism has been accepted in all industrialized societies and establishes a rationale for the distribution of jobs and income. (This point is especially important in the light of the lack of correspondence between schooling and occupational competence established in studies such as Ivar Berg's *Education and Jobs: The Great Training Robbery*.)

The endeavor to put all men through successive stages of enlightenment is rooted deeply in alchemy, the Great Art of the waning Middle Ages. John Amos Comenius, a Moravian bishop, self-styled Pansophist, and pedagogue, is rightly considered one of the founders of the modern schools. He was among the first to propose seven or twelve grades of compulsory learning. In his *Magna Didactica*, he described schools as devices to "teach everybody everything" and outlined a blueprint for the assembly-line production of knowledge, which according to his method would make education cheaper and better and make growth into full humanity possible for all. But Comenius was not only an early efficiency expert, he was an alchemist who adopted the technical language of his craft to describe the art of rearing children. The alchemist sought to refine base elements by leading their distilled spirits through twelve stages of successive enlightenment, so that for their own and all the world's benefit they might be transmuted into gold. Of course, alchemists failed no matter how often they tried, but each time their "science" yielded new reasons for their failure, and they tried again.

Pedagogy opened a new chapter in the history of Ars Magna.

Education became the search for an alchemic process that would bring forth a new type of man, who would fit into an environment created by scientific magic. But, no matter how much each generation spent on its schools, it always turned out that the majority of people were unfit for enlightenment by this process and had to be discarded as unprepared for life in a man-made world.

Educational reformers who accept the idea that schools have failed fall into three groups. The most respectable are certainly the great masters of alchemy who promise better schools. The most seductive are popular magicians, who promise to make every kitchen into an alchemic lab. The most sinister are the new Masons of the Universe, who want to transform the entire world into one huge temple of learning. Notable among today's masters of alchemy are certain research directors employed or sponsored by the large foundations who believe that schools, if they could somehow be improved, could also become economically more feasible than those that are now in trouble, and simultaneously could sell a larger package of services. Those who are concerned primarily with the curriculum claim that it is outdated or irrelevant. So the curriculum is filled with new packaged courses on African Culture, North American Imperialism, Women's Lib, Pollution, or the Consumer Society. Passive learning is wrong—it is indeed—so we graciously allow students to decide what and how they want to be taught. Schools are prison houses. Therefore, principals are authorized to approve teachouts, moving the school desks to a roped-off Harlem street. Sensitivity training becomes fashionable. So, we import group therapy into the classroom. School, which was supposed to teach everybody everything, now becomes all things to all children.

Other critics emphasize that schools make inefficient use of modern science. Some would administer drugs to make it easier for the instructor to change the child's behavior. Others would transform school into a stadium for educational gaming. Still others would electrify the classroom. If they are simplistic desciples of McLuhan, they replace blackboards and textbooks with multimedia happenings; if they follow Skinner, they claim to be able to modify behavior more efficiently than old-fashioned classroom practitioners can.

Most of these changes have, of course, some good effects. The experimental schools have fewer truants. Parents do have a greater feeling of participation in a decentralized district. Pupils assigned by their teacher to an apprenticeship, do often turn out more competent than those who stay in the classroom. Some children do improve their knowledge of Spanish in the language lab because they prefer playing with the knobs of a tape recorder to conversations with their Puerto Rican peers. Yet all these improvements operate within predictably narrow limits, since they leave the hidden curriculum of school intact.

Some reformers would like to shake loose from the hidden curriculum, but they rarely succeed. Free schools that lead to further free schools produce a mirage of freedom, even though the chain of attendance is frequently interrupted by long stretches of loafing. Attendance through seduction inculcates the need for educational treatment more persuasively than the reluctant attendance enforced by a truant officer. Permissive teachers in a padded classroom can easily render their pupils impotent to survive once they leave.

Learning in these schools often remains nothing more than the acquisition of socially valued skills defined, in this instance, by the consensus of a commune rather than by the decree of a school board. New presbyter is but old priest writ large.

Free schools, to be truly free, must meet two conditions: First, they must be run in a way to prevent the reintroduction of the hidden curriculum of graded attendance and certified students studying at the feet of certified teachers. And, more importantly, they must provide a framework in which all participants—staff and pupils—can free themselves from the hidden foundations of a schooled society. The first condition is frequently incorporated in the stated aims of a free school. The second condition is only rarely recognized, and is difficult to state as the goal of a free school.

It is useful to distinguish between the hidden curriculum, which I have described, and the occult foundations of schooling. The hidden curriculum is a ritual that can be considered the official initiation into modern society, institutionally established through the school. It is the purpose of this ritual to hide from its participants the contradictions between the myth of an egalitarian society and the class-conscious reality it certifies. Once they are recognized as such, rituals lose their power, and this is what is now beginning to happen to schooling. But there are certain fundamental assumptions about growing up—the occult foundations—which now find their expression in the ceremonial of schooling, and which could easily be reinforced by what free schools do.

Among these assumptions is what Peter Schrag calls the "immigration syndrome," which impels us to treat all people as if they were newcomers who must go through a naturalization process. Only certified consumers of knowledge are admitted to citizenship. Men are not born equal, but are made equal through gestation by Alma Mater.

The rhetoric of all schools states that they form a man for the future, but they do not release him for his task before he has developed a high level of tolerance to the ways of his elders: education *for* life rather than *in* everyday life. Few free schools can avoid doing precisely this. Nevertheless they are among the most important centers from which a new life-style radiates, not because of the effect their graduates will have but, rather, because elders who choose to bring up their children without the benefit of properly ordained teachers frequently belong to a radical minority and because their preoccupation with the rearing of their children sustains them in their new style.

The most dangerous category of educational reformer is one who argues that knowledge can be produced and sold more effectively on an open market than on one controlled by the school. These people argue that most skills can be easily acquired from skill-models if the learner is truly interested in their acquisition; that individual entitlements can provide a more equal purchasing power for education. They demand a careful separation of the process by which it is measured and certified. These seem to me obvious statements. But it would be a fallacy to believe that the establishment of a free market for knowledge would constitute a radical alternative in education.

The establishment of a free market would indeed abolish what I have previously called the hidden curriculum of present schooling—its age-specific attendance at a graded curriculum. Equally, a free market would at first give the appearance of counteracting what I have called the occult foundations of a schooled society: the "immigration syndrome," the institutional monopoly of teaching, and the ritual of linear initiation. But at the same time a free market in education would provide the alchemist with innumerable hidden hands to fit each man into the multiple, tight little niches a more complex technocracy can provide.

Many decades of reliance on schooling has turned knowledge into a commodity, a marketable staple of a special kind. Knowledge is now regarded simultaneously as a first necessity and also as society's most precious currency. (The transformation of knowledge into a commodity is reflected in a corresponding transformation of language. Words that formerly functioned as verbs are becoming nouns that designate possessions. Until recently dwelling and learning and even healing designated activities. They are now usually conceived as commodities or services to be delivered. We talk about the manufacture of housing or the delivery of medical care. Men are no longer regarded fit to house or heal themselves. In such a society people come to believe that professional services are more valuable than personal care. Instead of learning how to nurse grandmother, the teen-ager learns to picket the hospital that does not admit her.) This attitude could easily survive the disestablishment of school, just as affiliation with a church remained a condition for office long after the adoption of the First Amendment. It is even more evident that test batteries measuring complex knowledge-packages could easily survive the disestablishment of school—and with this would go the compulsion to obligate everybody to acquire a minimum package in the knowledge stock. The scientific measurement of each man's worth and the alchemic dream of each man's "educability to his full humanity" would finally coincide. Under the appearance of a "free" market, the global village would turn into an environmental womb where pedagogic therapists control the complex navel by which each man is nourished.

At present, schools limit the teacher's competence to the classroom. They prevent him from claiming man's whole life as his domain. The demise of school will remove this restriction and give a semblance of legitimacy to the life-long pedagogical invasion of everybody's privacy. It will open the way for a scramble for "knowledge" on a free market, which would lead us toward the paradox of a vulgar, albeit seemingly egalitarian, meritocracy. Unless the concept of knowledge is transformed, the disestablishment of school will lead to a wedding between a growing meritocratic system that separates learning from certification and a society committed to provide therapy for each man until he is ripe for the gilded age.

For those who subscribe to the technocratic ethos, whatever is technically possible must be made available at least to a few whether they want it or not. Neither the privation nor the frustration of the majority counts. If cobalt treatment is possible, then the city of Tegucigalpa needs one apparatus in each of its two major hospitals, at a cost that would free an important part of the population of Honduras from parasites. If supersonic speeds are possible, then it must speed the travel of some. If the flight to Mars can be conceived, then a rationale must be found to make it appear a necessity. In the technocratic ethos poverty is modernized: Not only are old alternatives closed off by new monopolies, but the lack of necessities is also compounded by a growing spread between those services that are technologically feasible and those that are in fact available to the majority.

A teacher turns "educator" when he adopts this technocratic ethos. He then acts as if education were a technological enterprise designed to make man fit into whatever environment the "progress" of science creates. He seems blind to the evidence that constant obsolescence of all commodities comes at a high price: the mounting cost of training people to know about them. He seems to forget that the rising cost of tools is purchased at a high price in education: They decrease the labor intensity of the economy, make learning on the job impossible or, at best, a privilege for a few. All over the world the cost of educating men for society rises faster than the productivity of the entire economy, and fewer people have a sense of intelligent participation in the commonweal.

A revolution against those forms of privilege and power, which are based on claims to professional knowledge, must start with a transformation of consciousness about the nature of learning. This means, above all, a shift of responsibility for teaching and learning. Knowledge can be defined as a commodity only as long as it is viewed as the result of institutional enterprise or as the fulfillment of institutional objectives. Only when a man recovers the sense of personal responsibility for what he learns and teaches can this spell be broken and the alienation of learning from living be overcome.

The recovery of the power to learn or to teach means that the teacher who takes the risk of interfering in somebody else's private affairs also assumes responsibility for the results. Similarly, the student who exposes himself to the influence of a teacher must take responsibility for his own education. For such purposes educational institutions —if they are at all needed—ideally take the form of facility centers where one can get a roof of the right size over his head, access to a piano or a kiln, and to records, books, or slides. Schools, TV stations, theaters, and the like are designed primarily for use by professionals. Deschooling society means above all the denial of professional status for the second-oldest profession, namely teaching. The certification of teachers now constitutes an undue restriction of the right to free speech: the corporate structure and professional pretentions of journalism an undue restriction on the right to free press. Compulsory attendance rules interfere with free assembly. The deschooling of society is nothing less than a cultural mutation by which a people recovers the effective use of its Constitutional freedoms: learning and teaching by men who know that they are born free rather than treated to freedom. Most people learn most of the time when they do whatever they enjoy; most people are curious and want to give meaning to whatever they come in contact with; and most people are capable of personal intimate intercourse with others unless they are stupefied by inhuman work or turned off by schooling.

The fact that people in rich countries do not learn much on their own constitutes no proof to the contrary. Rather it is a consequence of life in an environment from which, paradoxically, they cannot learn much, precisely because it is so highly programed. They are constantly frustrated by the structure of contemporary society in which the facts on which decisions can be made have become elusive. They live in an environment in which tools that can be used for creative purposes have become luxuries, an environment in which channels of communication serve a few to talk to many.

A modern myth would make us believe that the sense of impotence with which most men live today is a consequence of technology that cannot but create huge systems. But it is not technology that makes systems huge, tools immensely powerful, channels of communication one-directional. Quite the contrary: Properly controlled, technology could provide each man with the ability to understand his environment better, to shape it powerfully with his own hands, and to permit him full intercommunication to a degree never before possible. Such an alternative use of technology constitutes the central alternative in education.

If a person is to grow up he needs, first of all, access to things, to places and to processes, to events and to records. He needs to see, to touch, to tinker with, to grasp whatever there is in a meaningful setting. This access is now largely denied. When knowledge became a commodity, it acquired the protections of private property, and thus a principle designed to guard personal intimacy became a rationale for declaring facts off limits for people without the proper credentials. In schools teachers keep knowledge to themselves unless it fits into the day's program. The media inform, but exclude those things they regard as unfit to print. Information is locked into special languages, and specialized teachers live off its retranslation. Patents are protected by corporations, secrets are guarded by bureaucracies, and the power to keep others out of private preserves—be they cockpits, law offices, junkyards, or clinics— is jealously guarded by professions, institutions, and nations. Neither the political nor the professional structure of our societies, East and West, could withstand the elimination of the power to keep entire classes of people from facts that could serve them. The access to facts that I advocate goes far beyond truth in labeling. Access must be built into reality, while all we ask from advertising is a guarantee that it does not mislead. Access to reality constitutes a fundamental alternative in education to a system that only purports to teach *about* it.

Abolishing the right to corporate secrecy—even when professional opinion holds that this secrecy serves the common good—is, as shall presently appear, a much more radical political goal than the traditional demand for public ownership or control of the tools of production. The socialization of tools without the effective socialization of know-how in their use tends to put the knowledge-capitalist into the position formerly held by the financier. The technocrat's only claim to power is the stock he holds in some class of scarce and secret knowledge, and the best means to protect its value is a large and capital-intensive organization that renders access to know-how formidable and forbidding.

It does not take much time for the interested learner to acquire almost any skill that he wants to use. We tend to forget this in a society where professional teachers monopolize entrance into all fields, and thereby stamp teaching by uncertified individuals as quackery. There are few mechanical skills used in industry or research that are as demanding, complex, and dangerous as driving cars, a skill that most people quickly acquire from a peer. Not all people are suited for advanced logic, yet those who are make rapid progress if they are challenged to play mathematical games at an early age. One out of twenty kids in Cuernavaca can beat me at Wiff 'n' Proof after a couple of weeks' training. In four months all but a small percentage of motivated adults at our CIDOC center learn Spanish well enough to conduct academic business in the new language.

A first step toward opening up access to skills would be to provide various incentives for skilled individuals to share their knowledge. Inevitably, this would run counter to the interest of guilds and professions and unions. Yet, multiple apprenticeship is attractive: It provides everybody with an opportunity to learn something about almost anything. There is no reason why a person should not combine the ability to drive a car, repair telephones and toilets, act as a midwife, and function as an architectural draftsman. Special-interest groups and their disciplined consumers would, of course, claim that the public needs the protection of a professional guarantee. But this argument is now steadily being challenged by consumer protection associations. We have to take much more seriously the objection that economists raise to the radical socialization of skills: that "progress" will be impeded if knowledge—patents, skills, and all the rest—is democratized. Their argument can be faced only if we demonstrate to them the growth rate of futile diseconomies generated by any existing educational system.

Access to people willing to share their skills is no guarantee of learning. Such access is restricted not only by the monopoly of educational programs over learning and of unions over licensing but also by a technology of scarcity. The skills that count today are know-how in the use of highly specialized tools that were designed to be scarce. These tools produce goods or render services that everybody wants but only a few can enjoy, and which only a limited number of people know how to use. Only a few privileged individuals out of the total number of people who have a given disease ever benefit from the results of sophisticated medical technology, and even fewer doctors develop the skill to use it.

The same results of medical research have, however, also been employed to create a basic medical tool kit that permits Army and Navy medics, with only a few months of training, to obtain results, under battlefield conditions, that would have been beyond the expectations of full-fledged doctors during World War II. On an even simpler level any peasant girl could learn how to diagnose and treat most infections if medical scientists prepared dosages and instructions specifically for a given geographic area.

All these examples illustrate the fact that educational considerations alone suffice to demand a radical reduction of the professional structure that now impedes the mutual relationship between the scientist and the majority of people who want access to science. If this demand were heeded, all men could learn to use yesterday's tools, rendered more effective and durable by modern science, to create tomorrow's world.

Unfortunately, precisely the contrary trend prevails at present. I know a coastal area in South America where most people support themselves by fishing from small boats. The outboard motor is certainly the tool that has changed most dramatically the lives of these coastal fishermen. But in the area I have surveyed, half of all outboard motors that were purchased between 1945 and 1950 are still kept running by constant tinkering, while half the motors purchased in 1965 no longer run because they were not built to be repaired. Technological progress provides the majority of people with gadgets they cannot afford and deprives them of the simpler tools they need.

Metals, plastics, and ferro cement used in building have greatly improved since the 1940s and ought to provide more people the opportunity to create their own homes. But while in the United States, in 1948, more than 30 percent of all one-family homes were owner-built, by the end of the 1960s the percentage of those who acted as their own contractors had dropped to less than 20 percent.

The lowering of the skill level through so-called economic development becomes even more visible in Latin America. Here most people still build their own homes from floor to roof. Often they use mud, in the form of adobe, and thatchwork of unsurpassed utility in the moist, hot, and windy climate. In other places they make their dwellings out of cardboard, oil-drums, and other industrial refuse. Instead of providing people with simple tools and highly standardized, durable, and easily repaired components, all governments have gone in for the mass production of low-cost buildings. It is clear that not one single country can afford to provide satisfactory modern dwelling units for the majority of its people. Yet, everywhere this policy makes it progressively more difficult for the majority to acquire the knowledge and skills they need to build better houses for themselves.

Educational considerations permit us to formulate a second fundamental characteristic that any post-industrial society must possess: a basic tool kit that by its very nature counteracts technocratic control. For educational reasons we must work toward a society in which scientific knowledge is incorporated in tools and components that can be used meaningfully in units small enough to be within the reach of all. Only such tools favor temporary associations among those who want to use them for a specific occasion. Only such tools allow specific goals to emerge in the process of their use, as any tinkerer knows. Only the combination of guaranteed access to facts and of limited power in most tools renders it possible to envisage a subsistence economy capable of incorporating the fruits of modern science.

The development of such a scientific subsistence economy is unquestionably to the advantage of the overwhelming majority of all people in poor countries. It is also the only alternative to progressive pollution, exploitation, and opaqueness in rich countries. But, as we have seen, the dethroning of the GNP cannot be achieved without simultaneously subverting GNE (Gross National Education—usually conceived as manpower capitalization). An egalitarian economy cannot exist in a society in which the right to produce is conferred by schools.

The feasibility of a modern subsistence economy does not depend on new scientific inventions. It depends primarily on the ability of a society to agree on fundamental, self-chosen anti-bureaucratic and anti-technocratic restraints.

These restraints can take many forms, but they will not work unless they touch the basic dimensions of life. (The decision of Congress against development of the supersonic transport plane is one of the most encouraging steps in the right direction.) The substance of these voluntary social restraints would be very simple matters that can be fully understood and judged by any prudent man. The issues at stake in the SST controversy provide a good example. All such restraints would be chosen to promote stable and equal enjoyment of scientific know-how. The French say that it takes a thousand years to educate a peasant to deal with a cow. It would not take two generations to help all people in Latin America or Africa to use and repair outboard motors, simple cars, pumps, medicine kits, and ferro cement machines if their design does not change every few years. And since a joyful life is one of constant meaningful intercourse with others in a meaningful environment, equal enjoyment does translate into equal education.

At present a consensus on austerity is difficult to imagine. The reason usually given for the impotence of the majority is stated in terms of political or economic class. What is not usually understood is that the new class structure of a schooled society is even more powerfully controlled by vested interests. No doubt an imperialist and capitalist organization of society provides the social structure within which a minority can have disproportionate influence over the effective opinion of the majority. But in a technocratic society the power of a minority of knowledge capitalists can prevent the formation of true public opinion through control of scientific know-how and the media of communication. Constitutional guarantees of free speech, free press, and free assembly were meant to ensure government by the people. Modern electronics, photo-offset presses, time-sharing computers, and telephones have in principle provided the hardware that could give an entirely new meaning to these freedoms. Unfortunately, these things are used in modern media to increase the power of knowledge-bankers to funnel their program-packages through international chains to more people, instead of being used to increase true networks that provide equal opportunity for encounter among the members of the majority.

Deschooling the culture and social structure requires the use of technology to make participatory politics possible. Only on the basis of a majority coalition can limits to secrecy and growing power be determined without dictatorship. We need a new environment in which growing up can be classless, or we will get a brave new world in which Big Brother educates us all.

appendices

APPENDIX A

Contributing Authors

Stephen Arons, staff attorney, Center for Law and Education, Harvard University.

Emmanuel Bernstein holds a Ph.D. in counseling psychology, University of Oregon.

Hillel Black, author of *The American Schoolbook; Buy Now, Pay Later;* and other writings.

William Boyer, professor of education, University of Hawaii.

Myron Brenton, researcher in the social sciences.

Alexander Calandra, faculty member, Department of Physics, Washington University.

Harry Edwards, assistant professor, Department of Sociology, San Jose State College.

Jerry Farber, English teacher, San Jose State College.

Estelle Fuchs, associate professor of education, Hunter College.

George Gallup, founder and chairman, The American Institute of Public Opinion.

Gordon Gammack, reporter, *Des Moines Register and Tribune,* Iowa.

Paul Goodman, educator, social critic, and author of *Growing Up Absurd, People or Personnel, Adam and His Works,* and other writings.

Dick Gregory, first known as a comedian, now prominent in the black civil rights movement.

Max Gunther, freelance writer, author of *The Split-Level Trap, The Weekenders,* and other writings.

Merrill Harmin, a member of the Department of Psychology, Southern Illinois University at Edwardsville, best known for his work on values with Louis Raths and Sidney Simon.

Vivian Horner, assistant professor of psycholinguistics and education, Yeshiva University.

Ivan Illich, director, Center for Intercultural Documentation, Cuernavaca, Mexico, an educational organization devoted to improving the cultural and social environment of Latin American people.

Vera John, assistant professor of psychology and education, Yeshiva University.

David L. Kirp, director, Center for Law and Education, Harvard University; and assistant professor, Harvard Graduate School of Education.

Charles R. Kniker, assistant professor, College of Education, Iowa State University.

George Leonard, Jr., West Coast editorial manager and senior editor, *Look* magazine; he has won Educational Writers' Association and School Bell awards for his educational articles.

Gerald I. Levy, instructor, Department of Sociology, Adelphi University.

Hollis Limprecht, editor, *Magazine of the Midlands,* the Sunday magazine of the *Omaha World-Herald,* Nebraska.

Judith Martin, staff writer, *The Washington Post.*

Richard Martin, staff writer, *Wall Street Journal.*

Philip Meyer, Washington correspondent, Knight Newspapers, Inc.; he specializes in behavioral science applications to journalism; former Nieman Fellow (1966–67) and project director, Russell Sage Foundation (1969–70).

Patricia Michaels, member of the Bay Area Radical Teachers Organizing Committee.

A. S. Neill, founder, Summerhill School, Leiston, England, and author of *Summerhill: A Radical Approach to Child Rearing* and other writings.

Tim Parsons, urban education specialist, New Jersey State Department of Education.

Thomas F. Pettigrew, professor of social psychology, Department of Social Relations, Harvard University.

Joel T. Santoro, co-chairman, Physical Education Department, Isaac E. Young Junior High School, New Rochelle, New York.

Charles E. Silberman, member of the Board of Editors, *Fortune* magazine. He and his wife Arlene recently completed *Crisis in the Classroom.*

Sidney Simon, formerly assistant professor, Temple University; now at the University of Massachusetts.

Glenn Smith, associate professor, College of Education, Iowa State University.

Judy Socolor, editor and staff associate, Yeshiva University.

Anthony Tovatt, supervisor of English, Burris Laboratory School, Teachers College, Ball State University.

Eric Wentworth, staff writer, *The Washington Post,* and former congressional fellow of the American Political Science Association (1962–63).

John Oliver Wilson, director, Office of Planning, Research and Evaluation, U. S. Office of Economic Opportunity.

APPENDIX B

The Summerhill Society

The Summerhill Society, organized in February 1961 in New York City for the purpose of establishing a school in the United States based upon the work of A. S. Neill at his Summerhill School in Leiston, England, stimulated tremendous interest and a strong hope on the part of many parents that a similar educational opportunity might be made available for their children. For the next two and a half years, educators, psychologists, parents, and other people inspired by Neill's exciting achievements devoted much time and energy to laying the groundwork for this kind of education throughout the United States. Over seven hundred members, representing almost every state in the Union, sent contributions and "spread the word." In New York City, active committees worked on the many problems relevant to the goal.

Much of the Society's present focus has shifted to activities designed to promote greater public awareness of the dynamics of a truly democratic education. As part of its effort to disseminate information about free school developments, the Society puts together and periodically updates the following list of free schools. It is not the function of the Society to investigate, judge, or endorse any particular school. In listing these schools, the Society is expressing its belief in the right of every individual to choose from among many alternatives. For specific information about the basic philosophy, staff, fees, facilities, special programs, and scholarships, contact the schools directly. It is emphasized that none of the schools listed is officially endorsed or approved by A. S. Neill. No legal or other formal affiliation exists between the Summerhill Society and the schools, nor is there any such affiliation among the schools. They are all co-educational.

Barker Free School—day and boarding, ages 5 to 13. Bob Barker, 6251 Overstone Drive, West Vancouver, British Columbia, Canada.
Bay High School—day, high school. Glen Nimnicht, 1744 University Avenue, Berkeley, California 94703.
Bensalem, The Experimental College—residential, three-year program. Hamid Kizilbash, Fordham University, Bronx, New York 10458.

Used by permission of the Summerhill Society, 339 Lafayette Street, New York, New York 10012.

Berkeley School—day, ages 12 to 13 at present. Eugene Bergman, Box 418, Berkeley, California 94701.

Boston School for Human Resources—boarding, one-year program for high school graduates. Bob Doolittle, 174 St. Botolph Street, Boston, Massachusetts 02115.

Cambridge Free School—day, ages 3 to 5. John Davis, 5 Howard Street, Cambridge, Massachusetts 02139.

Celeste School—day and boarding, ages 5 to 12 at present. Mervyn Willard, 120 Yale Street SE, Albuquerque, New Mexico 87106.

Centers for Change—university without walls. Fred Newman, located in New York City (Manhattan).

Children's Community—day, ages 4 to 9 at present. Bill Ayers, 805 McKinley, Ann Arbor, Michigan 48103.

Clonlara—day, ages 3 to 6 at present. Pat Montgomery, 1265 Jewett, Ann Arbor, Michigan 48104.

Collaberg School—day and boarding, ages 3 to 17. John Carson, Theill's Road, Stony Point, New York 10980.

Craigdarroch School—day, ages 6 to 10. Joan Schwartz, P. O. Box 5132, Station B, Victoria, British Columbia, Canada.

Everdale Place—boarding, ages 9 to 17 at present. Jim Deacove, Rural Route #1, Hillsburgh, Ontario, Canada.

Fayerwether Street School—day, ages 4 to 13. Madison Judson, P. O. Box 287, Cambridge, Massachusetts 02138.

Fifteenth Street School—day, nursery to fourth grade at present. Orson Bean, 206 West 15th Street, New York, New York 10011.

Franconia College—four-year liberal arts college. Larry Lemmel, Franconia, New Hampshire 03580.

Friends World Institute—four-year liberal arts college. Harrow Hill, 5722 Northern Boulevard, East Norwich, New York 11732.

Freegarden School—day, ages 5 to 9 at present. Phyllis Tower, 204 West 83rd Street, New York, New York 10024.

Green Valley School—boarding, ages 4 to 21. George Von Hilsheimer, Box 606, Orange City, Florida 32763.

Greentree School—day, kindergarten to sixth grade. Joyce Townsend, Greentree School, RFD #1, Waverly, Ohio 45690.

Hidden Springs School—intentional community based boarding school, ages 5 to 20. Charles Cook, Robert Wallace, and William Nixon, South Acworth, New Hampshire 03607.

Independent School of Buffalo—day, ages 5 to 11. J. Douglas Wright, 157 Woodward Avenue, Buffalo, New York 14214. (Planned opening September 1969 in Williamsville, New York).

Lewis-Wadhams School—boarding, ages 6 to 18. Herb Snitzer, R. D. Westport, New York 12993.

Live Oak School—day and boarding, ages 4 to 12. Bennie Noyes, 1388 Orange Road, Ojai, California 93023.

Lorillard School—day, ages 3 to 7. Helene Aarons, 2390 Tiebout Street, Bronx, New York 10458. (Planned opening September 1969).

Minnesota Summerhill Community School—boarding, ages 6 to 17. Cortland Smith, Box 271, Spray Island, Spring Park, Minnesota 55384.

Modern Play School and Play Mountain Place—day, nursery and elementary grades. Phyllis Fleishman, 6063 Hargis Street, Los Angeles, California 94334.

Monmouth Modern Day School—day, ages 5 to 13. Diane Cabarga, 24 Union Hill Road, Morganville, New Jersey 07751. (Planned opening September 1969).

One Room School House—day, kindergarten to second grade at present. Al Krauss, 88 Middle Rincon Road, Santa Rosa, California 94505.

Open Community School—part- and full-time boarding, elementary grades. Bob McCormick, Claverack, New York 12513.

Pacific High School—day and boarding. Stanley Bean, Box 311, Palo Alto, California 94301.

Perry Street Kids School—day and boarding, ages 3 to 8. Bill Pigman and Su Negrin, 156 Perry Street, New York, New York 10014.

Peter Pan Playschool—day, ages 3 to 5½. Jean Fleming, 2513 Malama Place, Honolulu, Hawaii 96822.

Pinehenge School—boarding, ages 5 to 14. Glenna Plaisted, Box 1, Waterford, Maine 04088.

Pinel—day, ages 5 to 14. Bill Kenny, 3655 Reliez Valley Road, Martinez, California 94553.

Rochdale College—liberal arts college. Linda Bomphray, 341 Bloor Street West, Toronto 5, Ontario, Canada.

Roxbury Community School—day, ages 5 to 8 at present. Doreen Wilkinson, Box 175, 1 Leyland Street, Dorchester, Massachusetts 02125.

Santa Barbara Free School—ages 4 to 18. Harvey Haber, 3730 Calle Real, P. O. Box 3511, Santa Barbara, California 93105.

Santa Fe Community School—Marie Kimmey, P. O. Box 2241, Santa Fe, New Mexico 87501.

Saturna Island Free School—boarding, ages 5 to 17. Tom Durrie, Saturna Island, British Columbia, Canada.

Satya Community School—day, ages 5 to 19. Presently at Farrington Memorial, Route 2, Lincoln, Massachusetts.

Shire School—day, ages 5 to 13. T. White, 69⅓ Harriet Street, San Francisco, California.

Sudbury Valley School—day, ages 4 to 18. Daniel Greenberg, Winch Street, Framingham, Massachusetts 01701.

Summerhill Day School—Oliver Haskell, 4074 Vineland, North Hollywood, California 91604.

Summerhill Society—339 Lafayette Street, New York, New York 10012.

Summerhill West—day and boarding, ages 5 to 18. Frank Lindenfeld, 23859 Stagg Street, Canoga Park, California 91304.

Urban School of San Francisco—Bob Wilder, 2938 Washington Street, San Francisco, California 94115.

Viewpoint Non-School—boarding, ages 6 to 15. Chuck Valentine, Argenta, British Columbia, Canada.

Village School—William Anderson, Poppycock Farm, New Gloucester, Maine 04260. (Planned opening September 1969).

Walden Center School—day, elementary grades. Denny Wilcher, 2446 McKinley, Berkeley, California 94700.

APPENDIX C

Power Groups and the Schools

Whether one wishes merely to observe the phenomenon called American schooling or truly wants to effect changes in that institution, he has to comprehend the influence exerted by current power groups. Generalizations about the shoulds, oughts, and musts of curriculum, and cries for more humanistic teachers need to be supplemented by accurate information about those forces which usually determine the scope of the school today.

The list is only partial. Included are representatives of business organizations, civil rights groups, educational industries, foundations, political clubs, religious denominations, service clubs, teacher organizations, government agencies, and veterans' groups. Hopefully, the reader's interest will direct him to further information about specific groups which may be more significant in his locale.

Information about the organizations mentioned here has usually been obtained from the mailing address indicated. Because of the variety of responses to a mailed inquiry, parallel information cannot always be given. In some cases, we have used information found in *Encyclopedia of Associations*, vol. 1, National Organizations of the United States, Margaret Fisk (ed.), (Detroit, Michigan; Gale Research Company, 1970).

As editors we debated about the usefulness of this section if it contained only mailing addresses. We concluded that to be consistent with the purpose of the book and articles offering a variety of opinions, we should add our evaluations of the power groups. We expect, indeed hope, that our opinions will invite debate within classrooms and from group representatives.

AMERICAN CIVIL LIBERTIES UNION (ACLU)

National headquarters: 156 Fifth Avenue, New York, New York 10010.
Membership: 175,000. Staff 24. Affiliates: 48, in 45 states, with 400 sub-
    chapters.
Budget: $2.8 million (1971).
History: The ACLU was formed in the wake of World War I, when a
    thousand people were deported from the U. S. for political reasons,
    and when thousands of aliens were arrested.

Purposes: Briefly: the ACLU seeks to defend the whole Bill of Rights for everybody. Typically, this has meant defending the rights of unpopular individuals and causes—labor unions in the 1920s, Japanese-Americans in the 1940s, Communists in the 1950s, and civil rights demonstrators in the 1960s.

Policies and programs: According to their literature, the ACLU "champions the rights of man set forth in the Declaration of Independence and the Constitution: freedom of inquiry and expression—speech, press, assembly, and religion—for everybody." The ACLU works through the courts. In terms of school-related cases, the ACLU handles cases regarding academic freedom for instructors (1925 Scopes "monkey" trial), student conduct cases (length of hair), and church-state issues (1962 prayer case, more recently cases on financial aid to non-public schools).

Publication: Civil Liberties, six issues a year.

Comments: Membership is primarily made up of upper-middle-class whites, with lawyers representing a high percentage of local chapter membership. ACLU is commonly regarded as a liberal, if not radical, organization by school boards.

AMERICAN FARM BUREAU FEDERATION

National headquarters: 225 Touhy Avenue, Park Ridge, Illinois 60068.

Membership: Over 2,000,000. Staff 65. County Farm Bureaus: 2,820, in all states but Alaska. According to a 1970 survey, 37.6 percent of its membership had incomes over $20,000. Almost 90 percent are farm owners.

Budget: $2,870,000 (1970).

History: Although the national organization was not formed until 1919, many county bureaus were begun between 1912 and 1914. Many were formed to sponsor agricultural extension work called for by the Smith-Lever Act of 1914, which sought to make scientific information available to farmers.

Purposes: "To promote, protect and represent the economic, social and educational interests of American farm people in county, state, national and international affairs."

Policies and programs: Strong supporters of local control of schools, the Federation's state bureaus have usually fought reorganization and have consistently opposed federal grants for elementary and secondary schools. In Farm Bureau policies for 1970, members were urged to serve on local committees to aid schools in selecting "the course of study." Also urged was adoption of an amendment to the U. S. Constitution to guarantee the right to offer prayers and to read the Bible in public schools. The Farm Bureau urges teachers to offer periods of spiritual meditation and patriotic instruction at the beginning of the school day.

Publications: weekly Newsletter, and monthly *Nation's Agriculture.*

Comments: Through its state bureaus it wields considerable influence with state legislatures. It has influenced financing of schools, especially, and has often fought successfully for more rural control of state funds.

AMERICAN FEDERATION OF TEACHERS (AFT)

National headquarters: 1012 Fourteenth Street, N.W., Washington, D. C. 20005.

Membership: 250,000. Locals 1,000. The AFT is a classroom teachers' organization which is affiliated with the American Federation of Labor. Currently, supervisors who are empowered to hire, fire, or discipline teachers are not admitted to AFT membership.

Budget: $4 million (1971–1972).

History: Begun on April 15, 1916, when eight local unions of teachers met in Chicago to form a national organization.

Purposes: The AFT believes that teachers, to be truly professional, must speak for themselves in their organizations and should have a real voice in the management of schools and in determining their own wages.

Policies and programs: The "Action Program" of the AFT calls for: $25,000 in five annual increments, recognition of teachers' bargaining rights, a "More Effective Schools" program to provide sharply reduced class size in urban areas. The AFT has been opposed to merit pay.

Publications: American Teacher, monthly; *Changing Education,* quarterly.

Comments: Until the late 1960s more militant than NEA, the AFT likes to boast that its organization has obtained greater economic gains for its membership. It is urban-centered. Historically, AFT has fought for civil rights, but increasingly it seems to be a reactionary force since it is fighting to defend its power position from minority group challenges.

AMERICAN JEWISH CONGRESS (AJC)*

National headquarters: 15 East 84th Street, New York, New York 10028.

Membership: 300,000. Staff 110. Local groups 350.

Budget: $1 million, of which $100,000 is for litigation of church-state cases (1968).

History: Founded in 1918, when Jewish leaders wished to send delegates to the Paris Peace Conference. Since World War II, AJC has expanded its efforts from Jewish concerns to a range of civil liberties issues.

Purposes: The organization defines its purposes as "American Jews committed to the preservation and extension of the democratic way of life. . . ."

Policies and programs: An emphatic supporter of the separation of church and state, the AJC has either sponsored or served as a "friend of the court" (*amicus curie*) on such cases as *Engel vs Vitale* (the 1962 New York case which ruled that prescribed prayers were illegal), *Abington vs Schempp* (1963 Pennsylvania decision that devotional Bible readings in public schools were unconstitutional), and cases which sought to discontinue federal funds for non-public school textbooks and services (*Flast*, New York), and the 1971 Rhode Island case in which the Supreme Court declared illegal state monies which paid portions of parochial teachers' salaries in secular subjects.

Publications: Congress, biweekly; *Judaism,* quarterly.

Comments: Its appeal is to the upper-middle-class Jewish population. The liberal orientation of the AJC makes it a natural ally of the American Civil Liberties Union.

*Source: Encyclopedia of Associations, p. 907; and Richard Morgan, *The Politics of Religious Conflict* (New York: Pegasus, 1968), pp. 55–56.

AMERICAN LEGION

National headquarters: P. O. Box 1055, 700 North Pennsylvania Street, Indianapolis, Indiana 46206.

Membership: 2,700,000. Local posts 16,500. The Legion is open to honorably discharged war-time veterans, both male and female.

Budget: $8.4 million (1970).

History: Founded in 1919. In 1921, the Legion co-founded, with the National Education Association, American Education Week. It is best known as the political lobby that fought for passage of the 1944 G.I. Bill.

Purposes: Both social and service. The Legion has worked vigorously for bills which help returning veterans get job-training benefits.

Policies and programs: The Legion's "Americanism" Commission provides a suggested course for schools on patriotism. The Legion is also a sponsor of oratorical contests based on information in the U. S. Constitution. During summers, it organizes Boys' State and Girls' State conferences to help high school students understand governmental processes. The Legion has also backed vocational programs.

Comments: The Legion has been one of the most conservative voices regarding school values. Through newspaper comments and telephone campaigns, Legion members have urged school boards to release instructors who have participated in peace marches and other expressions of dissent. At its Boys' State and Girls' State conventions, it has also carried on an anticommunism theme.

CARNEGIE CORPORATION OF NEW YORK

National headquarters: 437 Madison Avenue, New York, New York 10022.
Membership: Staff 43.
Budget: Approximately $13.5 million in grants (1970).
History: Founded in 1911. "A grant-making educational foundation." In the past, related Carnegie organizations have wielded much influence over college policy; for example, in the early twentieth century, it agreed to start pension funds for faculty members, provided the institutions dropped tests of creed for faculty.
Purposes: "Grants are made chiefly to colleges and universities, professional associations, and other educational organizations to finance teaching and research programs in education, and in certain aspects of governmental affairs . . ." (*Encyclopedia of Associations,* p. 463).
Publications: Quarterly and annual reports.
Comments: The power of foundations such as the Carnegie Corporation perhaps is more indirect than direct (see David Horowitz, "Billion Dollar Brains," *Ramparts,* May 1969, pp. 36–44). By having the power to bestow large sums of money for research projects, which in turn generates publicity, foundations are able to influence certain school systems to offer approved innovative programs. "Sesame Street," the Philadelphia Parkway School, and the Ocean Hill-Brownsville Demonstration District in New York City had substantial help from foundations. The Ford Foundation has now become the largest private grantor for educational work.

CHAMBER OF COMMERCE OF THE UNITED STATES

National headquarters: 1615 H Street N.W., Washington, D. C. 20006.
Membership: 5,000,000. Nearly 4,000 local, state, and regional chambers. Staff 850, with over 400 of these in Washington.
Budget: Not available.
History: Founded in 1912.
Purposes: "A federation comprised of business and professional members. Its functions are to determine policy and to act as a national spokesman for American business" (source: a booklet, *The National Chamber*).
Policies and programs: The national office's functions include: research and analysis of national problems, policymaking, informing Con-

gress and federal agencies about what business is doing, and program development (providing models, guidelines, and general information about programs that might be used locally).

Publications: Washington Report, weekly; *Nation's Business*, monthly.

Comments: A status quo group, the Chamber has frequently been a conservative voice in the community. For years it opposed federal aid to education and it still is active to see that "communist" influence does not invade the schools. The most obvious evidence of Chamber interest in schools is the production of informational packets about school subjects. In some communities, the Chamber exerts a powerful school influence by serving as an unofficial screening agency for school board candidates and superintendents.

CITIZENS FOR EDUCATIONAL FREEDOM (CEF)

National headquarters: Suite 844, Washington Building, Fifteenth and New York streets, N.W., Washington, D. C. 20005.

Membership: 125,000. Local chapters 1000. It has been estimated that 90 percent of membership is Roman Catholic.

Budget: Approximately $500,000 (1968).

History: Founded in 1959 in St. Louis, CEF has been led by laymen rather than ordained priests.

Purposes: Billed as "a non-sectarian organization of parents and other individuals" to "secure participation by every parent and citizen-student in his own education," it has fought for full public support for church schools. In addition, CEF has opted for a "God-centered" curriculum.

Policies and programs: Primarily, CEF can be considered a "grass roots" movement, because it appears to be most effective at the local and state levels. Objectives which are central include sharing of government funds (state and federal especially) by all schools, a curriculum which stresses moral and spiritual values, and support of voucher plan.

Publication: Freedom in Education, monthly.

Comments: State legislators especially feel the impact of this group through mailings. In recent years, CEF has promoted bills to pay for busing parochial school children.

CONGRESS OF RACIAL EQUALITY (CORE)

National headquarters: 38 Park Row, New York, New York 10038.

Membership: 70,000. Local groups 180.

Budget: Not available.

History: Founded in 1942.

Purposes: "Persons of various races committed to the use of non-violent direct action in specific attacks on segregation and discrimination who are accepted through local groups after screening."

Policies and programs: In the South, CORE has concentrated on voter registration and full black rights. In the North, more work has been done on community problems—improved housing conditions, school curriculum changes, elimination of police brutality.

Publications: CORE-lator, bimonthly.

Comments: To compensate for a loss of power to other civil rights groups, CORE has become more militant. Black leadership has increased dramatically. In major cities, CORE has been active in community control movements, at times insisting that it is the best spokesman for the black cause.

EDUCATIONAL TESTING SERVICE (ETS)

National headquarters: Rosedale Road, Princeton, New Jersey 08540.

Membership: Trustees (1971–1972): John H. Fischer, President, Teachers College, Columbia University; Malcolm C. Moos, President, University of Minnesota; George F. Baughman, President, The College Foundation; Rev. Paul C. Reinert, S.J., President, St. Louis University; plus representatives of groups named below. Total membership: 1,700.

Budget: $39 million (1971–1972 fiscal year).

History: In 1947 three groups—American Council on Education, Carnegie Foundation for the Advancement of Teaching, and the College Entrance Examination Board—formed ETS. Today, this group is perhaps the national leader in determining standardized tests for the country's students, especially at the college level.

Purposes: Primarily, ETS provides measurement devices and pursues research in measurement theory.

Policies and programs: Believing that the future will see more individualized instruction, plus the need for more school system planning of more complex programs, ETS is working on research in measurement theory, creating new or improved measures which aid students in planning their own programs, and systems which help educational institutions evaluate students. Specifically, two programs now being researched relate to computer-assisted instruction which would have built-in diagnostic warning signals to alert the teacher to a student's difficulties; and a longitudinal study of the early education of disadvantaged children.

Comments: A prime example of a private organization which establishes public school standards. ETS seems to enjoy its lack of publicity.

4-H CLUBS

National headquarters: Federal Extension Service, U. S. Department of
    Agriculture, Washington, D. C. 20250.
Membership: 3,200,000. Volunteer adult leaders 500,000. Local chapters
    95,977. Members are boys and girls age 9 to 19 from rural and
    suburban areas.
Budget: Not available.
History: Founded in 1914, in climate which deplored the movement to
    the cities and sought to make rural life more appealing.
Purposes: "To foster character development and good citizenship,
    through a wide variety of plant and animal science, home making,
    community service and other projects which emphasize the 'head,
    heart, hands, and health' objectives of 4-H clubs."
Policies and programs: The 4-H has encouraged individual student pro-
    jects such as raising animals for boys and dressmaking for girls;
    but in recent years activities have grown to include service in
    the inner city and interest in ecology.
Comments: A straight organization with "wholesome" goals. Its Protes-
    tant work-ethic suggests an almost pristine form of middle-class
    values.

JOHN BIRCH SOCIETY*

National headquarters: 395 Concord Avenue, Belmont, Massachusetts
    02178.
Membership: 100,000 in 50 states and the District of Columbia. 800
    chapters. Requirements: "only men and women of good character,
    humane conscience, and religious ideals." Dues: $24 per year for
    men; $12 for women.
Budget: Not available.
History: Founded in 1958 by Robert Welch. John Birch Society members
    have always considered themselves an educational organization,
    viewing politics only as the mechanical means to change.
Purposes: "Less government, more responsibility, and—with God's
    help—a better world."
Policies and programs: Specifically, the society finds itself against the
    spirit of "collectivism" and seeks to bring about more individual
    freedom and local control. It has been opposed to the United
    Nations and to trade with the Soviet Union and its satellites. The
    Supreme Court leadership of Chief Justice Earl Warren was chal-
    lenged by the society. Lately, it has opposed sex education pro-
    grams in the schools, and some local chapters have led campaigns
    of book censorship.

Publication: American Opinion Magazine, monthly.
Comments: A highly conservative group, prone to see communist plots in experimental programs, the John Birch Society frequently charges professional educators with indoctrinating youth. Tactics have included telephone and letter campaigns promoting the society's viewpoints.
*Source: Robert Welch, "What Is the John Birch Society?" *American Opinion* reprint, 1970. Also, *Encyclopedia of Associations,* p. 756.

KIWANIS INTERNATIONAL*

National headquarters: 101 East Erie Street, Chicago, Illinois 60611.
Membership: 275,000. Local clubs 5,700. Staff 120. The Kiwanis are business and professional men united for service and social meetings.
Budget: Not available.
History: Founded in 1915.
Purposes: "Service to Youth, Community, and Nation." Meeting once a week for a meal, Kiwanis plan on working with boys and girls, with senior citizens, the ill, in a wide variety of projects, including such things as conservation practices, providing health aids, encouraging church attendance, and providing opportunities for students to get career guidance.
Policies and programs: A central program is the Key Club International for high school boys (95,000 members in 3,500 clubs) and Circle K International for college men (13,600 members in 800 clubs).
Publication: The Kiwanis Magazine, monthly.
Comments: Typical of the middle-class organizations school administrators belong to.
*Source: Encyclopedia of Associations, p. 1061; and "Kiwanis in Brief," a pamphlet from Kiwanis International, 1969.

LEAGUE OF WOMEN VOTERS OF THE UNITED STATES

National headquarters: 1730 M Street N.W., Washington, D. C. 20036.
Membership: 160,000. Staff 56. 50 state leagues. 1275 locals. The League is a voluntary organization of women citizens of voting age.
Budget: Not available.
History: Founded in 1920 as an outgrowth of the National American Woman Suffrage Association.
Purposes: "To promote political responsibility through informed and active participation of citizens in government." Members study selected issues at local, state, and national governmental levels and take legislative positions on issues if there is consensus among

membership at the respective levels. However, the League will not support or oppose candidates or political parties.

Publications: National Voter, 10 issues a year.

Comments: An upper-middle-class organization. Members are highly articulate on political issues. Typically, local chapters organize public forums to hear candidates for school boards, and spokesmen for and against school bond issue proposals.

NATIONAL ASSOCIATION FOR THE ADVANCEMENT OF COLORED PEOPLE (NAACP)

National headquarters: 1790 Broadway, New York, New York 10019; also a Washington bureau and four regional offices.

Membership: 450,673. Staff 125. Local groups 1730.

Budget: Approximately $4 million (1969).

History: Founded in 1909 by a small group disturbed over riots against blacks in Lincoln's hometown, Springfield, Illinois. W. E. B. DuBois became the first executive secretary.

Purposes: "To achieve, through peaceful and lawful means, equal citizenship rights for all American citizens by eliminating segregation and discrimination in housing, employment, voting, schools, the courts, transportation, recreation."

Policies and programs: NAACP has been active in such court cases as the desegregation case *Brown vs Topeka, Kansas, Board of Education* (1954); and *Hobsen vs Hansen* (Washington, D. C., 1967) on ability grouping. It also lobbied for the Civil Rights Laws of 1957, 1960, 1964, 1965, and 1968. NAACP is active in fighting de facto school segregation in the North and has maintained an information service for many years. The new Education Department is helping local groups analyze ESEA programs.

Publications: Crisis, monthly.

Comments: Radical blacks consider the Association an "Uncle Tom" organization—that is, a sellout group because it has opted to work within the system. The white community frequently regards this group as one of the "safest" groups to work with, because it uses legal channels.

NATIONAL ASSOCIATION OF MANUFACTURERS (NAM)*

National headquarters: 277 Park Avenue, New York, New York 10017.

Membership: 12,370 member companies. Staff 282. 385 state, trade, and national associations. "NAM's member companies account for approximately 75 percent of the nation's industrial output and provide a similar percentage of the nation's industrial employment."

Budget: Approximately $5,675,000 (1970).
History: Founded in 1895.
Purposes: To encourage individual freedom and support the American system of free enterprise. Objectives include promotion of the industrial interest of the United States and dissemination of information among the public with respect to the principles of individual liberty and ownership of property.
Policies and programs: For schools, NAM provides a wide range of films related to economic topics, all in support of the "American way." It conducts workshops for clergymen to help them understand (and disseminate) beliefs of American industry. NAM also lobbies in Washington, and they are strong supporters of technical-vocational programs.
Publications: "In Depth," a monthly bulletin.
Comments: Lately NAM has pushed for stronger technical-vocational programs. The educational goal of this business-oriented group is to support programs that aid students to become, in the words of one NAM filmstrip, "well educated consumer-citizens." It is considered a strong lobbying power. NAM has supported dropout prevention measures.
*Source: Encyclopedia of Associations, p. 161; "This is NAM," a pamphlet; and NAM Public Information Department fact sheet.

NATIONAL CONGRESS OF PARENTS AND TEACHERS (PTA)

National headquarters: 700 North Rush Street, Chicago, Illinois 60611.
Membership: 9,210,911. 52 branches. 40,194 local units. Person joins local unit, but does not need to be parent nor teacher.
Budget: Not available.
History: Founded in 1897 as the National Congress of Mothers. Name changed in 1925.
Purposes: "To promote the welfare of children and youth in home, school, church, and community. To raise the standards of home life; to secure adequate laws for the care and protection of children and youth; to bring into close relation the home and the school, that parents and teachers may cooperate intelligently in the training of the child; to develop between educators and the general public such united efforts as will secure for every child the highest advantages in physical, mental, social and spiritual education."
Policies and programs: Lately the PTA has stressed two special projects— Project RISE (Reading Improvement Services Everywhere) and Project PTSA, an effort to have students join their organization. Essentially an information-disseminating organization, the PTA has also worked on special education and drug abuse.
Comments: Probably the most overrated school-supporting group in this

list. Traditional PTA structure has not worked in inner cities, probably because it is almost exclusively a middle-class organization. It is not usually influential in decision-making about school policies. Administrators could well label it their school pacification program.

NATIONAL COUNCIL OF CHURCHES IN THE UNITED STATES (NCC)*

National headquarters: 475 Riverside Drive, New York, New York 10027.
Membership: 33 member denominations. Staff 700. *Encyclopedia of Associations* states: "A federation of 33 Protestant and Eastern Orthodox denominations, comprising 143,993 churches with 42,038,539 members" (p. 892).
Budget: $40,000 for lobbying (1968).
History: Founded in 1950.
Purposes: "To serve as a cooperative instrument of its constituent communions in manifesting oneness in Jesus Christ as Divine Lord and Savior and to do together those things which can better be done united than separated."
Policies and programs: Some 70 programs of a world-wide nature are now done cooperatively, such as the training and placement of missionaries. During the height of the civil rights movement in the 1960s, the NCC organized the Delta Ministry. NCC has a Department of Education which is now involved in promoting study of religion in the public schools. Traditionally, it has supported separation of church and state, becoming more lenient of public funds for non-public schools. It also produces some audio-visual material.
Comments: Definitely a liberal group in social pronouncements. Frequently its leadership, rather than membership at large, is for social change. Statements from NCC are not considered binding on members. Because of the large membership represented, NCC has a small but powerful lobby group in Washington that has a disproportionate influence. For example, its lobby power kept a prayer amendment in committee from 1962 to 1963.
Source: Encyclopedia of Associations, p. 889. Also, Richard E. Morgan, *The Politics of Religious Conflict* (New York: Pegasus, 1968), pp. 49–52.

NATIONAL EDUCATION ASSOCIATION (NEA)*

National headquarters: 1201 Sixteenth Street N.W., Washington, D. C. 20036.

Membership: 1,103,485. Staff 1447. State groups 50. Local chapters 8,949. NEA is a professional organization of elementary and secondary schoolteachers, college and university professors, principals, superintendents, and others interested in American schooling. In 1969, 75 percent were classroom teachers, 10 percent administrators; 63.8 percent were female. Almost 92 percent white membership.

Budget: $29,500,000 (1971–1972).

History: Founded in 1857.

Purposes: "To elevate the character and advance the interests of the profession of teaching and to promote the cause of popular education in the United States."

Policies and programs: To enhance the professional image, NEA has traditionally believed research to be the key to teachers having a larger voice in determining school policy. Historically, led by administrators the NEA has resisted making the salary level of teachers the most obvious problem to tackle. Because of AFT competition in recent years, the NEA has become much more prone to using the "withholding of services" option (sometimes called a strike).

Comments: NEA national headquarters in Washington is no accident. It has become one of the foremost lobbying groups in the nation. Increasingly its leaders speak on political issues. It still produces a large number of research bulletins. Silent for many years on civil rights (it had separate chapters for black members), NEA has recently been active in promoting integrated education. As it is a status quo organization, it has opposed radical experiments in schooling, such as the voucher plan and performance contracting.

*Source: Encyclopedia of Associations, p. 478; also, *NEA Handbook* and pamphlets from NEA.

NATIONAL URBAN LEAGUE

National headquarters: 55 East 52nd Street, New York, New York 10022.

Membership: 50,000. Staff 800. Local groups 98. The League is an interracial social work agency.

Budget: $14,900,571 (1970).

History: Founded in 1910.

Purposes: "To eliminate from American life all forms of segregation and discrimination based on race or color, and to secure for Negro citizens and other economically disadvantaged groups, equal opportunity to develop their fullest potential and to share equitably the rewards and responsibilities of American citizenship."

Policies and programs: The League primarily works with job development and employment, housing, and education causes. In school work it has developed the street academies in New York City, where school dropouts are brought to work in an informal atmosphere toward degrees. With foundation funds and business grants, the League also started the Harlem Prep Academy, a highly structured and rigorous private high school.

Comments: Considered the most middle-class of the civil rights groups identified with the Black cause. The late Whitney Young, former director, was considered an excellent bargainer with whites around the union tables and at government conferences. The new leadership appears to be more militant.

OFFICE OF ECONOMIC OPPORTUNITY (OEO)*

National headquarters: 1200 19th Street N.W., Washington, D.C. 20506; 10 regional offices.

Budget: Obligations $889.4 million total (fiscal 1971).

History: Established in 1964 by Act of Congress as a government agency whose head reports directly to the Executive Office of the President.

Purposes: "To strengthen, supplement, and coordinate efforts to further the policy of the United States to 'eliminate the paradox of poverty in the midst of plenty in this Nation by opening to everyone the opportunity for education and training, the opportunity to work, and the opportunity to live in decency and dignity.' "

Policies and programs: Using federal legislation (e.g., housing laws, economic aids), this agency has opened many doors for the poverty class in America. Some of the programs it is responsible for include the Job Corps, VISTA, day care programs, bilingual schools, and education loan fund administration. Lately, OEO has taken up the educational voucher plan.

Comments: Because of its skillful control of some federal funds and its expertise in working with power groups from the ranks of the poor, OEO has become more influential now in the determination of "educational" programs than any other federal agency.

*Source: U.S. Government Organization Manual, 1970–71 (Washington: U. S. Government Printing Office, 1971), pp. 63–67.

ROTARY INTERNATIONAL*

National headquarters: 1600 Ridge Avenue, Evanston, Illinois 60201.

Membership: 704,500. Staff 249. Local clubs 13,615 in 149 countries. Three-fifths of members are college graduates with median annual incomes of $20,083. One-quarter are on boards of directors of companies other than their own; nine of ten own their own homes, half of these worth more than $32,000. More than two-thirds live in a community of less than 50,000 population.

Budget: Approximately $4.2 million (1971–1972).

History: Founded in 1905. Primarily a service organization of businessmen who hold weekly meetings. Activities include sponsoring
fund-raising drives for countries around the world.

Purposes: "To encourage and foster the ideal of service as a basis of
worthy enterprise . . . especially high ethical standards in business
and professions . . . and the advancement of international understanding."

Publications: The Rotarian.

Policies and programs: (1) Offers some graduate scholarships and awards
which provide students with opportunity to study in another country; (2) no educational policies nationally stated.

Comments: A very high group in the pecking order of businessmen's
clubs. Probably more school decisions are made at their noon
luncheons than at the school board meetings.

*Source: From Rotary files, especially "A Market for the '70s," a profile
of the readers of *The Rotarian.*

UNITED STATES CATHOLIC CONFERENCE (USCC)

National headquarters: 1312 Massachusetts Avenue, N.W., Washington,
D. C. 20025.

Membership: Staff 350. "Civil entity of the American Catholic Bishops."

Budget: Not available.

History: Founded in 1919 to aid Roman Catholic servicemen.

Purposes: "Provides an organizational structure and the resources needed
to insure coordination, cooperation and assistance in the public,
educational and social concerns of the church. . . ." (*Encyclopedia
of Associations,* p. 889).

Policies and programs: In the educational field, USCC is an active ac-
commodationist group seeking federal and state funds for parochial schools.

Comments: While it determines certain policies for the Roman Catholic
system nationally, such as curriculum, it is not as effective on a
local level as is the CEF. The lobby in Washington has some power,
stopping the Elementary and Secondary Education Act of 1965 until
children in parochial schools were guaranteed some federal financial assistance.

UNITED STATES OFFICE OF EDUCATION (USOE)

National headquarters: 400 Maryland Avenue, S.W., Washington, D. C.
20202; 10 field offices.

Budget: $2.668 billion elementary; $1.395 billion secondary; $266 million vocational; $1.368 billion manpower training; $925 million other education (estimated 1970).

History: Created in 1867 as a non-Cabinet department, USOE is now part of the Department of Health, Education and Welfare.

Purposes: "To collect statistics and facts as shall show the condition and progress of education in the United States. . . ." Also, in more recent times, USOE has been asked to "aid in establishment of an efficient school system."

Policies and programs: Lately, USOE has been made responsible for federal financial assistance to schools. Frequently, it conducts special studies and research projects on educational change.

Comments: The Commissioner of Education's post is a political position. USOE is a status quo bureau.

Index